FAMILY STYLE

MEMORIES OF AN AMERICAN FROM VIETNAM

Thien Pham

FAMILY STYLE

MEMORIES OF AN AMERICAN FROM VIETNAM

First Second
NEW YORK

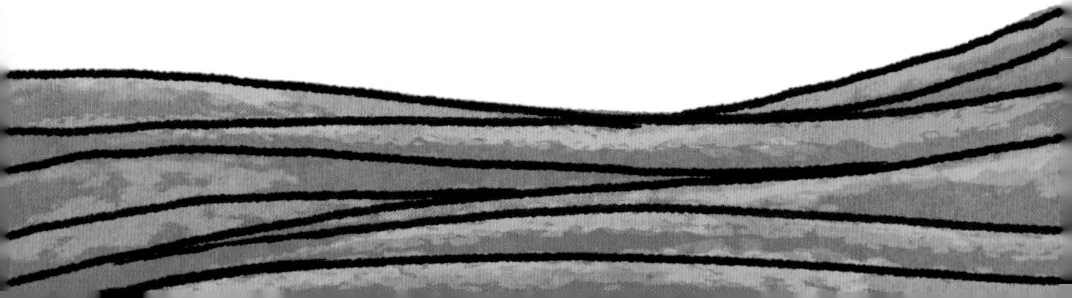

CHAPTER 1: RICE AND FISH

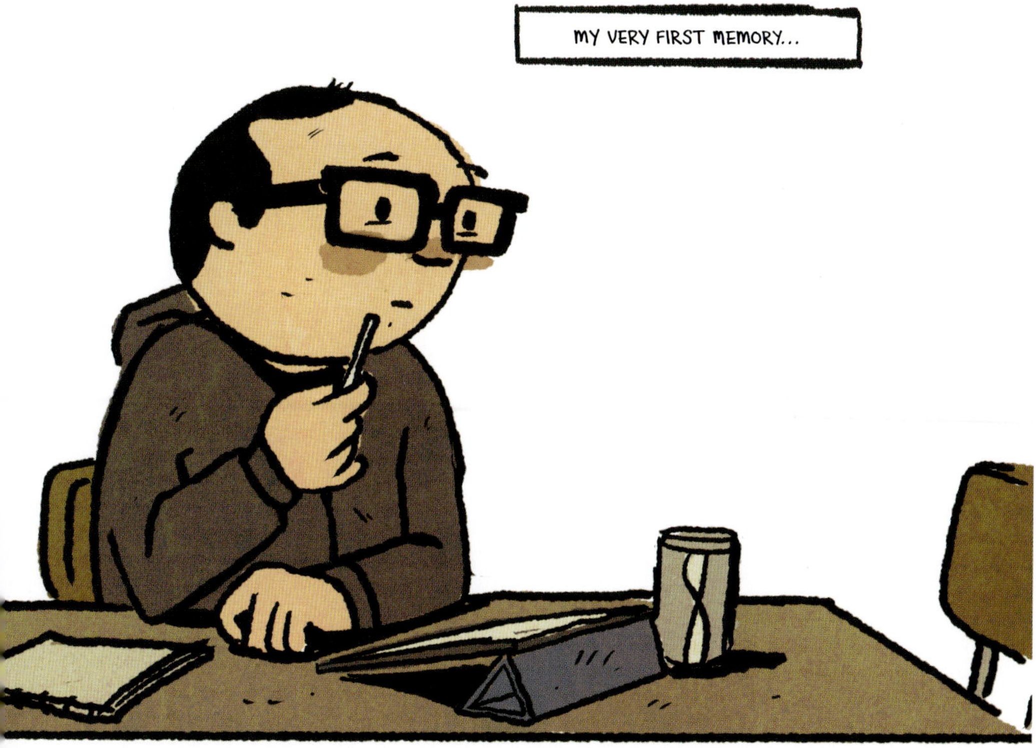
MY VERY FIRST MEMORY...

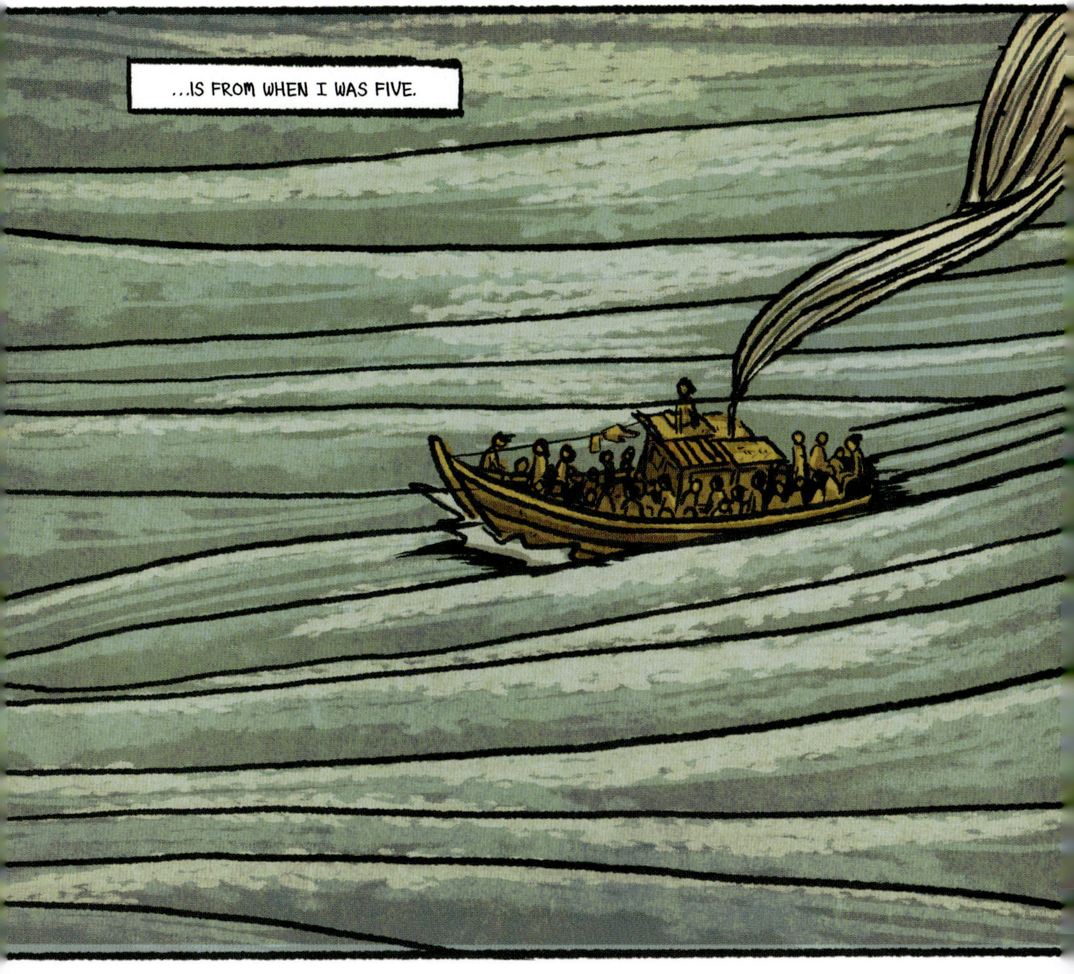
...IS FROM WHEN I WAS FIVE.

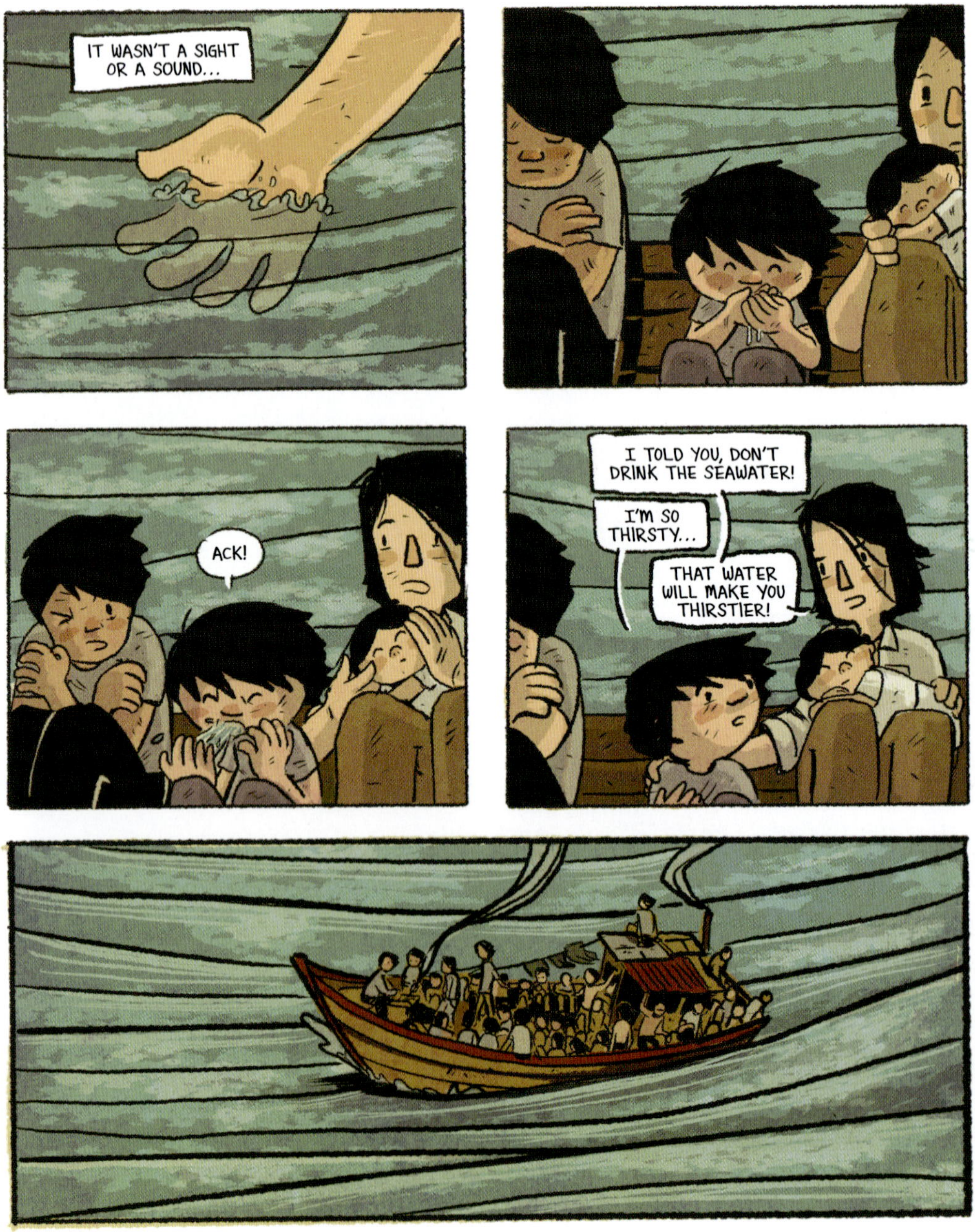
IT WASN'T A SIGHT OR A SOUND...
ACK!
I TOLD YOU, DON'T DRINK THE SEAWATER!
I'M SO THIRSTY...
THAT WATER WILL MAKE YOU THIRSTIER!

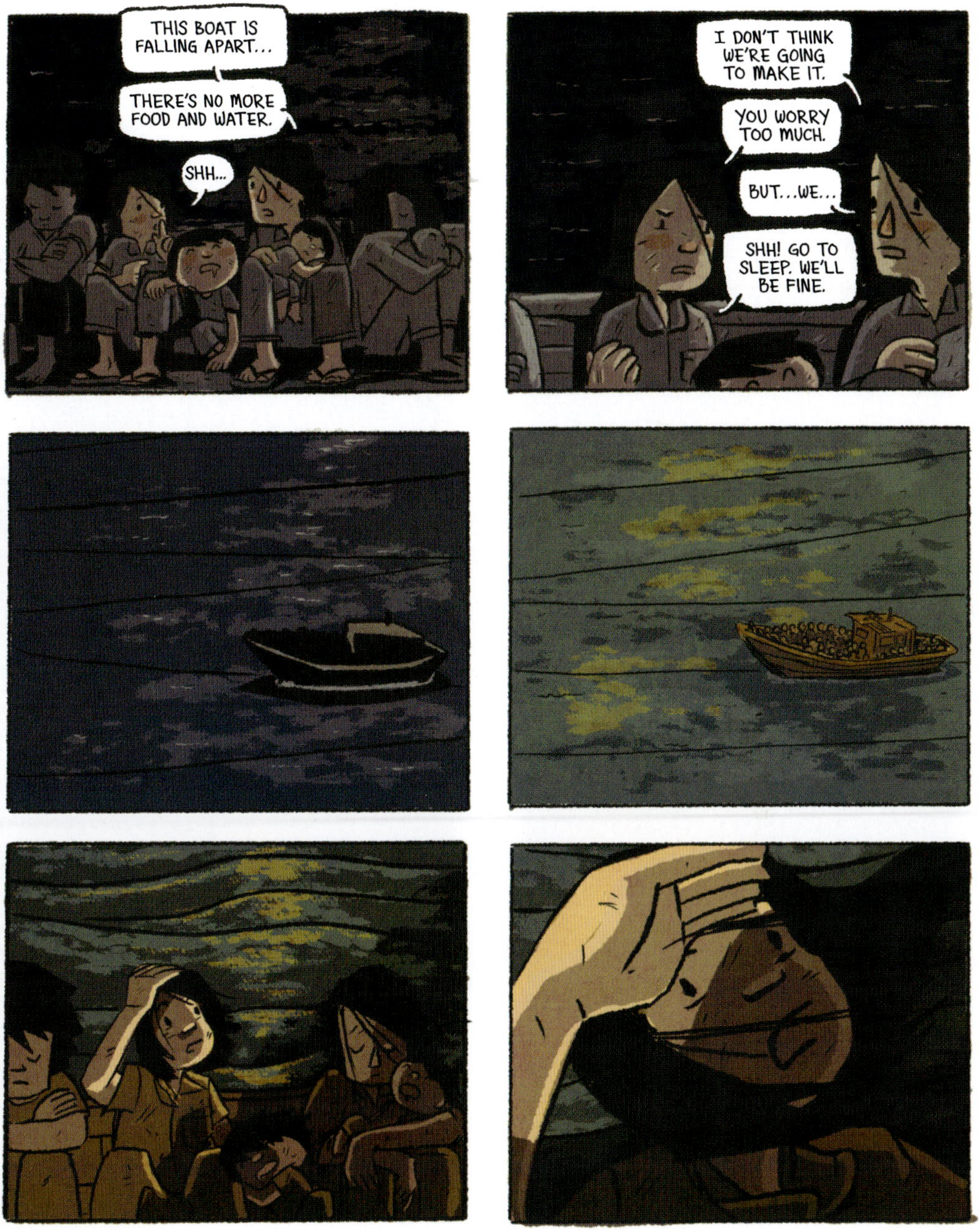
THIS BOAT IS FALLING APART...
THERE'S NO MORE FOOD AND WATER.
SHH...
I DON'T THINK WE'RE GOING TO MAKE IT.
YOU WORRY TOO MUCH.
BUT...WE...
SHH! GO TO SLEEP. WE'LL BE FINE.

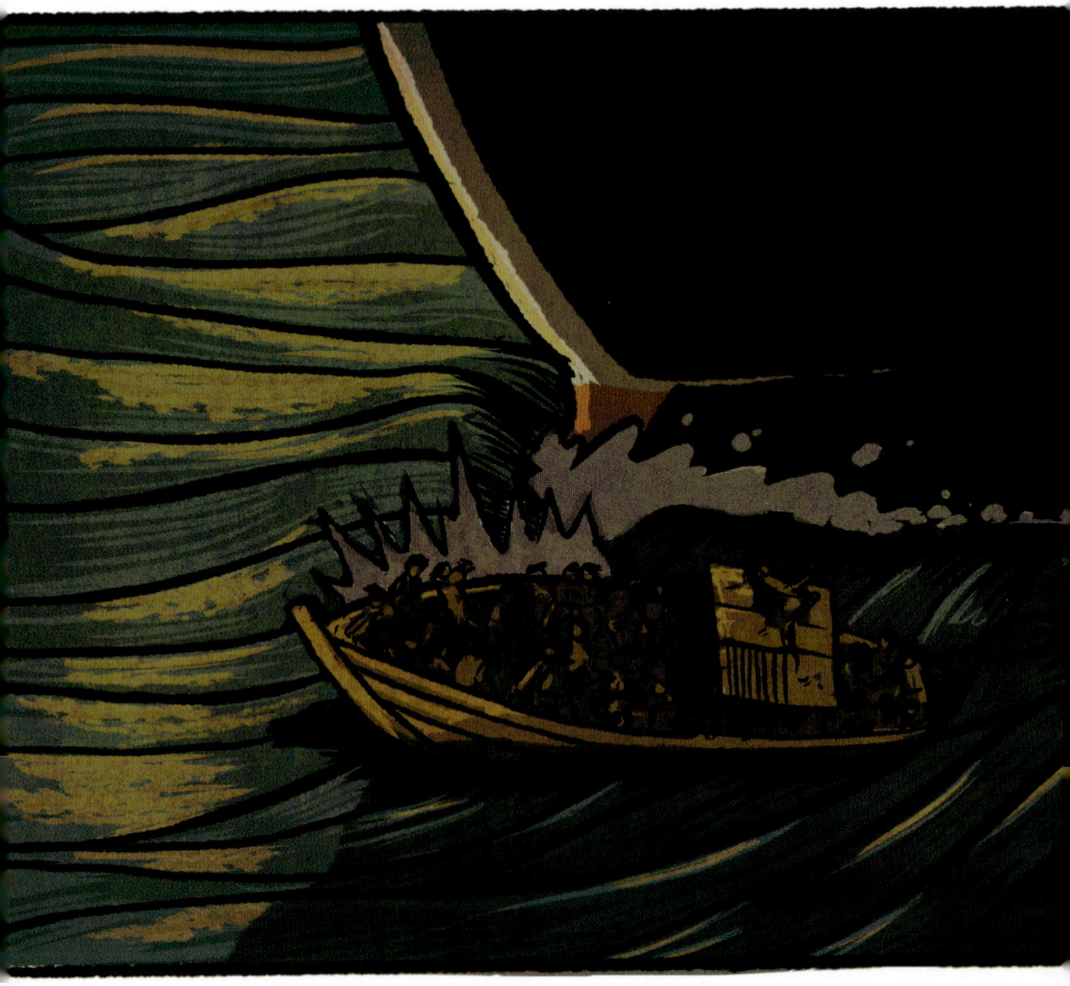

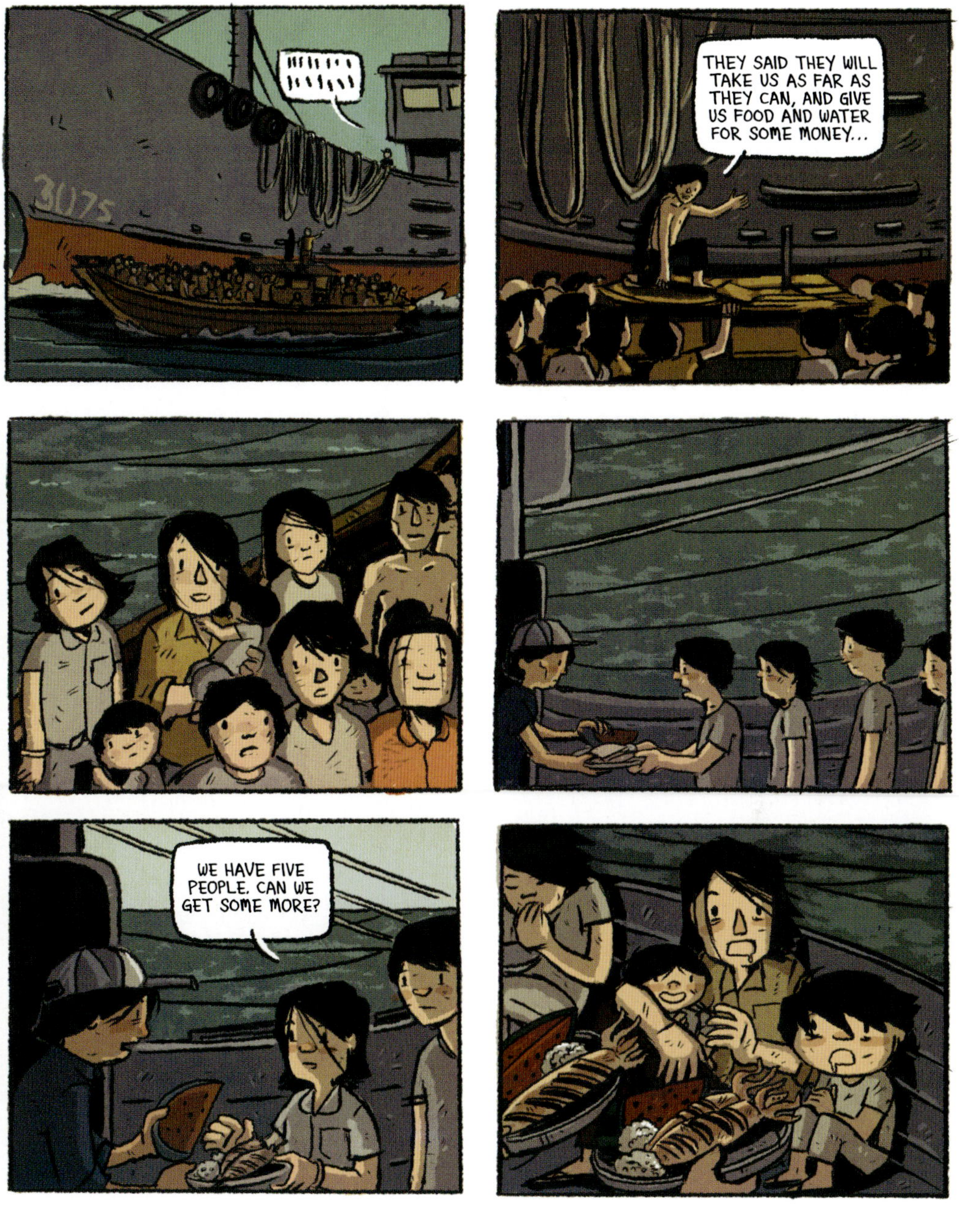
THEY SAID THEY WILL TAKE US AS FAR AS THEY CAN, AND GIVE US FOOD AND WATER FOR SOME MONEY...
WE HAVE FIVE PEOPLE. CAN WE GET SOME MORE?

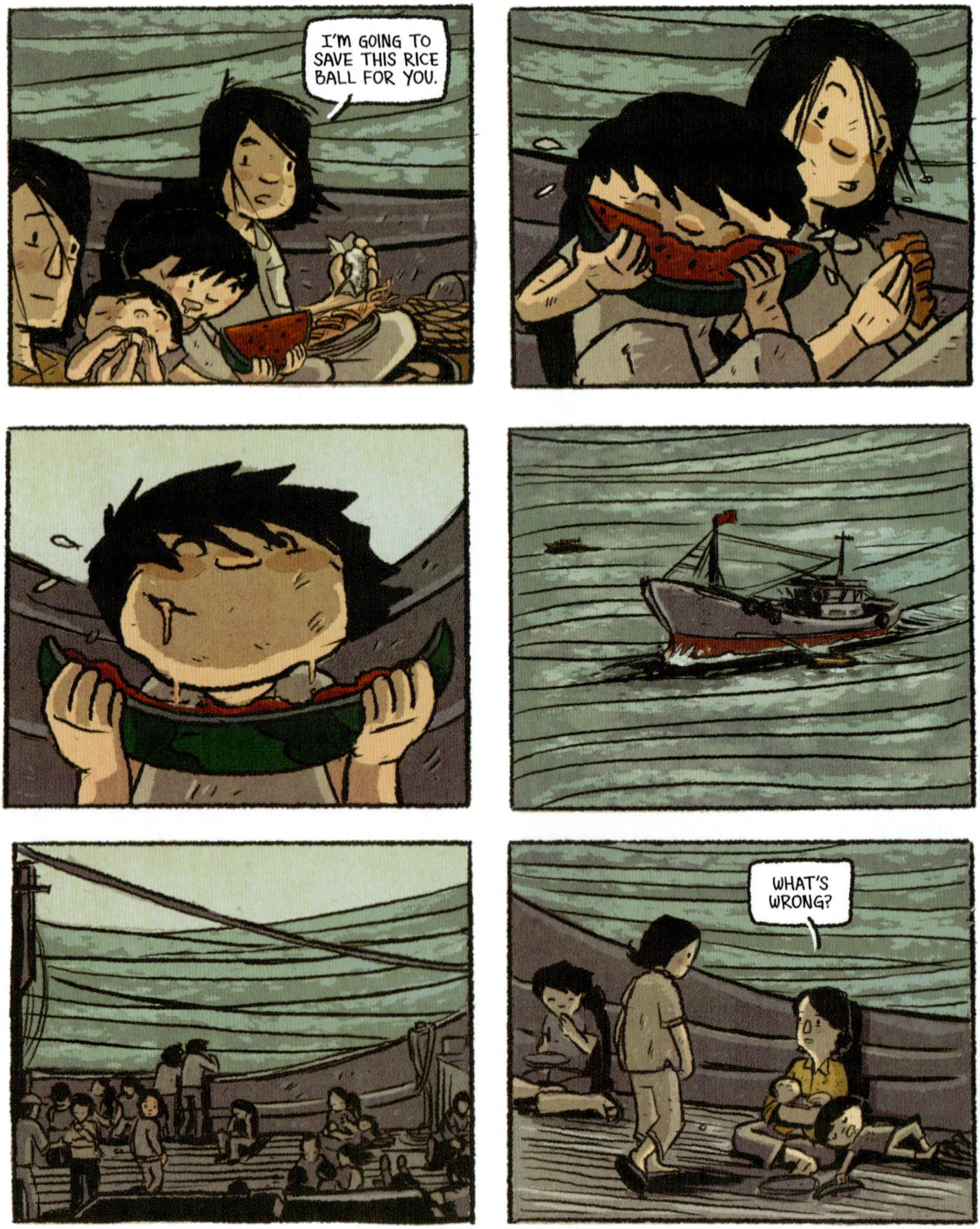
I'M GOING TO SAVE THIS RICE BALL FOR YOU.
WHAT'S WRONG?

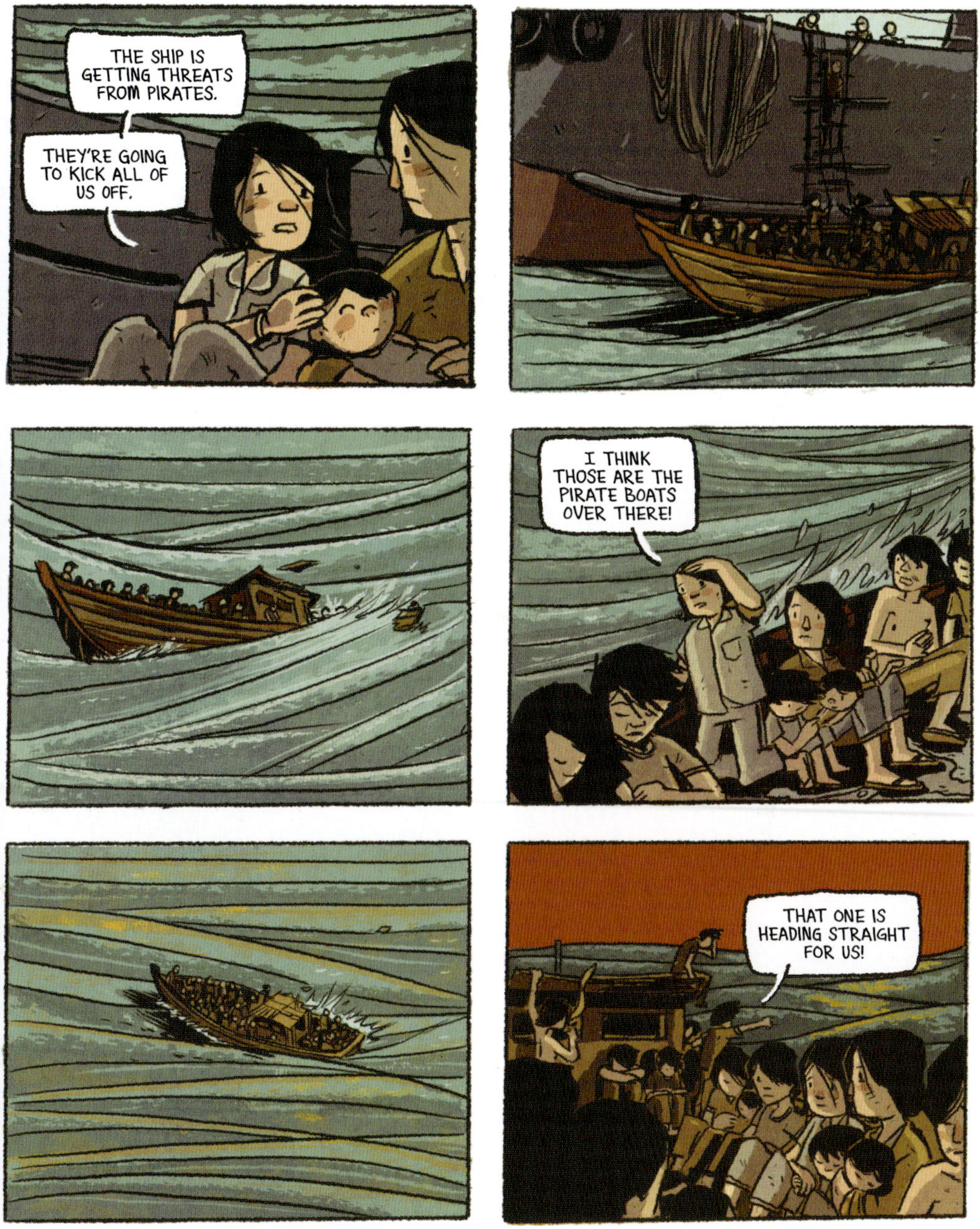
THE SHIP IS GETTING THREATS FROM PIRATES.
THEY'RE GOING TO KICK ALL OF US OFF.
I THINK THOSE ARE THE PIRATE BOATS OVER THERE!
THAT ONE IS HEADING STRAIGHT FOR US!

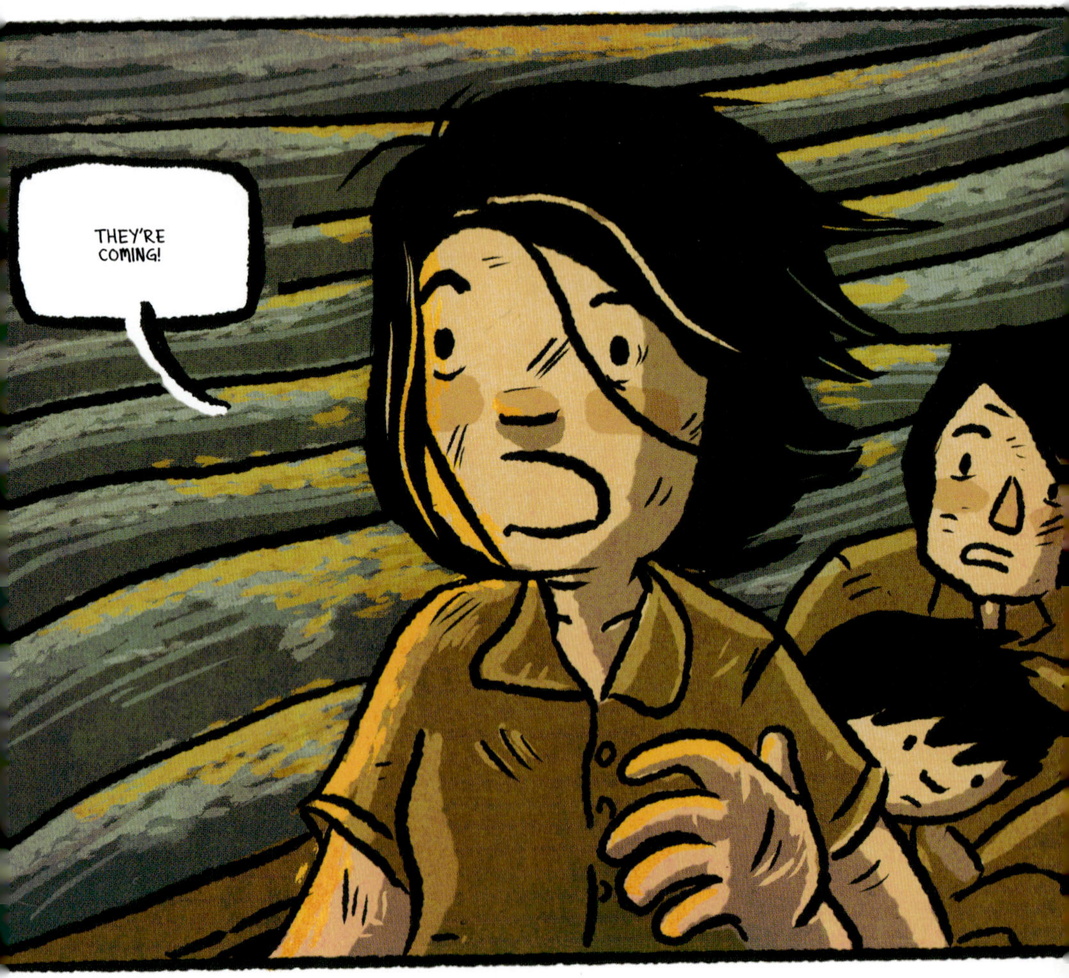
THEY'RE COMING!

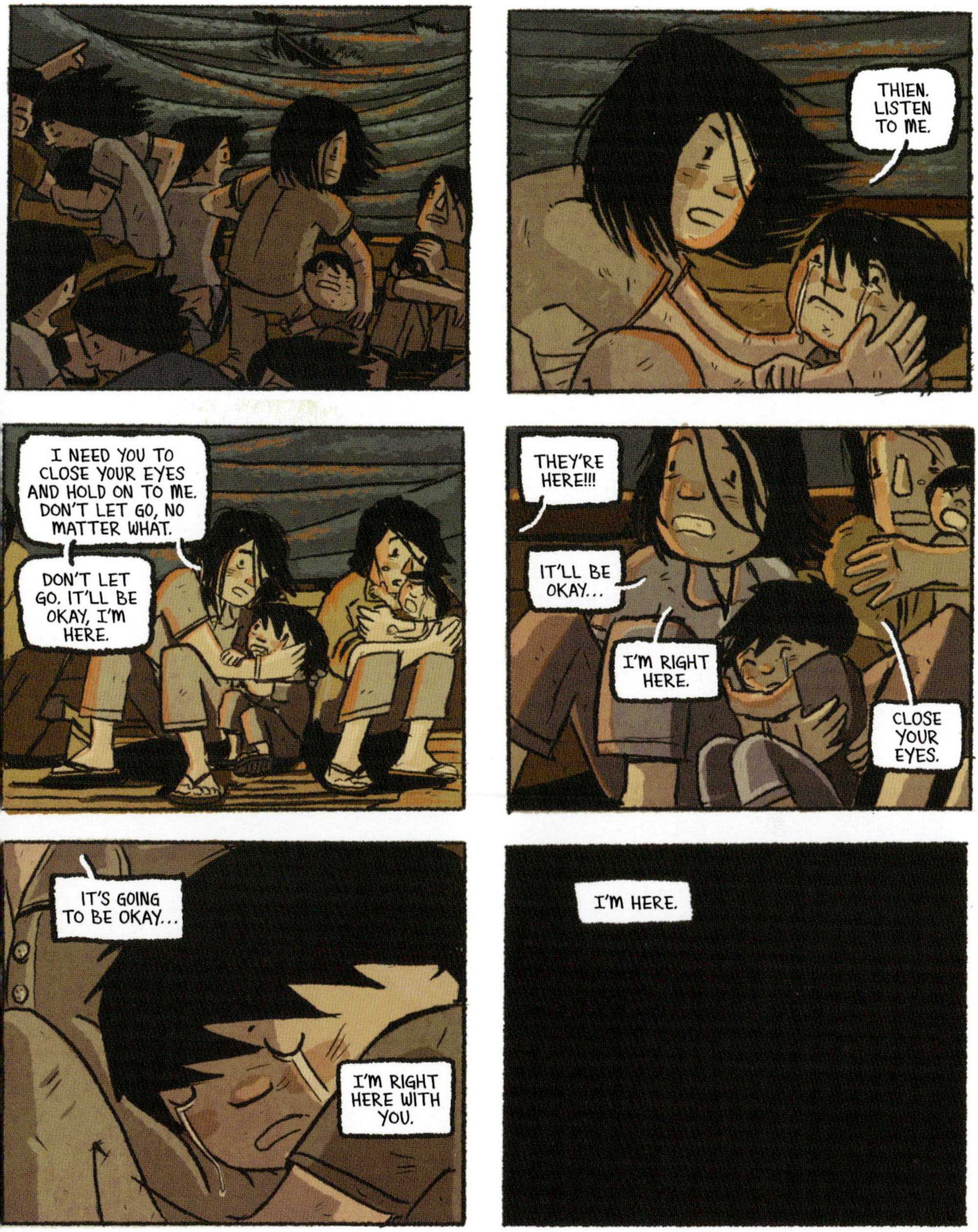
THIEN. LISTEN TO ME.
I NEED YOU TO CLOSE YOUR EYES AND HOLD ON TO ME. DON'T LET GO, NO MATTER WHAT.
DON'T LET GO. IT'LL BE OKAY, I'M HERE.
THEY'RE HERE!!!
IT'LL BE OKAY...
I'M RIGHT HERE.
CLOSE YOUR EYES.
IT'S GOING TO BE OKAY...
I'M RIGHT HERE WITH YOU.
I'M HERE.

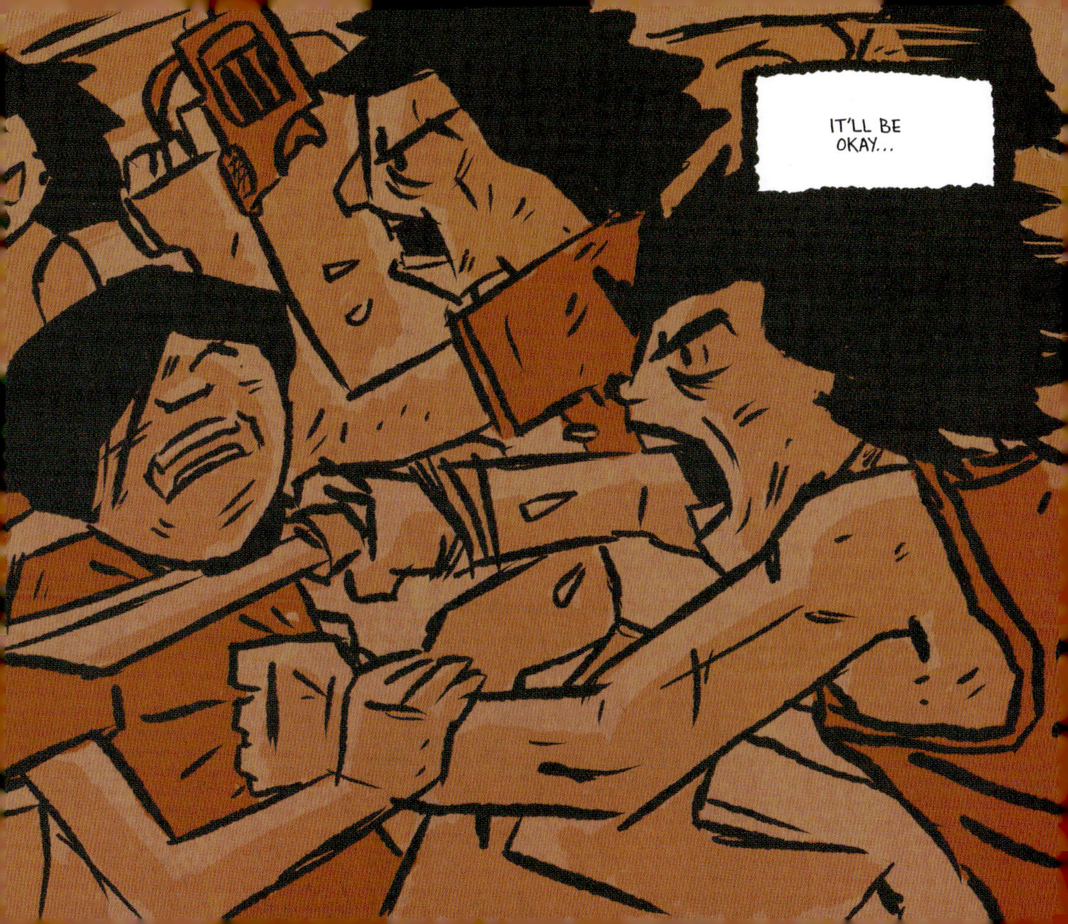
IT'LL BE OKAY...

I'M RIGHT HERE.

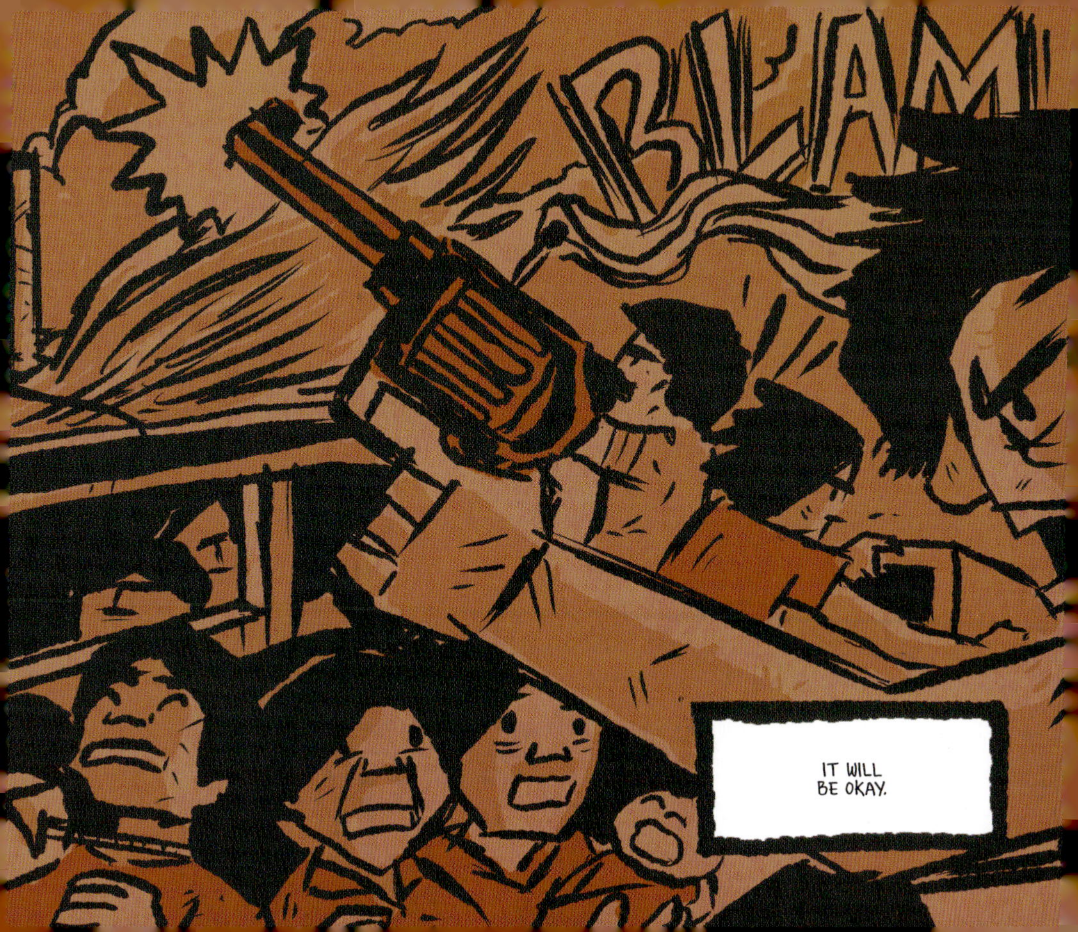
BLAM
IT WILL BE OKAY.

I'M RIGHT HERE.

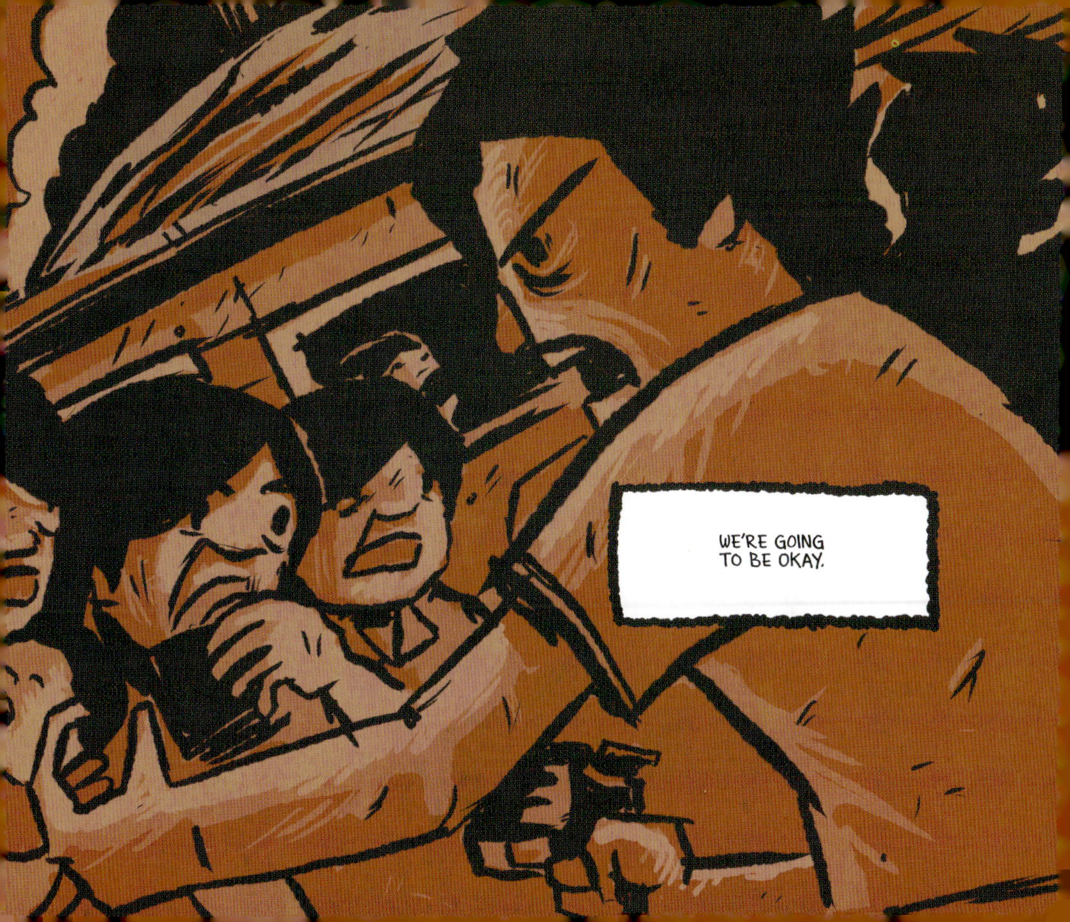
WE'RE GOING TO BE OKAY.

I'M RIGHT HERE WITH YOU.

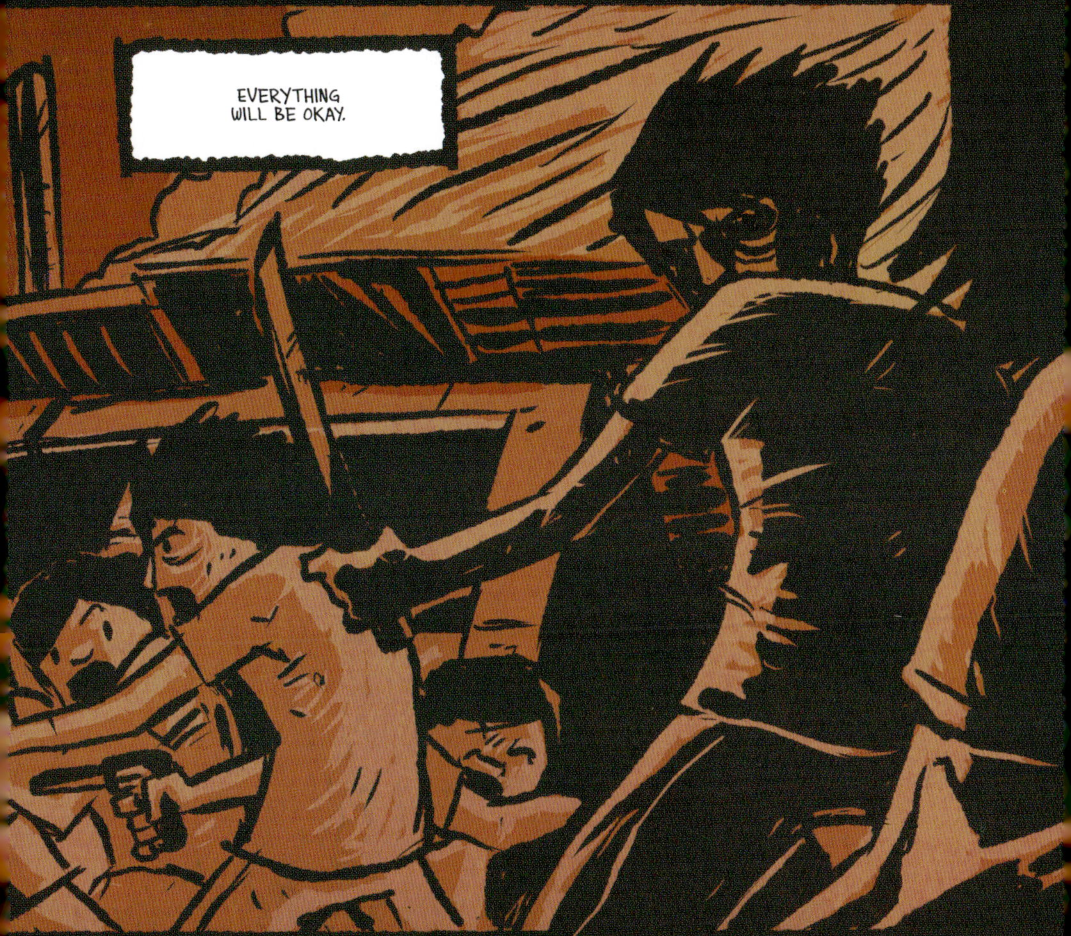
EVERYTHING WILL BE OKAY.

I'M HERE.

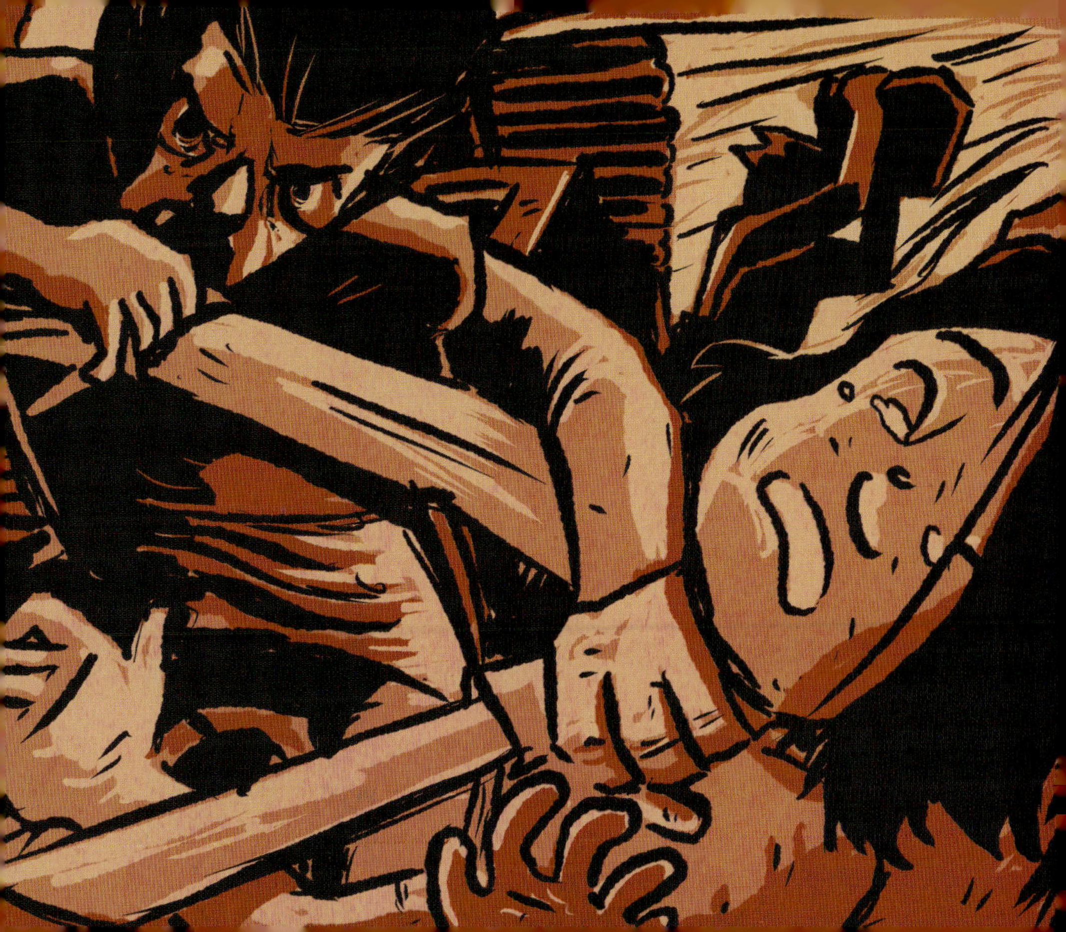

THIEN.
THEY'RE GONE. YOU CAN OPEN YOUR EYES NOW.
WE'RE STILL HERE.
WE'LL BE OKAY.

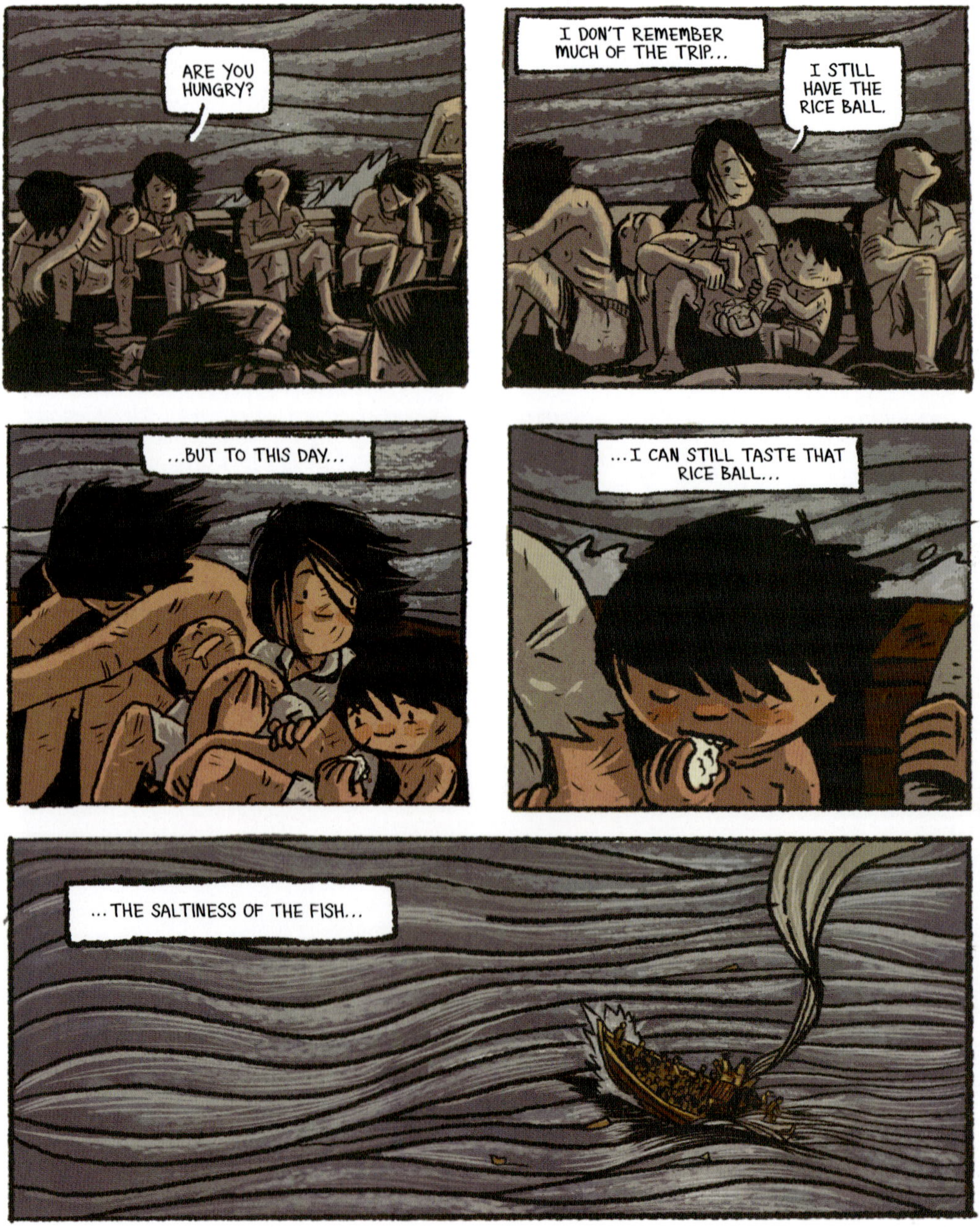
ARE YOU HUNGRY?
I DON'T REMEMBER MUCH OF THE TRIP...
I STILL HAVE THE RICE BALL.
...BUT TO THIS DAY...
...I CAN STILL TASTE THAT RICE BALL...
...THE SALTINESS OF THE FISH...

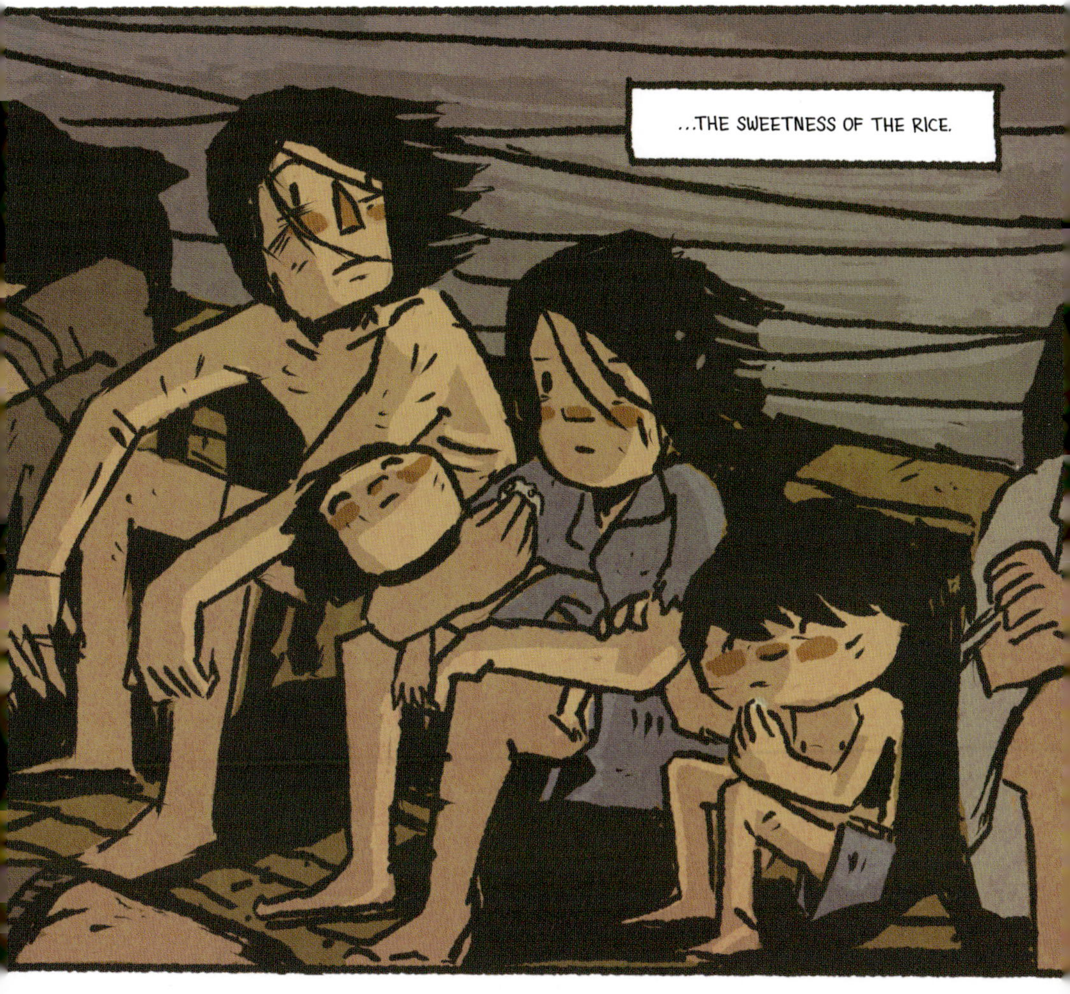
...THE SWEETNESS OF THE RICE.

CHAPTER 2: BÁNH CUỐN

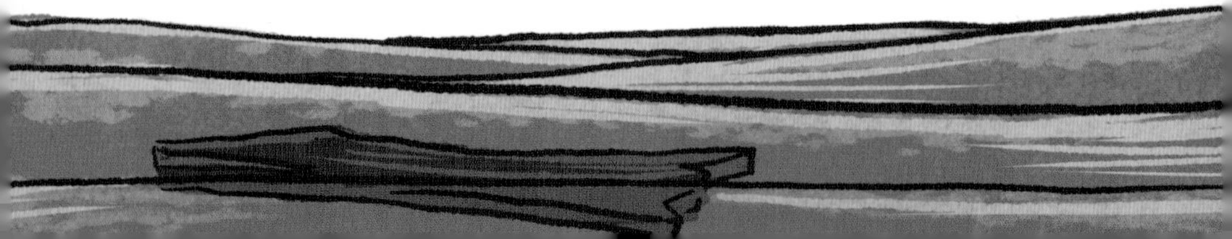

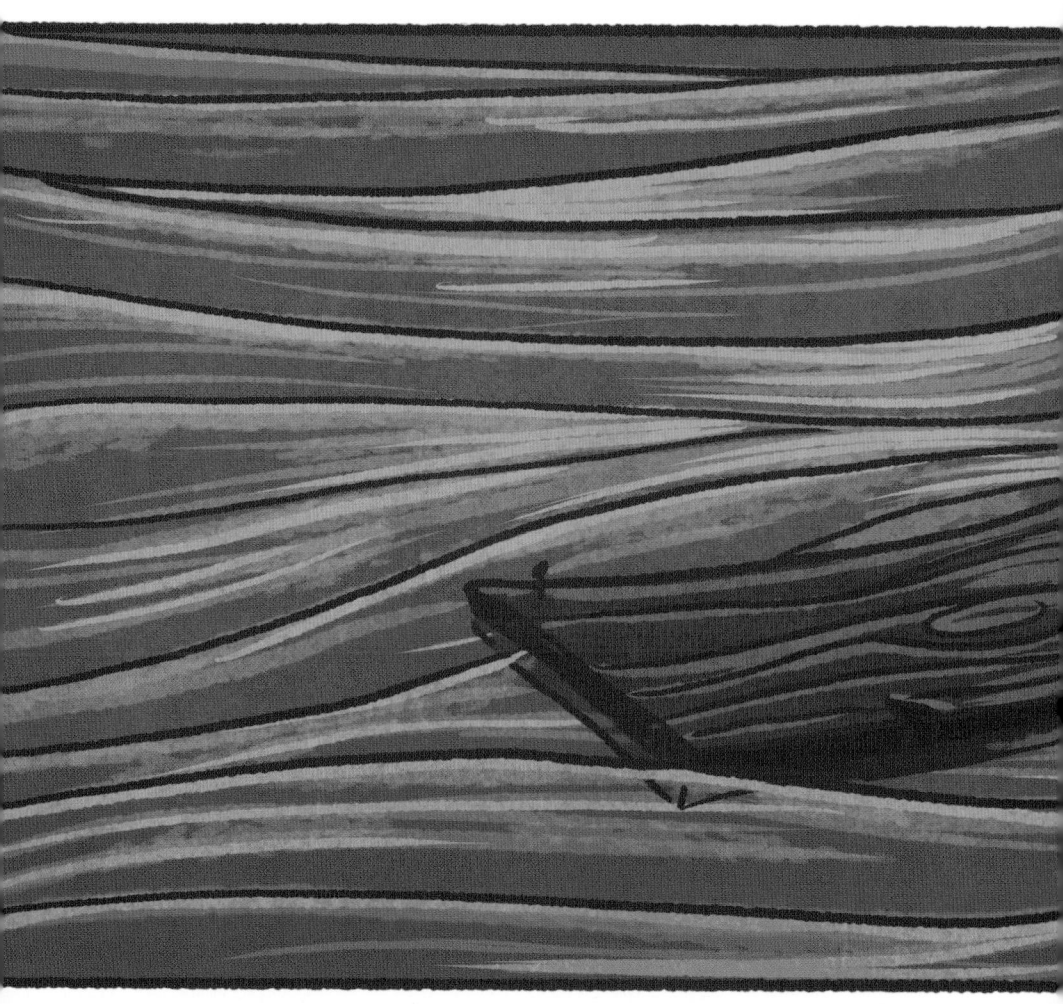

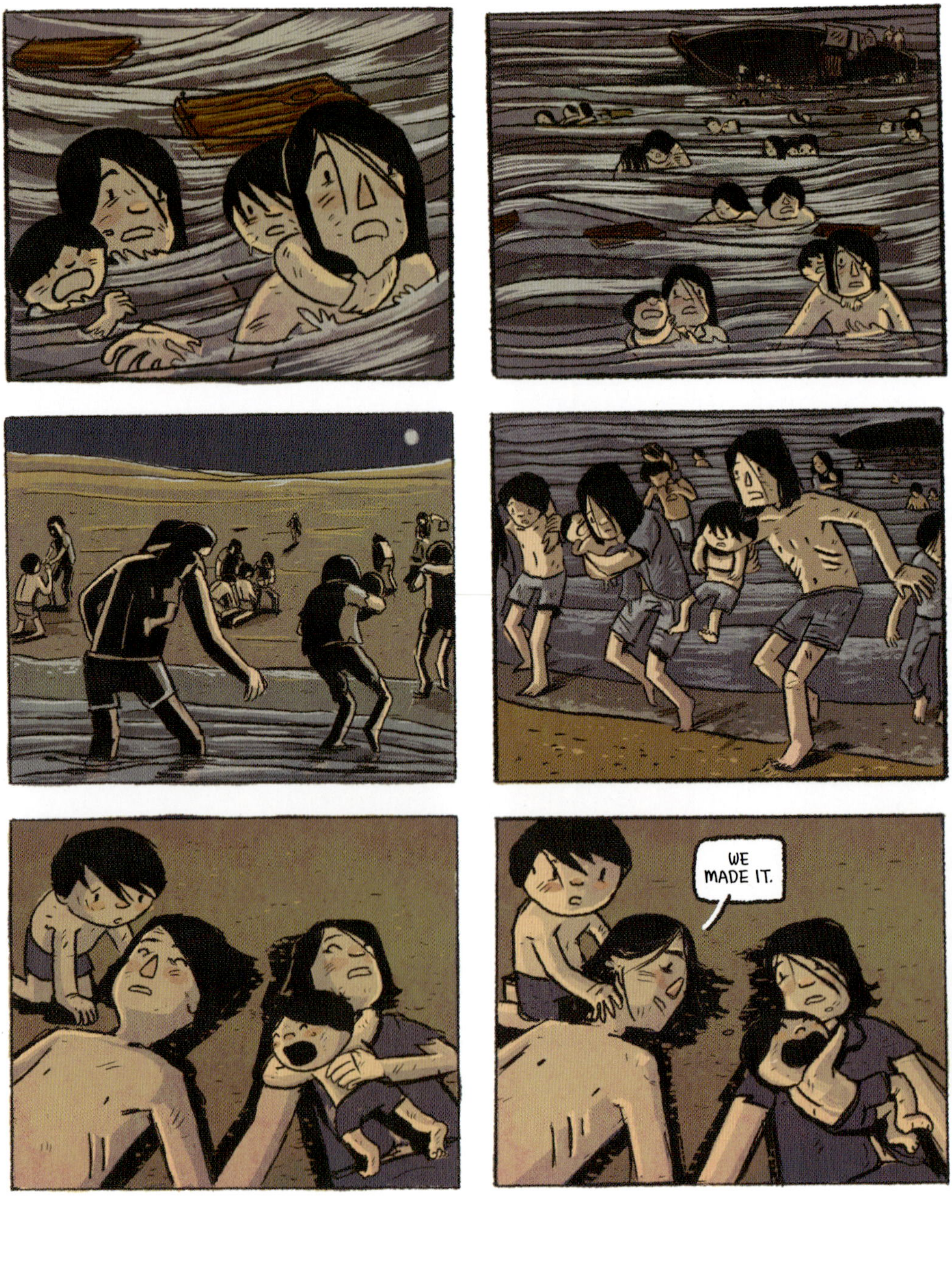
WE MADE IT.

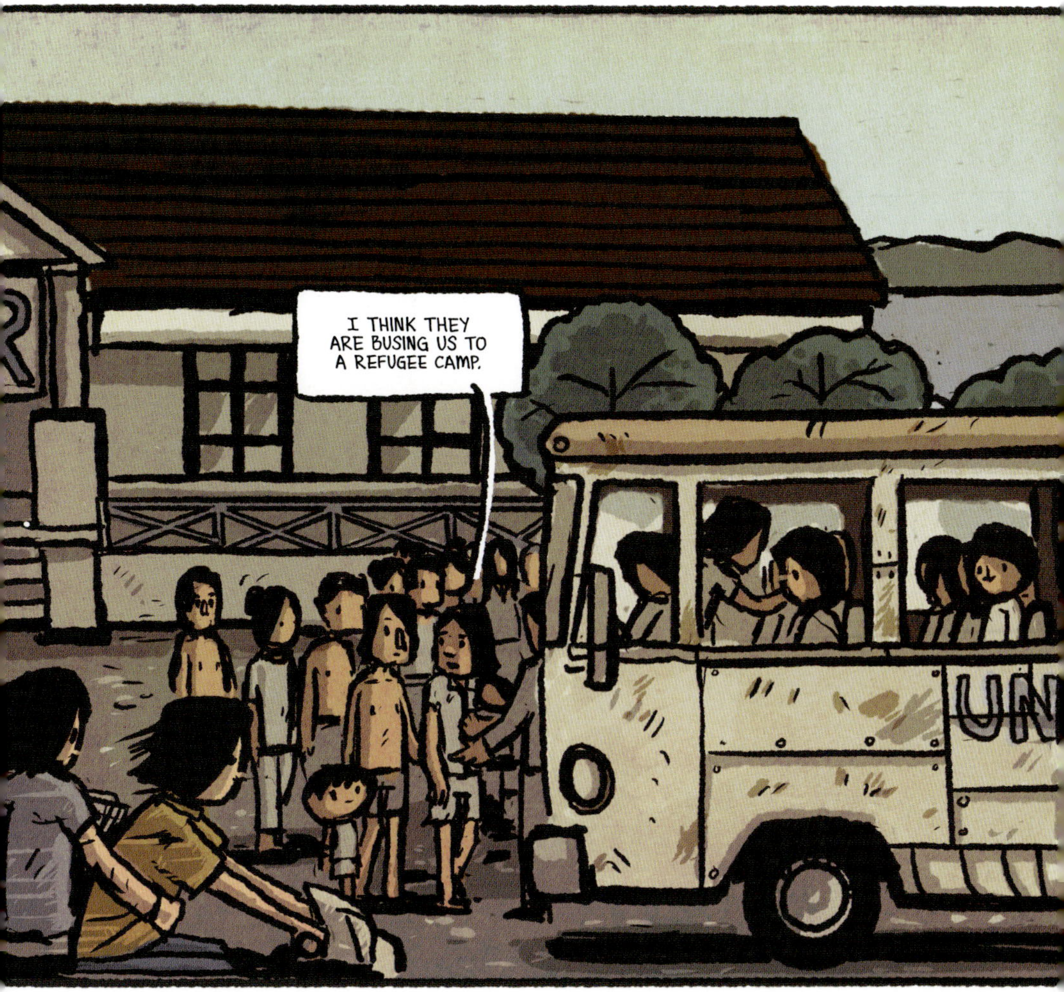
I THINK THEY ARE BUSING US TO A REFUGEE CAMP.
UN

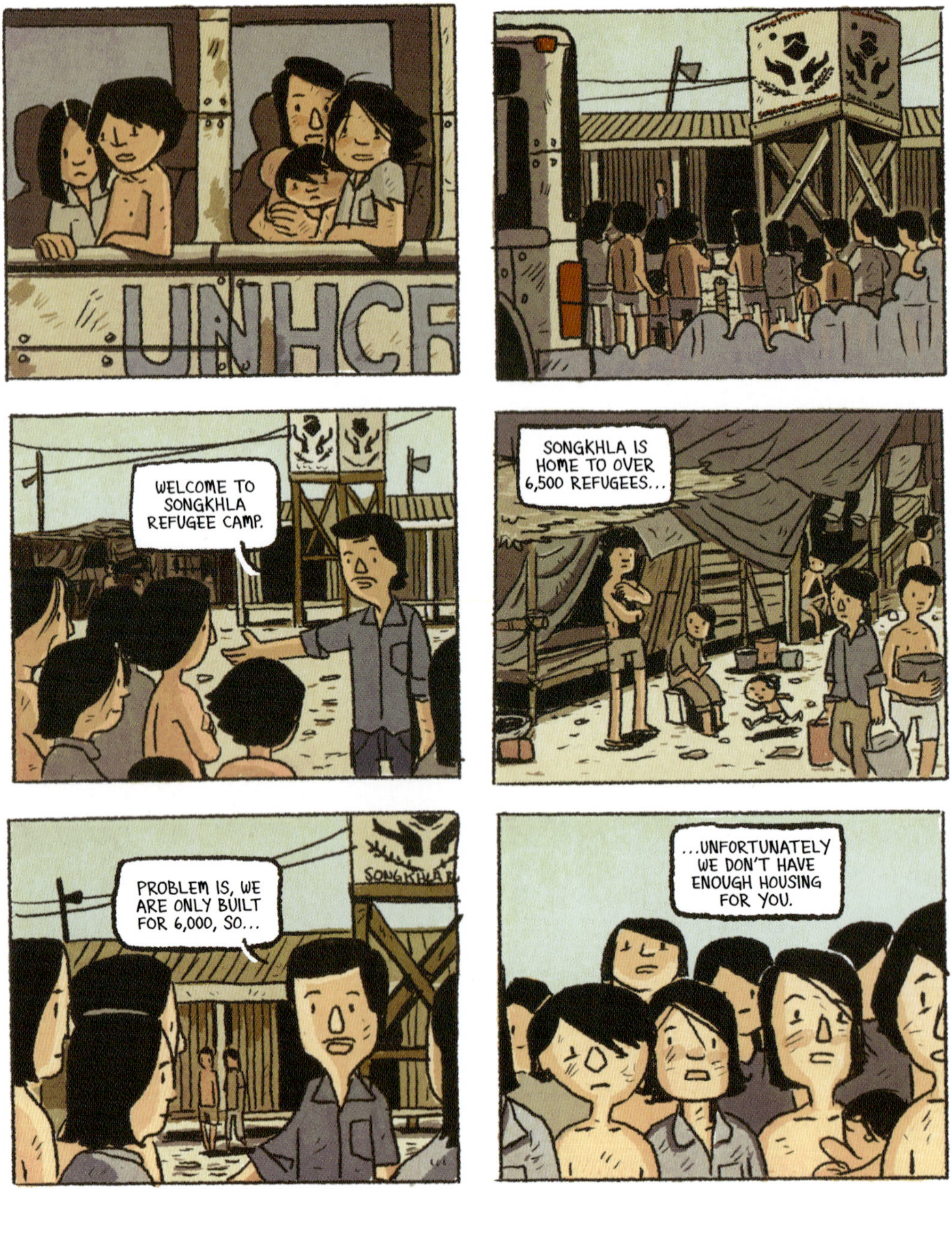
UNHCR
WELCOME TO SONGKHLA REFUGEE CAMP.
SONGKHLA IS HOME TO OVER 6,500 REFUGEES...
PROBLEM IS, WE ARE ONLY BUILT FOR 6,000, SO...
...UNFORTUNATELY WE DON'T HAVE ENOUGH HOUSING FOR YOU.

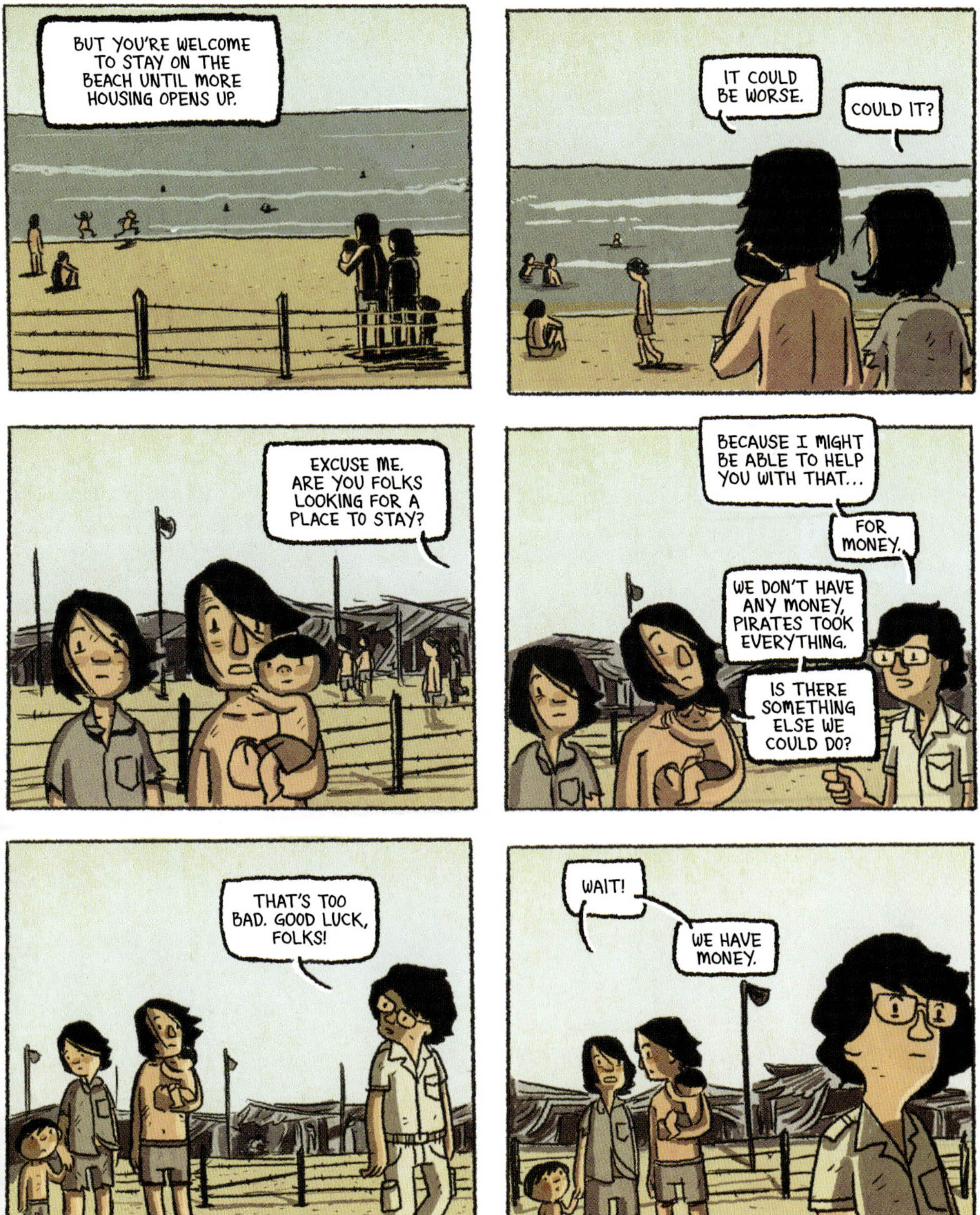
BUT YOU'RE WELCOME TO STAY ON THE BEACH UNTIL MORE HOUSING OPENS UP.
IT COULD BE WORSE.
COULD IT?
EXCUSE ME. ARE YOU FOLKS LOOKING FOR A PLACE TO STAY?
BECAUSE I MIGHT BE ABLE TO HELP YOU WITH THAT...
FOR MONEY.
WE DON'T HAVE ANY MONEY, PIRATES TOOK EVERYTHING.
IS THERE SOMETHING ELSE WE COULD DO?
THAT'S TOO BAD. GOOD LUCK, FOLKS!
WAIT!
WE HAVE MONEY.

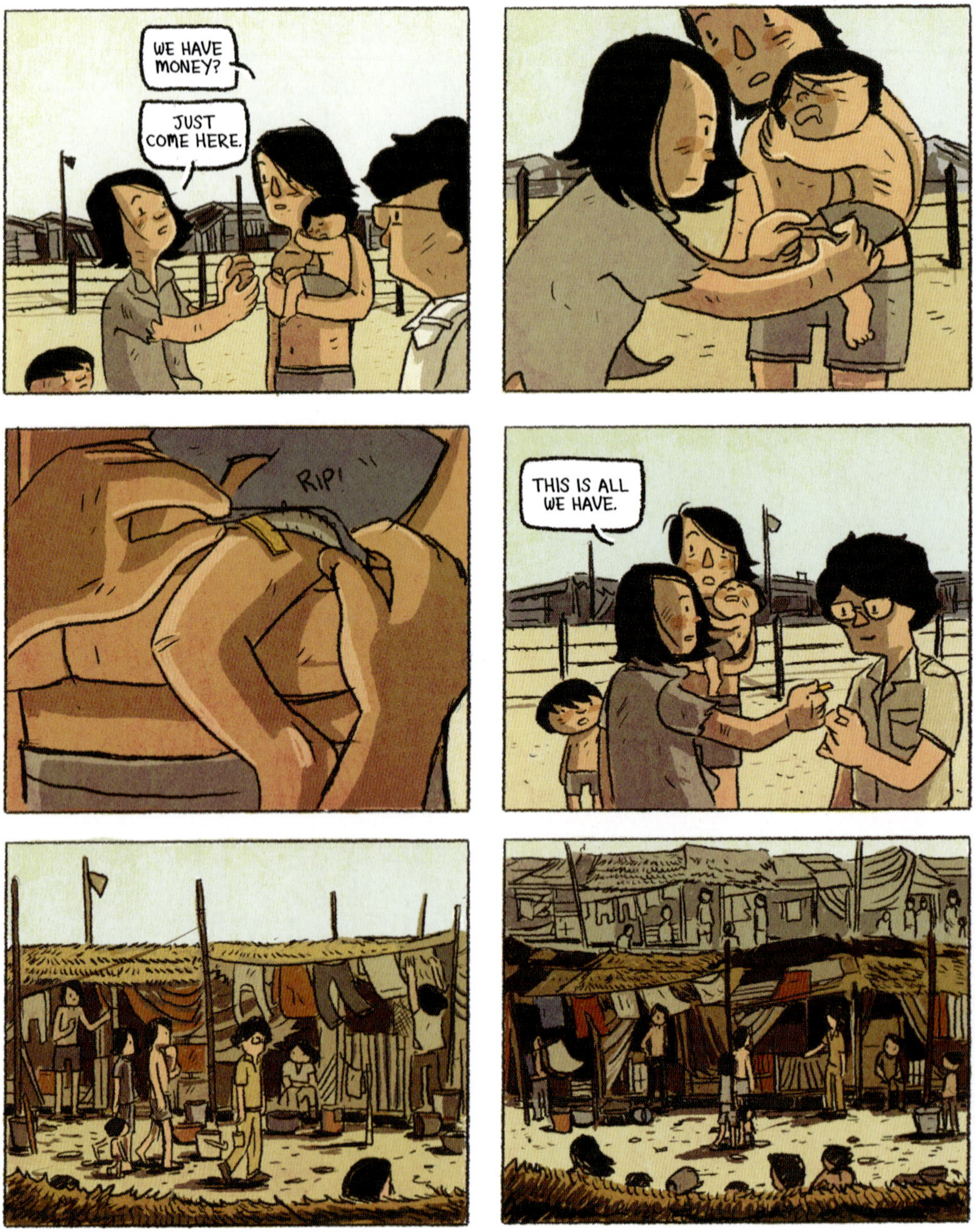
WE HAVE MONEY?
JUST COME HERE.
RIP!
THIS IS ALL WE HAVE.

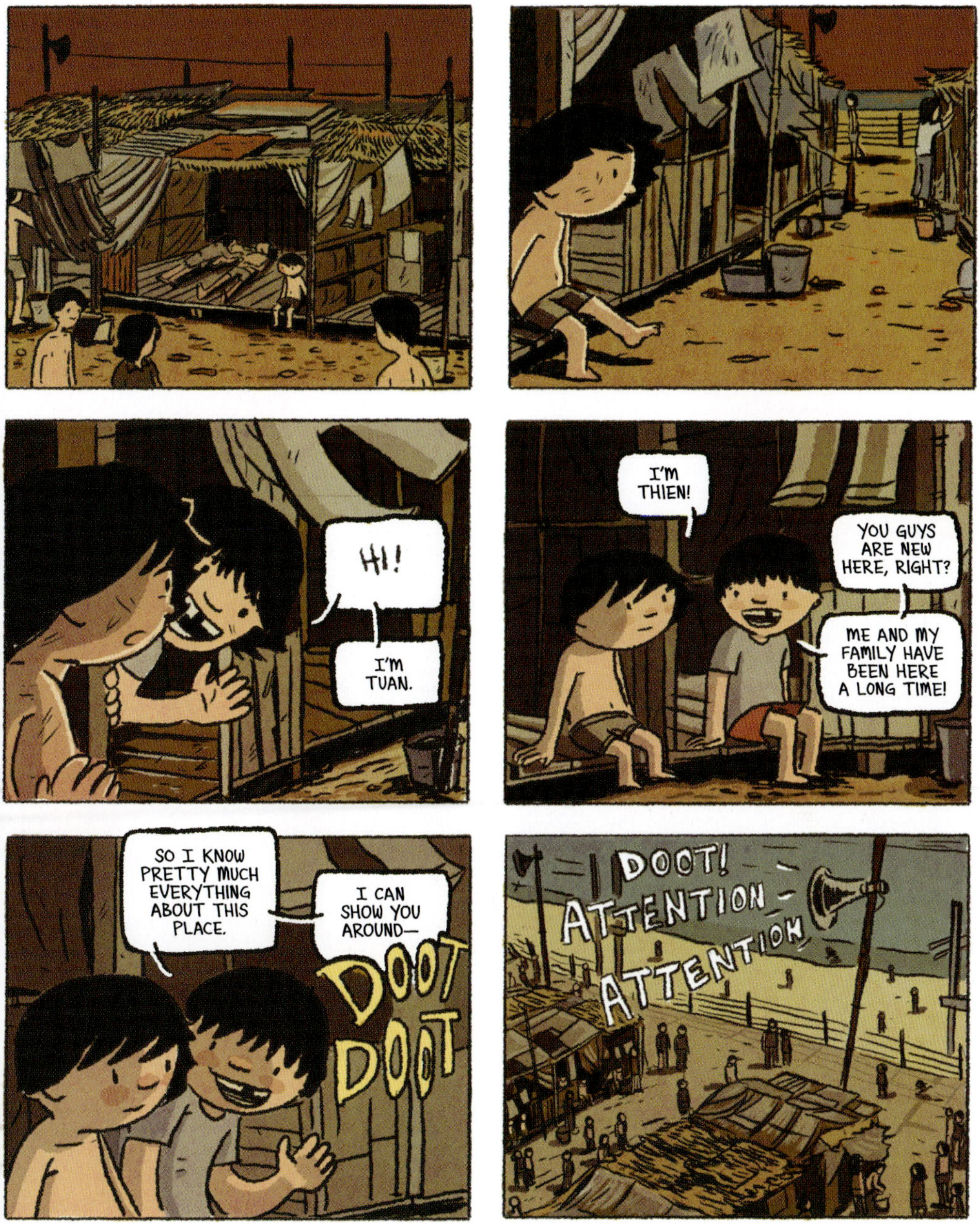
HI!
I'M TUAN.
I'M THIEN!
YOU GUYS ARE NEW HERE, RIGHT?
ME AND MY FAMILY HAVE BEEN HERE A LONG TIME!
SO I KNOW PRETTY MUCH EVERYTHING ABOUT THIS PLACE.
I CAN SHOW YOU AROUND—
DOOT DOOT
DOOT!
ATTENTION
ATTENTION

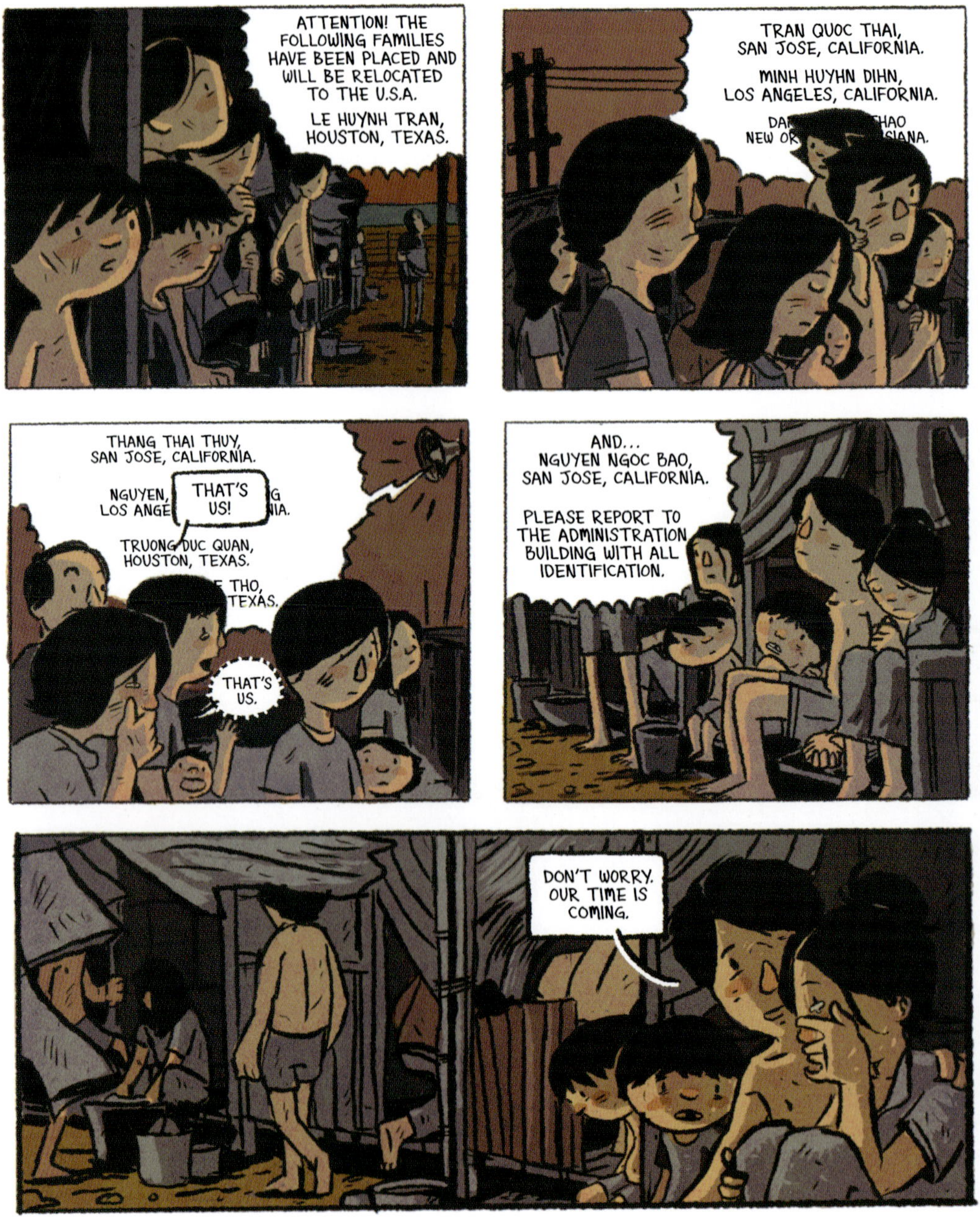
ATTENTION! THE FOLLOWING FAMILIES HAVE BEEN PLACED AND WILL BE RELOCATED TO THE U.S.A.
LE HUYNH TRAN, HOUSTON, TEXAS.
TRAN QUOC THAI, SAN JOSE, CALIFORNIA.
MINH HUYHN DIHN, LOS ANGELES, CALIFORNIA.
THANG THAI THUY, SAN JOSE, CALIFORNIA.
THAT'S US!
TRUONG DUC QUAN, HOUSTON, TEXAS.
THAT'S US.
AND... NGUYEN NGOC BAO, SAN JOSE, CALIFORNIA.
PLEASE REPORT TO THE ADMINISTRATION BUILDING WITH ALL IDENTIFICATION.
DON'T WORRY. OUR TIME IS COMING.

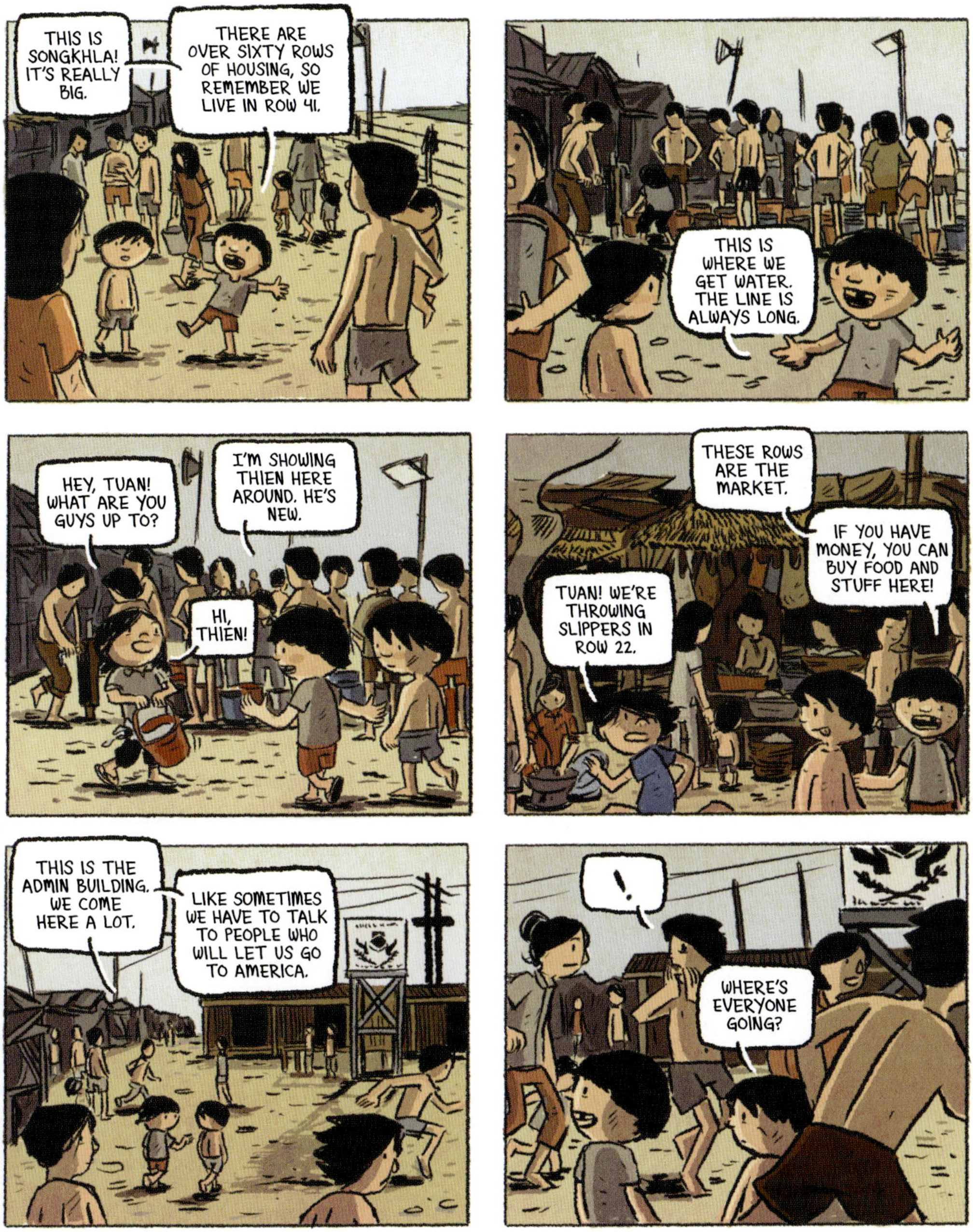

THIS IS SONGKHLA! IT'S REALLY BIG.
THERE ARE OVER SIXTY ROWS OF HOUSING, SO REMEMBER WE LIVE IN ROW 41.
THIS IS WHERE WE GET WATER. THE LINE IS ALWAYS LONG.
HEY, TUAN! WHAT ARE YOU GUYS UP TO?
I'M SHOWING THIEN HERE AROUND. HE'S NEW.
HI, THIEN!
THESE ROWS ARE THE MARKET.
IF YOU HAVE MONEY, YOU CAN BUY FOOD AND STUFF HERE!
TUAN! WE'RE THROWING SLIPPERS IN ROW 22.
THIS IS THE ADMIN BUILDING. WE COME HERE A LOT.
LIKE SOMETIMES WE HAVE TO TALK TO PEOPLE WHO WILL LET US GO TO AMERICA.
!
WHERE'S EVERYONE GOING?

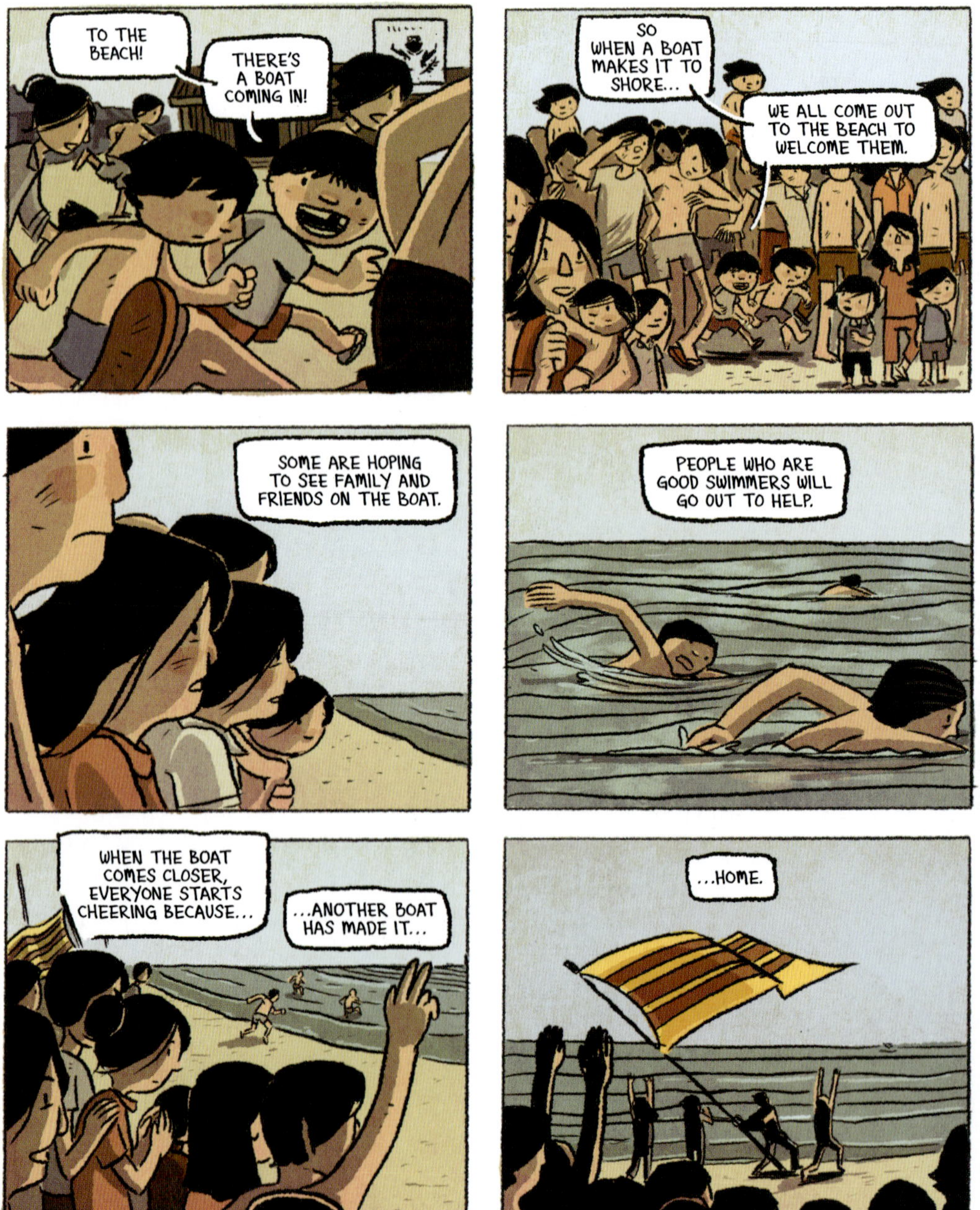
TO THE BEACH!
THERE'S A BOAT COMING IN!
SO WHEN A BOAT MAKES IT TO SHORE...
WE ALL COME OUT TO THE BEACH TO WELCOME THEM.
SOME ARE HOPING TO SEE FAMILY AND FRIENDS ON THE BOAT.
PEOPLE WHO ARE GOOD SWIMMERS WILL GO OUT TO HELP.
WHEN THE BOAT COMES CLOSER, EVERYONE STARTS CHEERING BECAUSE...
...ANOTHER BOAT HAS MADE IT...
...HOME.

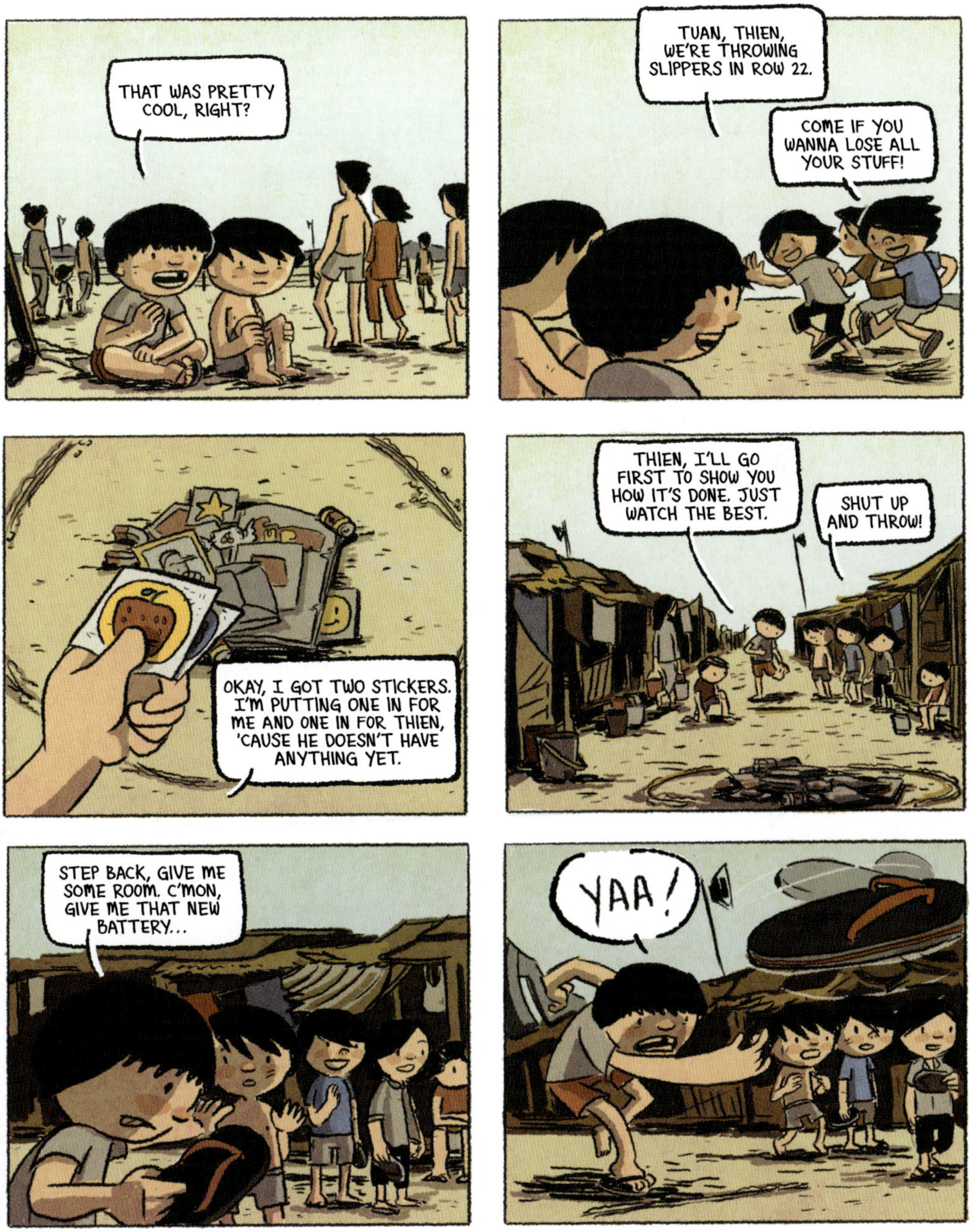
THAT WAS PRETTY COOL, RIGHT?
TUAN, THIEN, WE'RE THROWING SLIPPERS IN ROW 22.
COME IF YOU WANNA LOSE ALL YOUR STUFF!
OKAY, I GOT TWO STICKERS. I'M PUTTING ONE IN FOR ME AND ONE IN FOR THIEN, 'CAUSE HE DOESN'T HAVE ANYTHING YET.
THIEN, I'LL GO FIRST TO SHOW YOU HOW IT'S DONE. JUST WATCH THE BEST.
SHUT UP AND THROW!
STEP BACK, GIVE ME SOME ROOM. C'MON, GIVE ME THAT NEW BATTERY...
YAA!

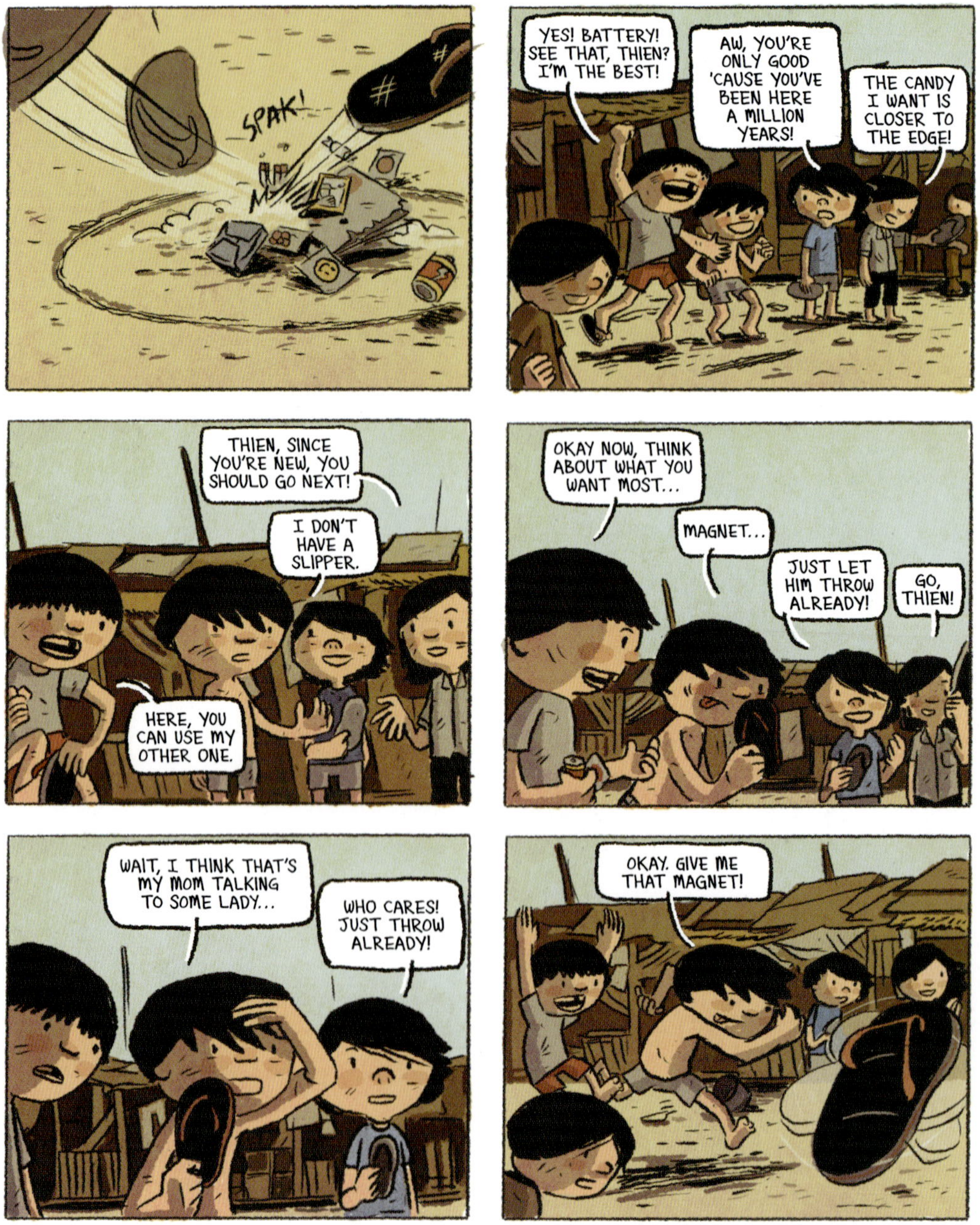
SPAK!
YES! BATTERY! SEE THAT, THIEN? I'M THE BEST!
AW, YOU'RE ONLY GOOD 'CAUSE YOU'VE BEEN HERE A MILLION YEARS!
THE CANDY I WANT IS CLOSER TO THE EDGE!
THIEN, SINCE YOU'RE NEW, YOU SHOULD GO NEXT!
I DON'T HAVE A SLIPPER.
HERE, YOU CAN USE MY OTHER ONE.
OKAY NOW, THINK ABOUT WHAT YOU WANT MOST...
MAGNET...
JUST LET HIM THROW ALREADY!
GO, THIEN!
WAIT, I THINK THAT'S MY MOM TALKING TO SOME LADY...
WHO CARES! JUST THROW ALREADY!
OKAY. GIVE ME THAT MAGNET!

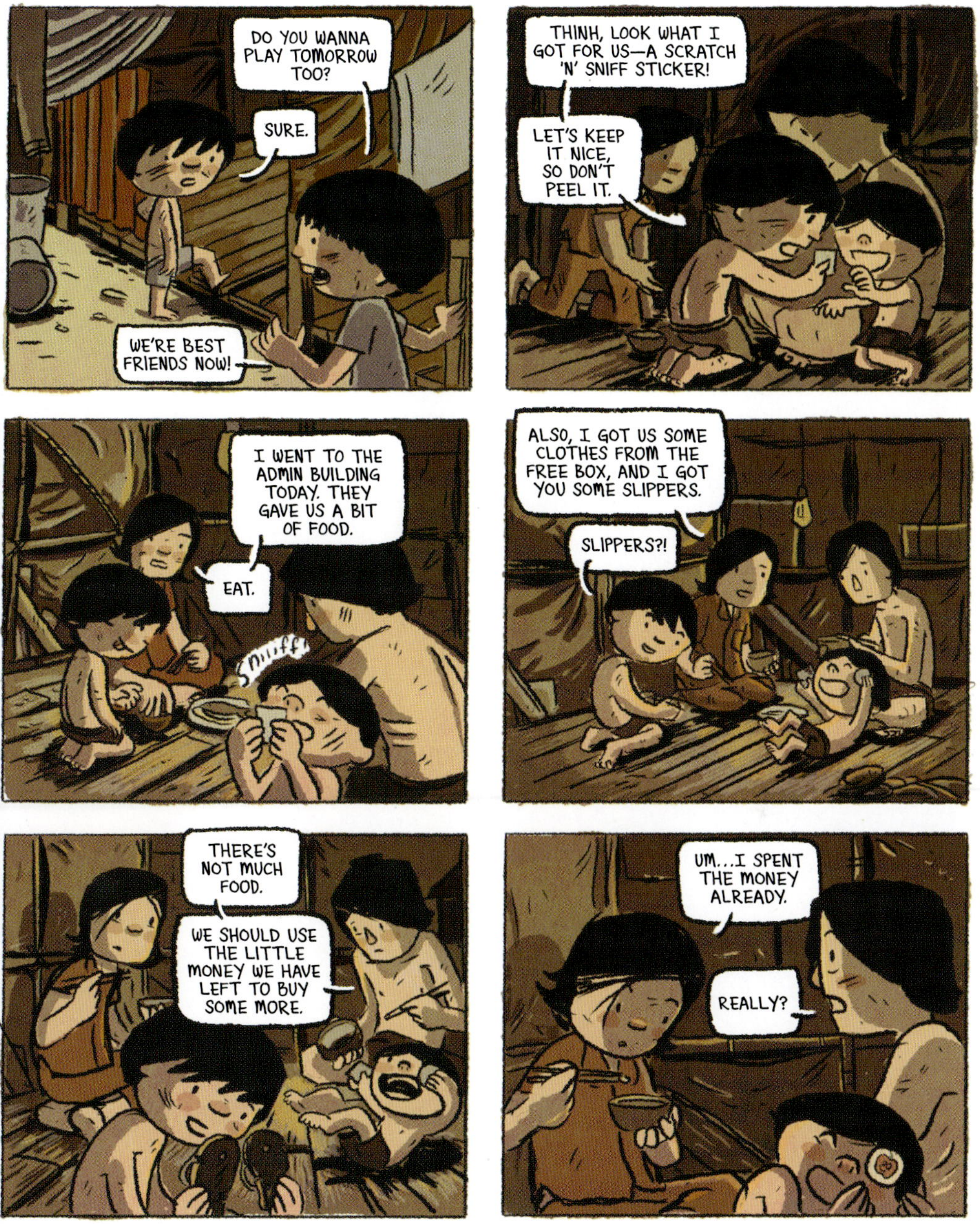
DO YOU WANNA PLAY TOMORROW TOO?
SURE.
WE'RE BEST FRIENDS NOW!
THINH, LOOK WHAT I GOT FOR US—A SCRATCH 'N' SNIFF STICKER!
LET'S KEEP IT NICE, SO DON'T PEEL IT.
I WENT TO THE ADMIN BUILDING TODAY. THEY GAVE US A BIT OF FOOD.
EAT.
SNIFF!
ALSO, I GOT US SOME CLOTHES FROM THE FREE BOX, AND I GOT YOU SOME SLIPPERS.
SLIPPERS?!
THERE'S NOT MUCH FOOD.
WE SHOULD USE THE LITTLE MONEY WE HAVE LEFT TO BUY SOME MORE.
UM...I SPENT THE MONEY ALREADY.
REALLY?

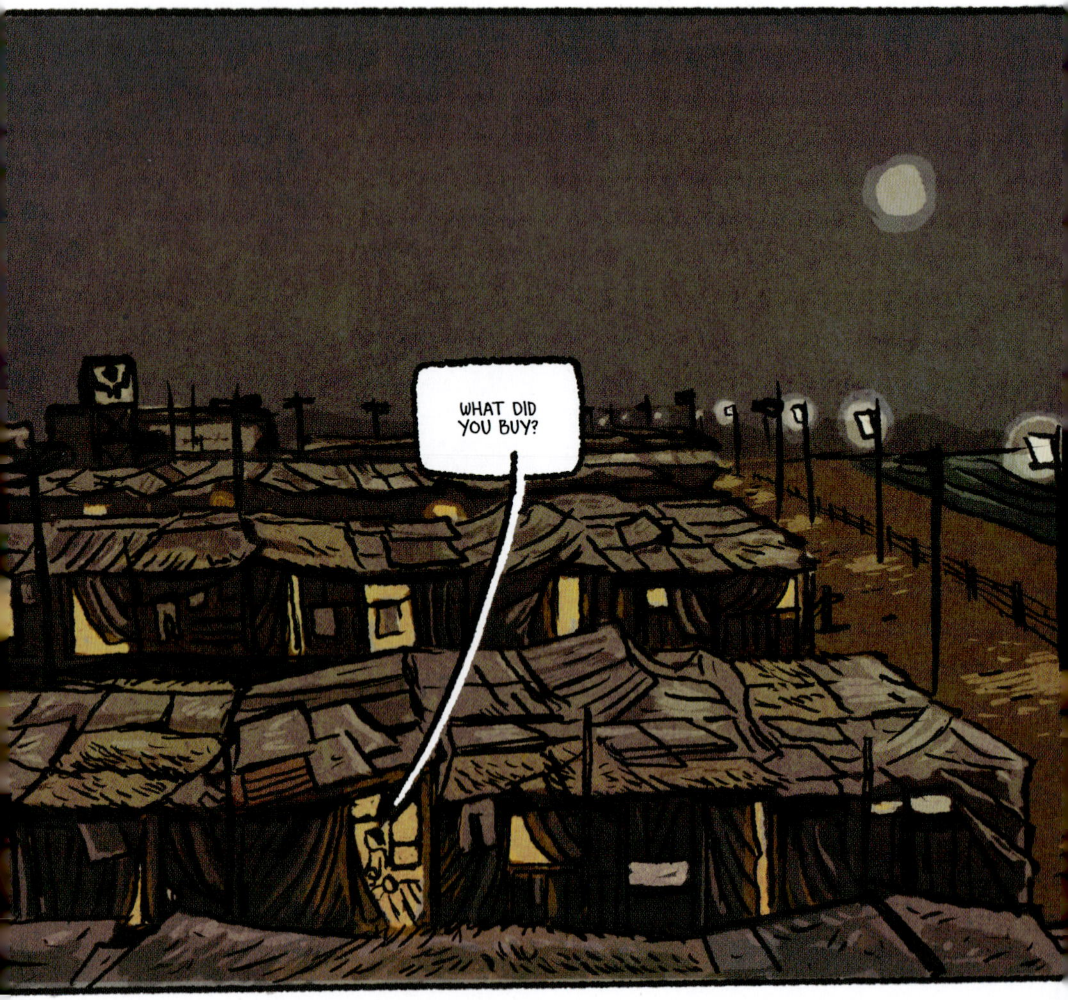
WHAT DID
YOU BUY?

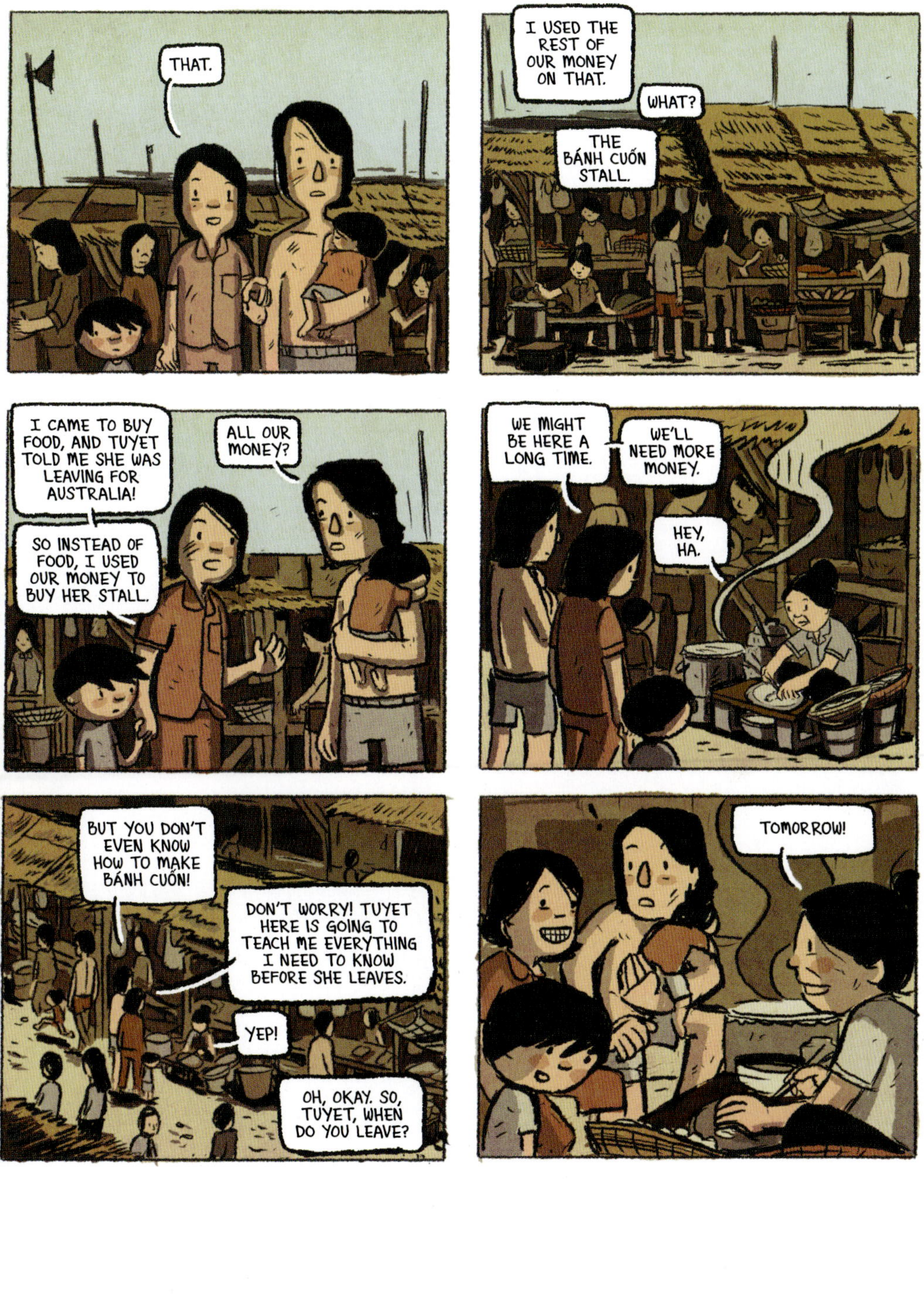
THAT.
I USED THE REST OF OUR MONEY ON THAT.
WHAT?
THE BÁNH CUỐN STALL.
I CAME TO BUY FOOD, AND TUYET TOLD ME SHE WAS LEAVING FOR AUSTRALIA!
SO INSTEAD OF FOOD, I USED OUR MONEY TO BUY HER STALL.
ALL OUR MONEY?
WE MIGHT BE HERE A LONG TIME.
WE'LL NEED MORE MONEY.
HEY, HA.
BUT YOU DON'T EVEN KNOW HOW TO MAKE BÁNH CUỐN!
DON'T WORRY! TUYET HERE IS GOING TO TEACH ME EVERYTHING I NEED TO KNOW BEFORE SHE LEAVES.
YEP!
OH, OKAY. SO, TUYET, WHEN DO YOU LEAVE?
TOMORROW!

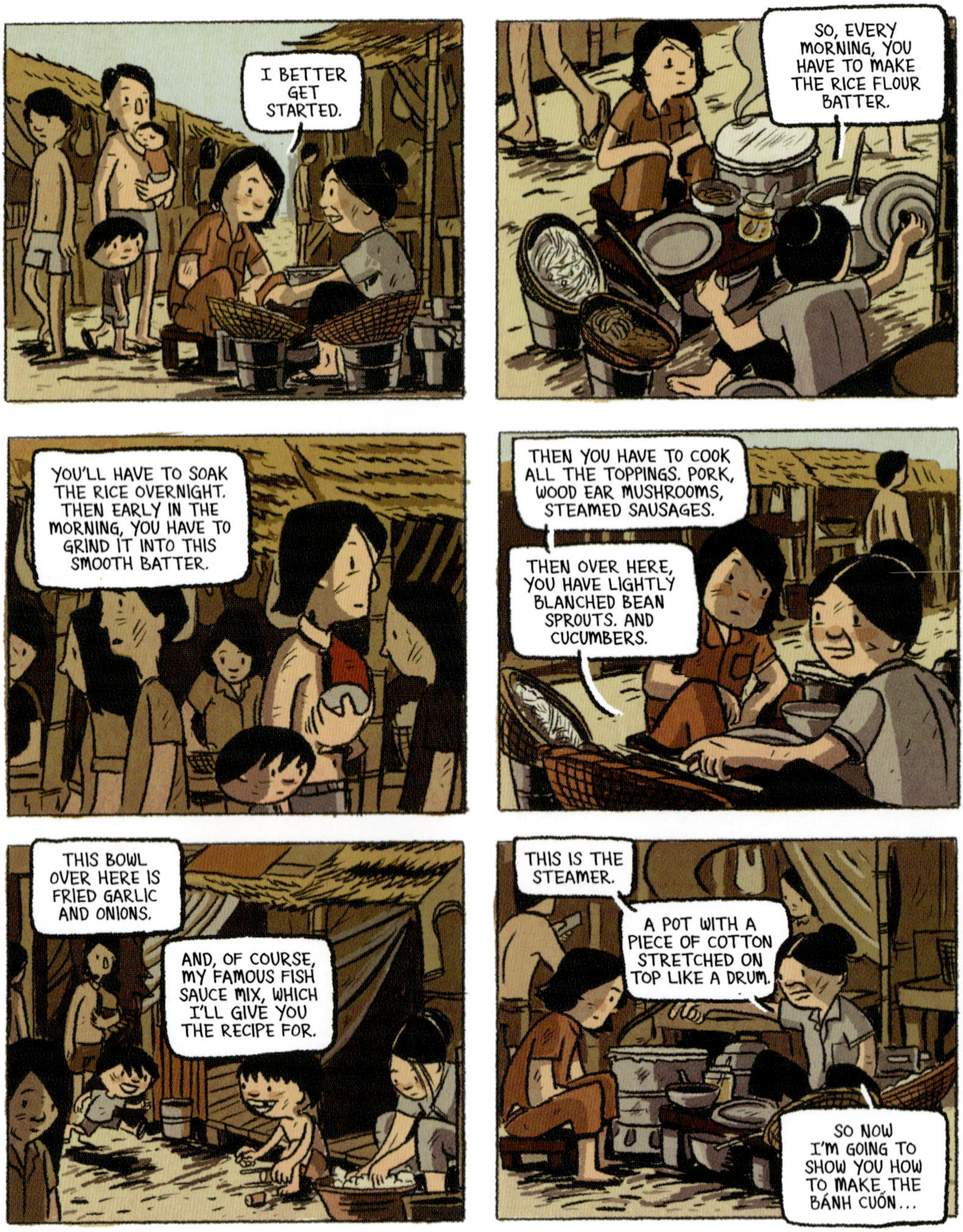
I BETTER GET STARTED.
SO, EVERY MORNING, YOU HAVE TO MAKE THE RICE FLOUR BATTER.
YOU'LL HAVE TO SOAK THE RICE OVERNIGHT. THEN EARLY IN THE MORNING, YOU HAVE TO GRIND IT INTO THIS SMOOTH BATTER.
THEN YOU HAVE TO COOK ALL THE TOPPINGS. PORK, WOOD EAR MUSHROOMS, STEAMED SAUSAGES.
THEN OVER HERE, YOU HAVE LIGHTLY BLANCHED BEAN SPROUTS. AND CUCUMBERS.
THIS BOWL OVER HERE IS FRIED GARLIC AND ONIONS.
AND, OF COURSE, MY FAMOUS FISH SAUCE MIX, WHICH I'LL GIVE YOU THE RECIPE FOR.
THIS IS THE STEAMER.
A POT WITH A PIECE OF COTTON STRETCHED ON TOP LIKE A DRUM.
SO NOW I'M GOING TO SHOW YOU HOW TO MAKE THE BÁNH CUỐN...

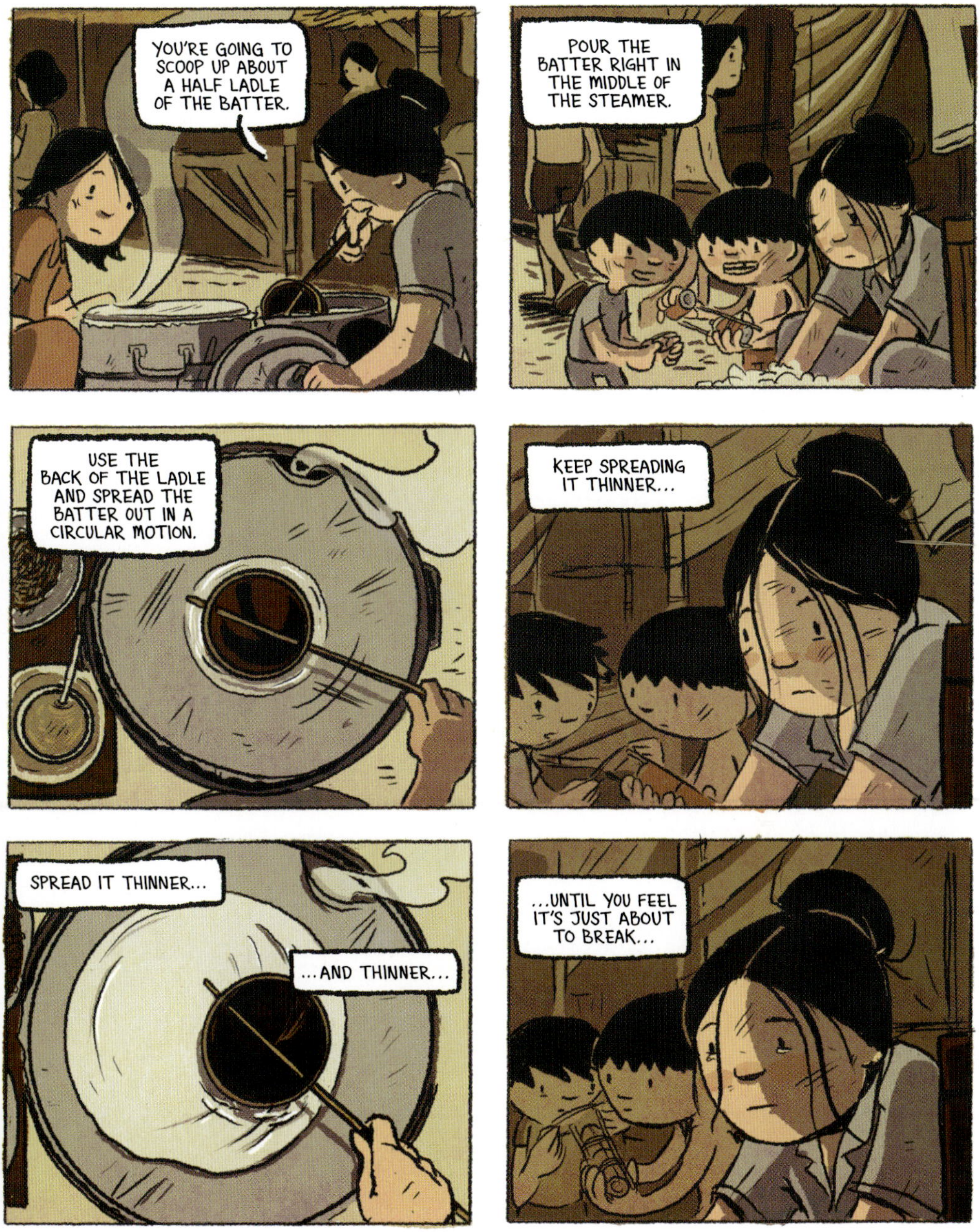
YOU'RE GOING TO SCOOP UP ABOUT A HALF LADLE OF THE BATTER.
POUR THE BATTER RIGHT IN THE MIDDLE OF THE STEAMER.
USE THE BACK OF THE LADLE AND SPREAD THE BATTER OUT IN A CIRCULAR MOTION.
KEEP SPREADING IT THINNER...
SPREAD IT THINNER...
...AND THINNER...
...UNTIL YOU FEEL IT'S JUST ABOUT TO BREAK...

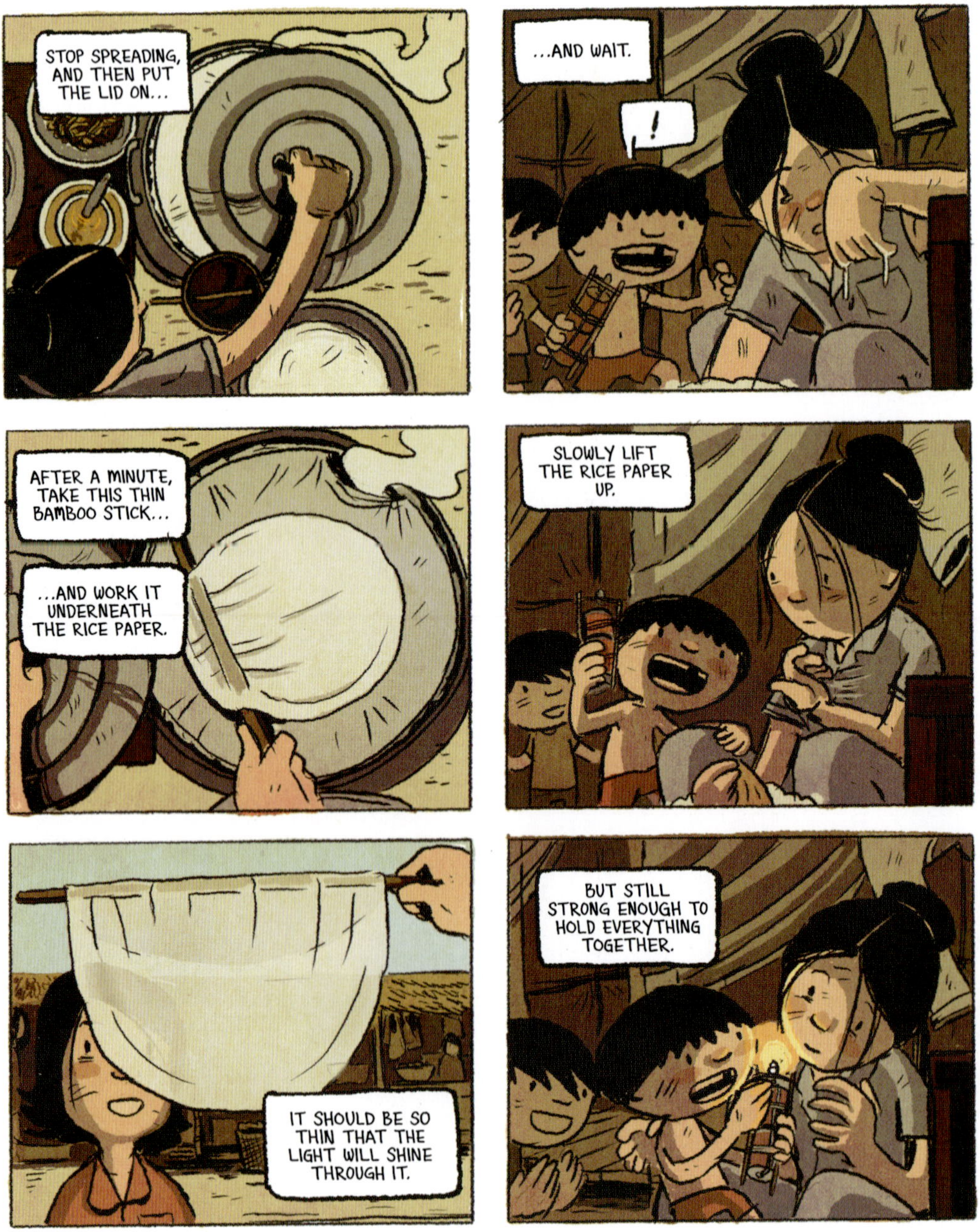
STOP SPREADING, AND THEN PUT THE LID ON...
...AND WAIT.
!
AFTER A MINUTE, TAKE THIS THIN BAMBOO STICK...
...AND WORK IT UNDERNEATH THE RICE PAPER.
SLOWLY LIFT THE RICE PAPER UP.
IT SHOULD BE SO THIN THAT THE LIGHT WILL SHINE THROUGH IT.
BUT STILL STRONG ENOUGH TO HOLD EVERYTHING TOGETHER.

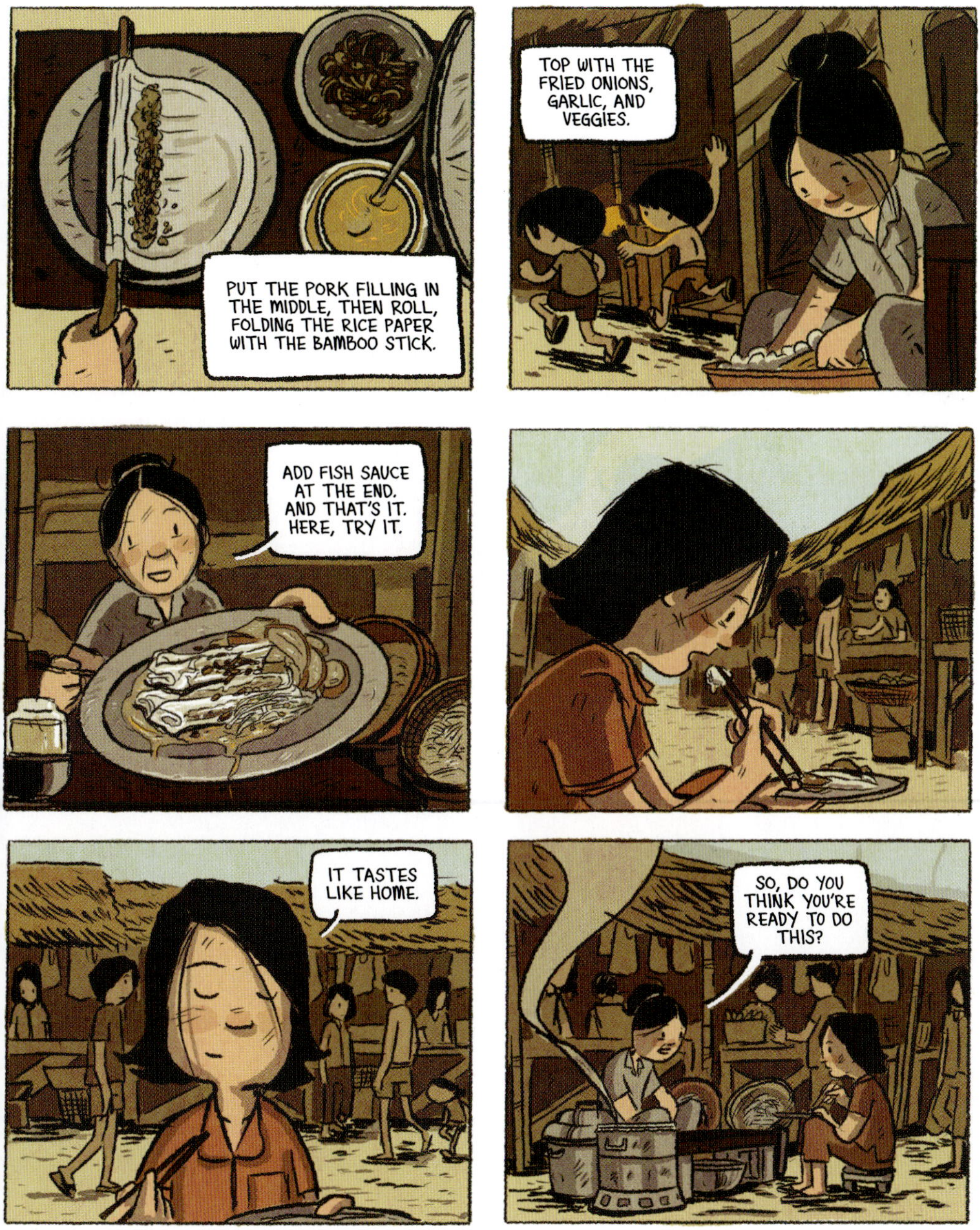
PUT THE PORK FILLING IN THE MIDDLE, THEN ROLL, FOLDING THE RICE PAPER WITH THE BAMBOO STICK.
TOP WITH THE FRIED ONIONS, GARLIC, AND VEGGIES.
ADD FISH SAUCE AT THE END. AND THAT'S IT. HERE, TRY IT.
IT TASTES LIKE HOME.
SO, DO YOU THINK YOU'RE READY TO DO THIS?

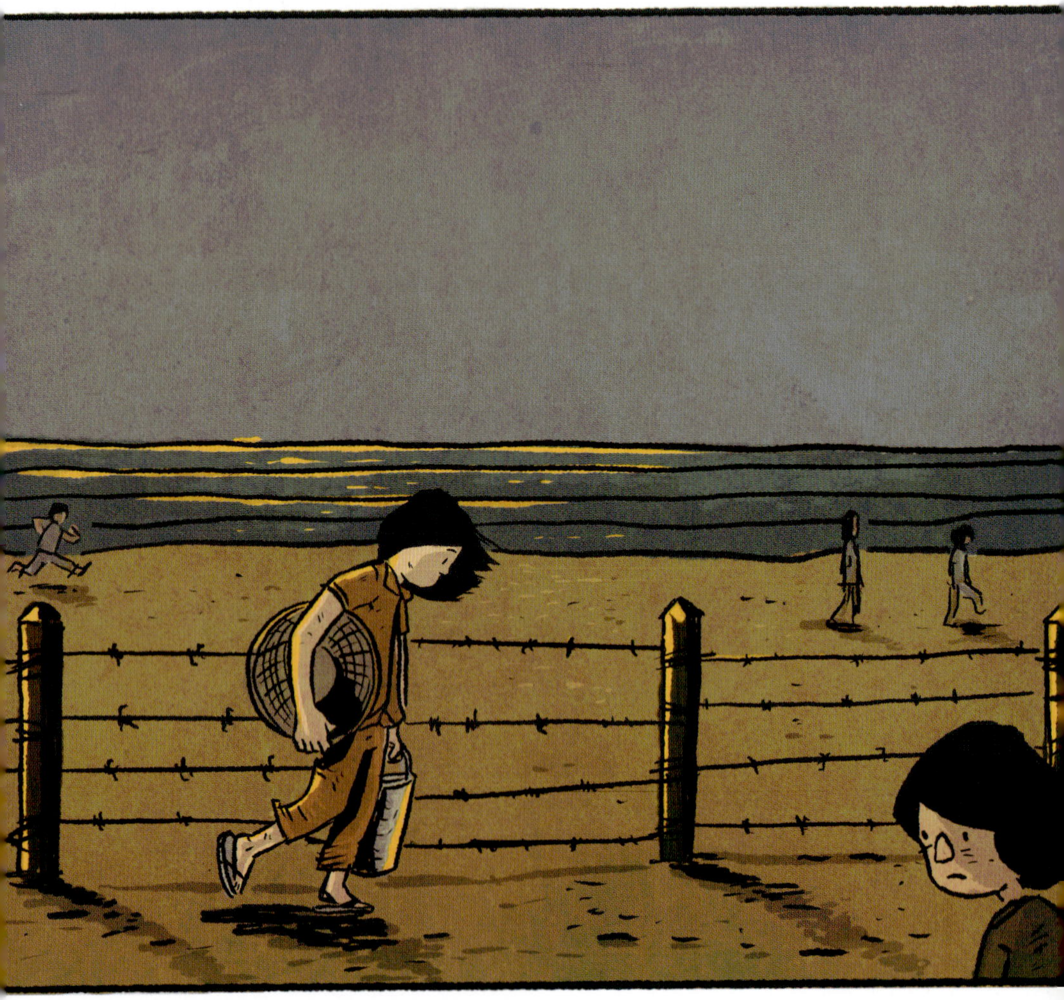

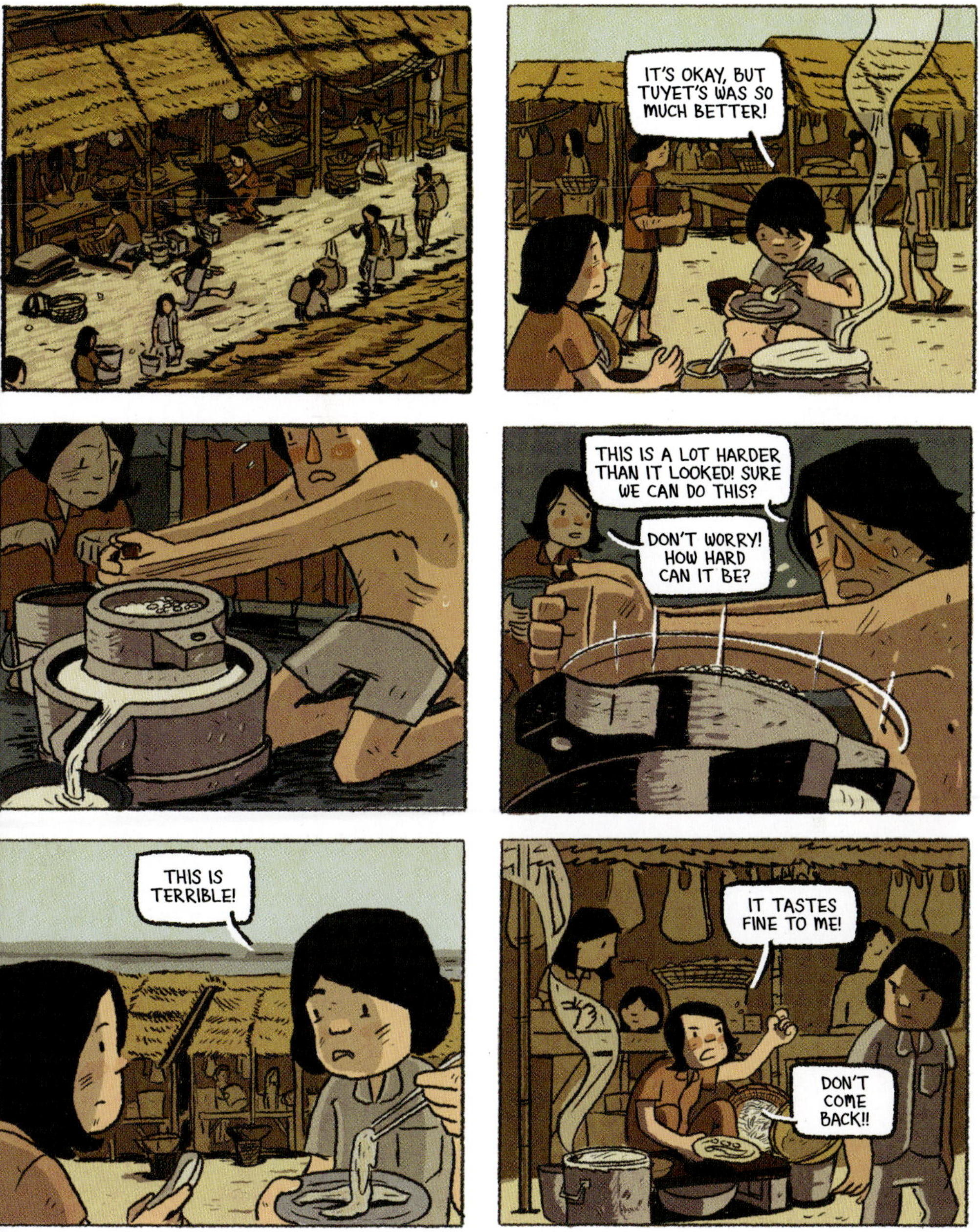
IT'S OKAY, BUT TUYET'S WAS SO MUCH BETTER!
THIS IS A LOT HARDER THAN IT LOOKED! SURE WE CAN DO THIS?
DON'T WORRY! HOW HARD CAN IT BE?
THIS IS TERRIBLE!
IT TASTES FINE TO ME!
DON'T COME BACK!!

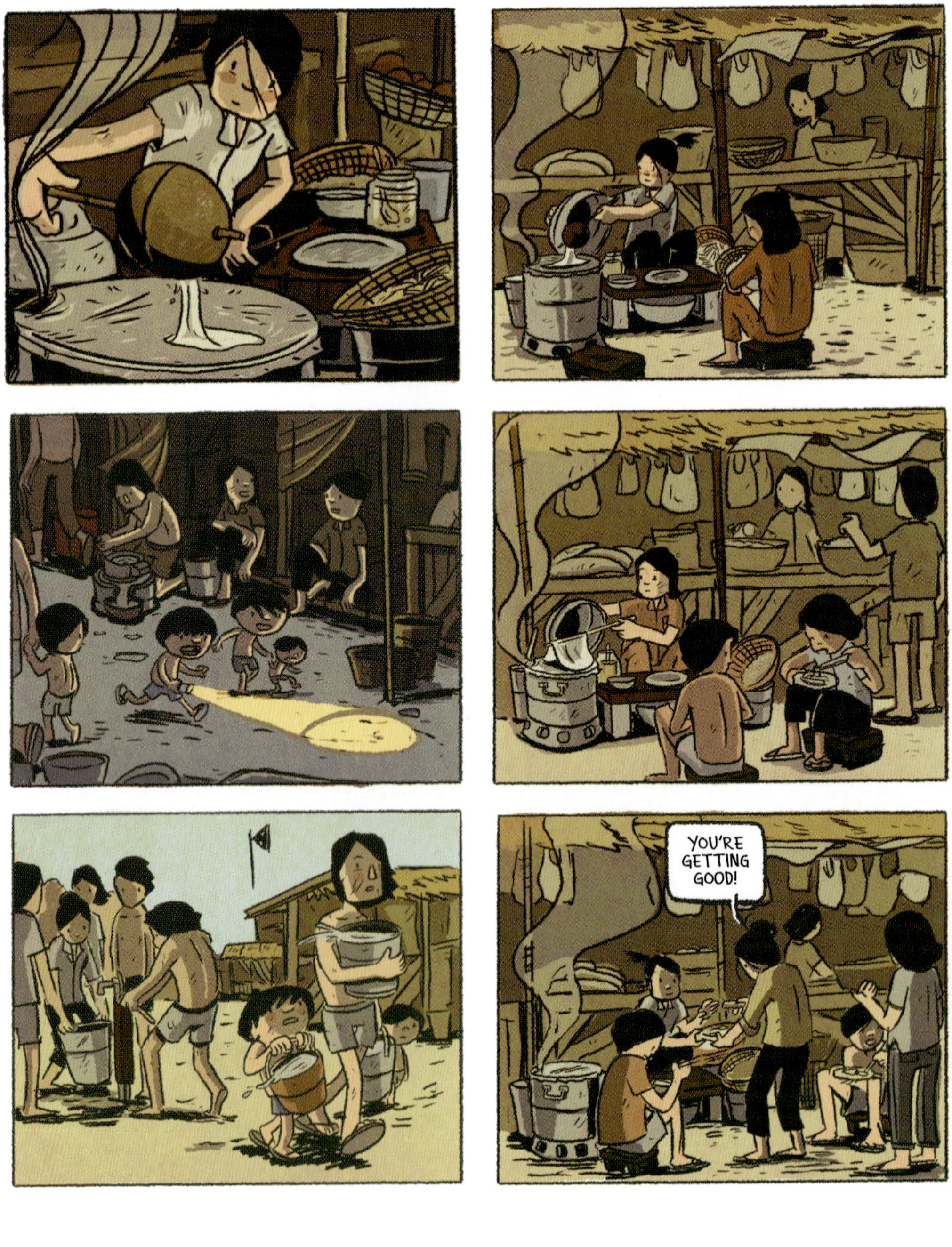
YOU'RE GETTING GOOD!

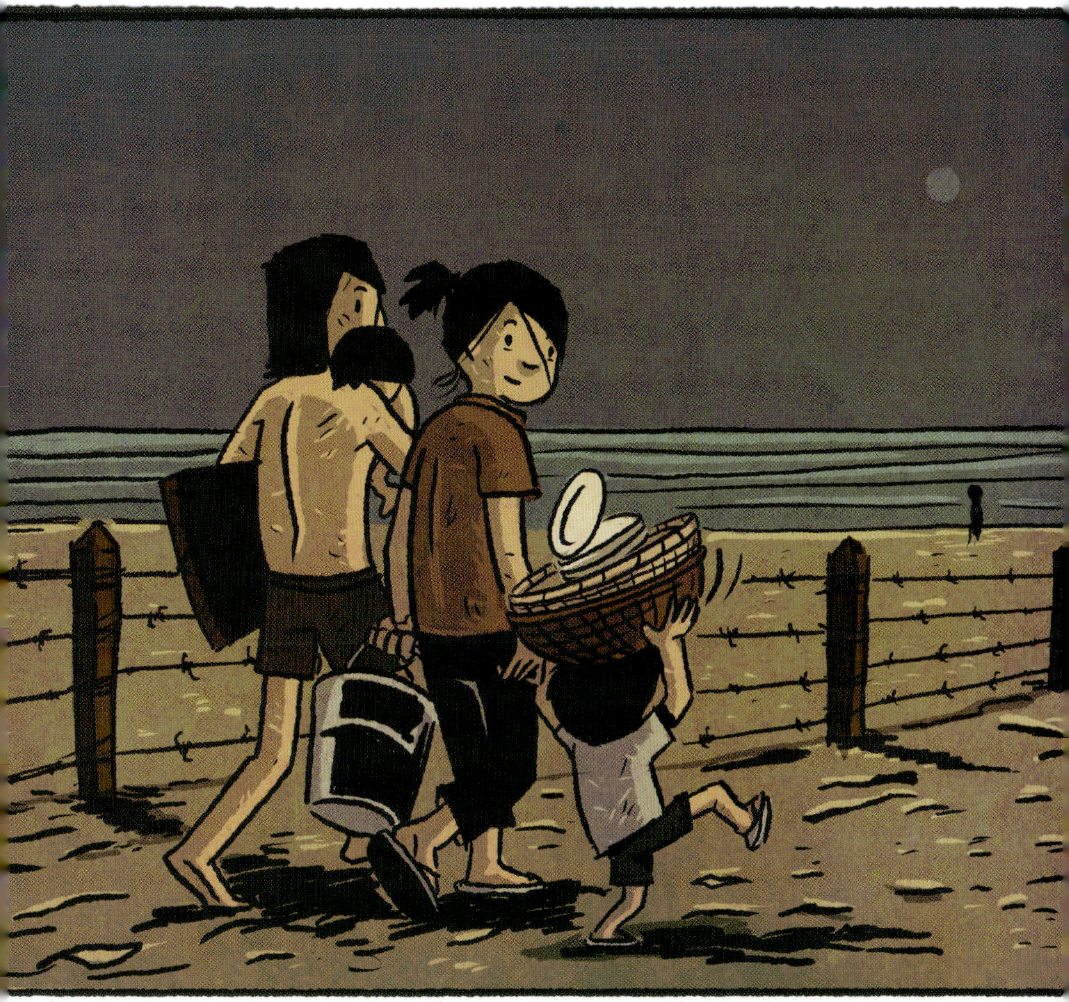

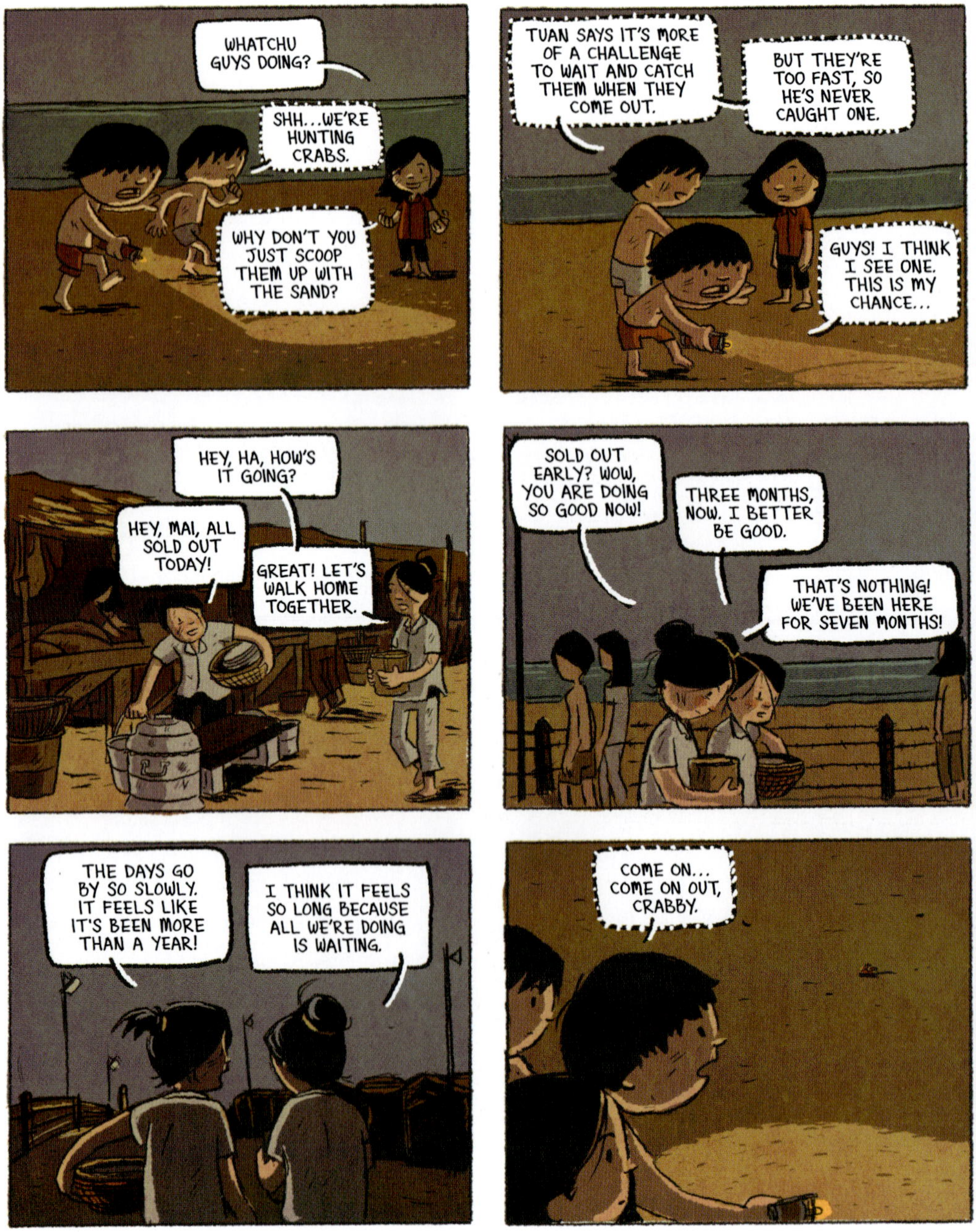
WHATCHU GUYS DOING?
SHH...WE'RE HUNTING CRABS.
WHY DON'T YOU JUST SCOOP THEM UP WITH THE SAND?
TUAN SAYS IT'S MORE OF A CHALLENGE TO WAIT AND CATCH THEM WHEN THEY COME OUT.
BUT THEY'RE TOO FAST, SO HE'S NEVER CAUGHT ONE.
GUYS! I THINK I SEE ONE. THIS IS MY CHANCE...
HEY, HA, HOW'S IT GOING?
HEY, MAI, ALL SOLD OUT TODAY!
GREAT! LET'S WALK HOME TOGETHER.
SOLD OUT EARLY? WOW, YOU ARE DOING SO GOOD NOW!
THREE MONTHS, NOW. I BETTER BE GOOD.
THAT'S NOTHING! WE'VE BEEN HERE FOR SEVEN MONTHS!
THE DAYS GO BY SO SLOWLY. IT FEELS LIKE IT'S BEEN MORE THAN A YEAR!
I THINK IT FEELS SO LONG BECAUSE ALL WE'RE DOING IS WAITING.
COME ON... COME ON OUT, CRABBY.

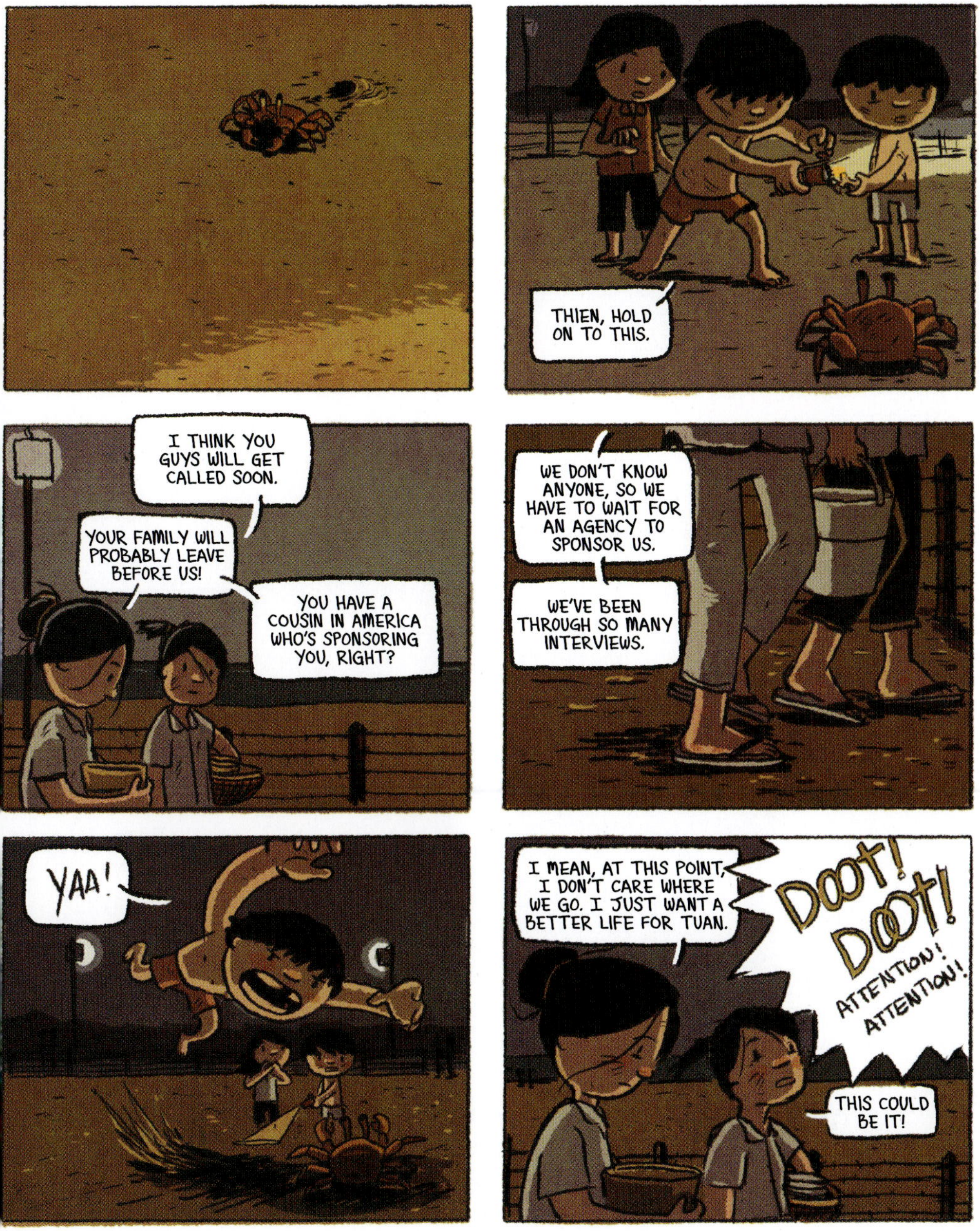
THIEN, HOLD ON TO THIS.
I THINK YOU GUYS WILL GET CALLED SOON.
YOUR FAMILY WILL PROBABLY LEAVE BEFORE US!
YOU HAVE A COUSIN IN AMERICA WHO'S SPONSORING YOU, RIGHT?
WE DON'T KNOW ANYONE, SO WE HAVE TO WAIT FOR AN AGENCY TO SPONSOR US.
WE'VE BEEN THROUGH SO MANY INTERVIEWS.
YAA!
I MEAN, AT THIS POINT, I DON'T CARE WHERE WE GO. I JUST WANT A BETTER LIFE FOR TUAN.
DOOT! DOOT!
ATTENTION! ATTENTION!
THIS COULD BE IT!

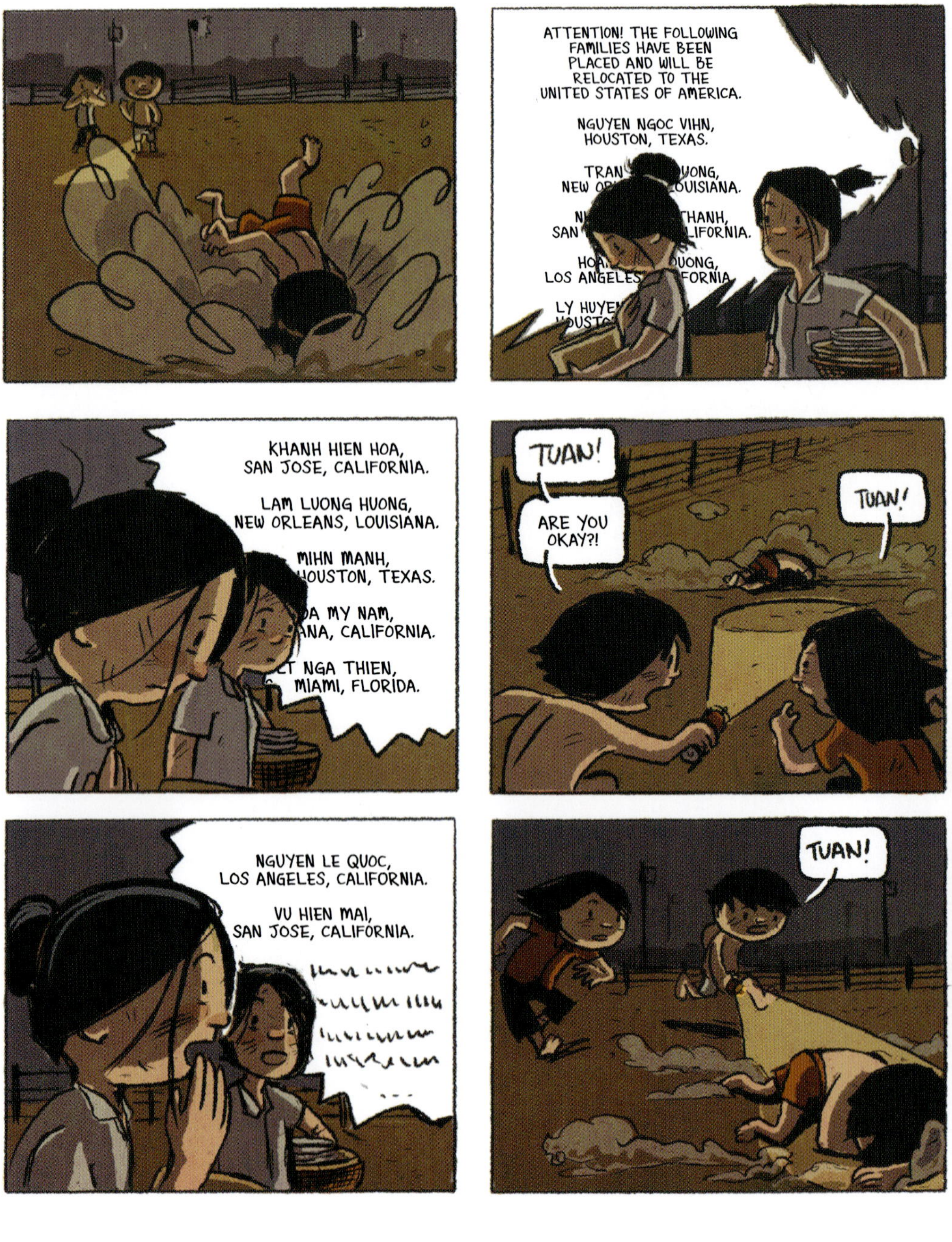

ATTENTION! THE FOLLOWING FAMILIES HAVE BEEN PLACED AND WILL BE RELOCATED TO THE UNITED STATES OF AMERICA.
NGUYEN NGOC VIHN, HOUSTON, TEXAS.
KHANH HIEN HOA, SAN JOSE, CALIFORNIA.
LAM LUONG HUONG, NEW ORLEANS, LOUISIANA.
MIHN MANH,
MIAMI, FLORIDA.
TUAN!
ARE YOU OKAY?!
TUAN!
NGUYEN LE QUOC, LOS ANGELES, CALIFORNIA.
VU HIEN MAI, SAN JOSE, CALIFORNIA.
TUAN!

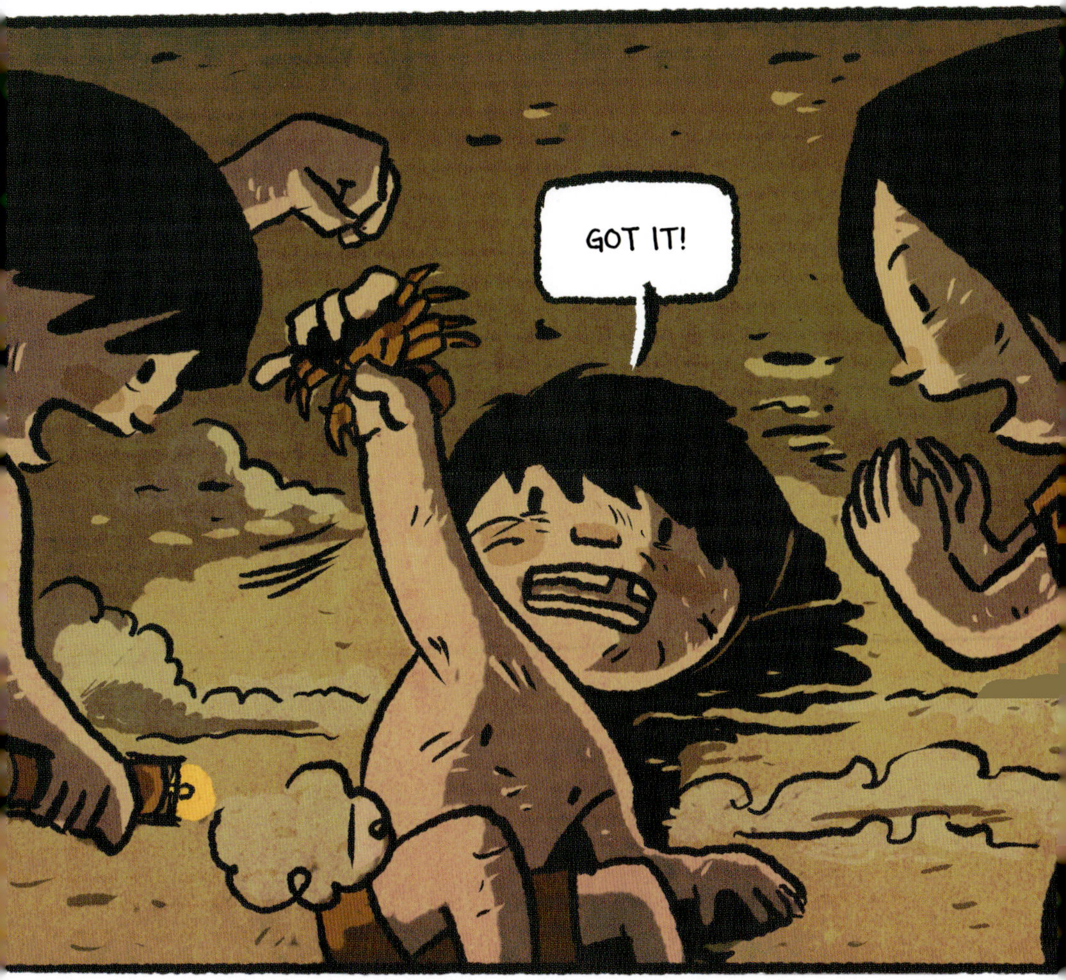
GOT IT!

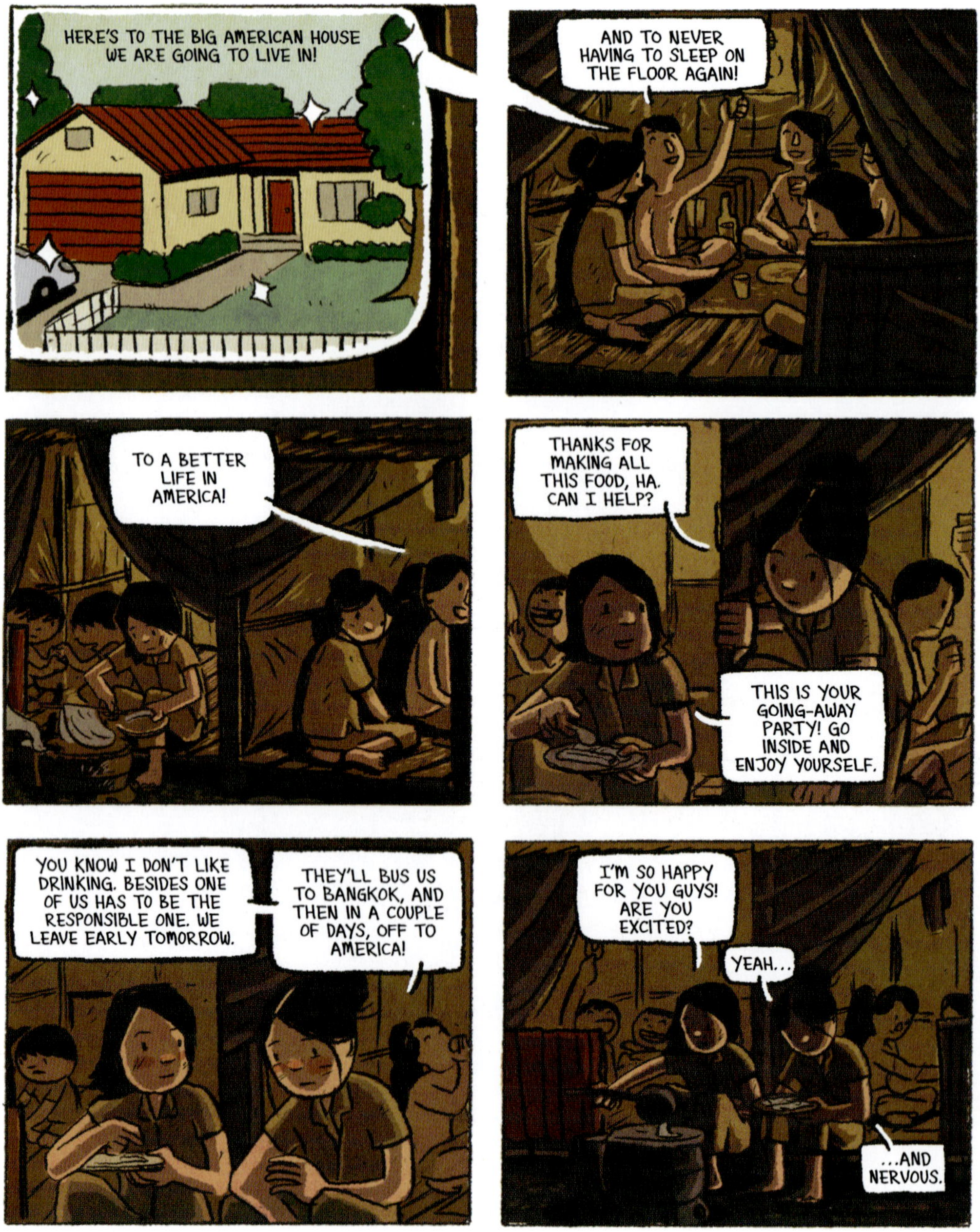
HERE'S TO THE BIG AMERICAN HOUSE WE ARE GOING TO LIVE IN!
AND TO NEVER HAVING TO SLEEP ON THE FLOOR AGAIN!
TO A BETTER LIFE IN AMERICA!
THANKS FOR MAKING ALL THIS FOOD, HA. CAN I HELP?
THIS IS YOUR GOING-AWAY PARTY! GO INSIDE AND ENJOY YOURSELF.
YOU KNOW I DON'T LIKE DRINKING. BESIDES ONE OF US HAS TO BE THE RESPONSIBLE ONE. WE LEAVE EARLY TOMORROW.
THEY'LL BUS US TO BANGKOK, AND THEN IN A COUPLE OF DAYS, OFF TO AMERICA!
I'M SO HAPPY FOR YOU GUYS! ARE YOU EXCITED?
YEAH...
...AND NERVOUS.

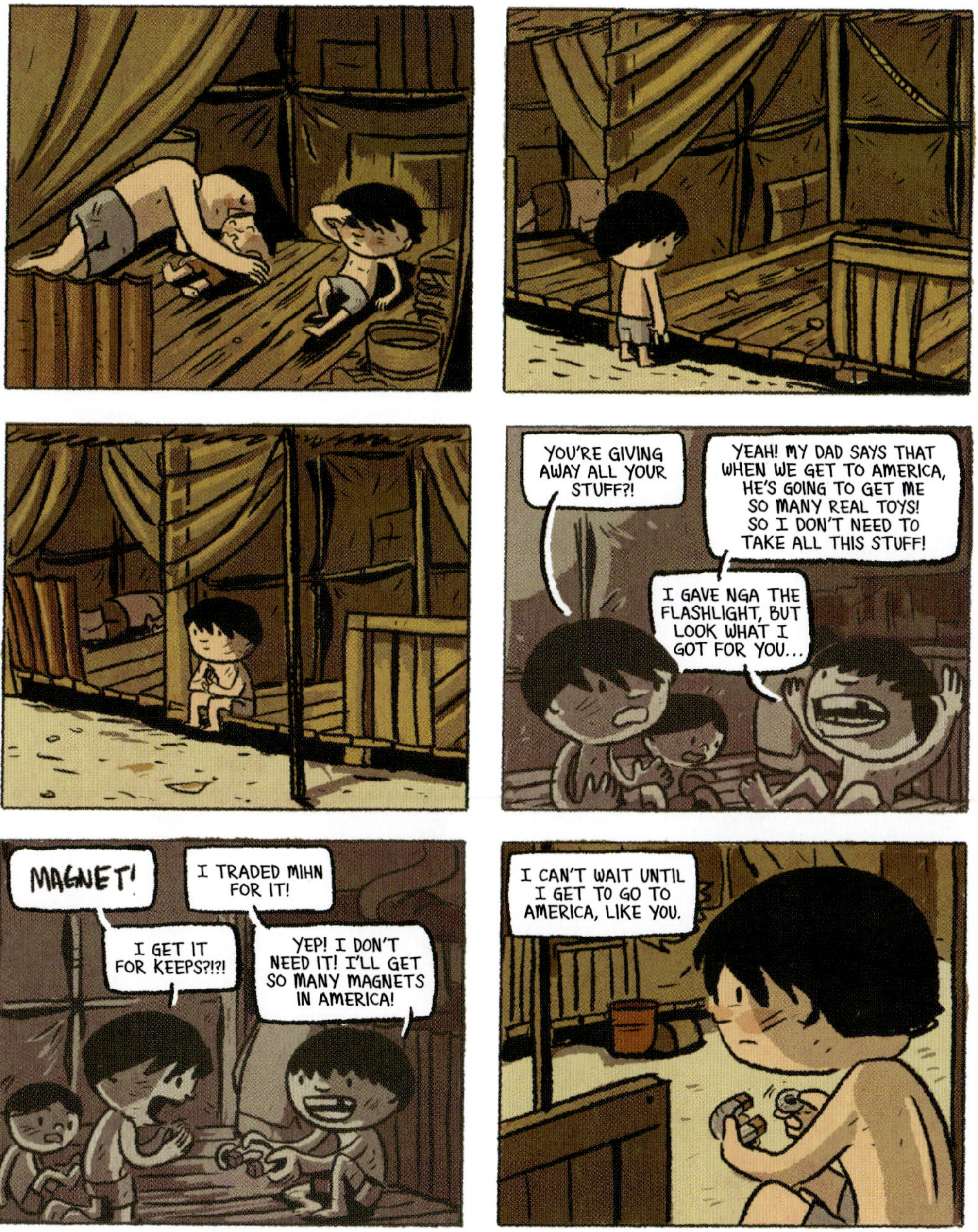
YOU'RE GIVING AWAY ALL YOUR STUFF?!
YEAH! MY DAD SAYS THAT WHEN WE GET TO AMERICA, HE'S GOING TO GET ME SO MANY REAL TOYS! SO I DON'T NEED TO TAKE ALL THIS STUFF!
I GAVE NGA THE FLASHLIGHT, BUT LOOK WHAT I GOT FOR YOU...
MAGNET!
I TRADED MIHN FOR IT!
I GET IT FOR KEEPS?!?!
YEP! I DON'T NEED IT! I'LL GET SO MANY MAGNETS IN AMERICA!
I CAN'T WAIT UNTIL I GET TO GO TO AMERICA, LIKE YOU.

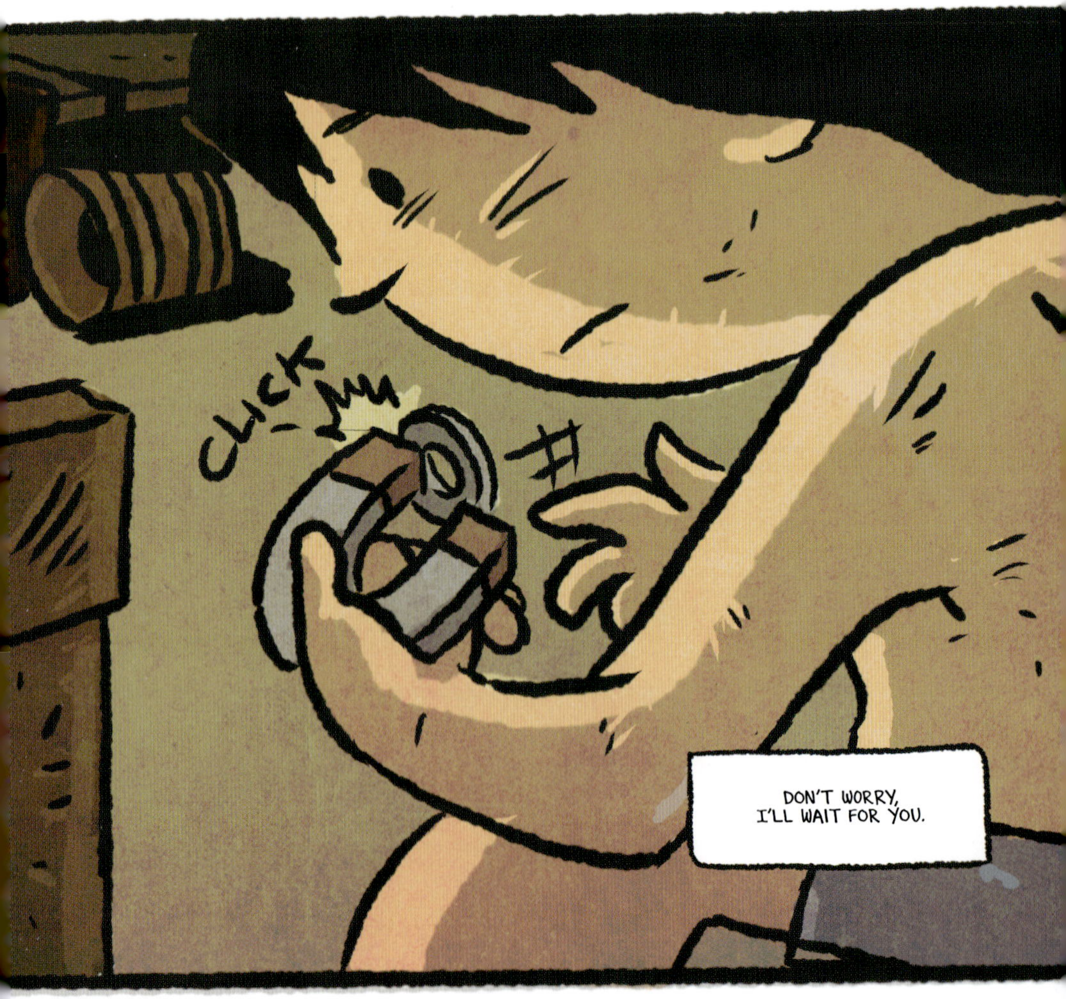
CLICK
DON'T WORRY,
I'LL WAIT FOR YOU.

CHAPTER 3: STEAK AND POTATOES

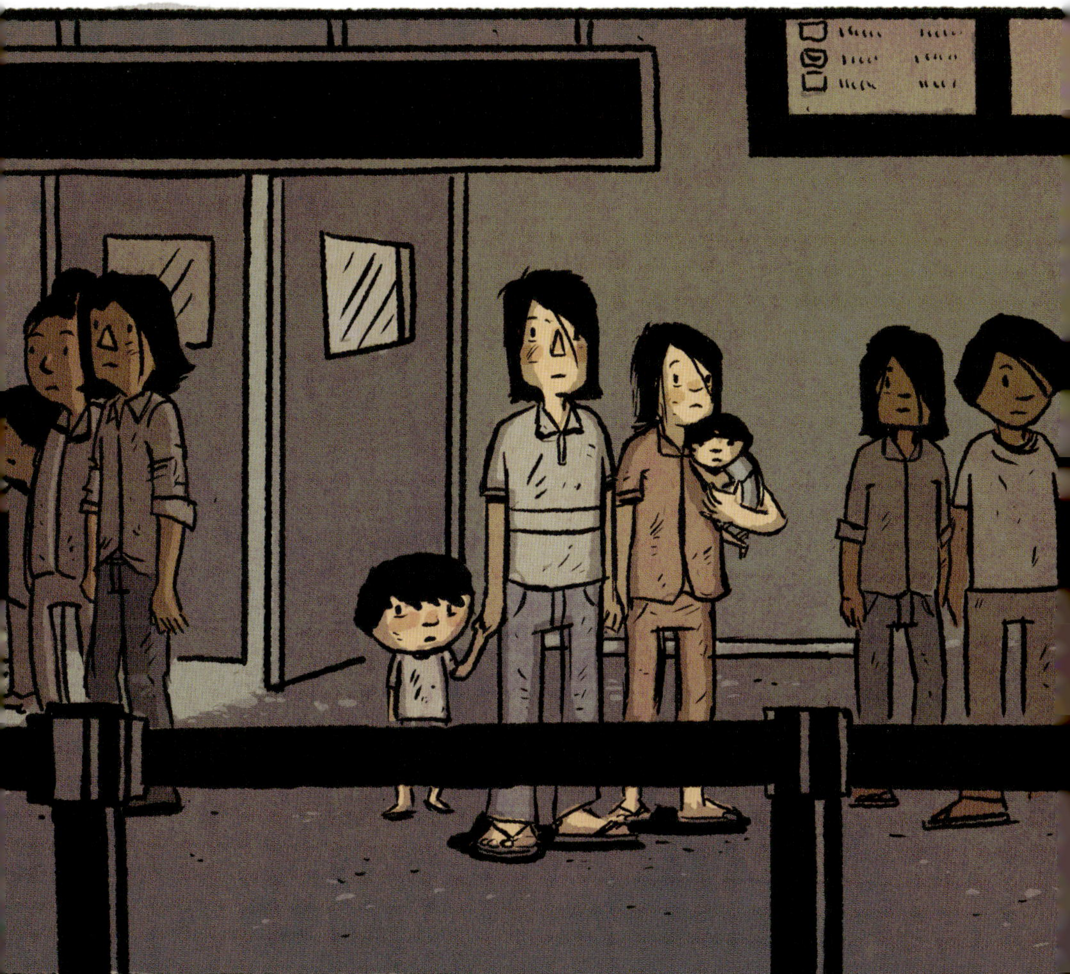

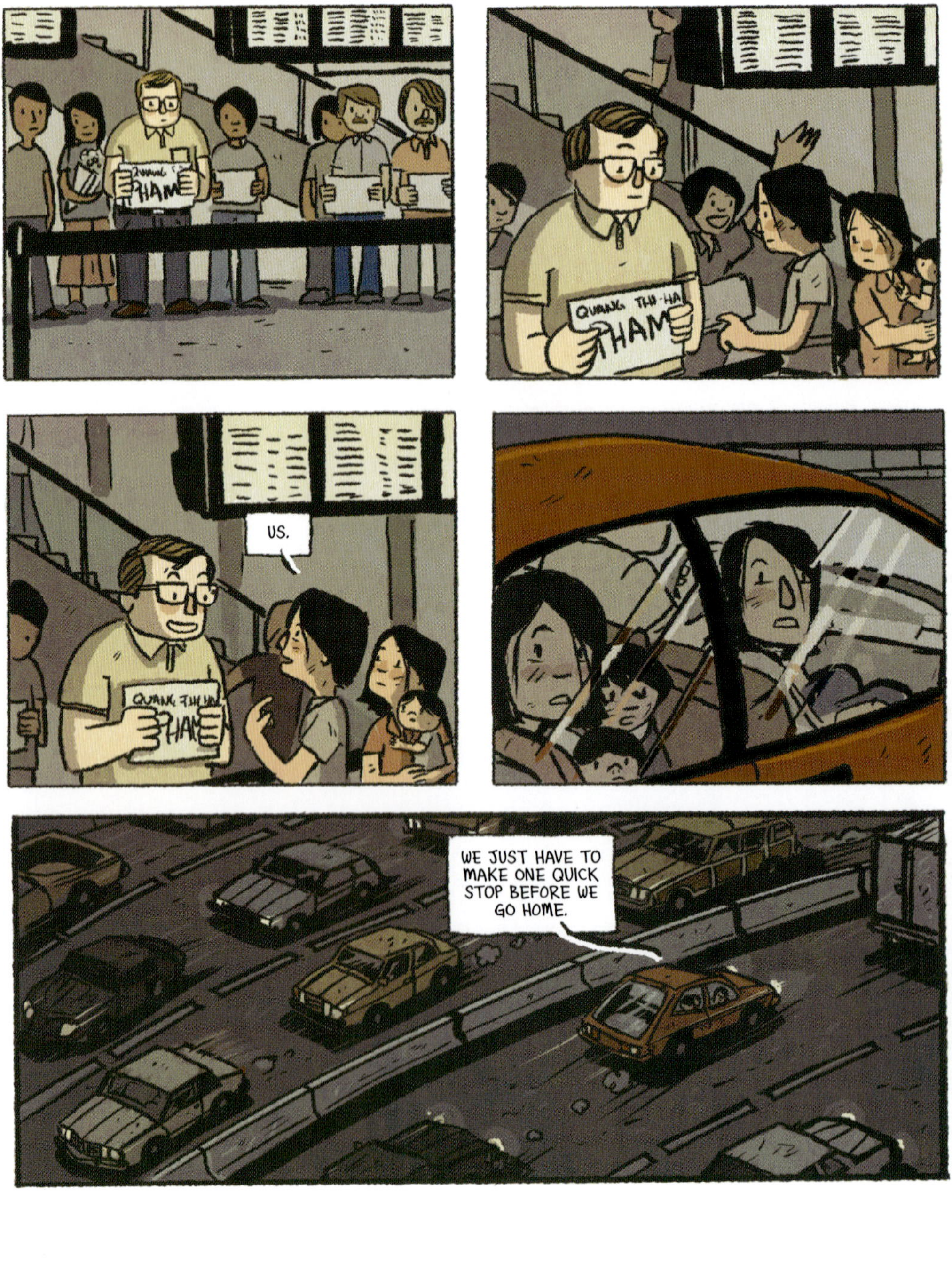
QUANG THI-HA
HAM
US.
WE JUST HAVE TO MAKE ONE QUICK STOP BEFORE WE GO HOME.

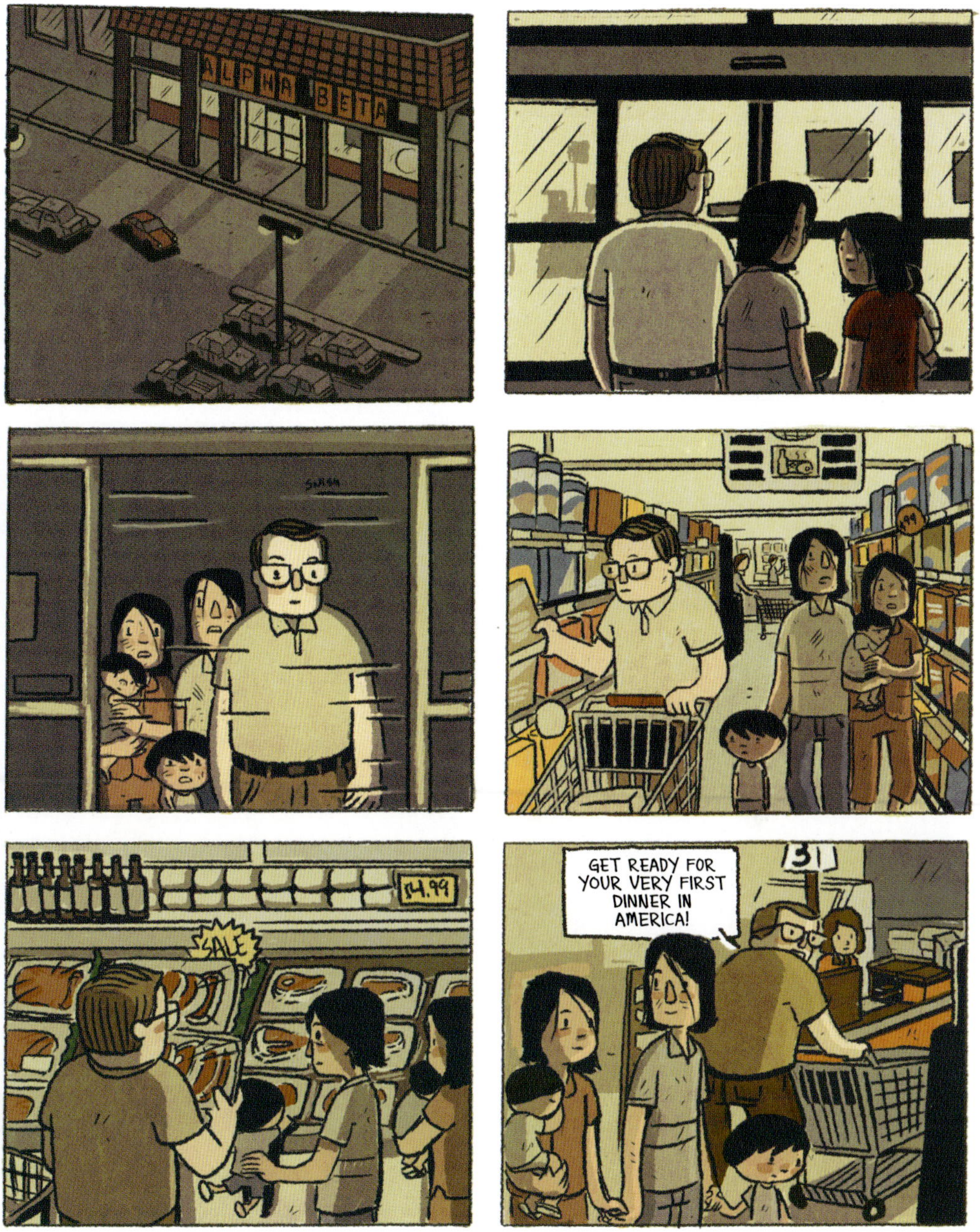
ALPHA BETA
$4.99
SALE
GET READY FOR YOUR VERY FIRST DINNER IN AMERICA!

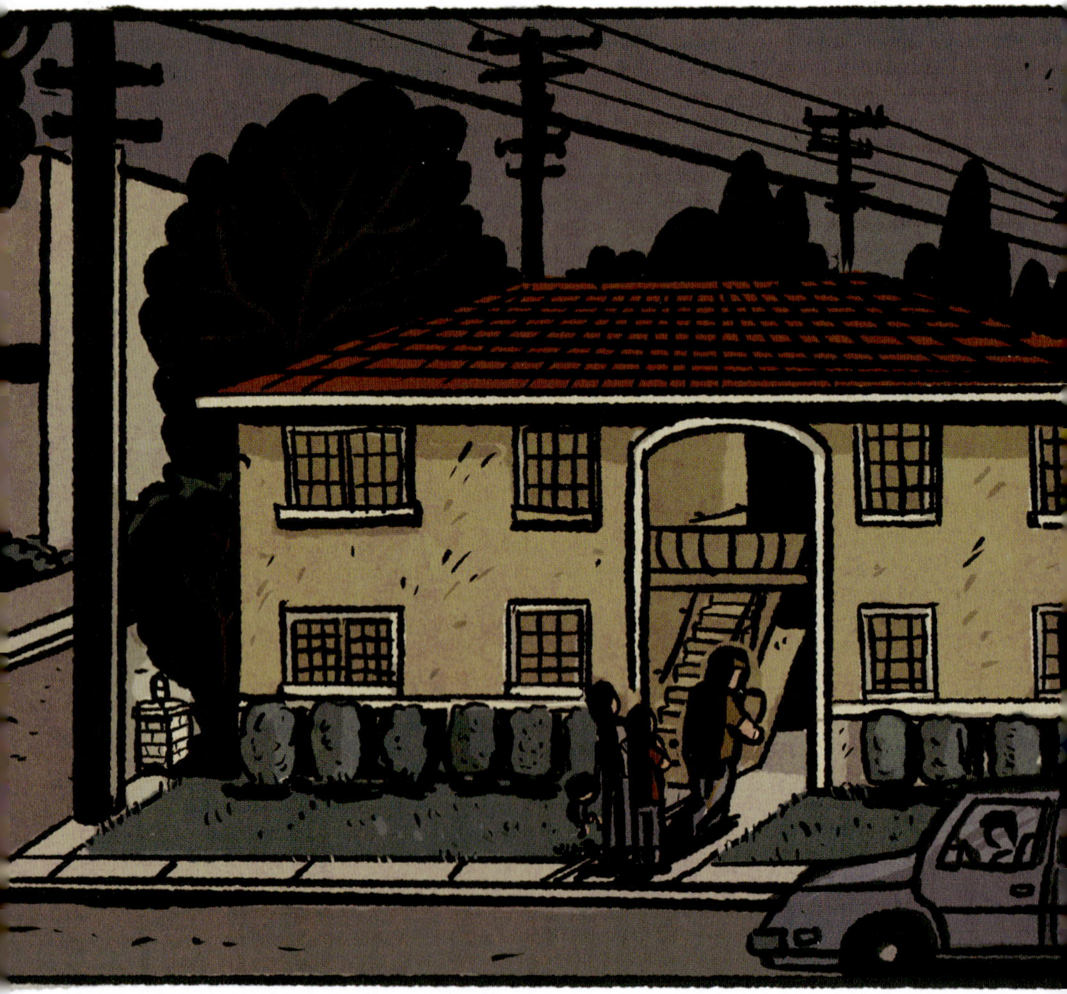

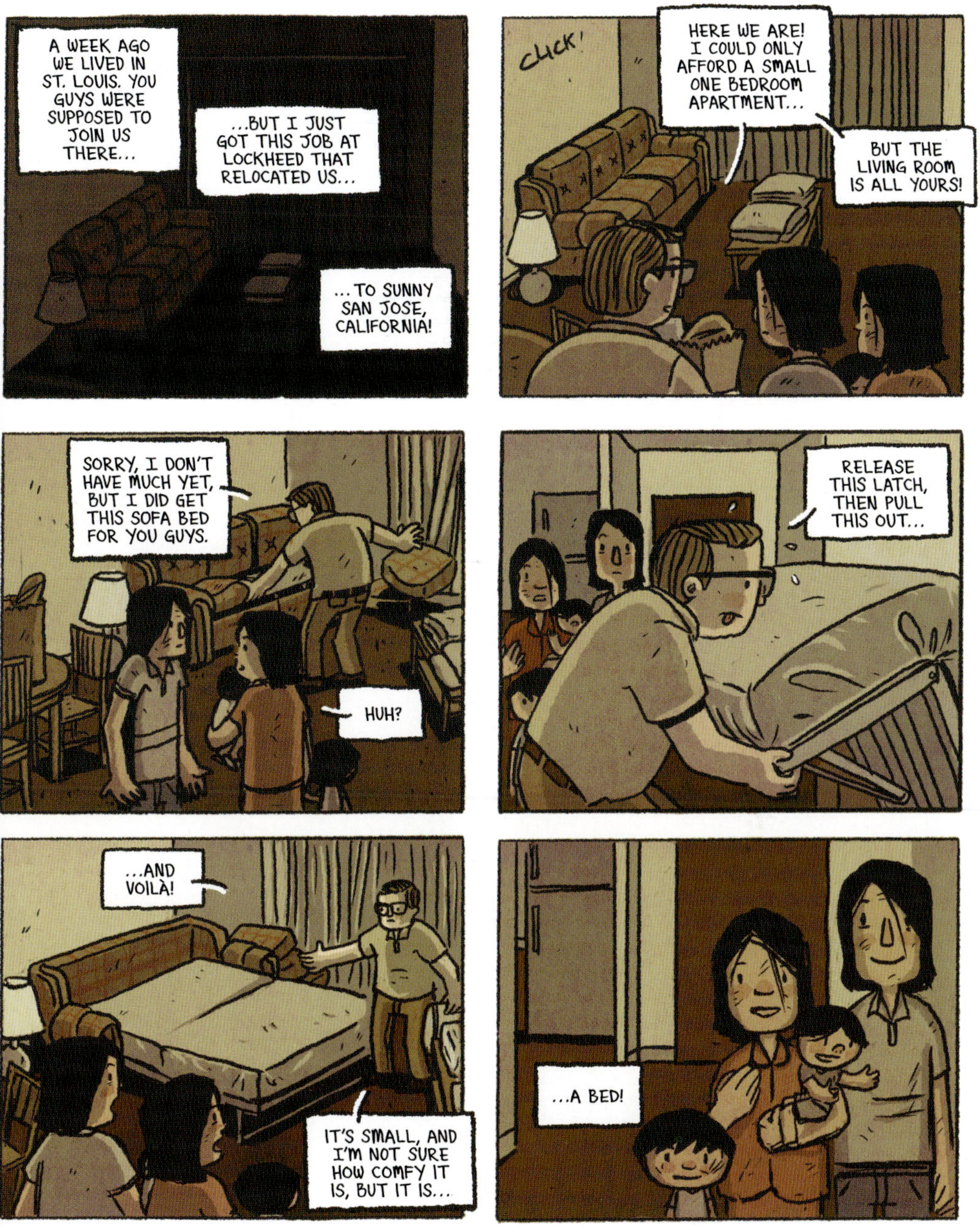
A WEEK AGO WE LIVED IN ST. LOUIS. YOU GUYS WERE SUPPOSED TO JOIN US THERE...
...BUT I JUST GOT THIS JOB AT LOCKHEED THAT RELOCATED US...
...TO SUNNY SAN JOSE, CALIFORNIA!
CLICK!
HERE WE ARE! I COULD ONLY AFFORD A SMALL ONE BEDROOM APARTMENT...
BUT THE LIVING ROOM IS ALL YOURS!
SORRY, I DON'T HAVE MUCH YET, BUT I DID GET THIS SOFA BED FOR YOU GUYS.
HUH?
RELEASE THIS LATCH, THEN PULL THIS OUT...
...AND VOILÀ!
IT'S SMALL, AND I'M NOT SURE HOW COMFY IT IS, BUT IT IS...
...A BED!

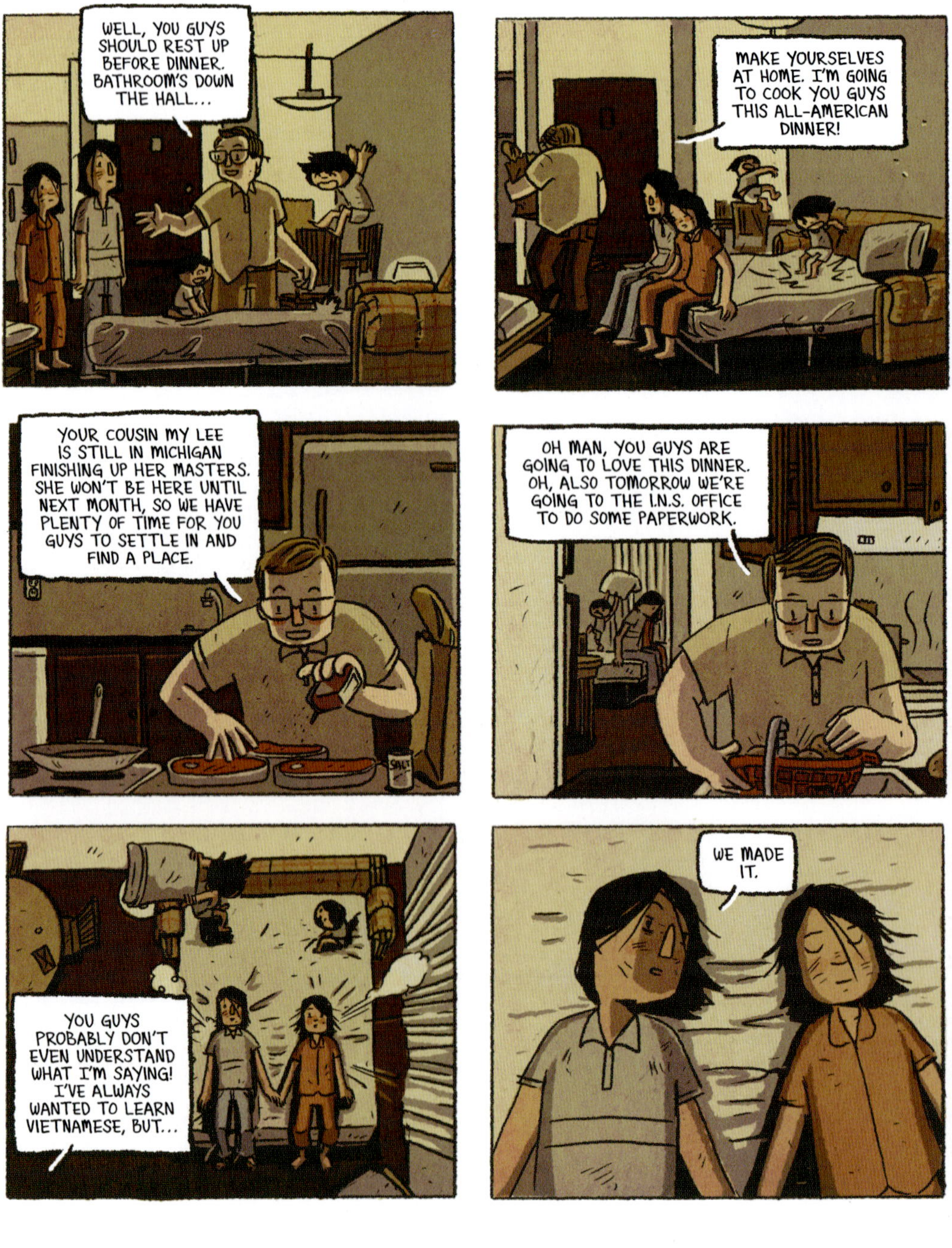
WELL, YOU GUYS SHOULD REST UP BEFORE DINNER. BATHROOM'S DOWN THE HALL...
MAKE YOURSELVES AT HOME. I'M GOING TO COOK YOU GUYS THIS ALL-AMERICAN DINNER!
YOUR COUSIN MY LEE IS STILL IN MICHIGAN FINISHING UP HER MASTERS. SHE WON'T BE HERE UNTIL NEXT MONTH, SO WE HAVE PLENTY OF TIME FOR YOU GUYS TO SETTLE IN AND FIND A PLACE.
SALT
OH MAN, YOU GUYS ARE GOING TO LOVE THIS DINNER. OH, ALSO TOMORROW WE'RE GOING TO THE I.N.S. OFFICE TO DO SOME PAPERWORK.
YOU GUYS PROBABLY DON'T EVEN UNDERSTAND WHAT I'M SAYING! I'VE ALWAYS WANTED TO LEARN VIETNAMESE, BUT...
WE MADE IT.

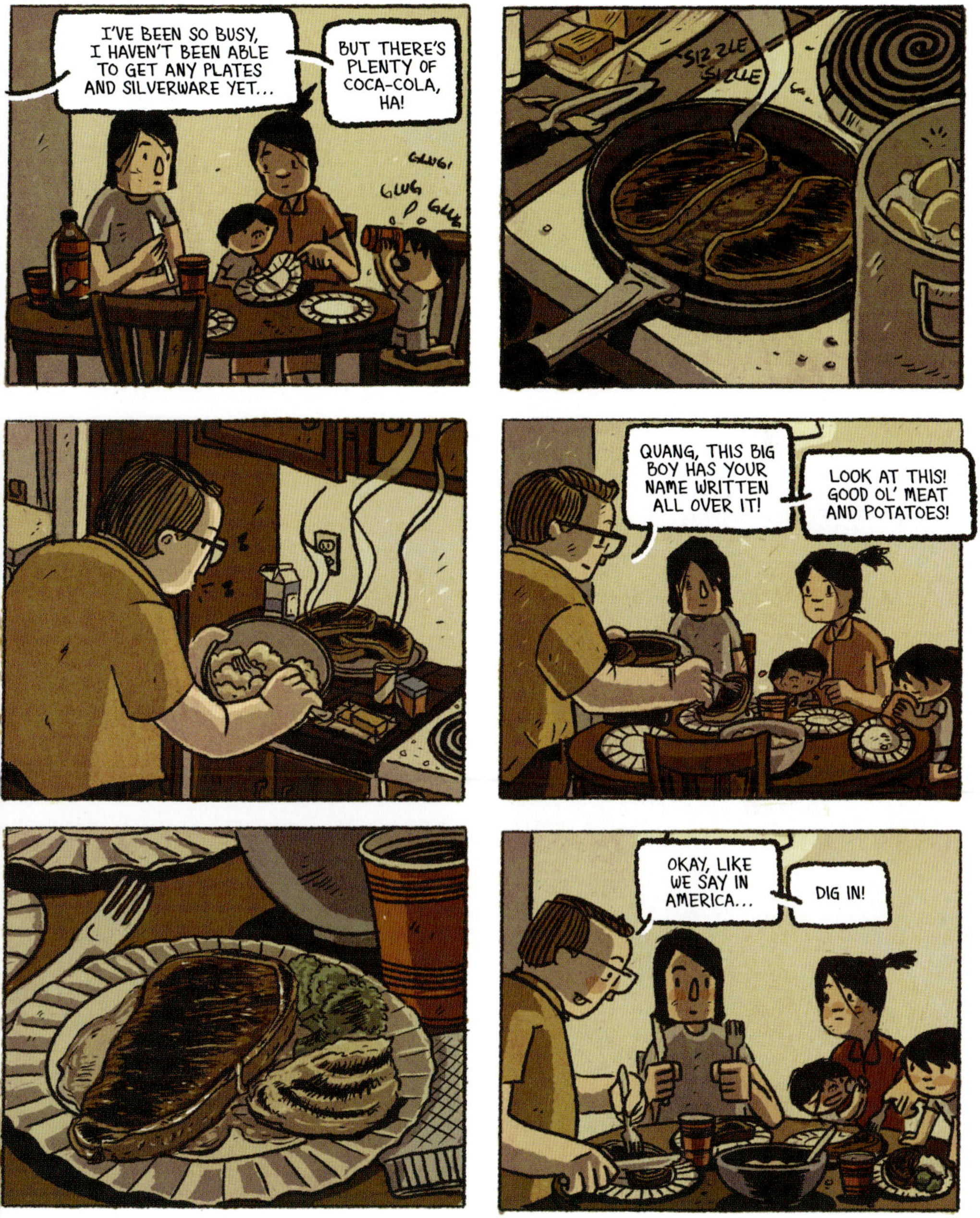
I'VE BEEN SO BUSY, I HAVEN'T BEEN ABLE TO GET ANY PLATES AND SILVERWARE YET...
BUT THERE'S PLENTY OF COCA-COLA, HA!
GLUG!
GLUG
GLUG
SIZZLE
SIZZLE
QUANG, THIS BIG BOY HAS YOUR NAME WRITTEN ALL OVER IT!
LOOK AT THIS! GOOD OL' MEAT AND POTATOES!
OKAY, LIKE WE SAY IN AMERICA...
DIG IN!

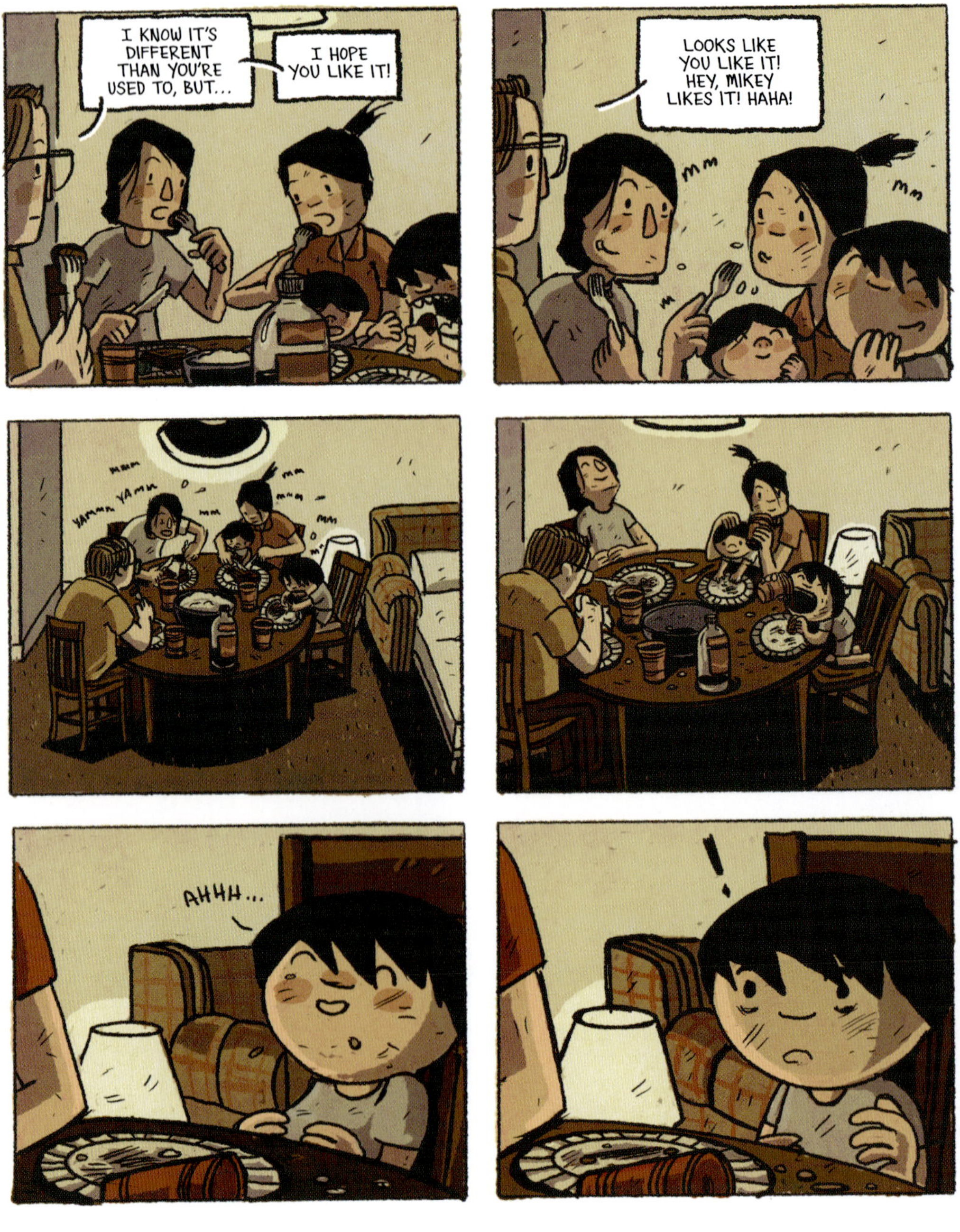
I KNOW IT'S DIFFERENT THAN YOU'RE USED TO, BUT...
I HOPE YOU LIKE IT!
LOOKS LIKE YOU LIKE IT! HEY, MIKEY LIKES IT! HAHA!
MM
MM
MM
MMM
YAMM YAMM
MM
AHHH...
!

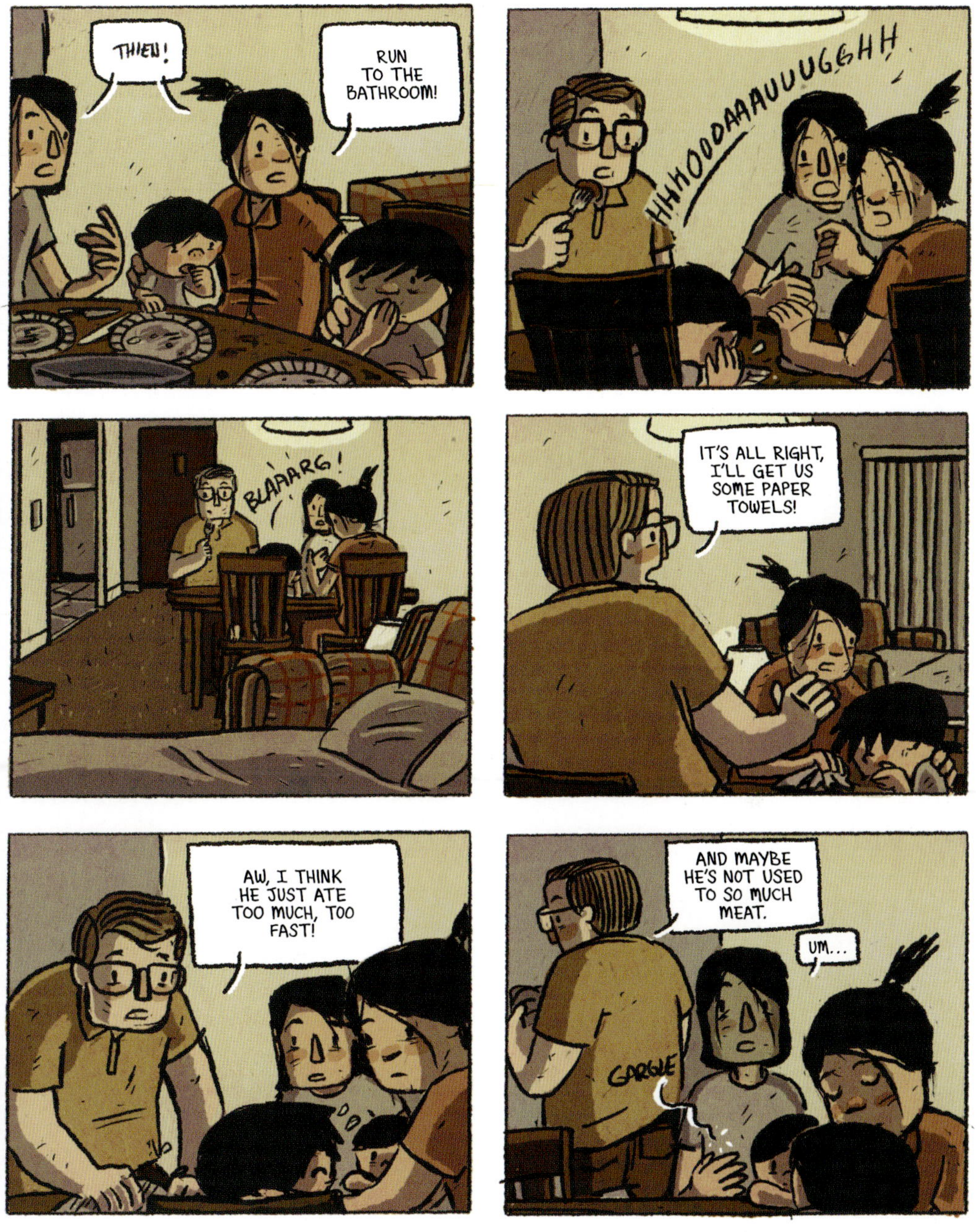
THIEN!
RUN TO THE BATHROOM!
HHHOOOAAAAUUUUGGHH
BLAAARG!
IT'S ALL RIGHT, I'LL GET US SOME PAPER TOWELS!
AW, I THINK HE JUST ATE TOO MUCH, TOO FAST!
AND MAYBE HE'S NOT USED TO SO MUCH MEAT.
UM...
GARGLE

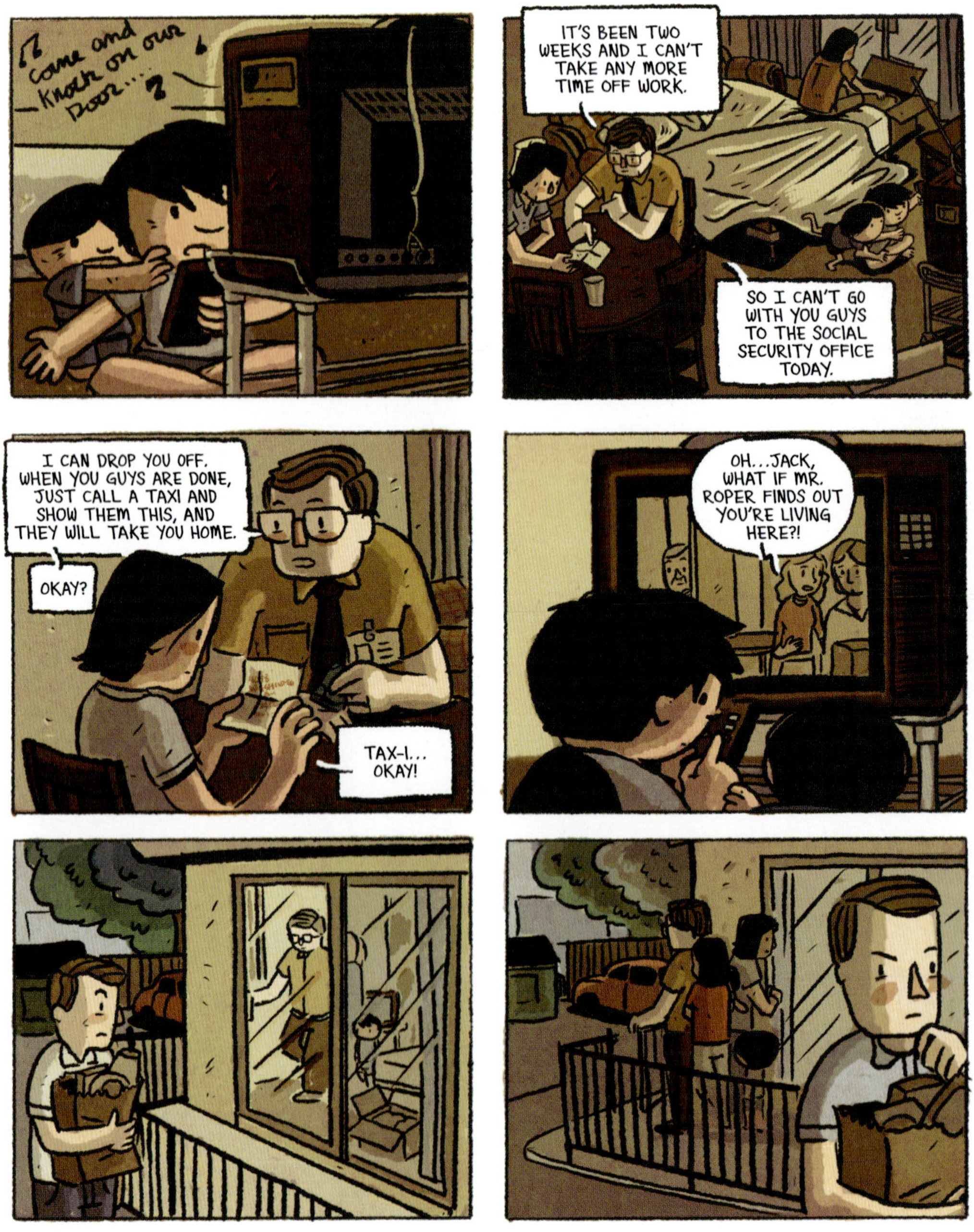
Come and Knock on our Door...
IT'S BEEN TWO WEEKS AND I CAN'T TAKE ANY MORE TIME OFF WORK.
SO I CAN'T GO WITH YOU GUYS TO THE SOCIAL SECURITY OFFICE TODAY.
I CAN DROP YOU OFF. WHEN YOU GUYS ARE DONE, JUST CALL A TAXI AND SHOW THEM THIS, AND THEY WILL TAKE YOU HOME.
OKAY?
TAX-I... OKAY!
OH...JACK, WHAT IF MR. ROPER FINDS OUT YOU'RE LIVING HERE?!

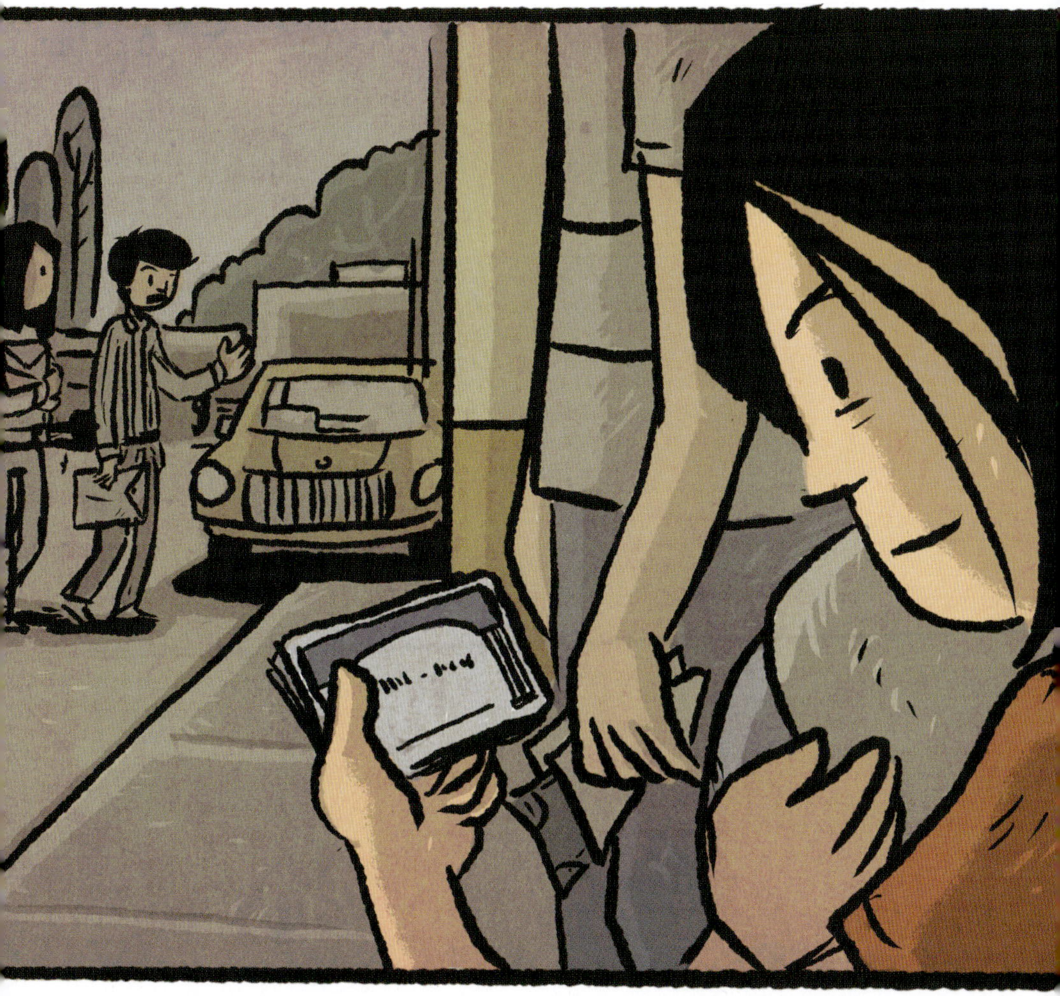

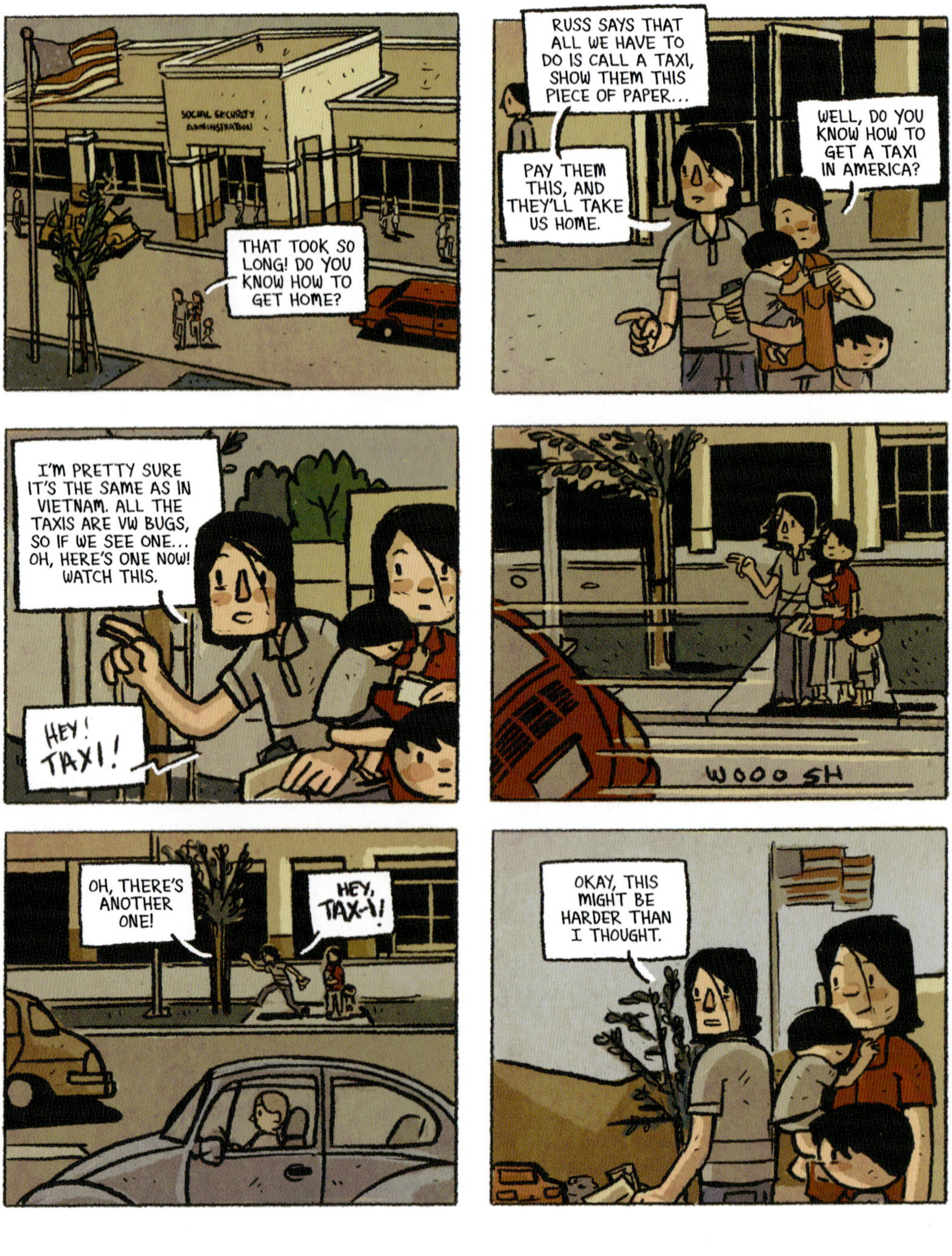
SOCIAL SECURITY ADMINISTRATION
THAT TOOK SO LONG! DO YOU KNOW HOW TO GET HOME?
RUSS SAYS THAT ALL WE HAVE TO DO IS CALL A TAXI, SHOW THEM THIS PIECE OF PAPER...
PAY THEM THIS, AND THEY'LL TAKE US HOME.
WELL, DO YOU KNOW HOW TO GET A TAXI IN AMERICA?
I'M PRETTY SURE IT'S THE SAME AS IN VIETNAM. ALL THE TAXIS ARE VW BUGS, SO IF WE SEE ONE... OH, HERE'S ONE NOW! WATCH THIS.
HEY! TAXI!
WOOOSH
OH, THERE'S ANOTHER ONE!
HEY, TAX-I!
OKAY, THIS MIGHT BE HARDER THAN I THOUGHT.

HEY, RUSS.
YOU HAVE A PERSONAL PHONE CALL.
WHO IS IT?
YOUR LANDLORD?
YOU HAVE TO TAKE THE CALL OUTSIDE THE SECURE AREA.
HELLO? YES. THIS IS RUSS. WHAT CAN I DO FOR YOU?
OH, YES. WELL...
OH.
OH! OKAY, I SEE...

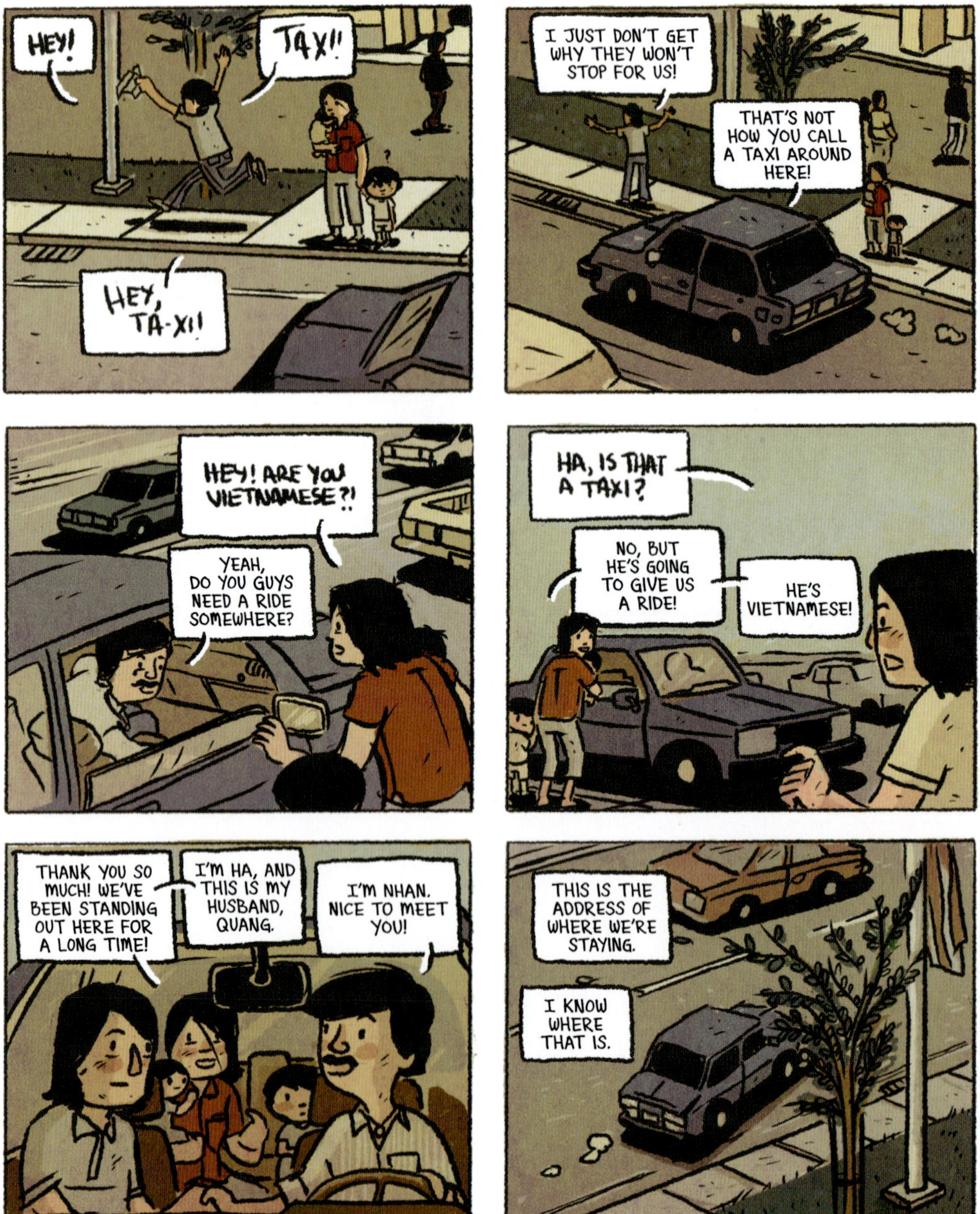
HEY!
TAXI!!
HEY, TA-XI!
I JUST DON'T GET WHY THEY WON'T STOP FOR US!
THAT'S NOT HOW YOU CALL A TAXI AROUND HERE!
HEY! ARE YOU VIETNAMESE?!
YEAH, DO YOU GUYS NEED A RIDE SOMEWHERE?
HA, IS THAT A TAXI?
NO, BUT HE'S GOING TO GIVE US A RIDE!
HE'S VIETNAMESE!
THANK YOU SO MUCH! WE'VE BEEN STANDING OUT HERE FOR A LONG TIME!
I'M HA, AND THIS IS MY HUSBAND, QUANG.
I'M NHAN. NICE TO MEET YOU!
THIS IS THE ADDRESS OF WHERE WE'RE STAYING.
I KNOW WHERE THAT IS.

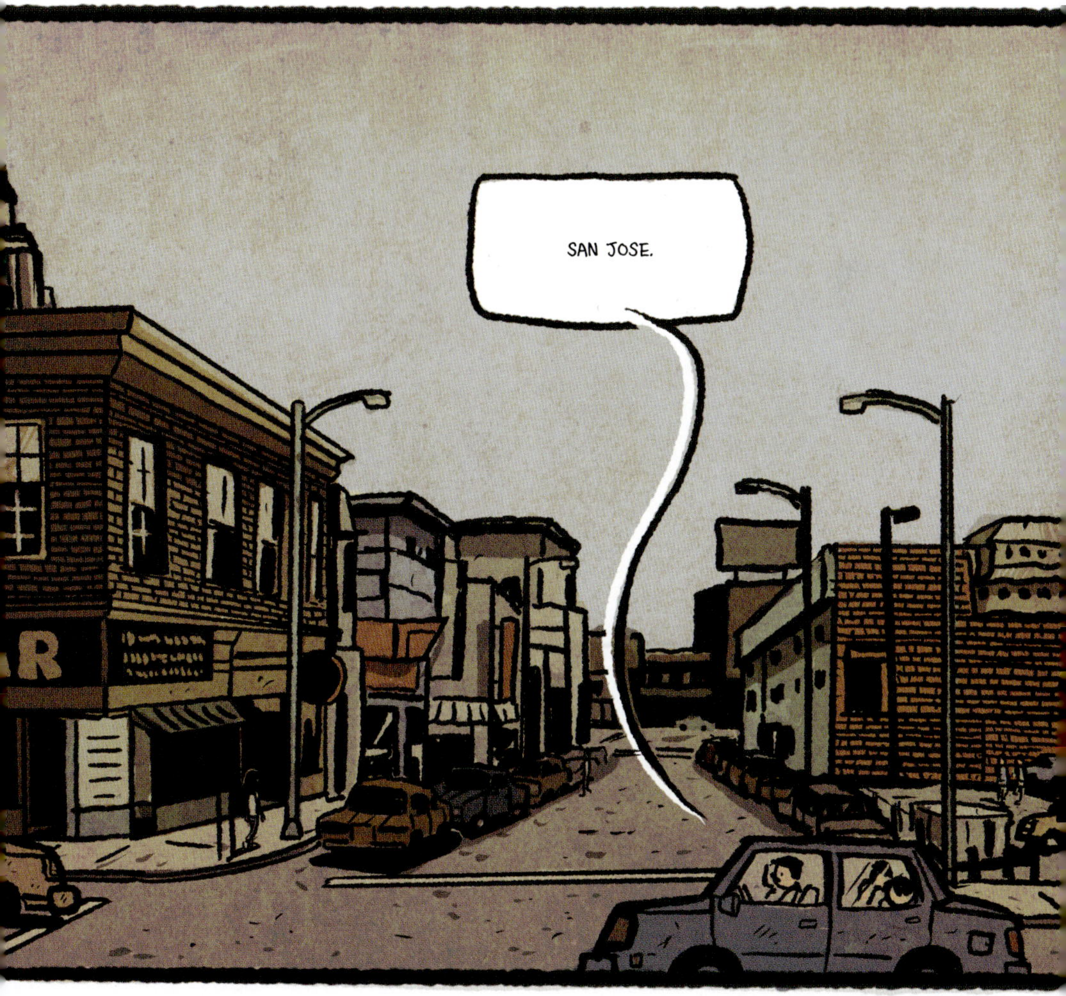
SAN JOSE.

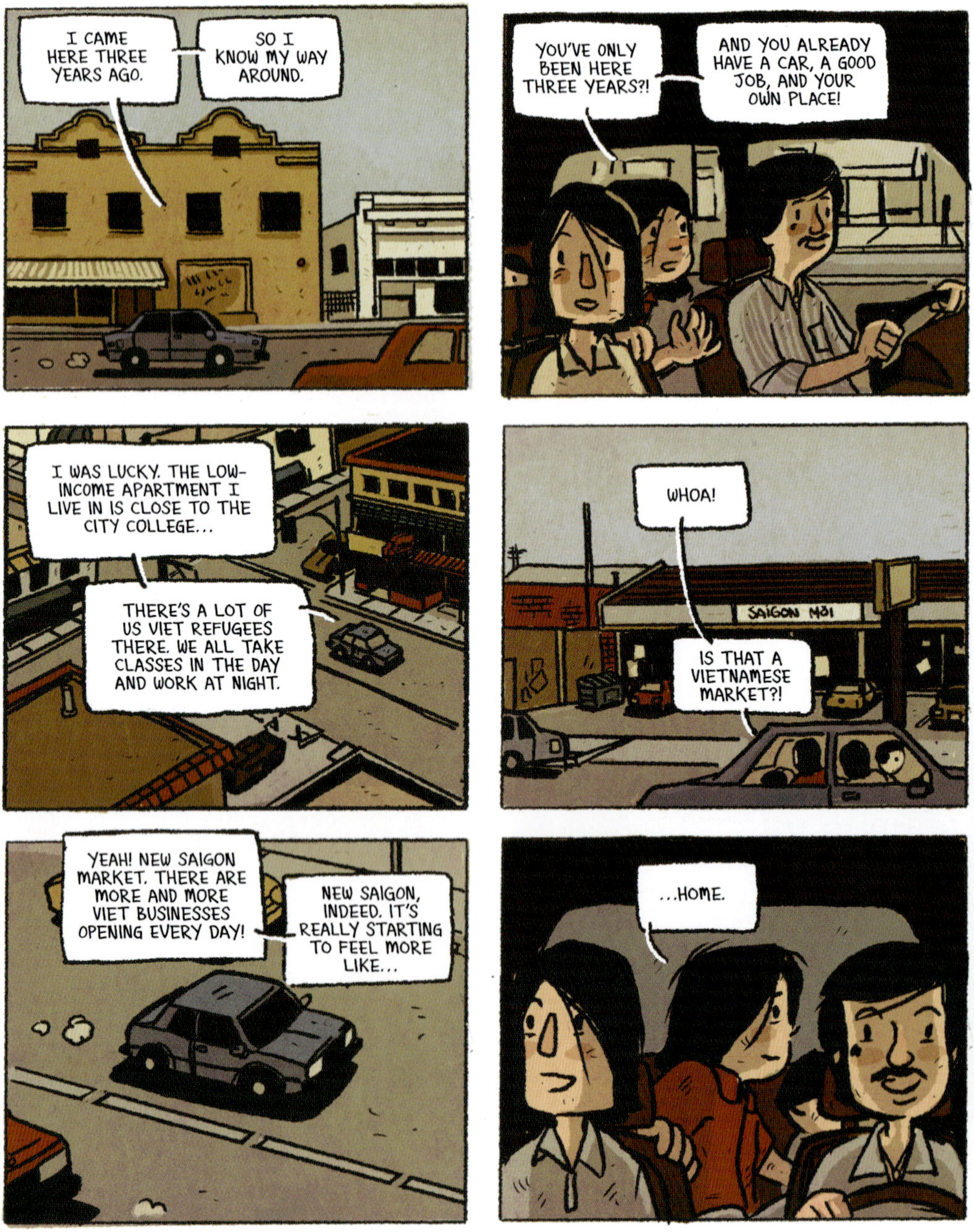

I CAME HERE THREE YEARS AGO.
SO I KNOW MY WAY AROUND.
YOU'VE ONLY BEEN HERE THREE YEARS?!
AND YOU ALREADY HAVE A CAR, A GOOD JOB, AND YOUR OWN PLACE!
I WAS LUCKY. THE LOW-INCOME APARTMENT I LIVE IN IS CLOSE TO THE CITY COLLEGE...
THERE'S A LOT OF US VIET REFUGEES THERE. WE ALL TAKE CLASSES IN THE DAY AND WORK AT NIGHT.
WHOA!
SAIGON MỚI
IS THAT A VIETNAMESE MARKET?!
YEAH! NEW SAIGON MARKET. THERE ARE MORE AND MORE VIET BUSINESSES OPENING EVERY DAY!
NEW SAIGON, INDEED. IT'S REALLY STARTING TO FEEL MORE LIKE...
...HOME.

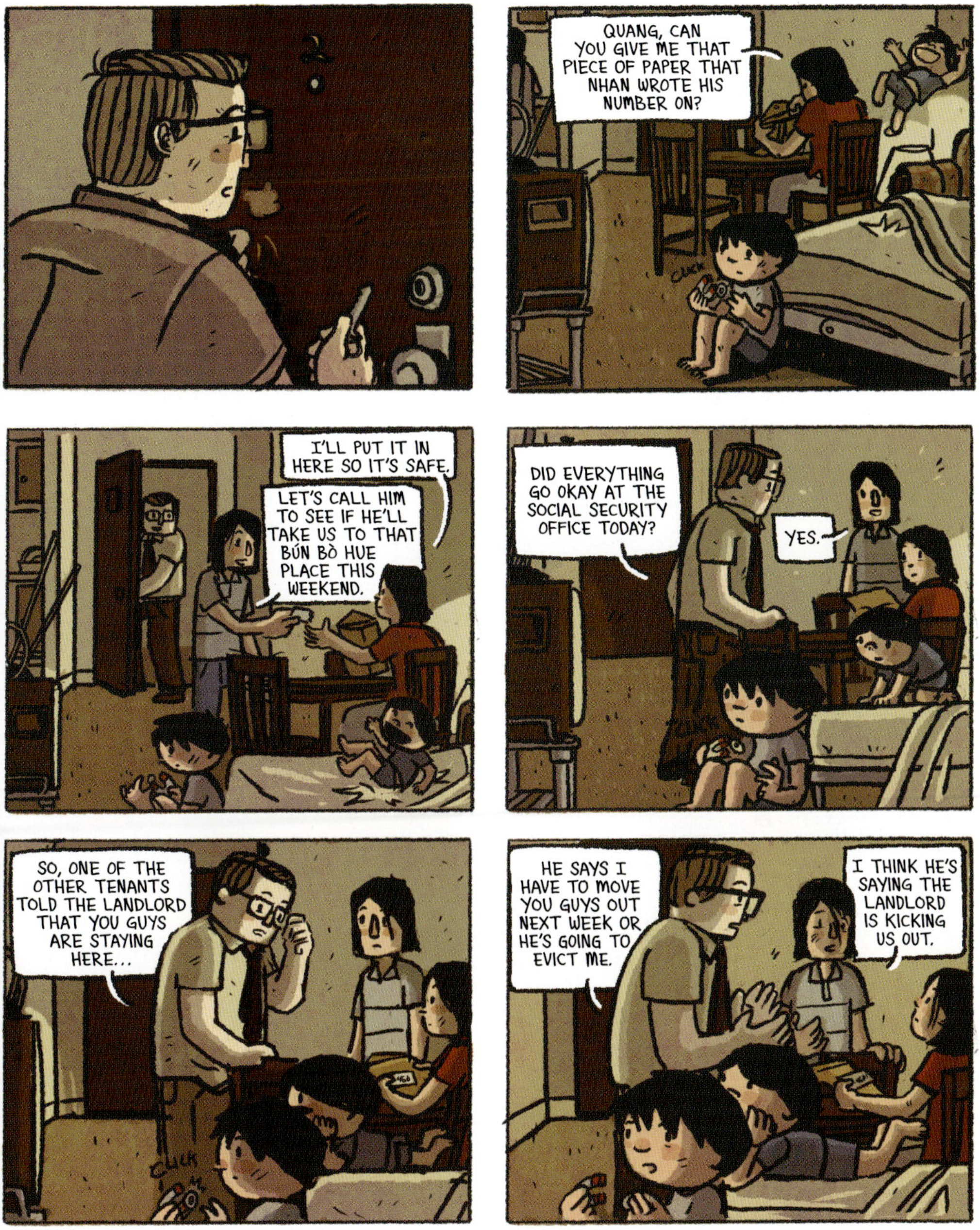
QUANG, CAN YOU GIVE ME THAT PIECE OF PAPER THAT NHAN WROTE HIS NUMBER ON?
CLICK
I'LL PUT IT IN HERE SO IT'S SAFE.
LET'S CALL HIM TO SEE IF HE'LL TAKE US TO THAT BÚN BÒ HUE PLACE THIS WEEKEND.
DID EVERYTHING GO OKAY AT THE SOCIAL SECURITY OFFICE TODAY?
YES.
SO, ONE OF THE OTHER TENANTS TOLD THE LANDLORD THAT YOU GUYS ARE STAYING HERE...
CLICK
HE SAYS I HAVE TO MOVE YOU GUYS OUT NEXT WEEK OR HE'S GOING TO EVICT ME.
I THINK HE'S SAYING THE LANDLORD IS KICKING US OUT.

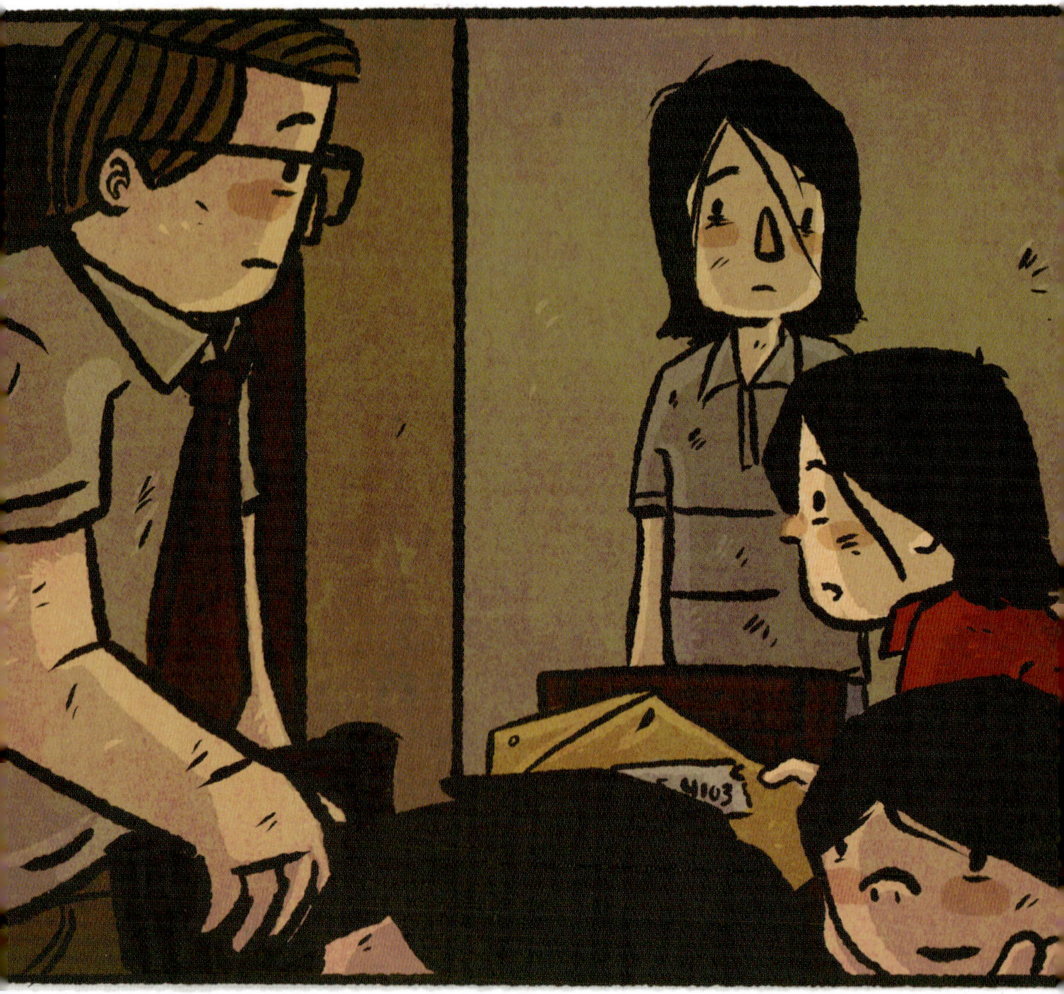

CHAPTER 4: STRAWBERRIES AND POTATO CHIPS

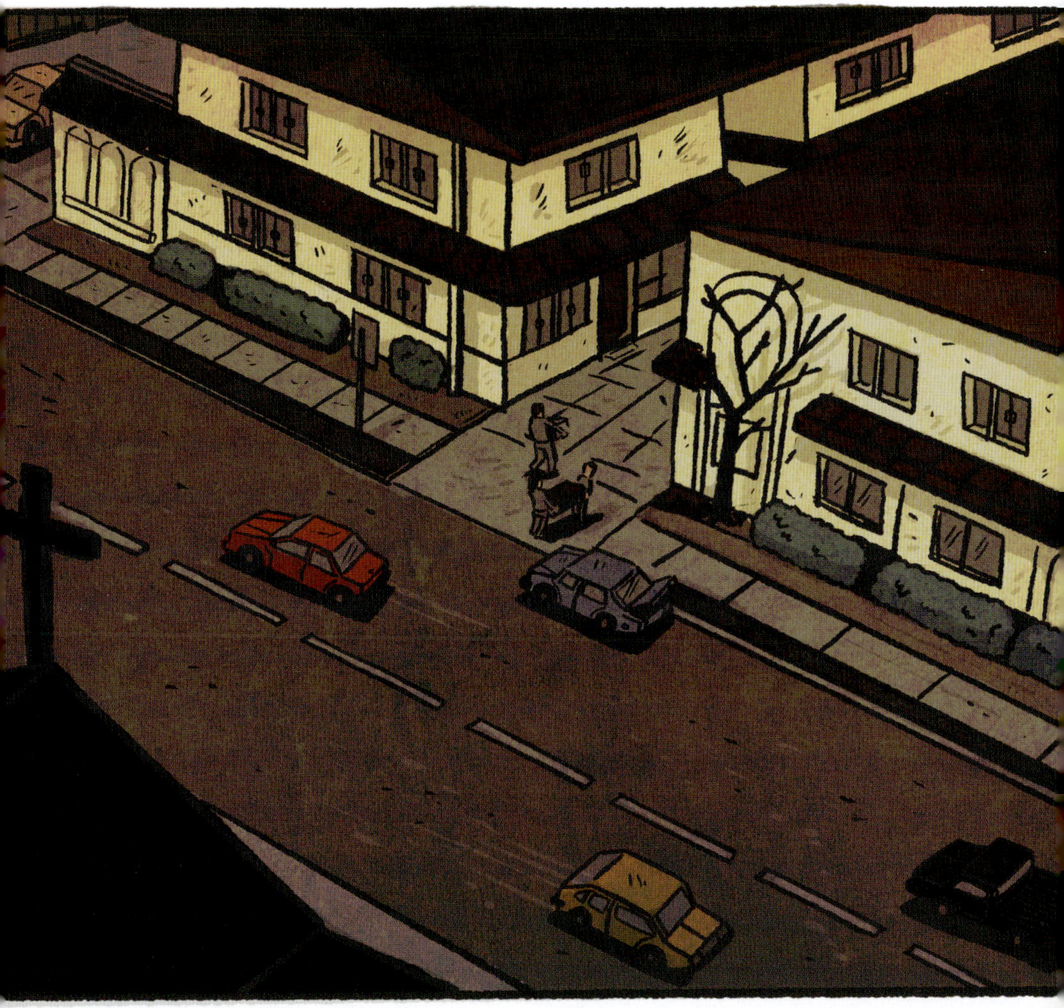

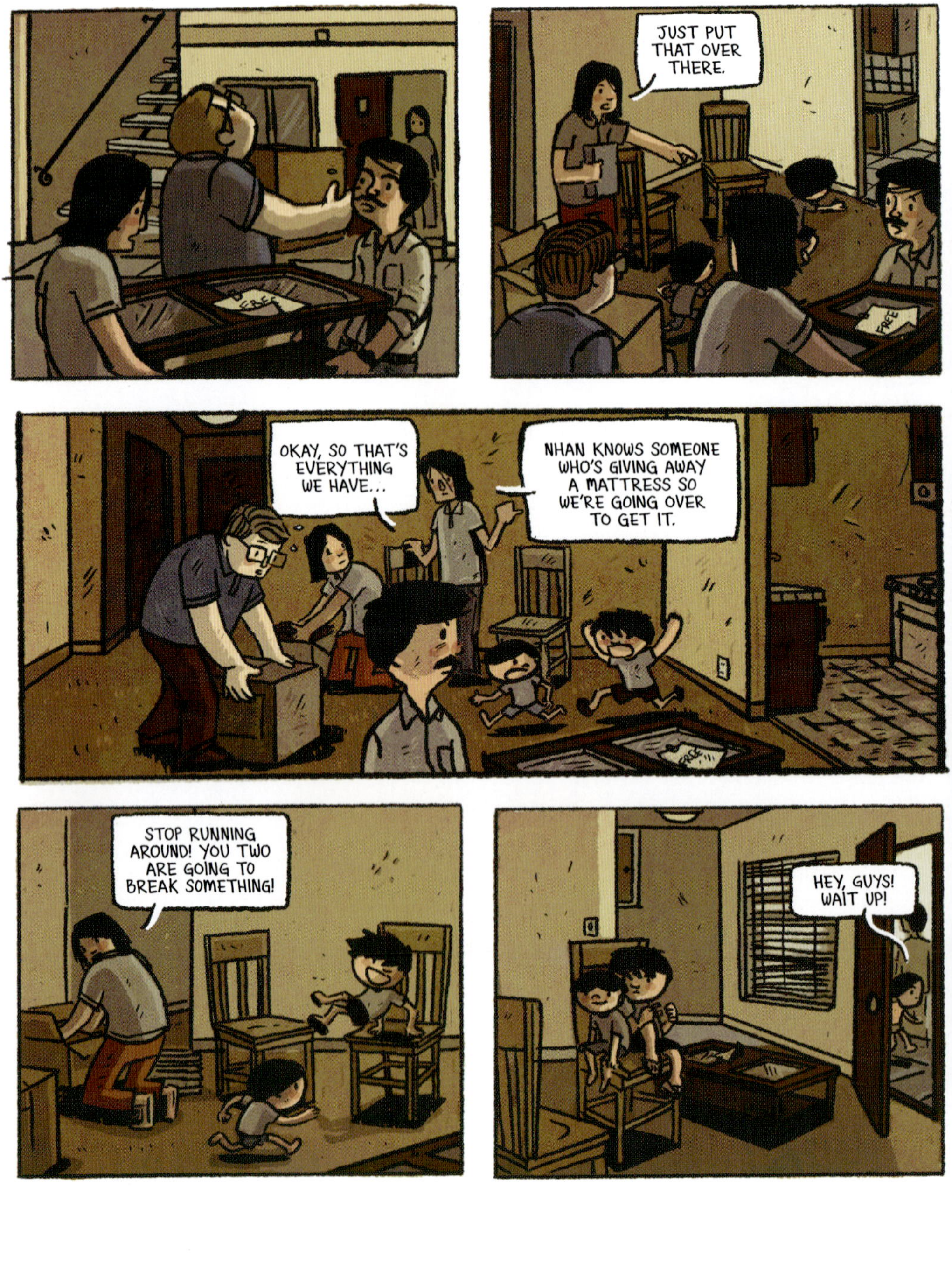
JUST PUT THAT OVER THERE.
OKAY, SO THAT'S EVERYTHING WE HAVE...
NHAN KNOWS SOMEONE WHO'S GIVING AWAY A MATTRESS SO WE'RE GOING OVER TO GET IT.
STOP RUNNING AROUND! YOU TWO ARE GOING TO BREAK SOMETHING!
HEY, GUYS! WAIT UP!

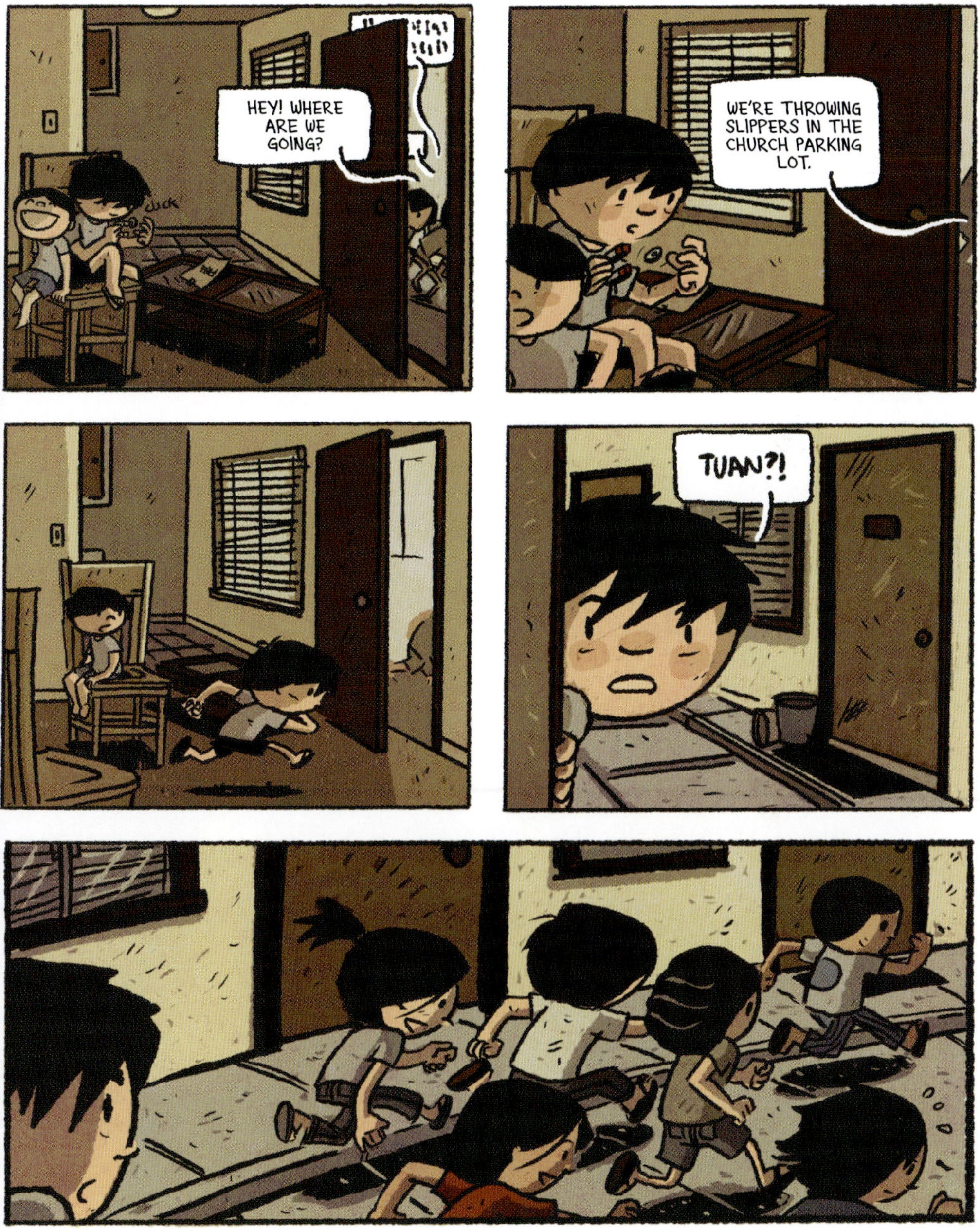
HEY! WHERE ARE WE GOING?
WE'RE THROWING SLIPPERS IN THE CHURCH PARKING LOT.
TUAN?!

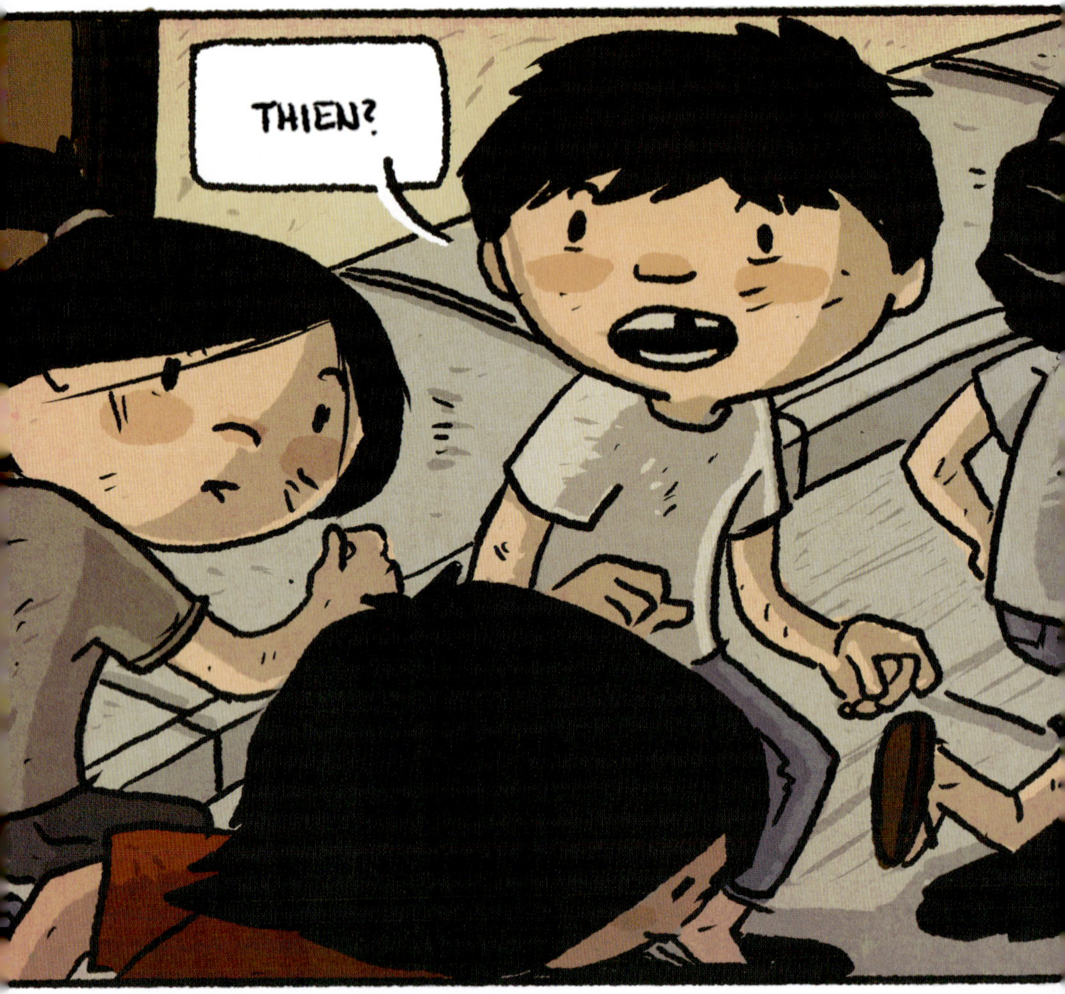
THIEN?

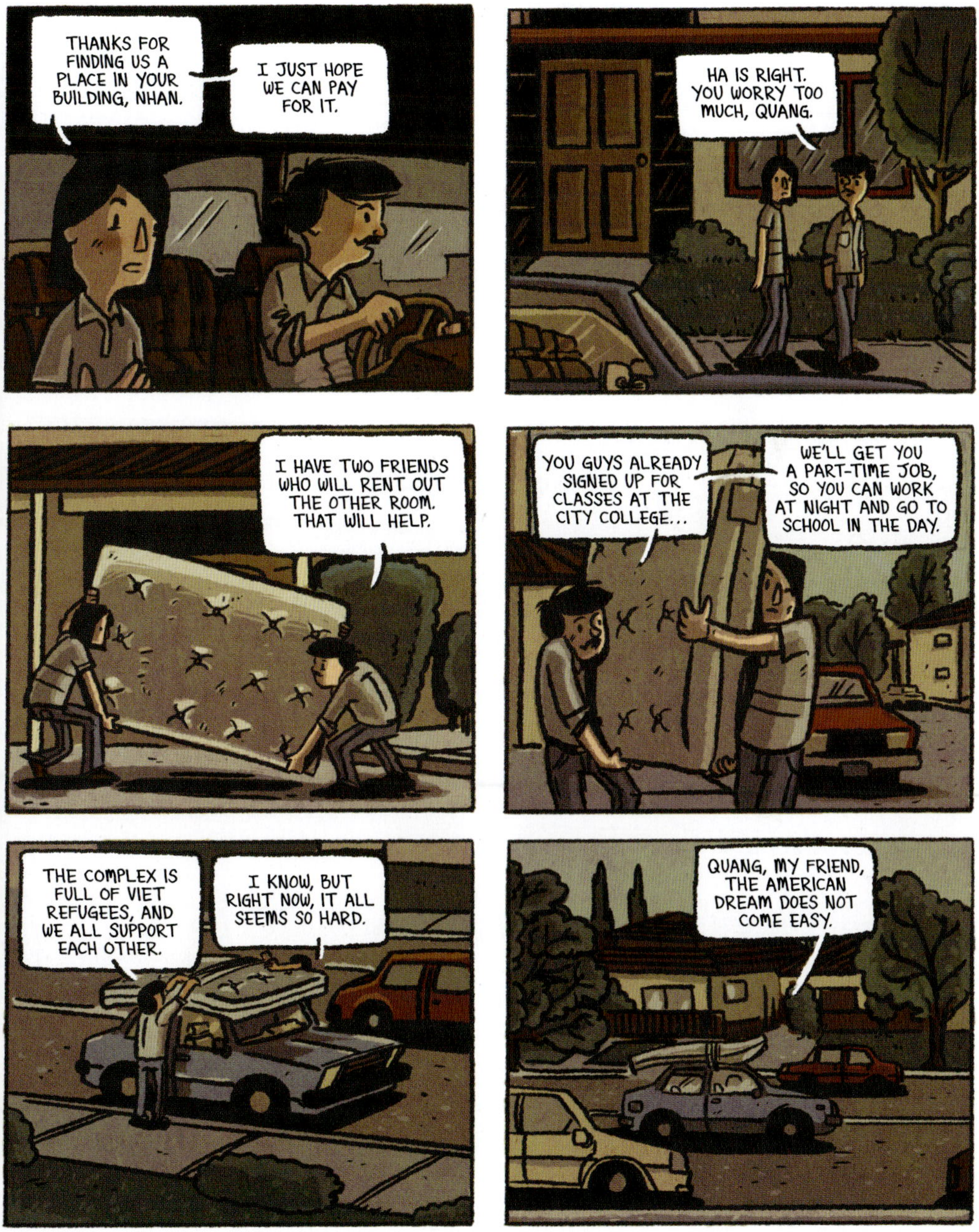
THANKS FOR FINDING US A PLACE IN YOUR BUILDING, NHAN.
I JUST HOPE WE CAN PAY FOR IT.
HA IS RIGHT. YOU WORRY TOO MUCH, QUANG.
I HAVE TWO FRIENDS WHO WILL RENT OUT THE OTHER ROOM. THAT WILL HELP.
YOU GUYS ALREADY SIGNED UP FOR CLASSES AT THE CITY COLLEGE...
WE'LL GET YOU A PART-TIME JOB, SO YOU CAN WORK AT NIGHT AND GO TO SCHOOL IN THE DAY.
THE COMPLEX IS FULL OF VIET REFUGEES, AND WE ALL SUPPORT EACH OTHER.
I KNOW, BUT RIGHT NOW, IT ALL SEEMS SO HARD.
QUANG, MY FRIEND, THE AMERICAN DREAM DOES NOT COME EASY.

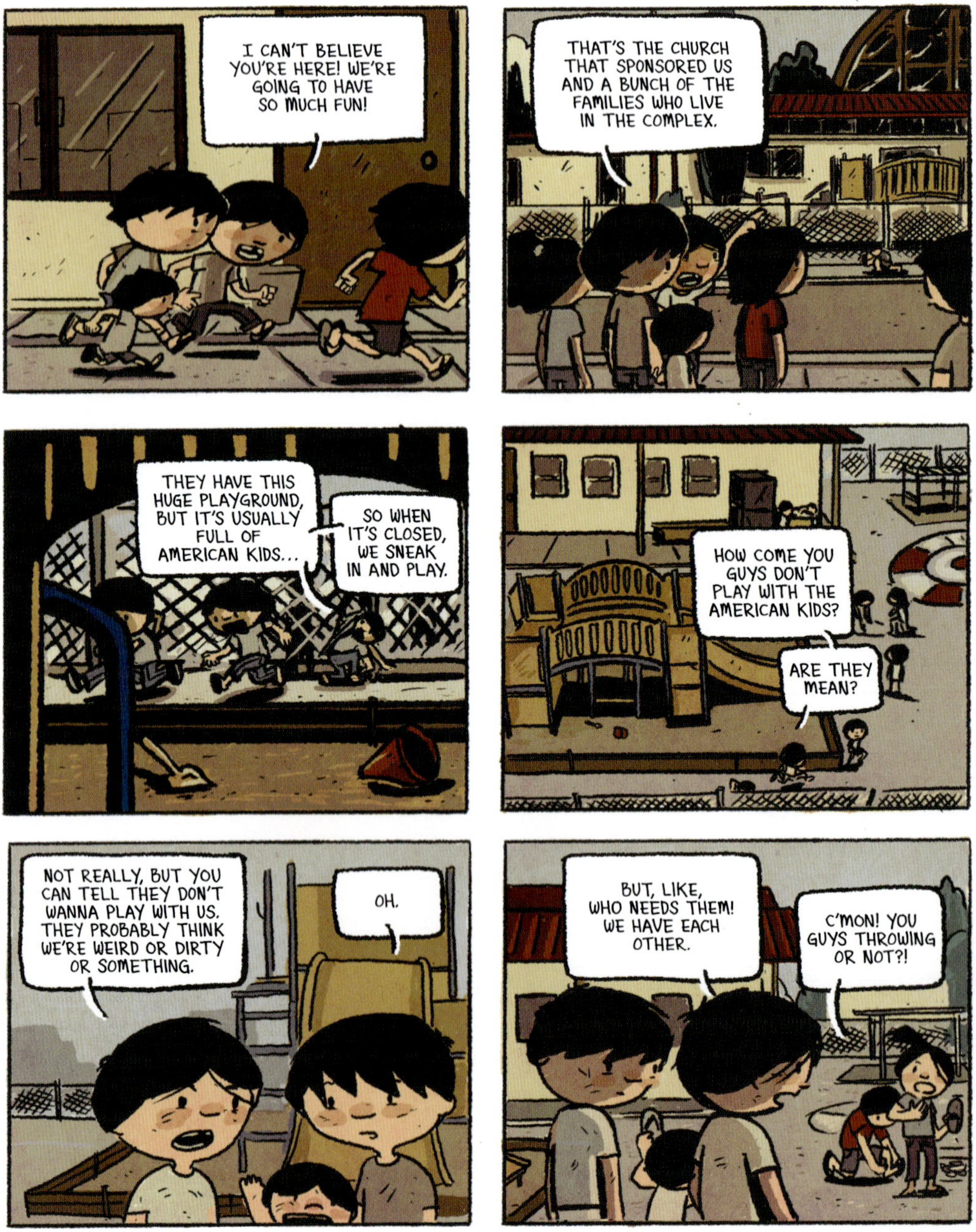
I CAN'T BELIEVE YOU'RE HERE! WE'RE GOING TO HAVE SO MUCH FUN!
THAT'S THE CHURCH THAT SPONSORED US AND A BUNCH OF THE FAMILIES WHO LIVE IN THE COMPLEX.
THEY HAVE THIS HUGE PLAYGROUND, BUT IT'S USUALLY FULL OF AMERICAN KIDS...
SO WHEN IT'S CLOSED, WE SNEAK IN AND PLAY.
HOW COME YOU GUYS DON'T PLAY WITH THE AMERICAN KIDS?
ARE THEY MEAN?
NOT REALLY, BUT YOU CAN TELL THEY DON'T WANNA PLAY WITH US. THEY PROBABLY THINK WE'RE WEIRD OR DIRTY OR SOMETHING.
OH.
BUT, LIKE, WHO NEEDS THEM! WE HAVE EACH OTHER.
C'MON! YOU GUYS THROWING OR NOT?!

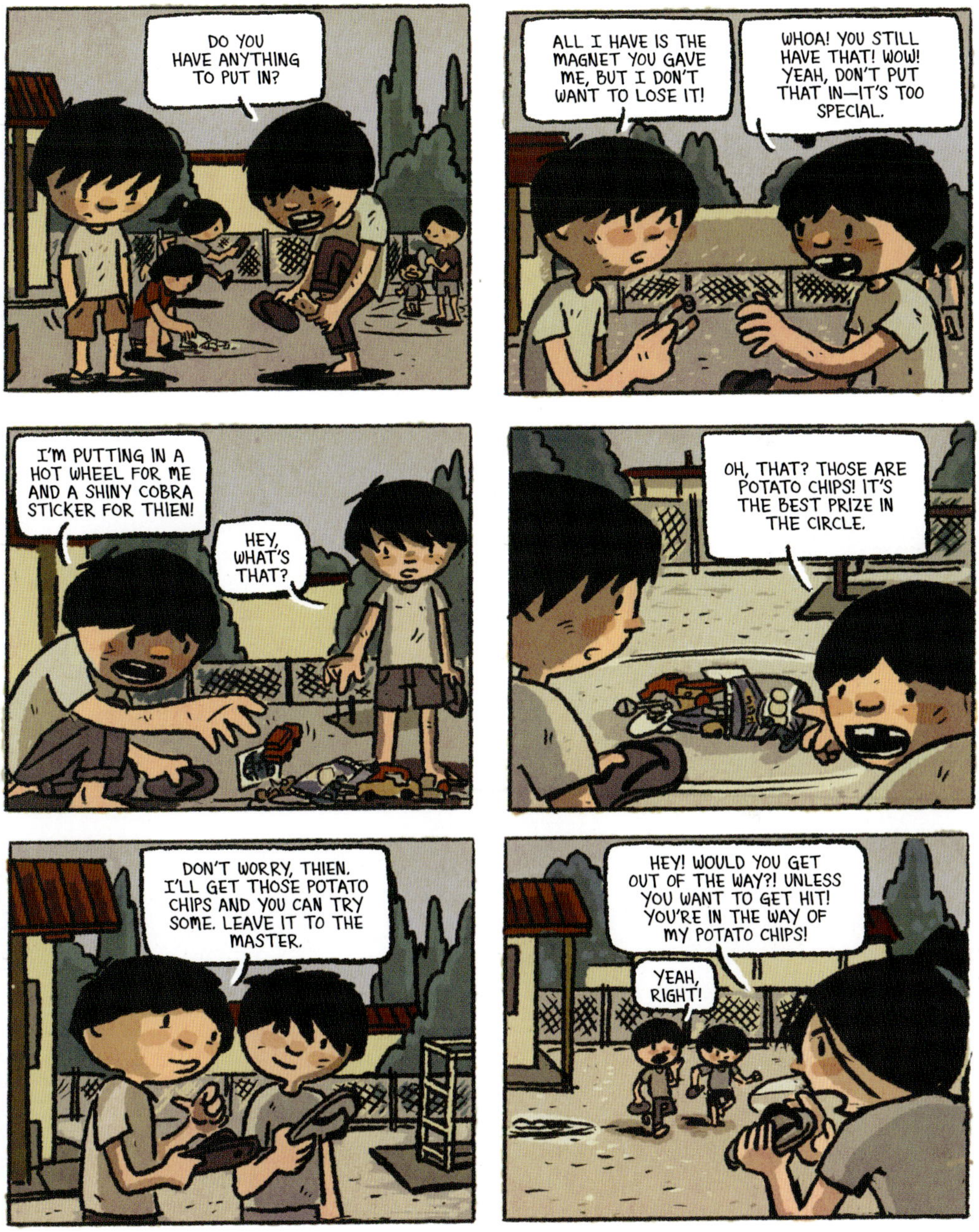
DO YOU HAVE ANYTHING TO PUT IN?
ALL I HAVE IS THE MAGNET YOU GAVE ME, BUT I DON'T WANT TO LOSE IT!
WHOA! YOU STILL HAVE THAT! WOW! YEAH, DON'T PUT THAT IN—IT'S TOO SPECIAL.
I'M PUTTING IN A HOT WHEEL FOR ME AND A SHINY COBRA STICKER FOR THIEN!
HEY, WHAT'S THAT?
OH, THAT? THOSE ARE POTATO CHIPS! IT'S THE BEST PRIZE IN THE CIRCLE.
DON'T WORRY, THIEN. I'LL GET THOSE POTATO CHIPS AND YOU CAN TRY SOME. LEAVE IT TO THE MASTER.
HEY! WOULD YOU GET OUT OF THE WAY?! UNLESS YOU WANT TO GET HIT! YOU'RE IN THE WAY OF MY POTATO CHIPS!
YEAH, RIGHT!

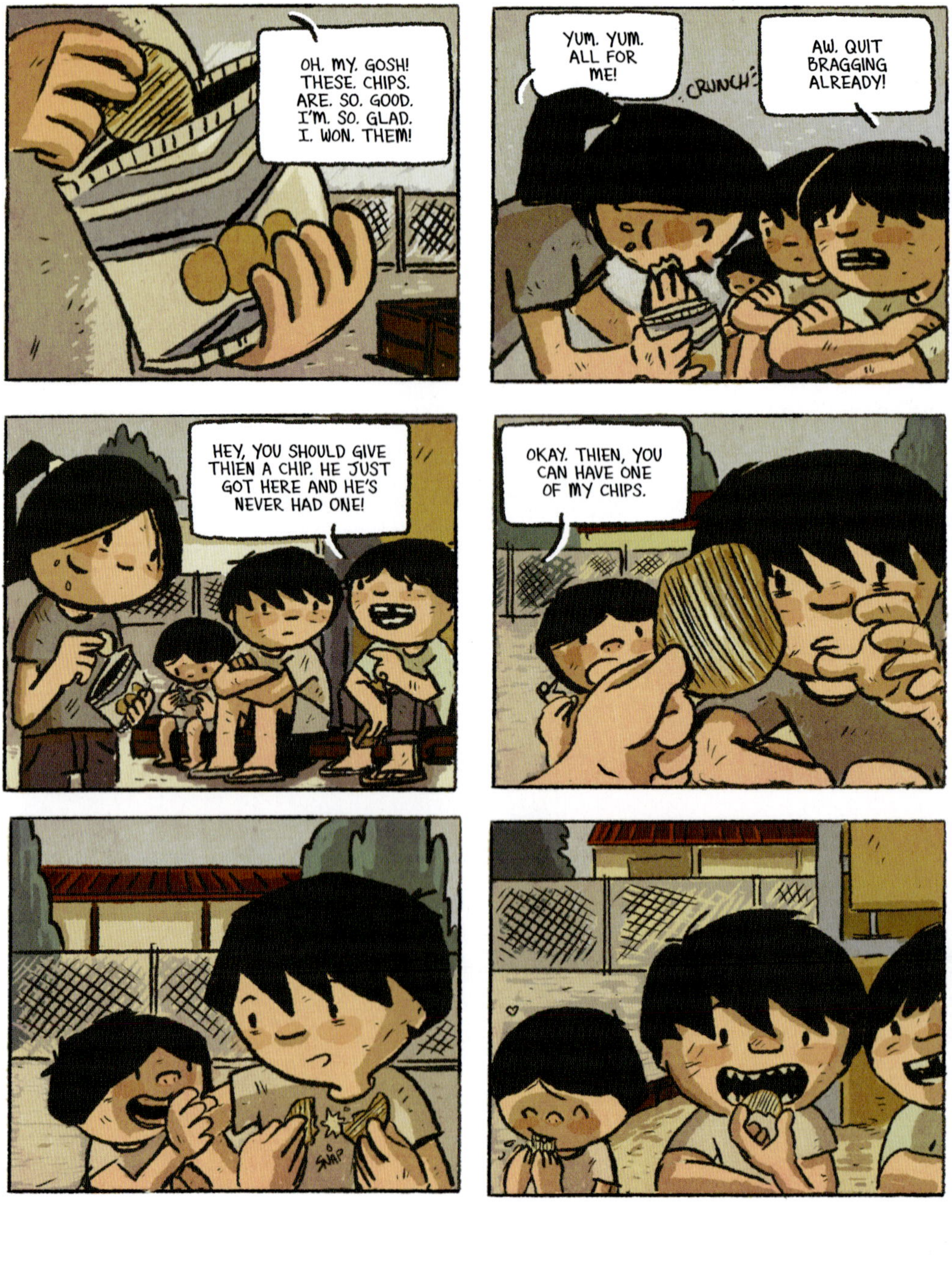
OH. MY. GOSH! THESE. CHIPS. ARE. SO. GOOD. I'M. SO. GLAD. I. WON. THEM!
YUM. YUM. ALL FOR ME!
CRUNCH
AW. QUIT BRAGGING ALREADY!
HEY, YOU SHOULD GIVE THIEN A CHIP. HE JUST GOT HERE AND HE'S NEVER HAD ONE!
OKAY. THIEN, YOU CAN HAVE ONE OF MY CHIPS.
SNAP

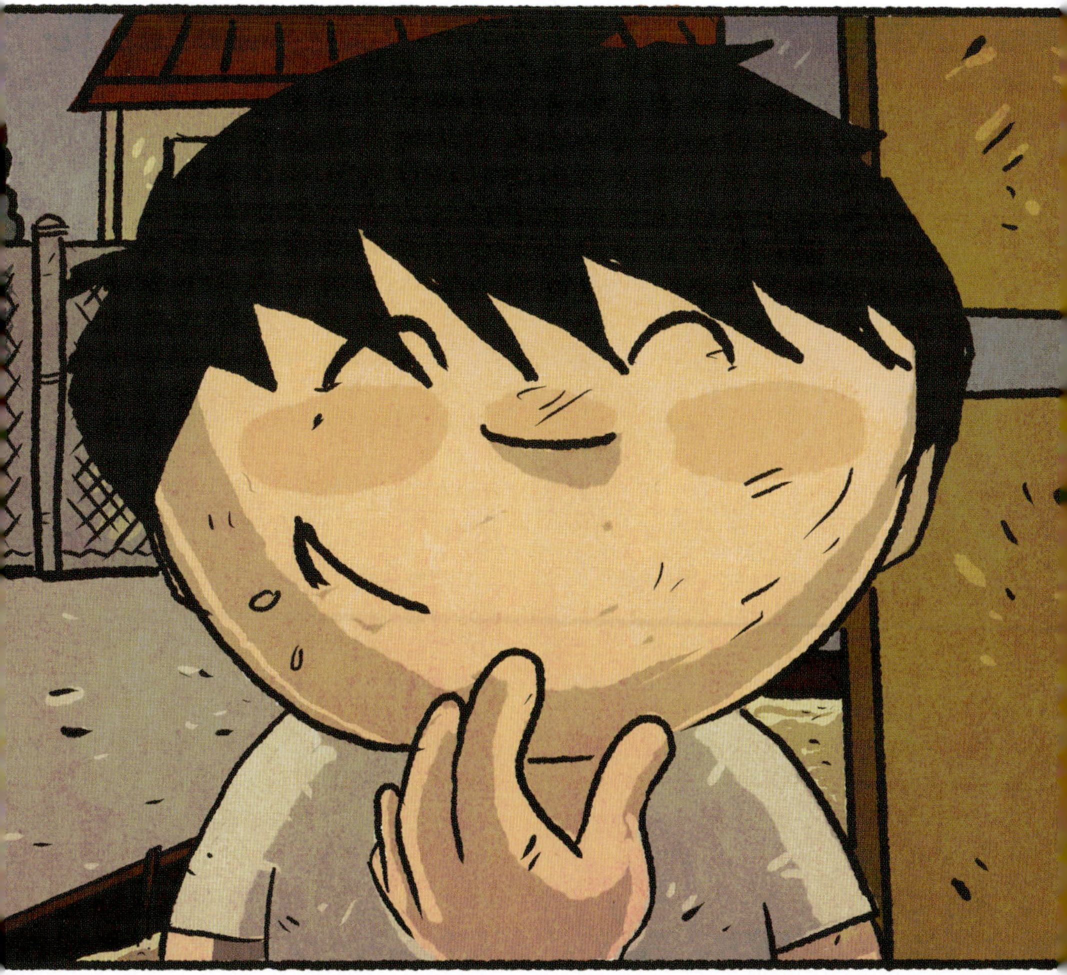

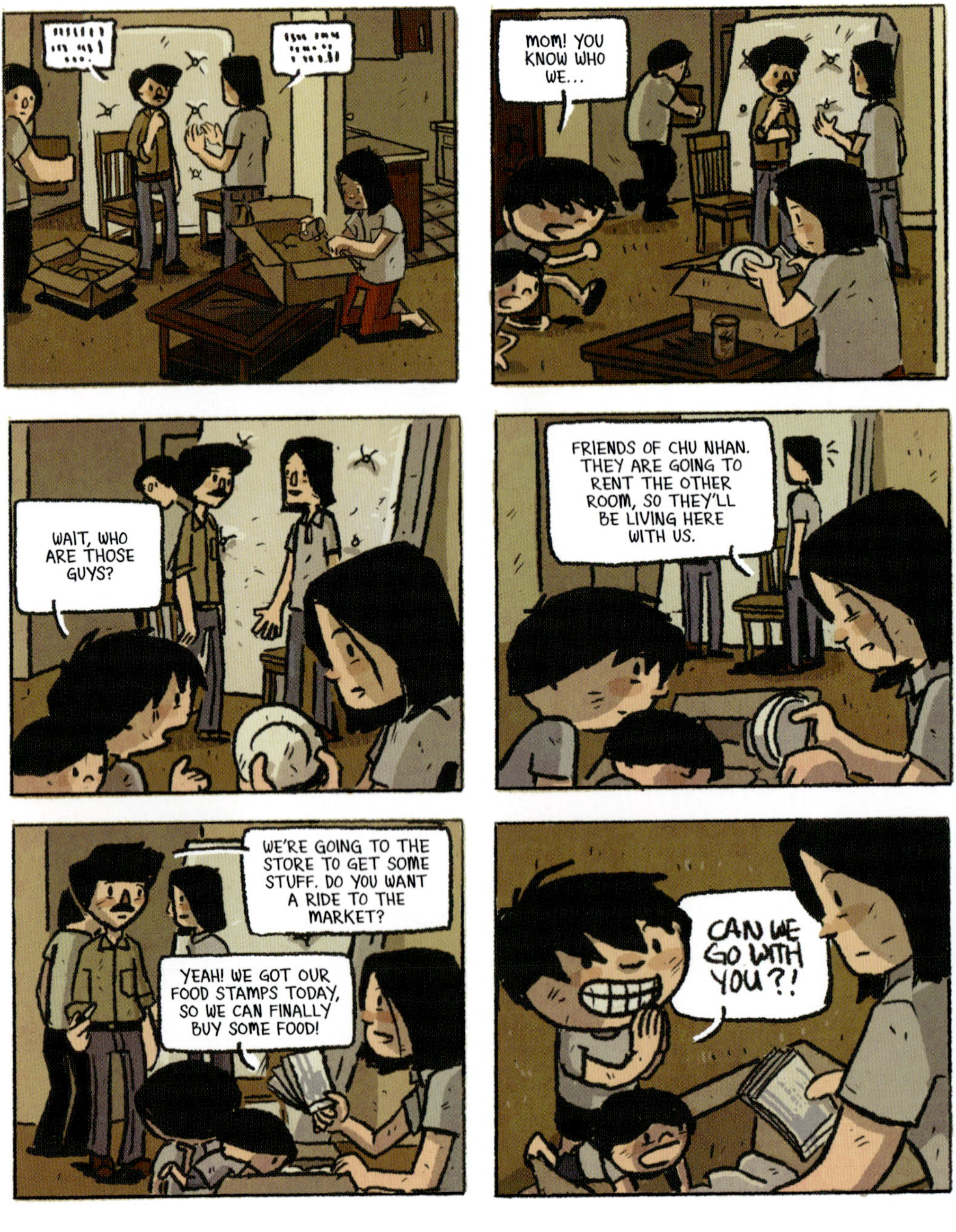
MOM! YOU KNOW WHO WE...
WAIT, WHO ARE THOSE GUYS?
FRIENDS OF CHU NHAN. THEY ARE GOING TO RENT THE OTHER ROOM, SO THEY'LL BE LIVING HERE WITH US.
WE'RE GOING TO THE STORE TO GET SOME STUFF. DO YOU WANT A RIDE TO THE MARKET?
YEAH! WE GOT OUR FOOD STAMPS TODAY, SO WE CAN FINALLY BUY SOME FOOD!
CAN WE GO WITH YOU?!

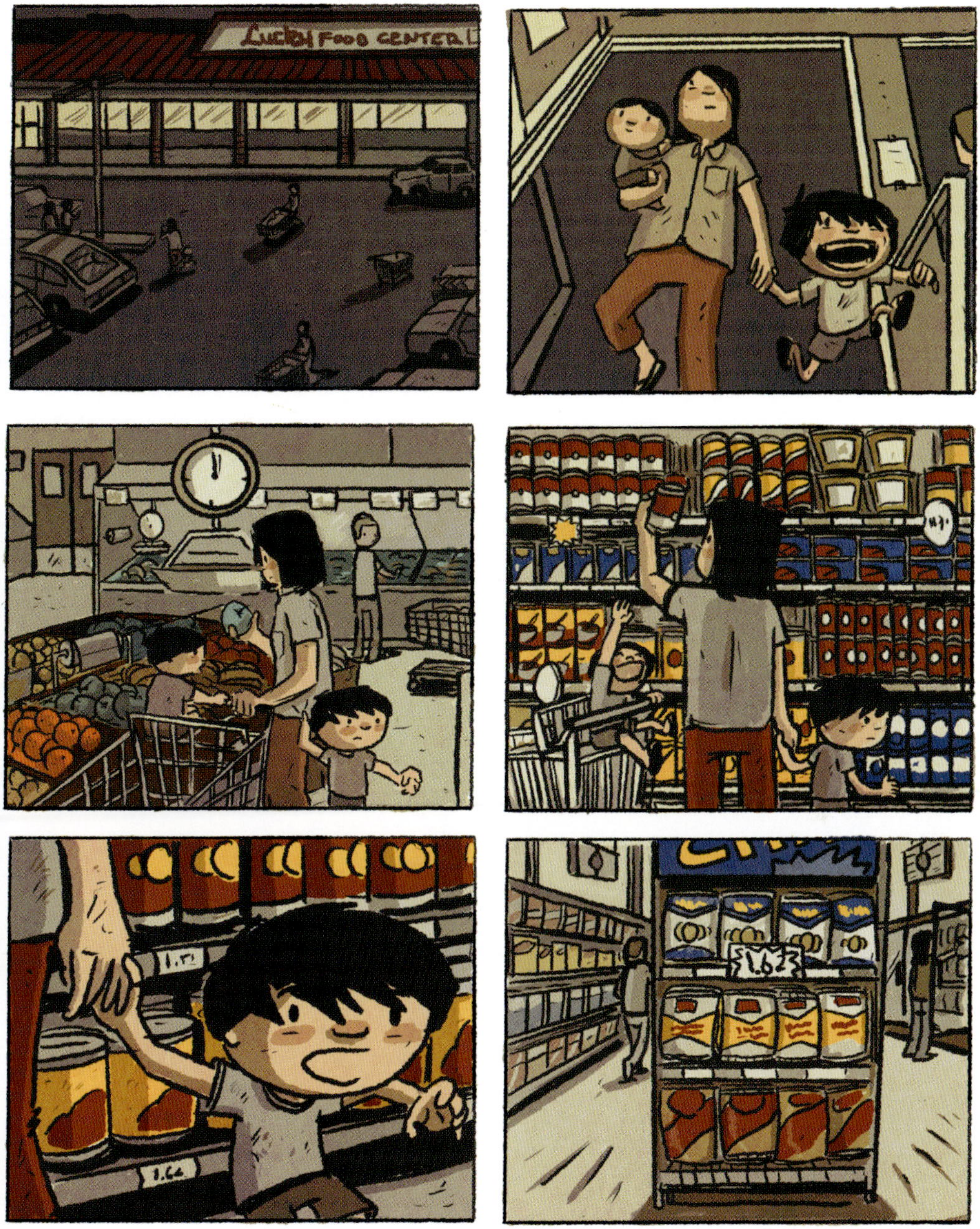
LUCKY FOOD CENTER
1.62

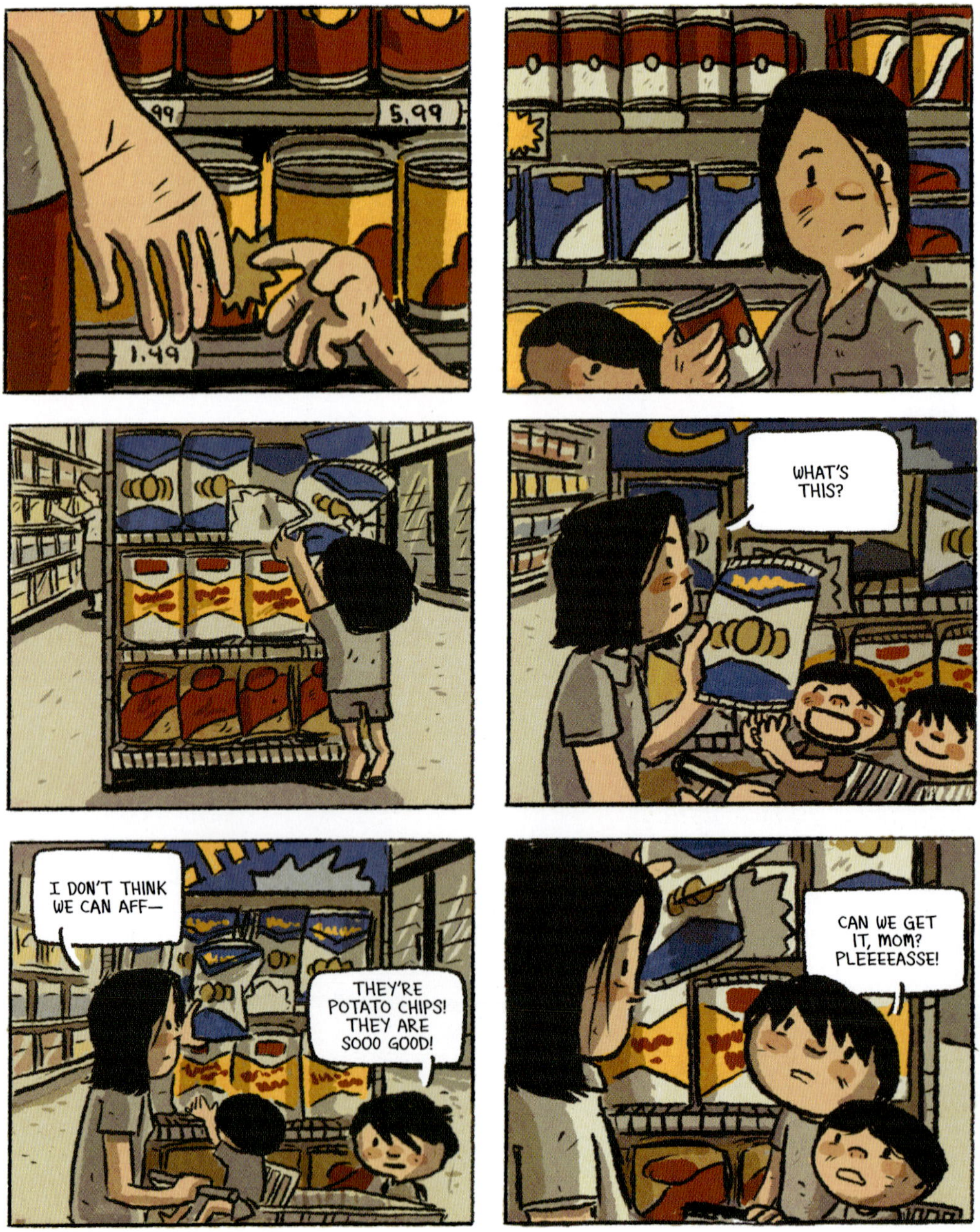
5.99
1.49
WHAT'S THIS?
I DON'T THINK WE CAN AFF—
THEY'RE POTATO CHIPS! THEY ARE SOOO GOOD!
CAN WE GET IT, MOM? PLEEEEASSE!

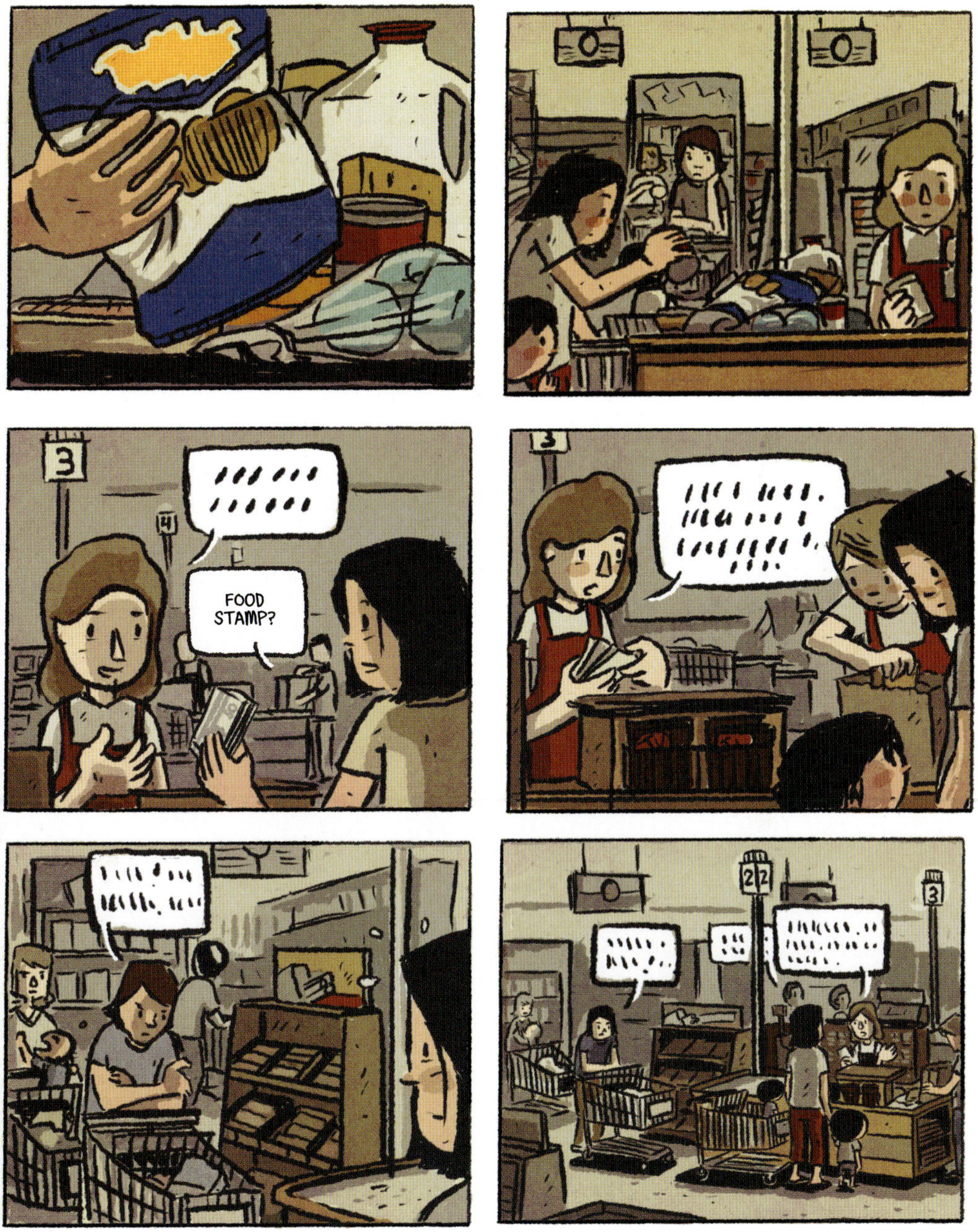
FOOD STAMP?

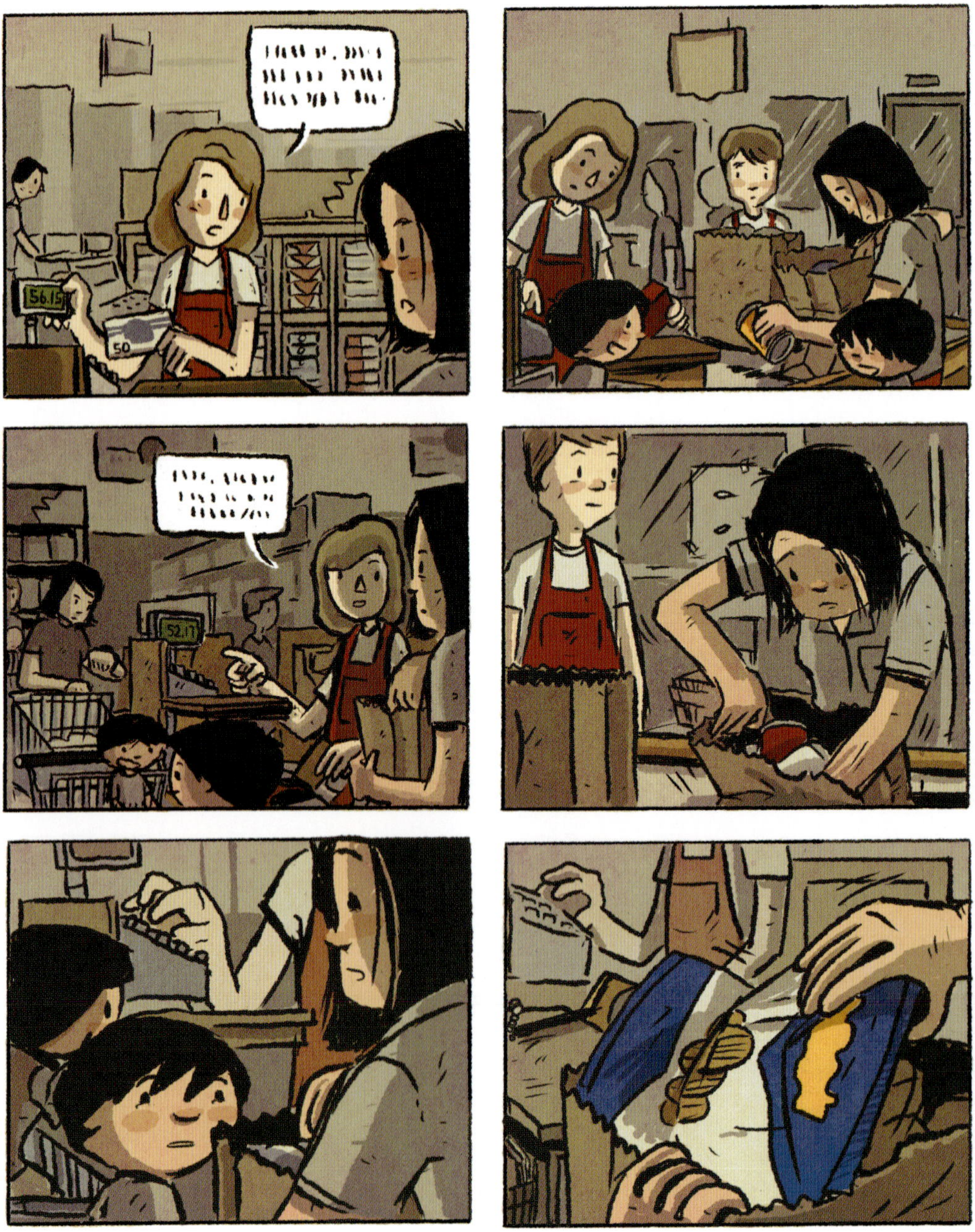
56.15
50
52.17

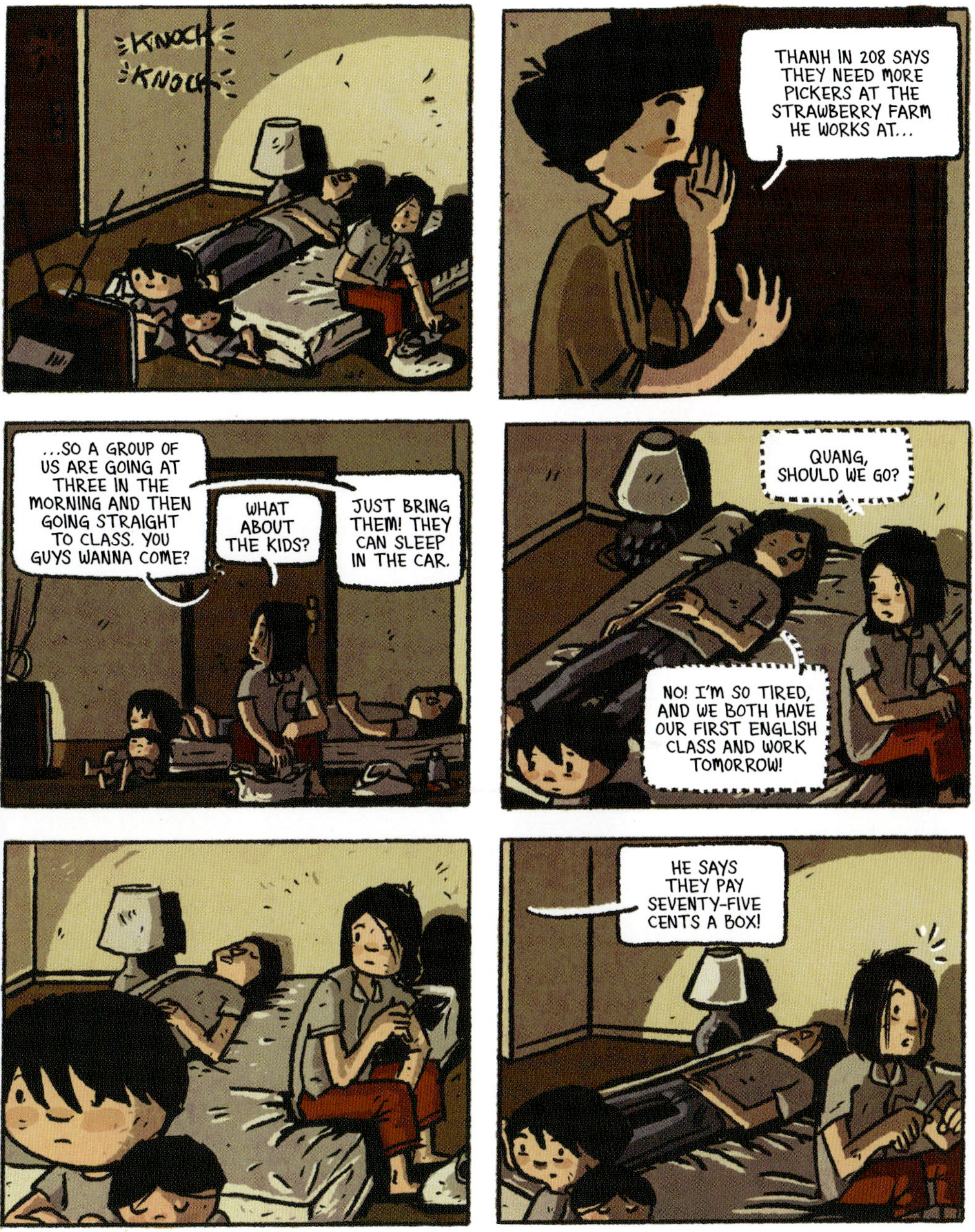
KNOCK
KNOCK
THANH IN 208 SAYS THEY NEED MORE PICKERS AT THE STRAWBERRY FARM HE WORKS AT...
...SO A GROUP OF US ARE GOING AT THREE IN THE MORNING AND THEN GOING STRAIGHT TO CLASS. YOU GUYS WANNA COME?
WHAT ABOUT THE KIDS?
JUST BRING THEM! THEY CAN SLEEP IN THE CAR.
QUANG, SHOULD WE GO?
NO! I'M SO TIRED, AND WE BOTH HAVE OUR FIRST ENGLISH CLASS AND WORK TOMORROW!
HE SAYS THEY PAY SEVENTY-FIVE CENTS A BOX!

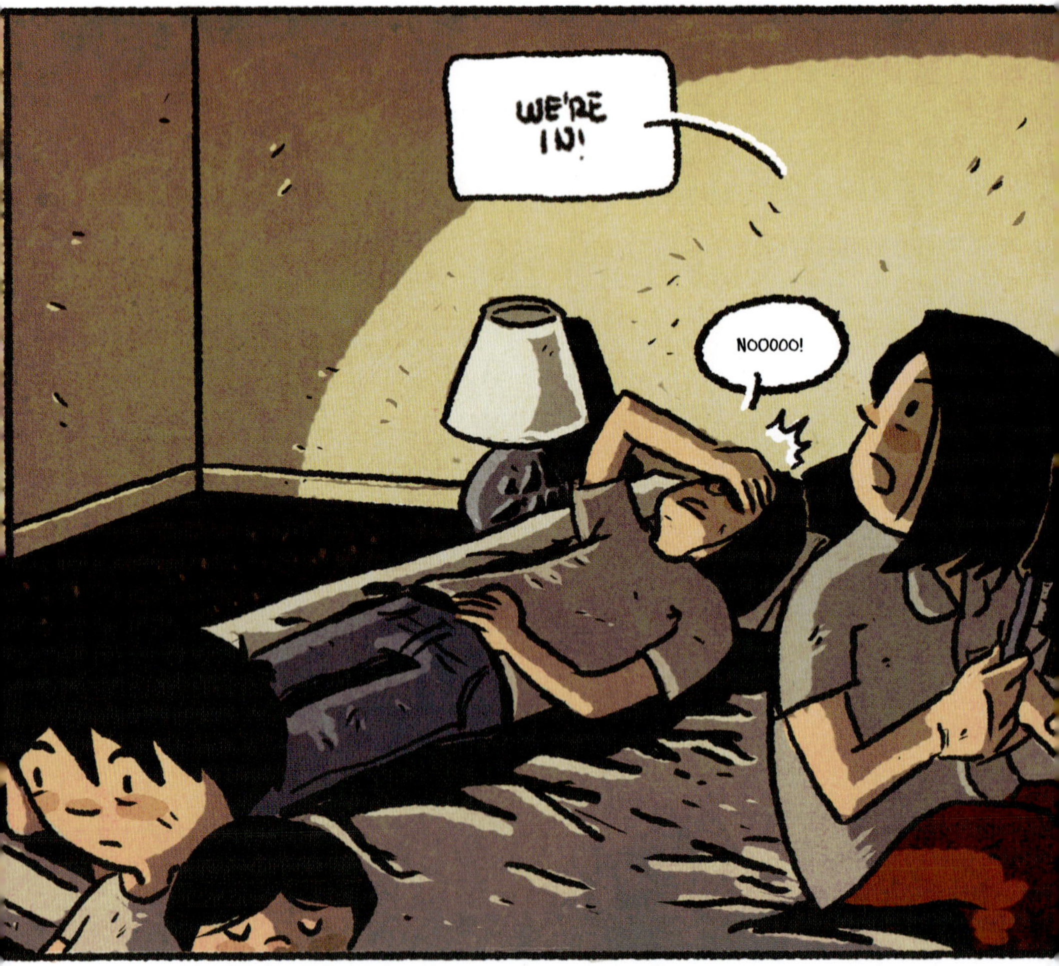
WE'RE IN!
NOOOOO!

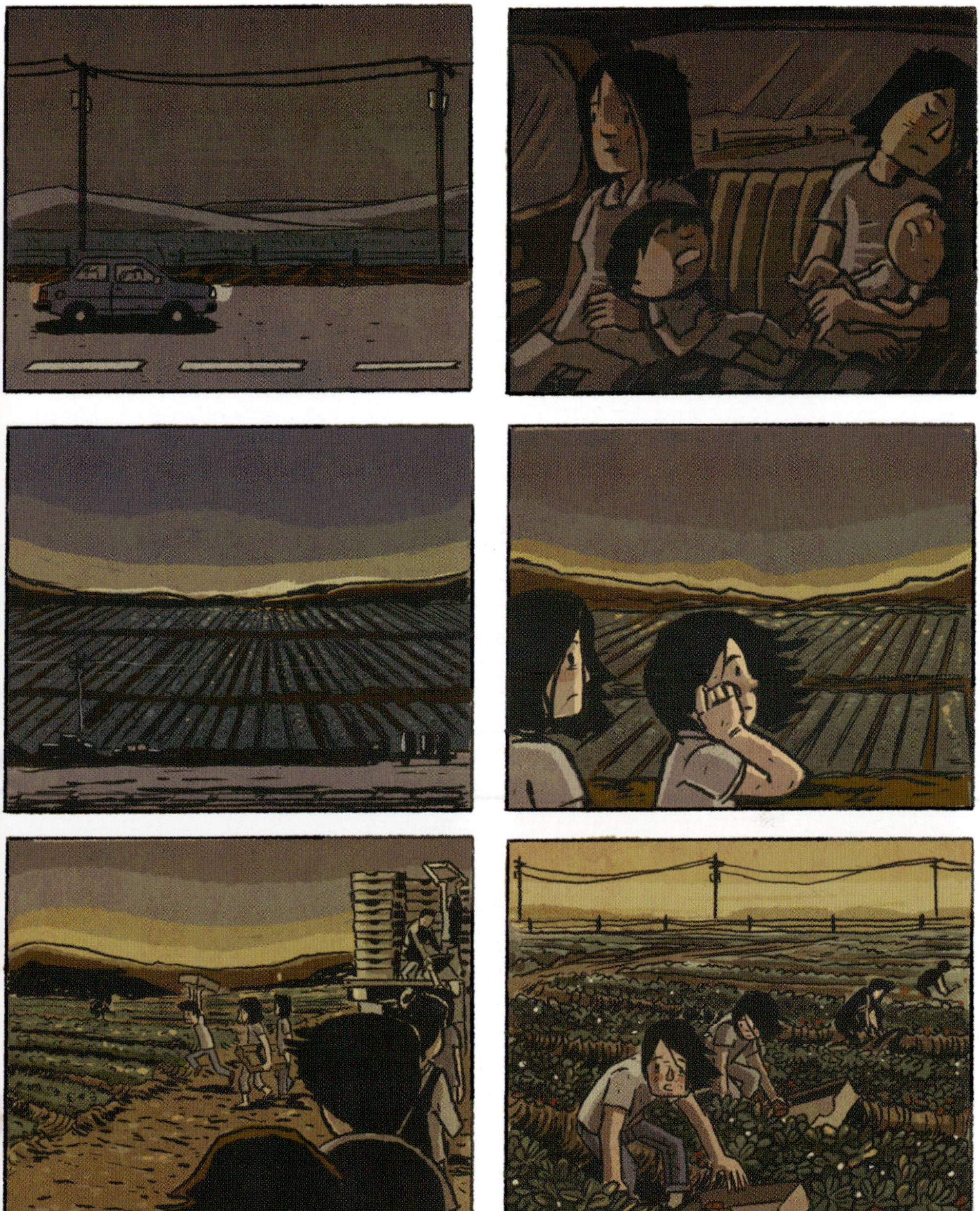

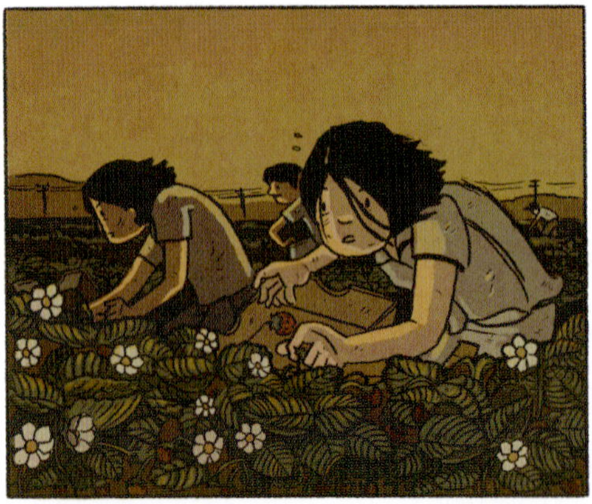

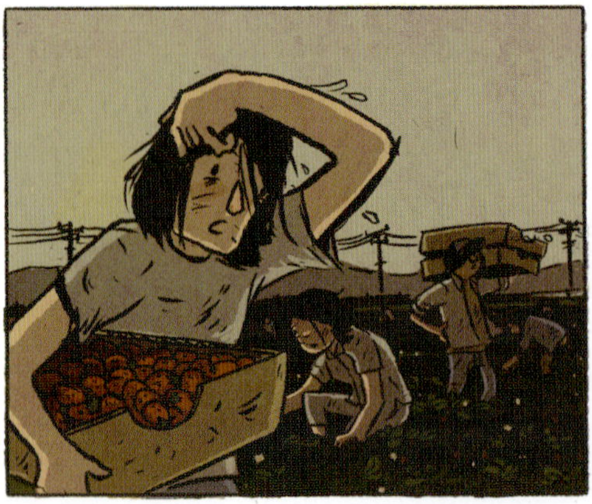

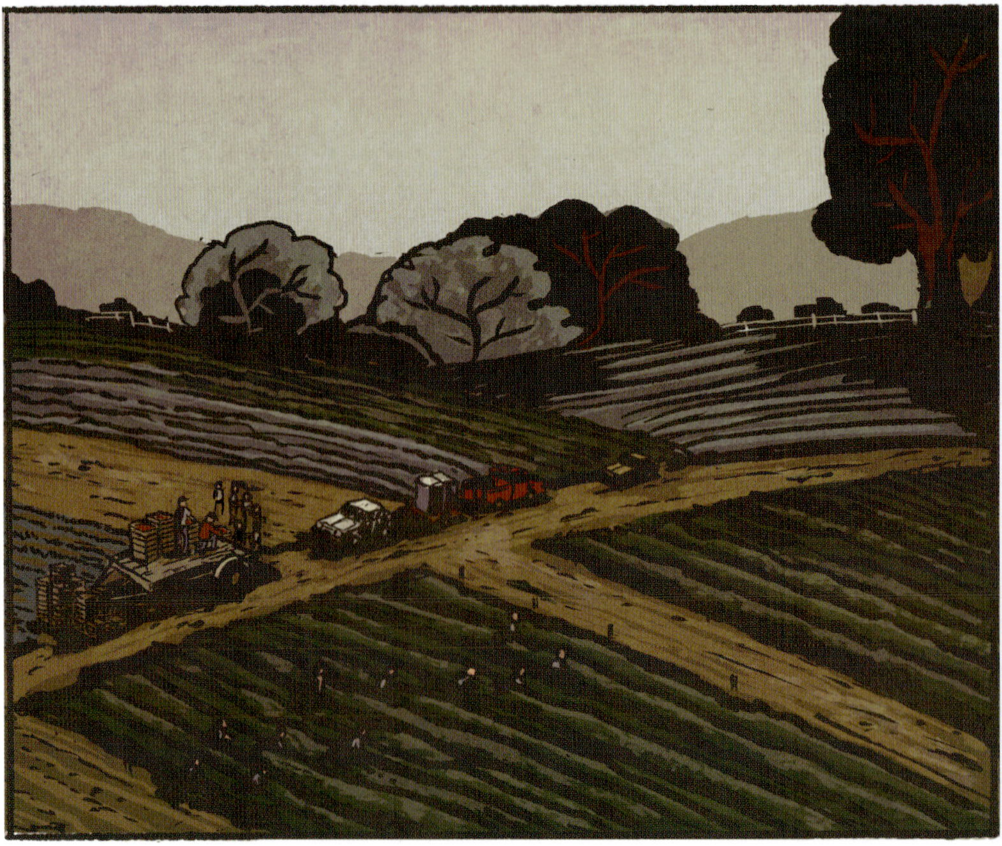

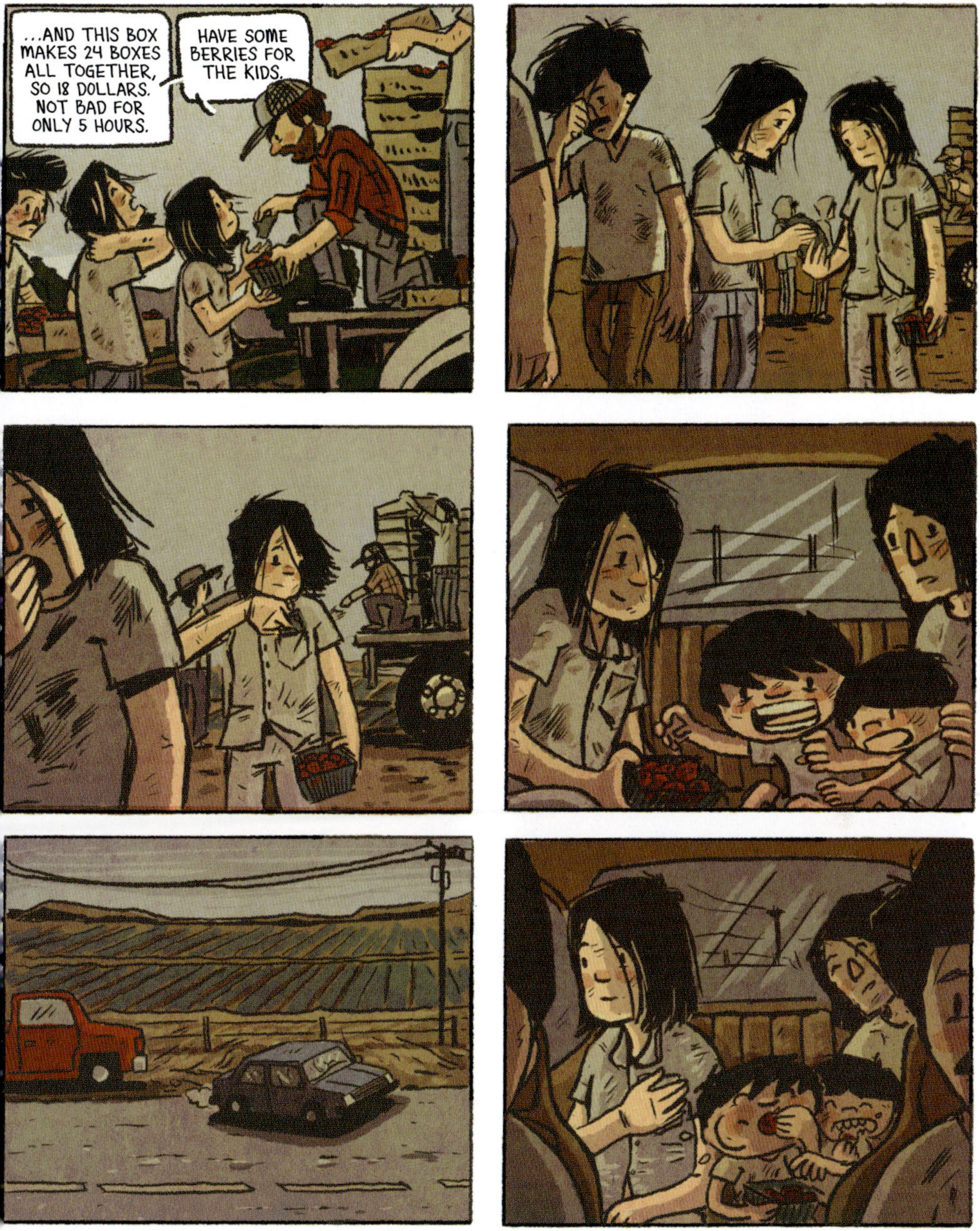
...AND THIS BOX MAKES 24 BOXES ALL TOGETHER, SO 18 DOLLARS. NOT BAD FOR ONLY 5 HOURS.
HAVE SOME BERRIES FOR THE KIDS.

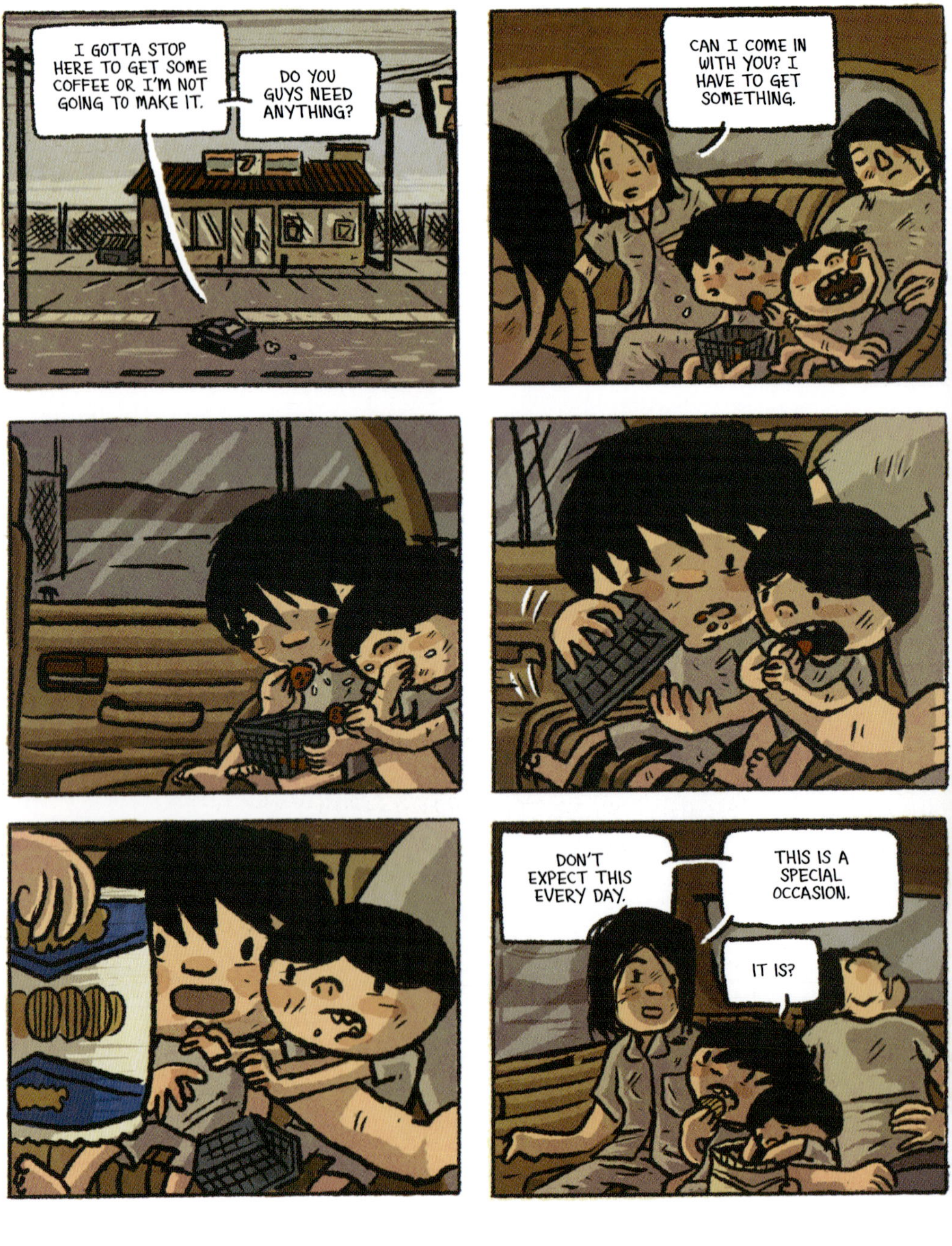
I GOTTA STOP HERE TO GET SOME COFFEE OR I'M NOT GOING TO MAKE IT.
DO YOU GUYS NEED ANYTHING?
CAN I COME IN WITH YOU? I HAVE TO GET SOMETHING.
DON'T EXPECT THIS EVERY DAY.
THIS IS A SPECIAL OCCASION.
IT IS?

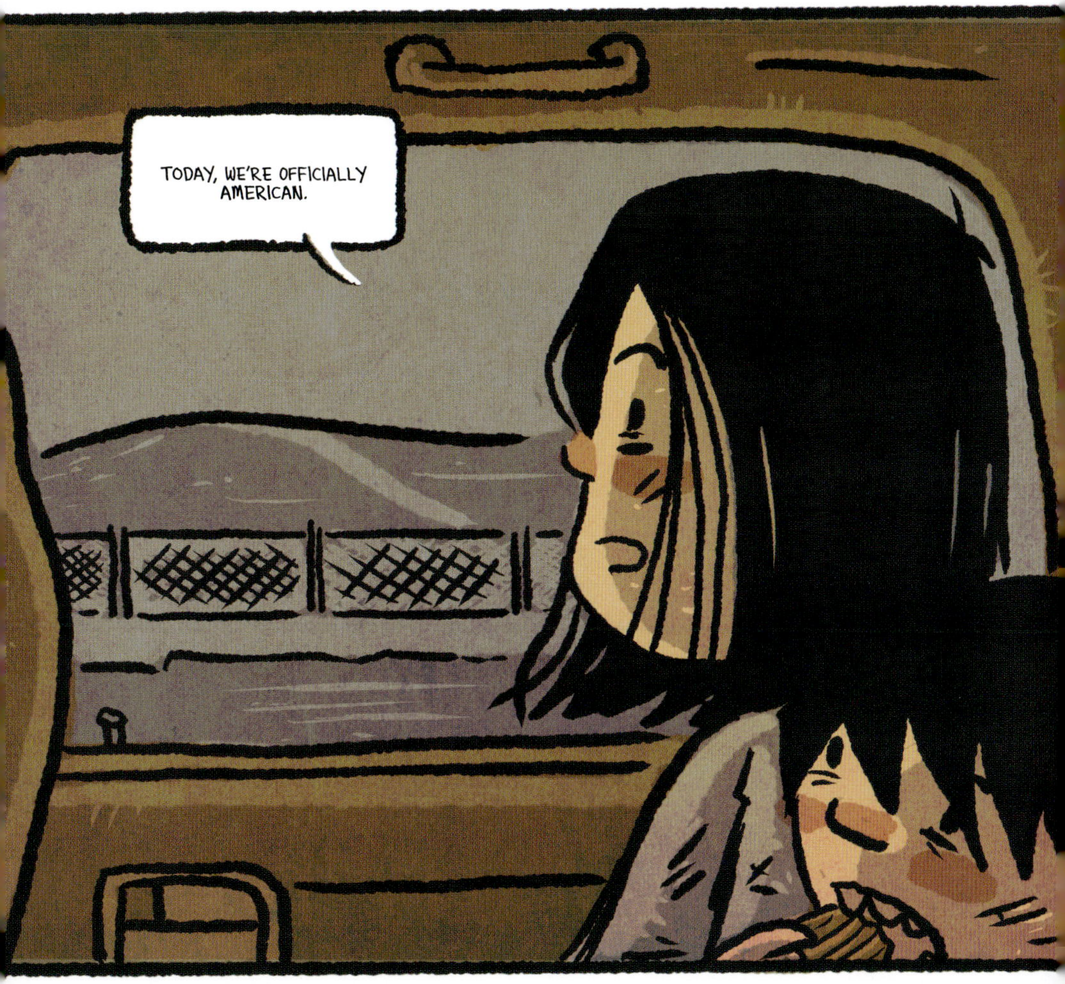
TODAY, WE'RE OFFICIALLY AMERICAN.

CHAPTER 5: SALISBURY STEAK

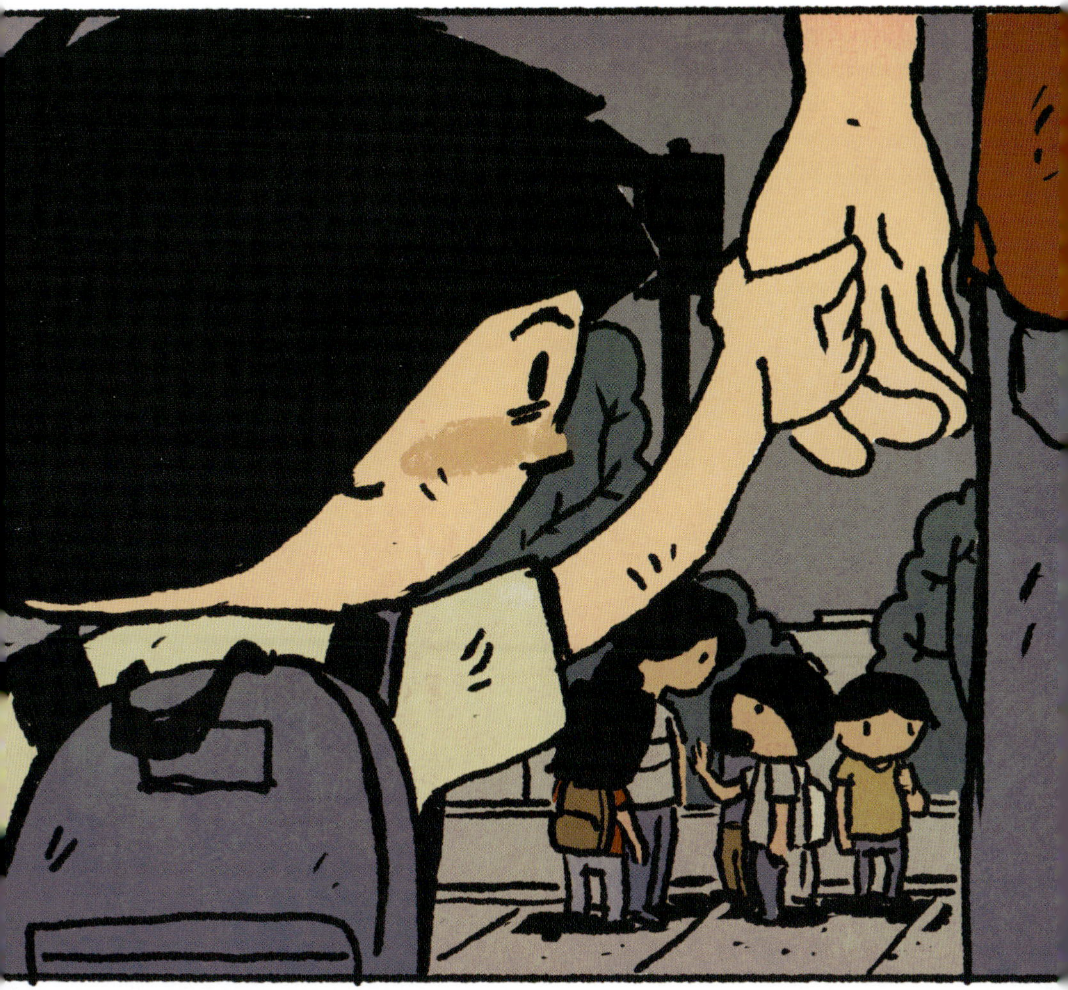

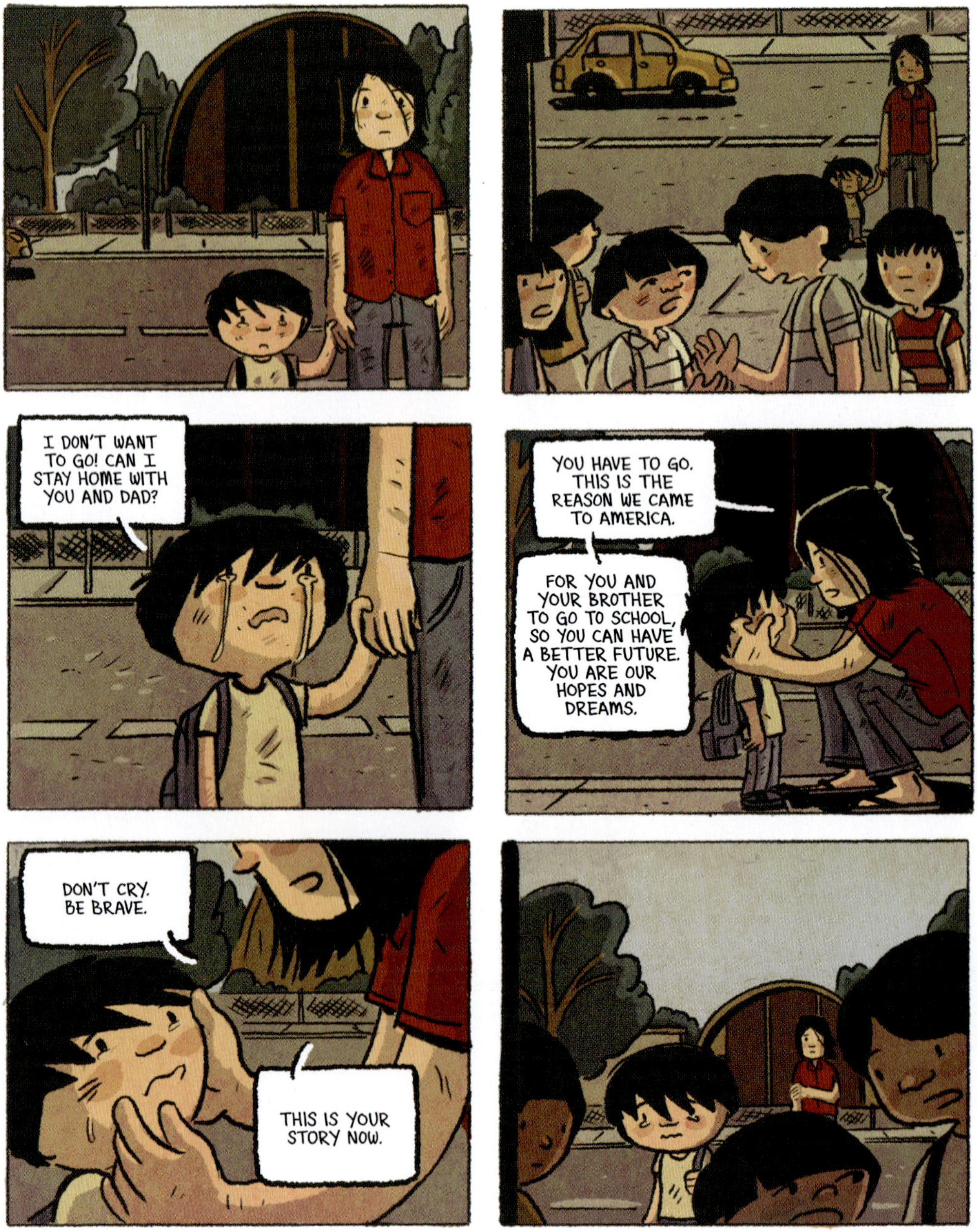
I DON'T WANT TO GO! CAN I STAY HOME WITH YOU AND DAD?
YOU HAVE TO GO. THIS IS THE REASON WE CAME TO AMERICA.
FOR YOU AND YOUR BROTHER TO GO TO SCHOOL, SO YOU CAN HAVE A BETTER FUTURE. YOU ARE OUR HOPES AND DREAMS.
DON'T CRY. BE BRAVE.
THIS IS YOUR STORY NOW.

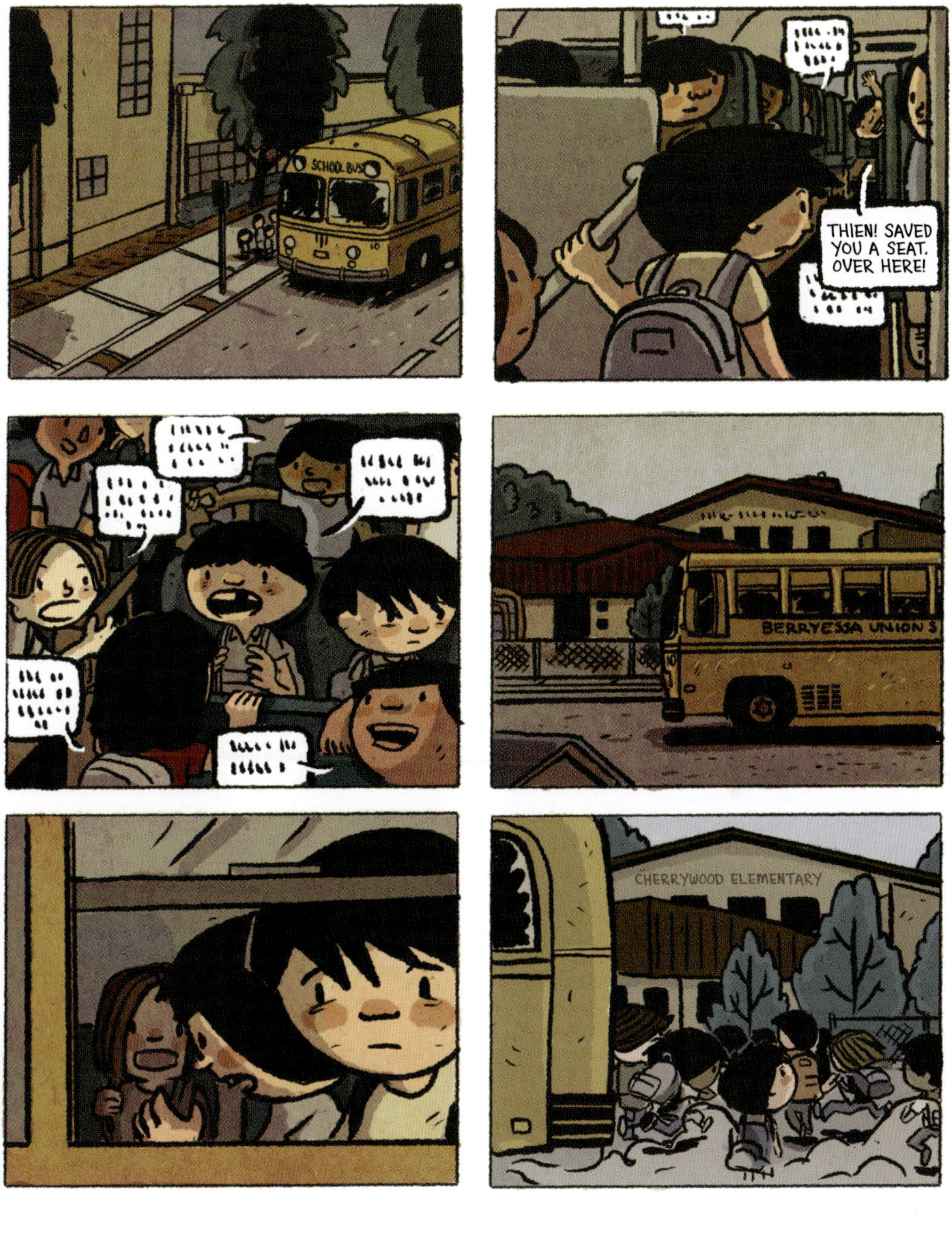
SCHOOL BUS
THIEN! SAVED YOU A SEAT. OVER HERE!
BERRYESSA UNION S
CHERRYWOOD ELEMENTARY

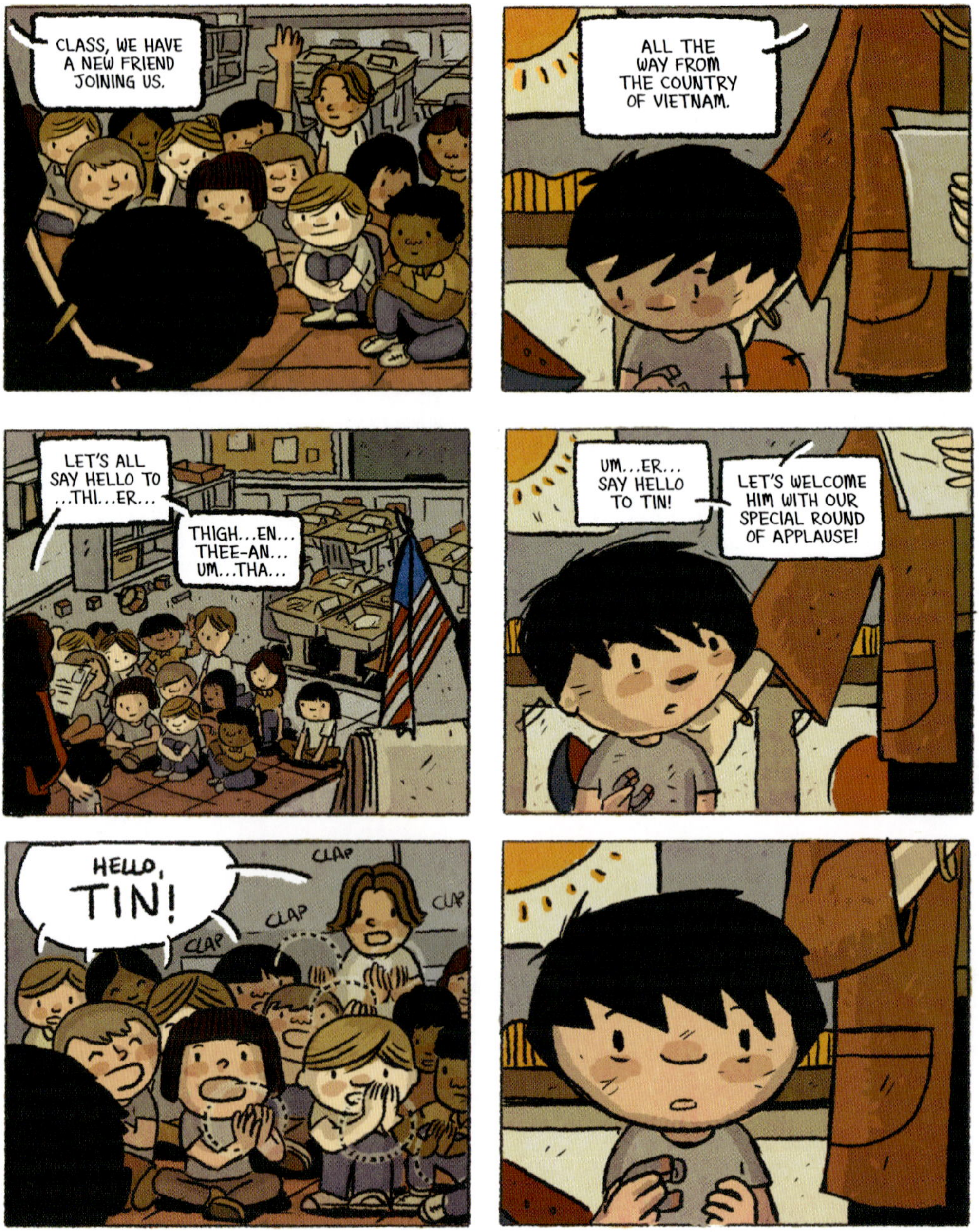
CLASS, WE HAVE A NEW FRIEND JOINING US.
ALL THE WAY FROM THE COUNTRY OF VIETNAM.
LET'S ALL SAY HELLO TO ...THI...ER...
THIGH...EN... THEE-AN... UM...THA...
UM...ER... SAY HELLO TO TIN!
LET'S WELCOME HIM WITH OUR SPECIAL ROUND OF APPLAUSE!
HELLO, TIN!
CLAP
CLAP
CLAP
CLAP

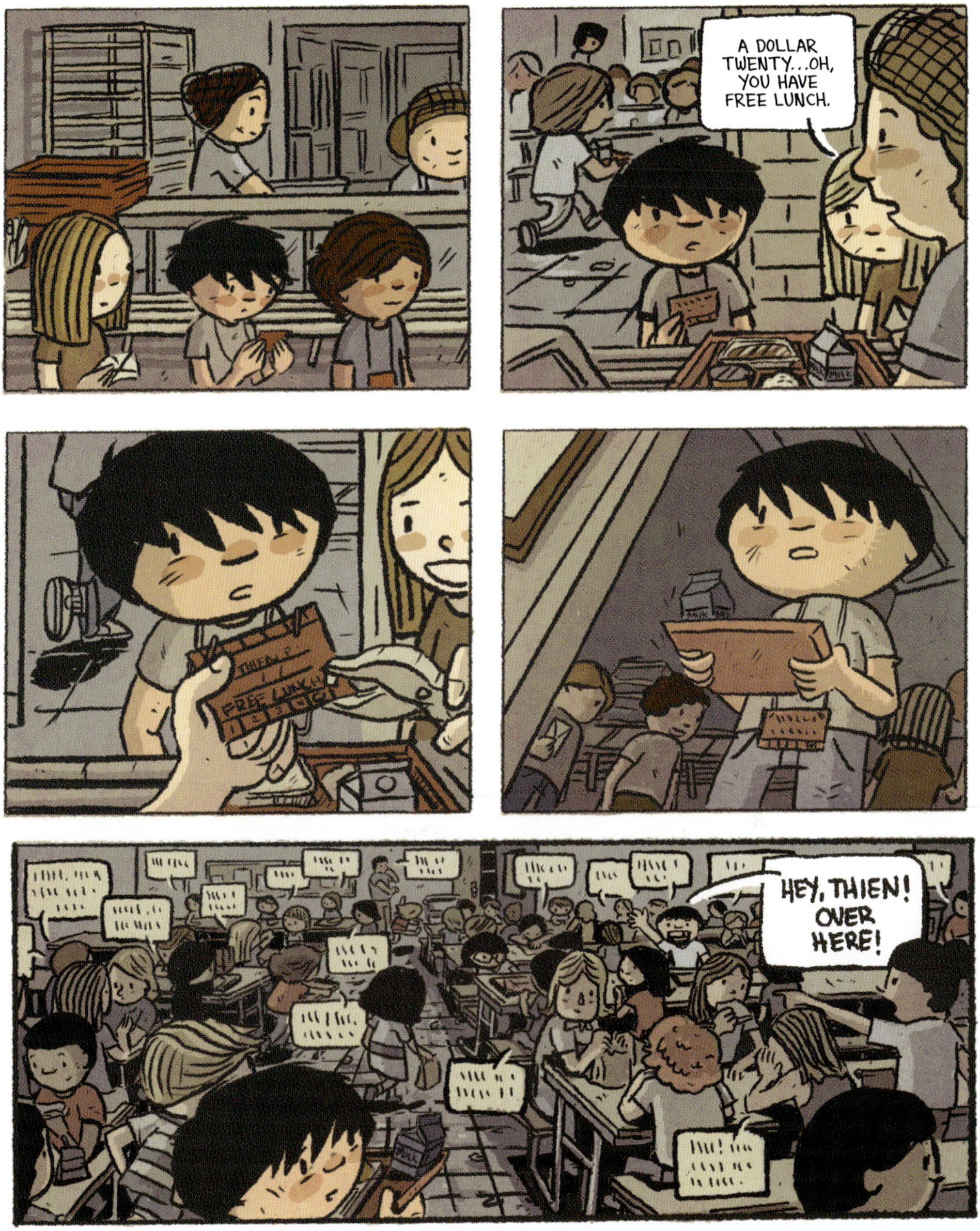
A DOLLAR TWENTY...OH, YOU HAVE FREE LUNCH.
HEY, THIEN! OVER HERE!

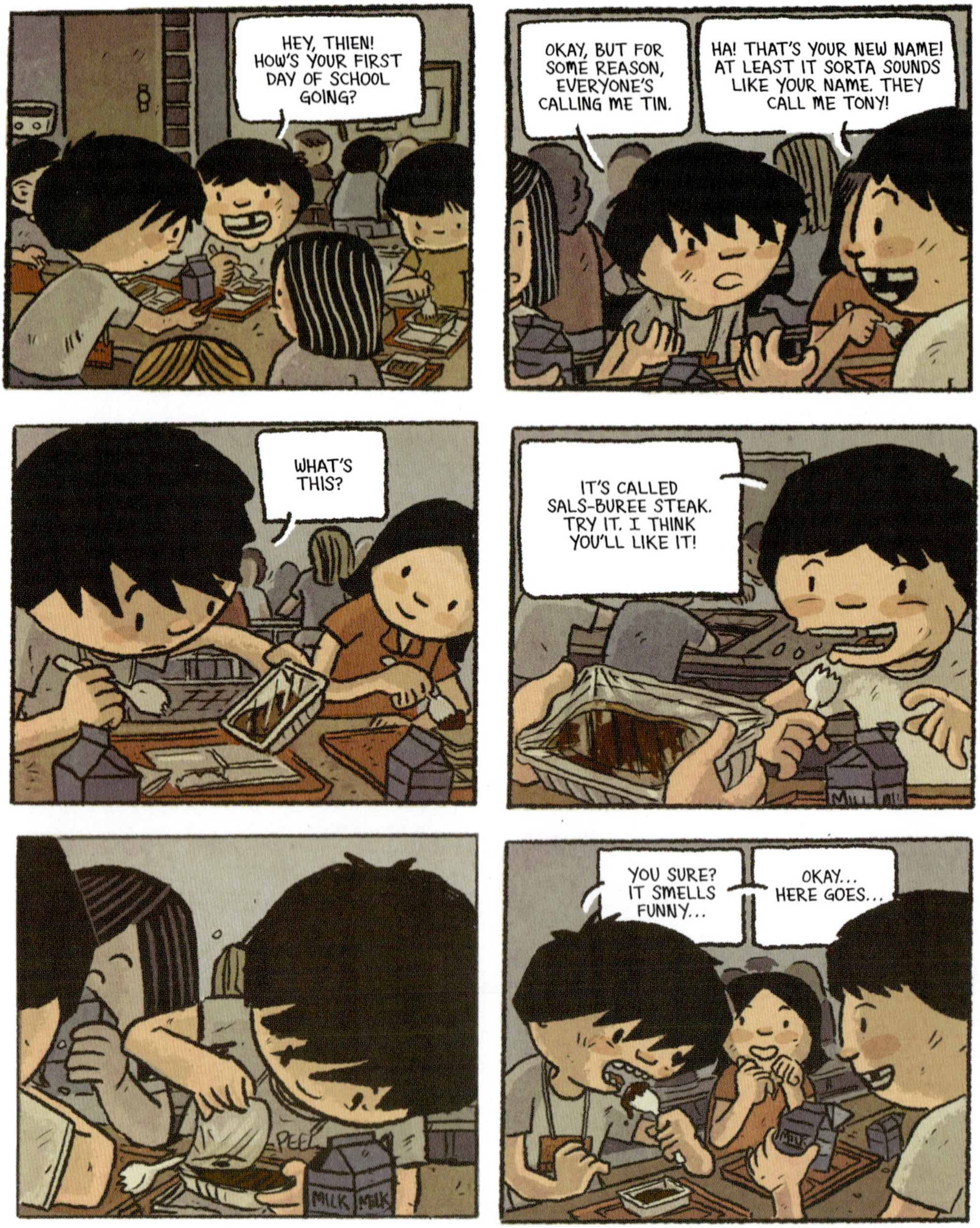
HEY, THIEN! HOW'S YOUR FIRST DAY OF SCHOOL GOING?
OKAY, BUT FOR SOME REASON, EVERYONE'S CALLING ME TIN.
HA! THAT'S YOUR NEW NAME! AT LEAST IT SORTA SOUNDS LIKE YOUR NAME. THEY CALL ME TONY!
WHAT'S THIS?
IT'S CALLED SALS-BUREE STEAK. TRY IT. I THINK YOU'LL LIKE IT!
PEEL
MILK MILK
YOU SURE? IT SMELLS FUNNY...
OKAY... HERE GOES...

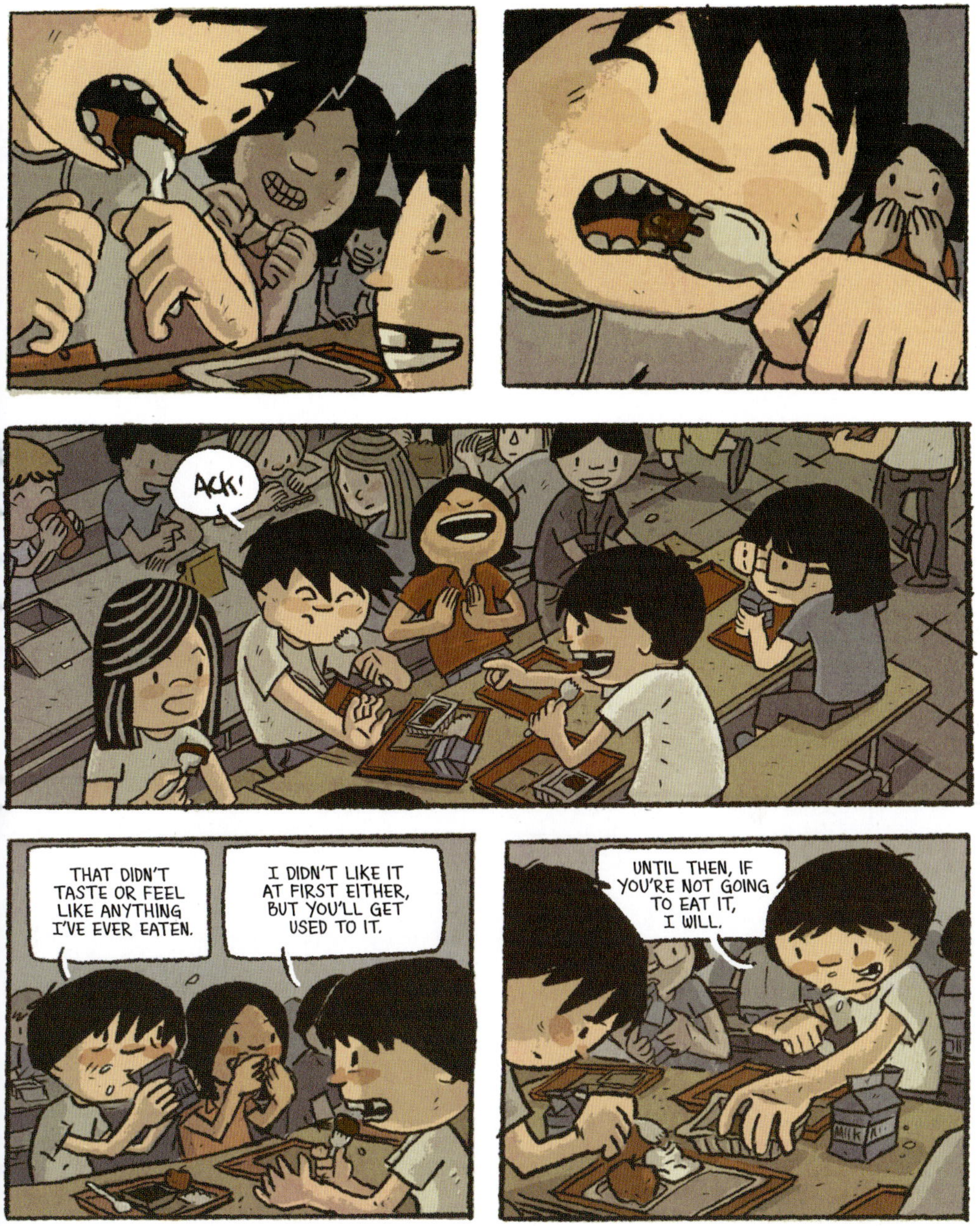
ACK!
THAT DIDN'T TASTE OR FEEL LIKE ANYTHING I'VE EVER EATEN.
I DIDN'T LIKE IT AT FIRST EITHER, BUT YOU'LL GET USED TO IT.
UNTIL THEN, IF YOU'RE NOT GOING TO EAT IT, I WILL.
MILK

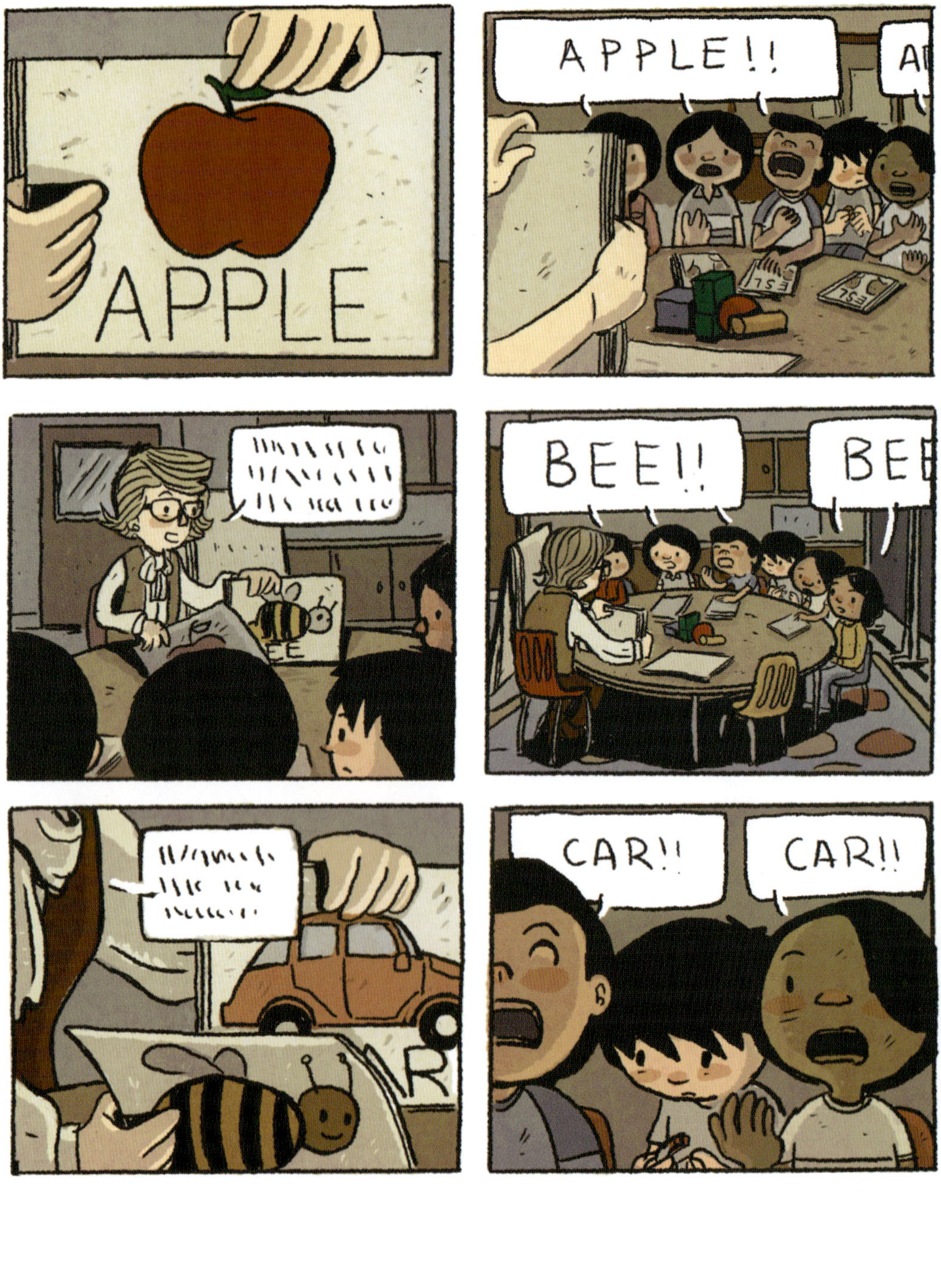
APPLE
APPLE!!
ESL
BEE!!
CAR!!
CAR!!

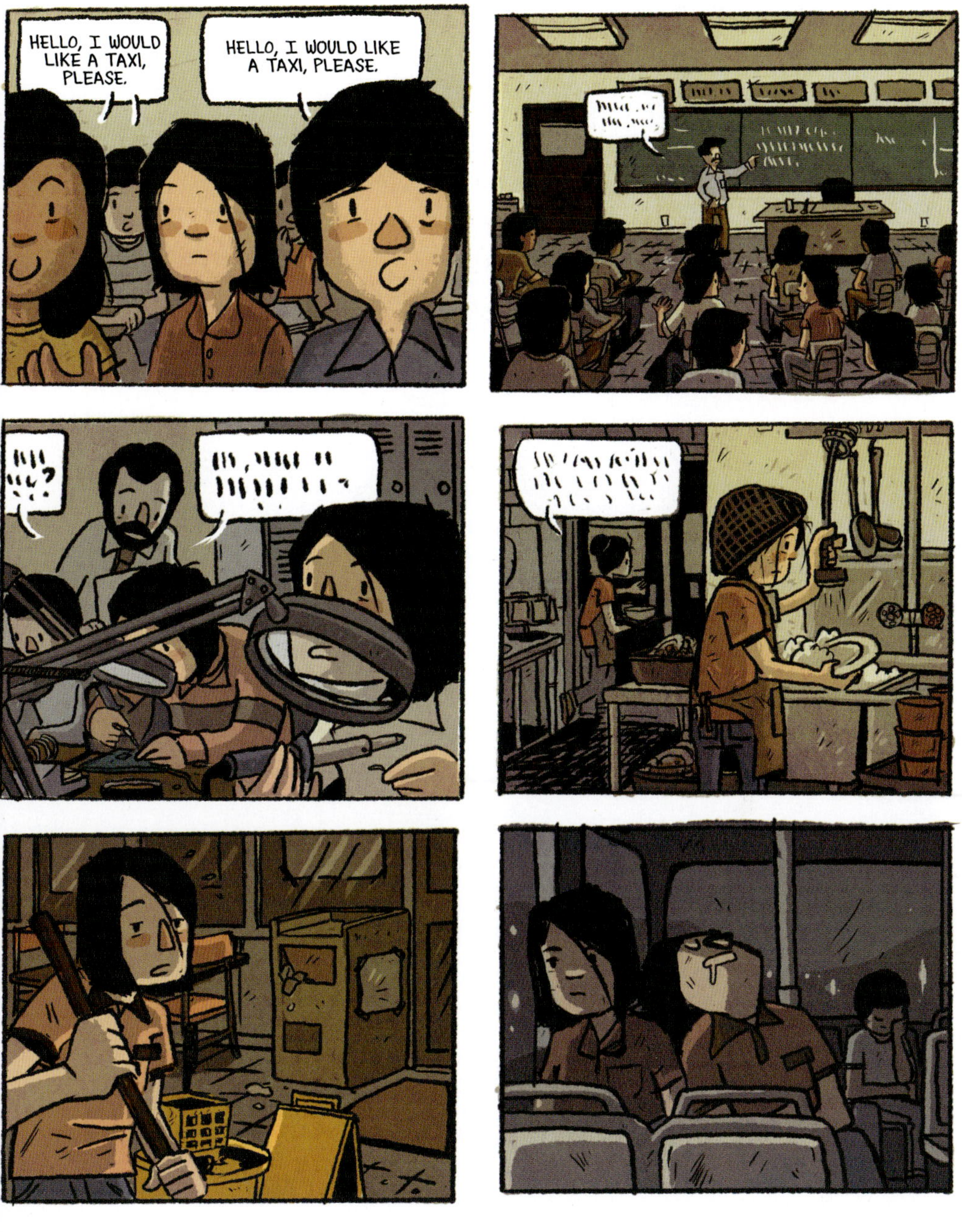
HELLO, I WOULD LIKE A TAXI, PLEASE.
HELLO, I WOULD LIKE A TAXI, PLEASE.

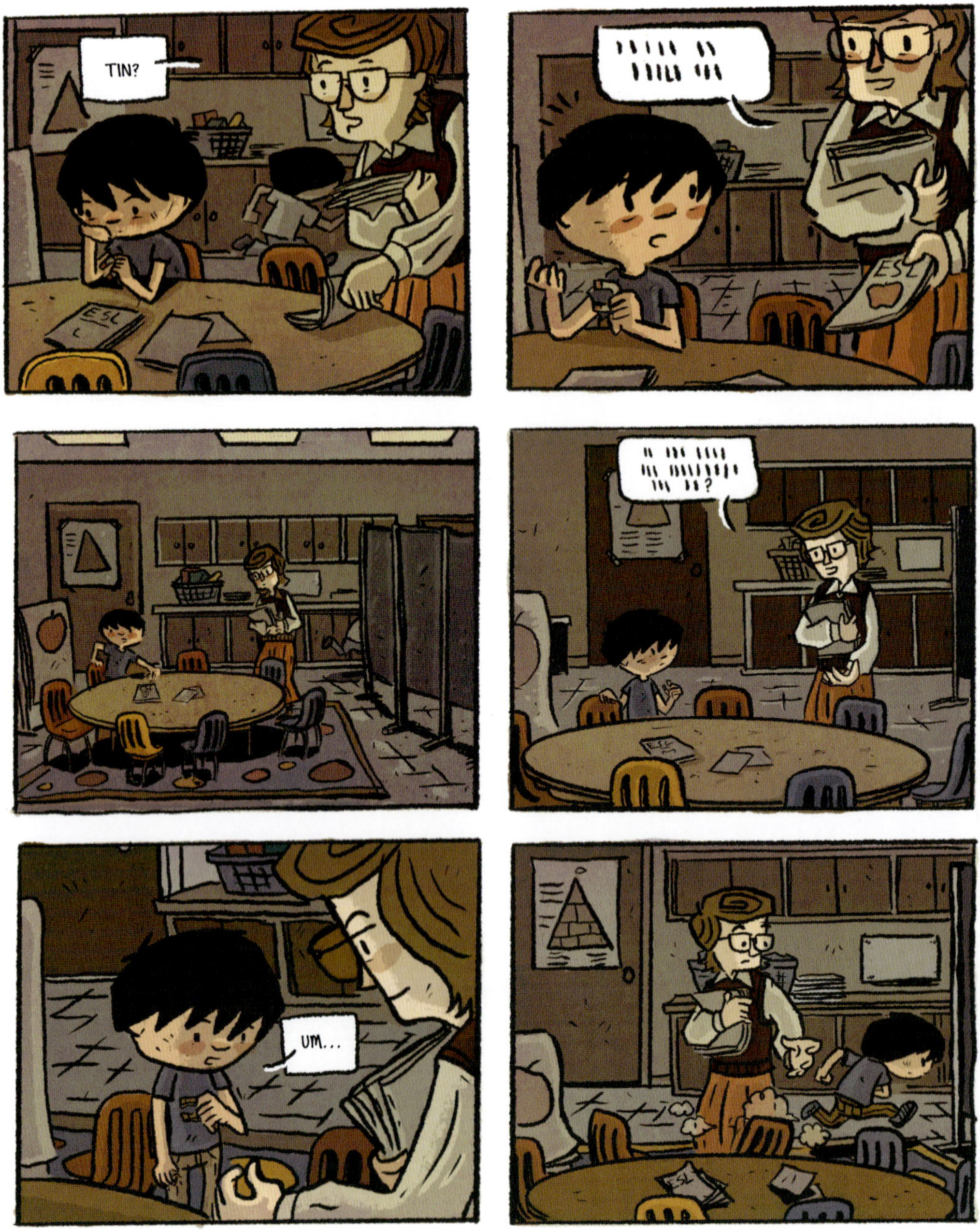
TIN?
UM...

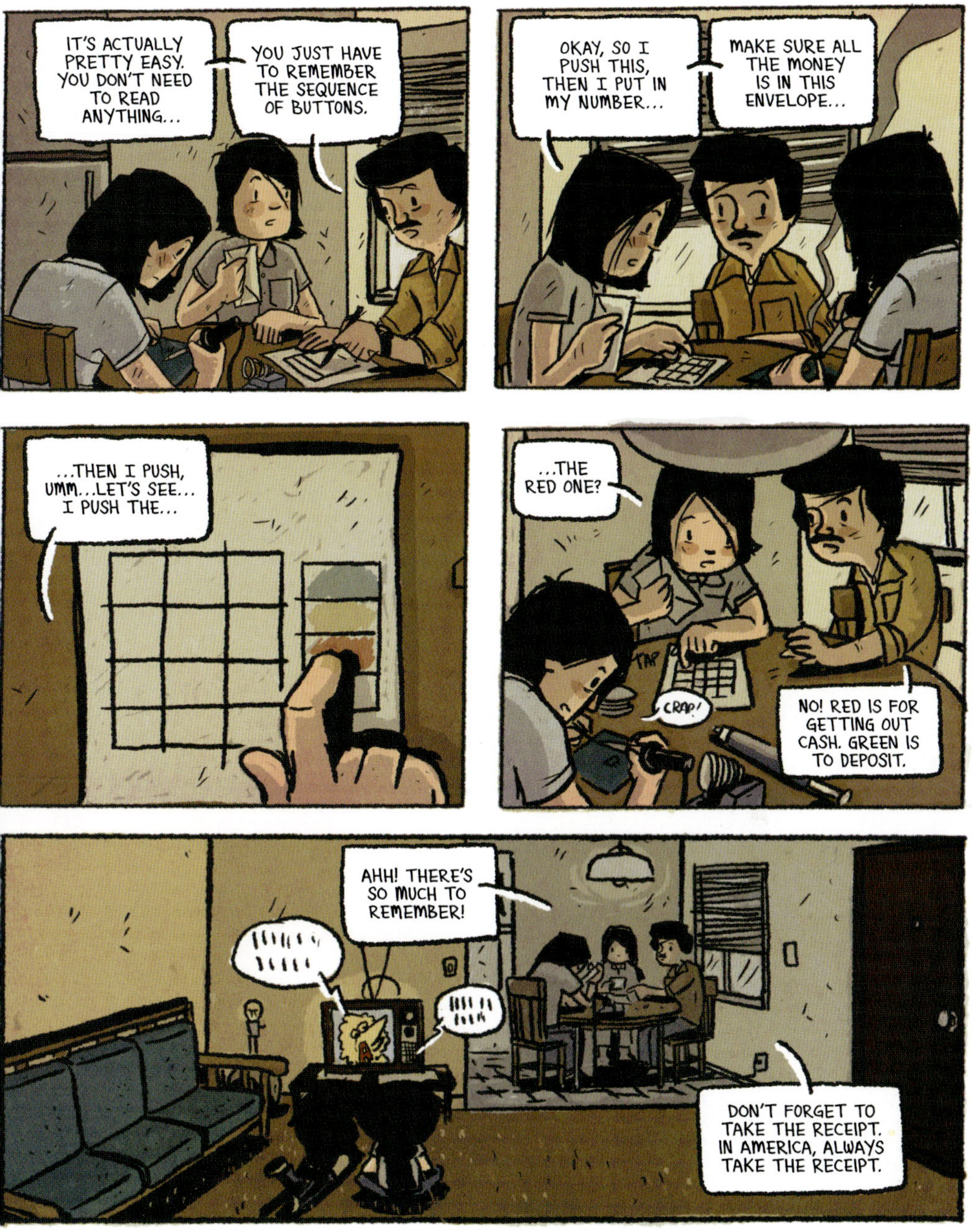

IT'S ACTUALLY PRETTY EASY. YOU DON'T NEED TO READ ANYTHING...
YOU JUST HAVE TO REMEMBER THE SEQUENCE OF BUTTONS.
OKAY, SO I PUSH THIS, THEN I PUT IN MY NUMBER...
MAKE SURE ALL THE MONEY IS IN THIS ENVELOPE...
...THEN I PUSH, UMM...LET'S SEE... I PUSH THE...
...THE RED ONE?
TAP
CRAP!
NO! RED IS FOR GETTING OUT CASH. GREEN IS TO DEPOSIT.
AHH! THERE'S SO MUCH TO REMEMBER!
DON'T FORGET TO TAKE THE RECEIPT. IN AMERICA, ALWAYS TAKE THE RECEIPT.

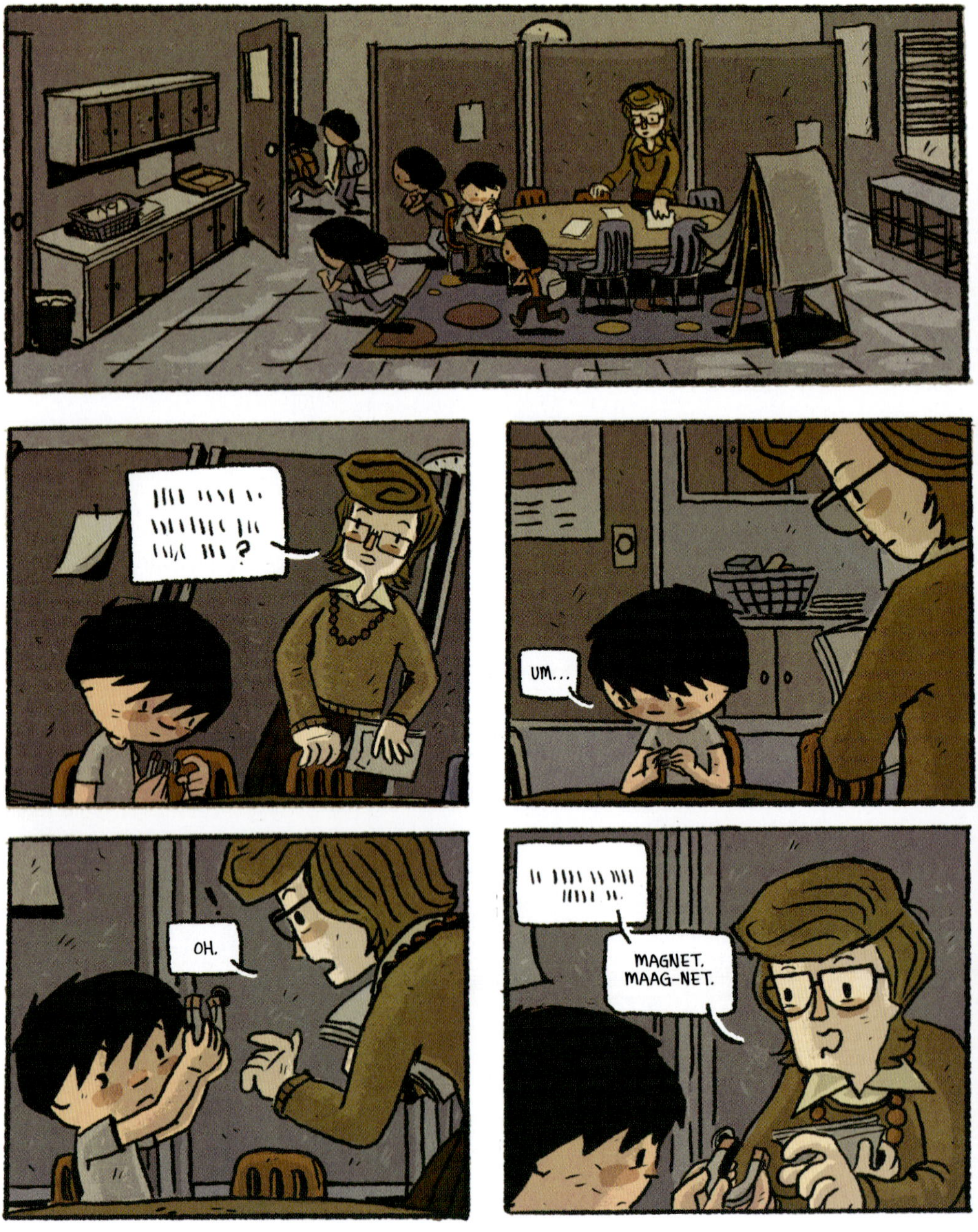
UM...
OH.
MAGNET.
MAAG-NET.

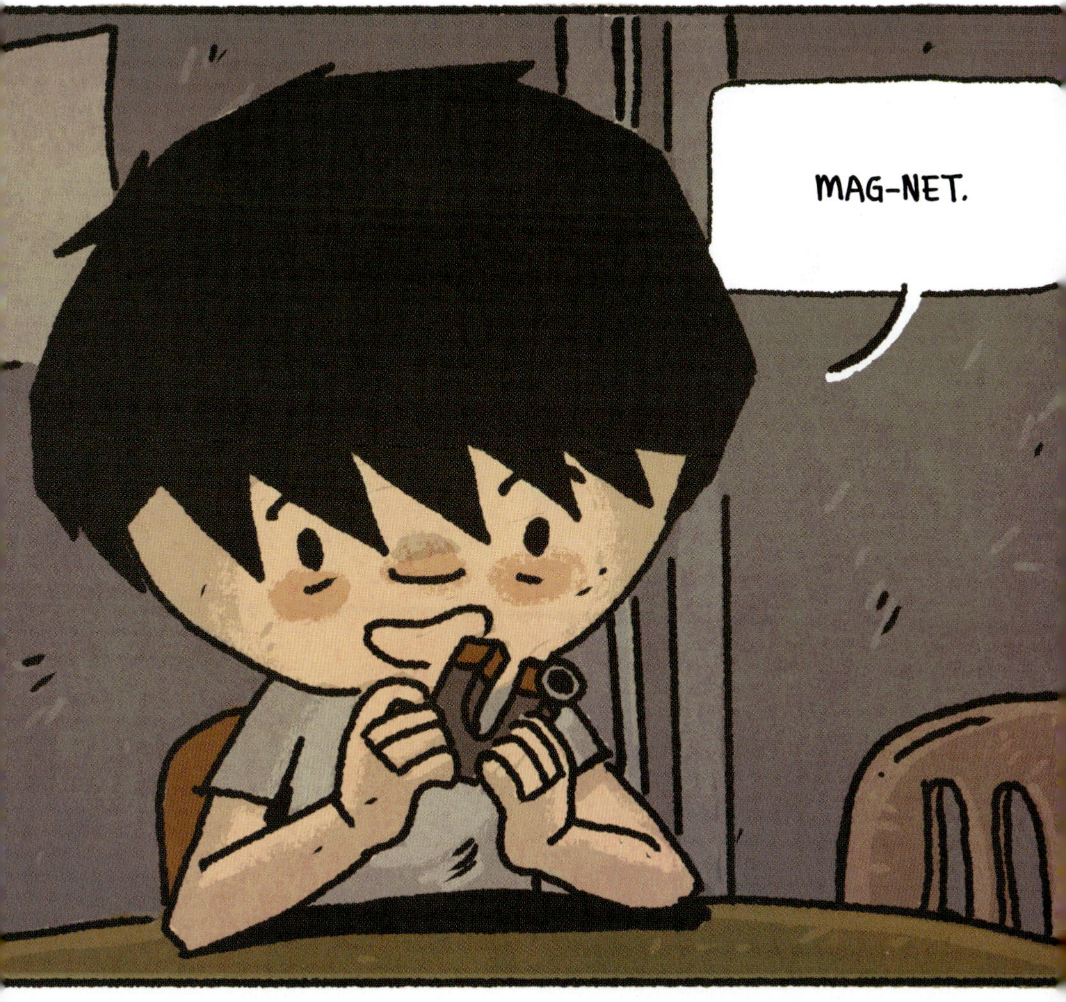
MAG-NET.

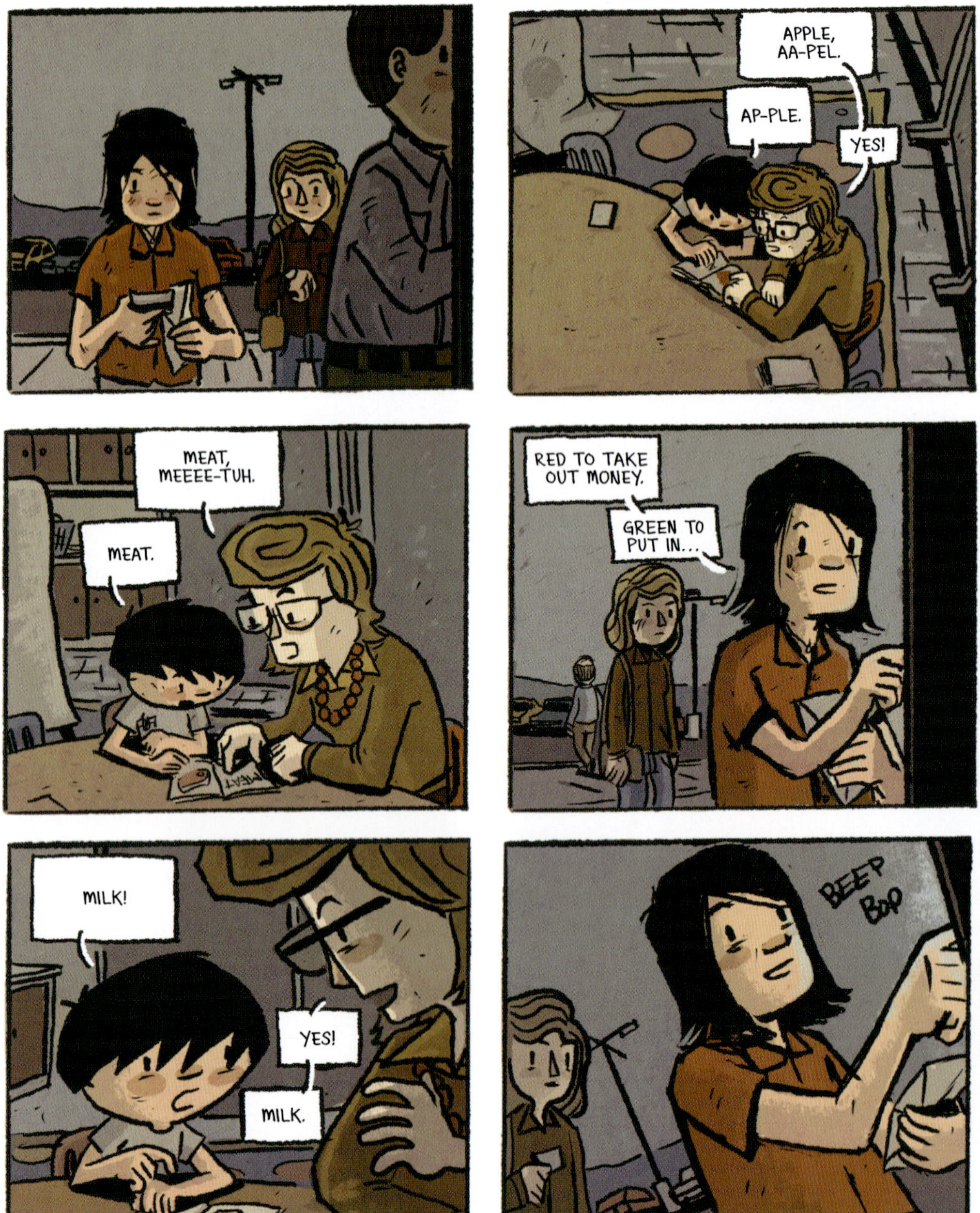
APPLE, AA-PEL.
AP-PLE.
YES!
MEAT, MEEEE-TUH.
MEAT.
RED TO TAKE OUT MONEY.
GREEN TO PUT IN...
MILK!
YES!
MILK.
BEEP BOP

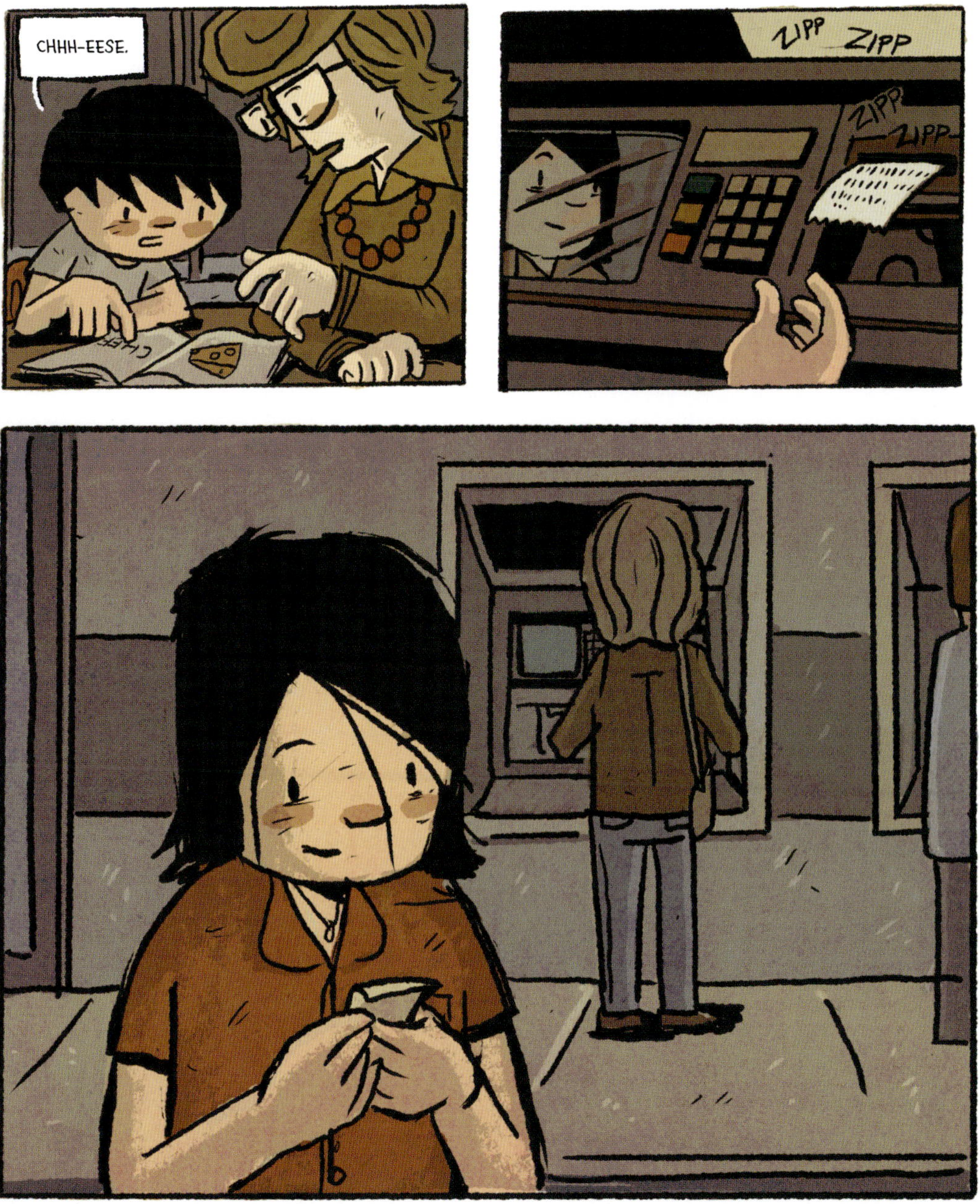
CHHH-EESE.
ZIPP ZIPP
ZIPP
ZIPP

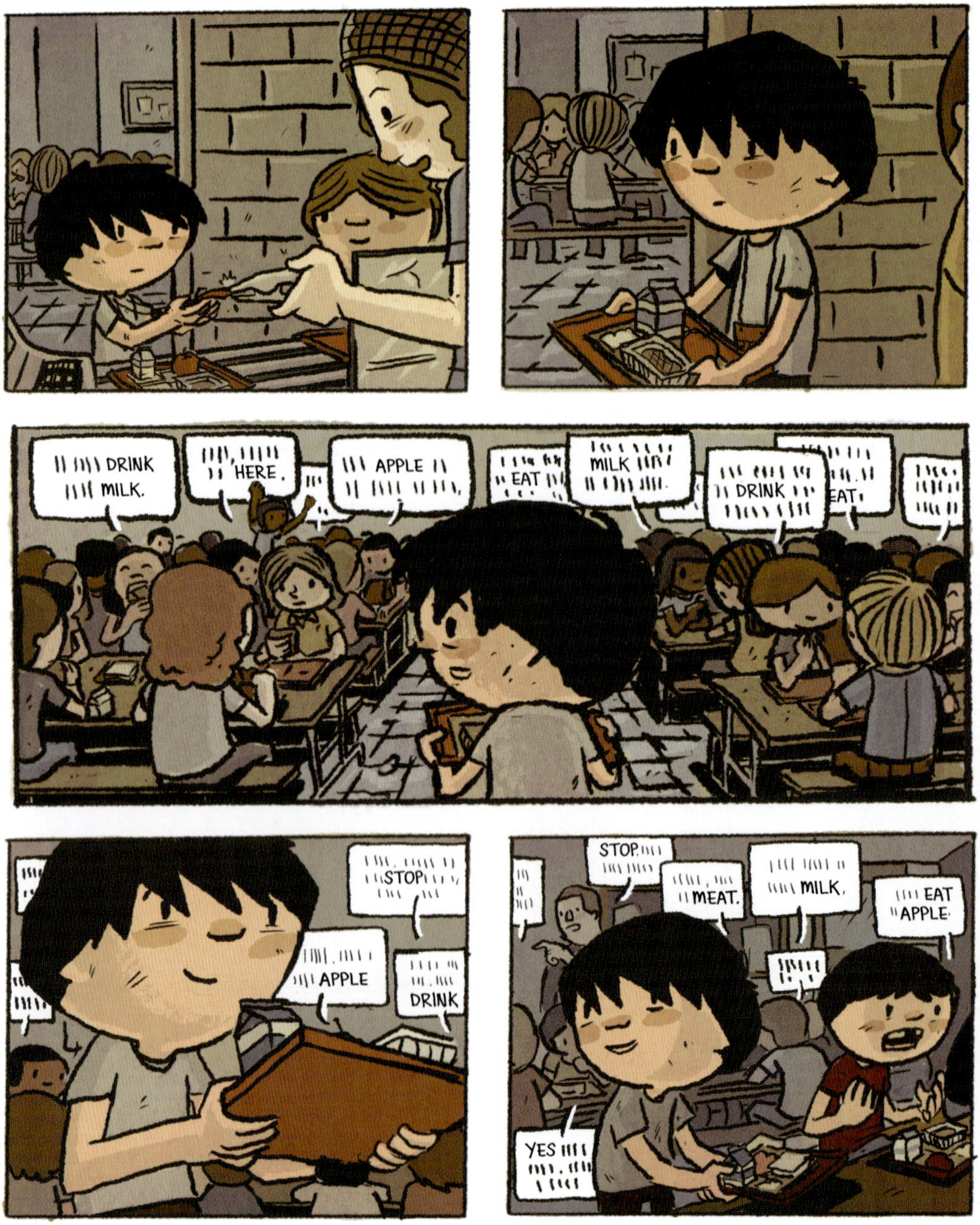
DRINK
MILK.
HERE.
APPLE
EAT
MILK
DRINK
EAT
STOP
APPLE
DRINK
STOP.
MEAT.
MILK.
EAT
APPLE.
YES

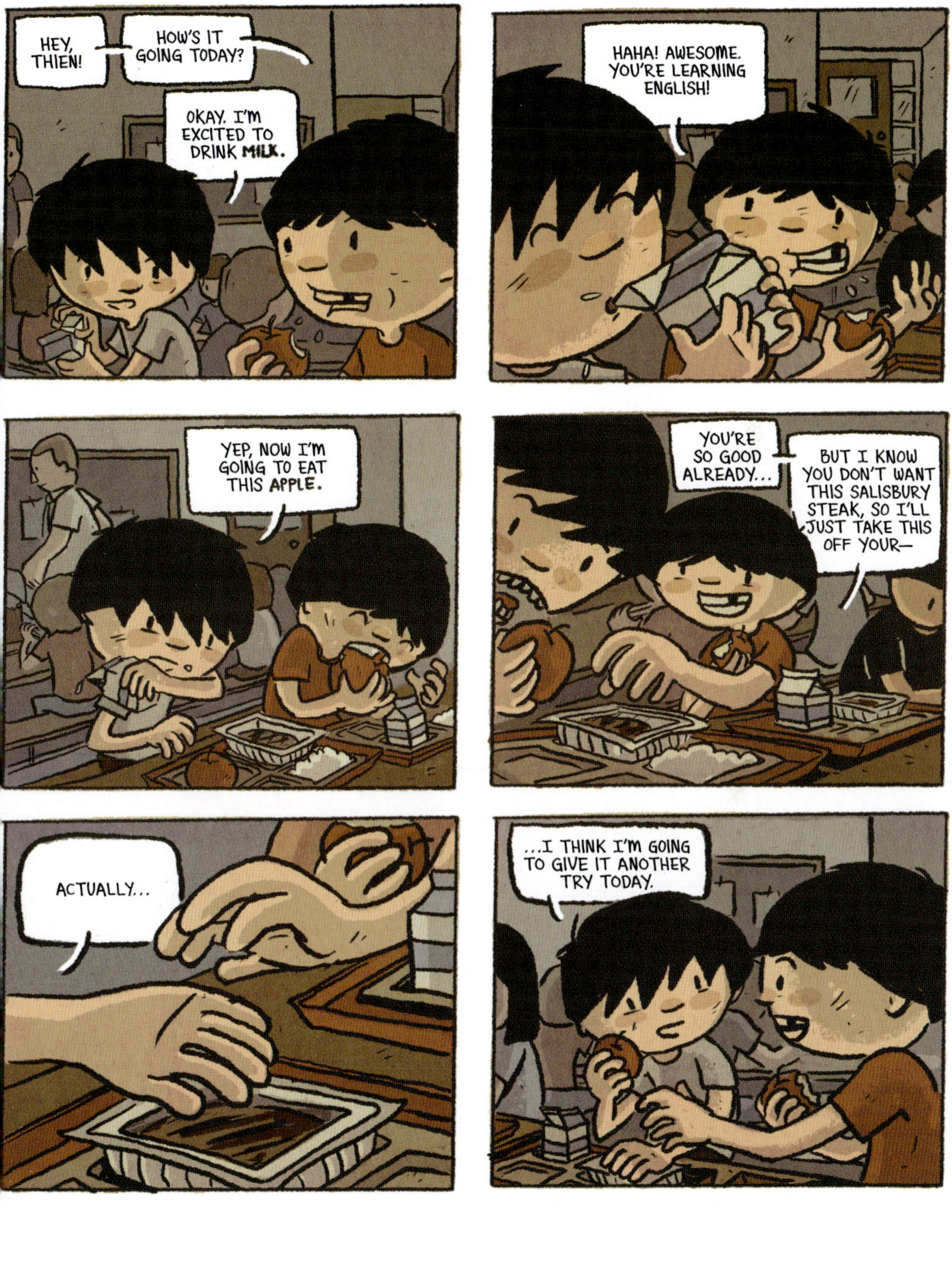

HEY, THIEN!
HOW'S IT GOING TODAY?
OKAY. I'M EXCITED TO DRINK MILK.
HAHA! AWESOME. YOU'RE LEARNING ENGLISH!
YEP, NOW I'M GOING TO EAT THIS APPLE.
YOU'RE SO GOOD ALREADY...
BUT I KNOW YOU DON'T WANT THIS SALISBURY STEAK, SO I'LL JUST TAKE THIS OFF YOUR—
ACTUALLY...
...I THINK I'M GOING TO GIVE IT ANOTHER TRY TODAY.

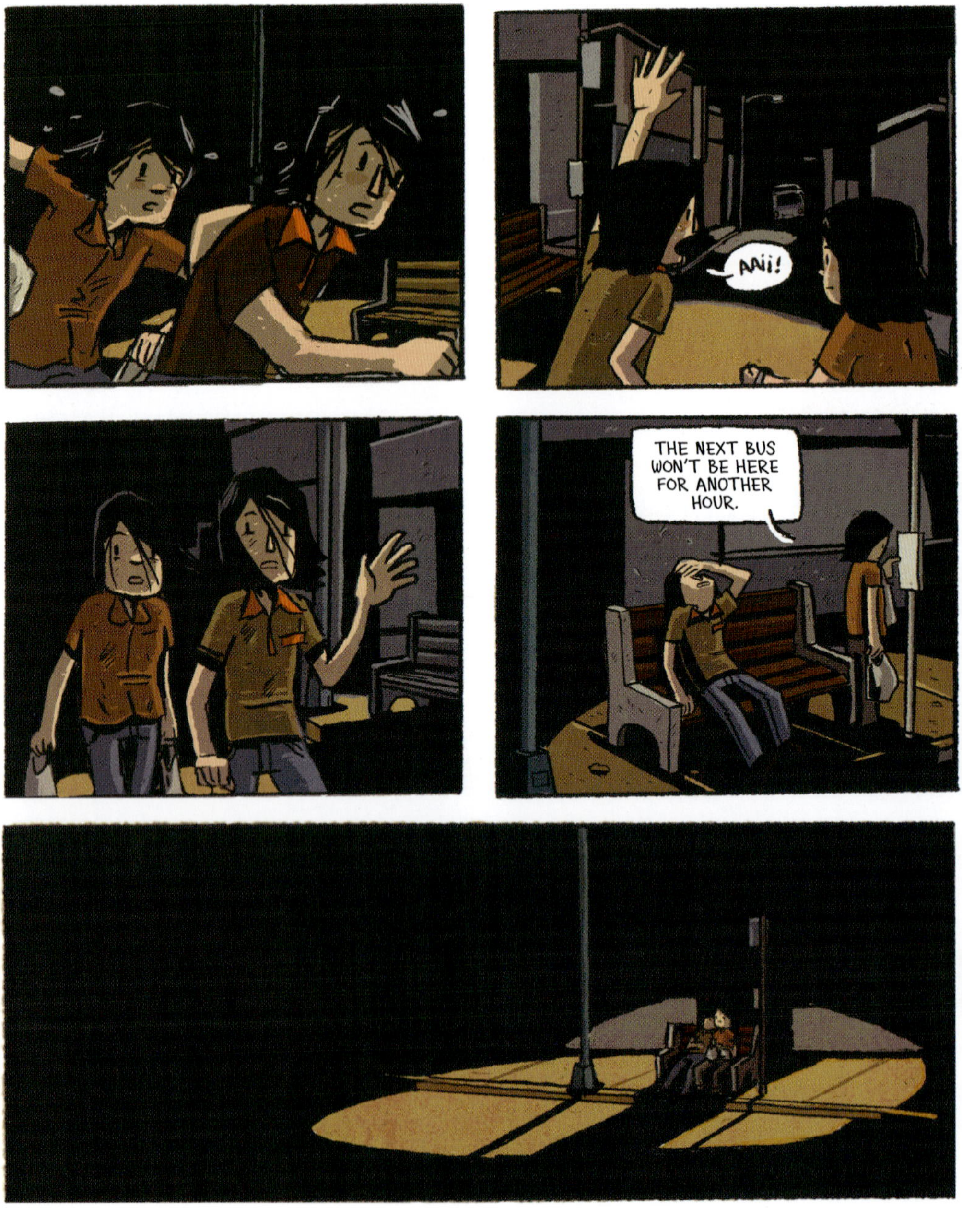
AAII!
THE NEXT BUS WON'T BE HERE FOR ANOTHER HOUR.

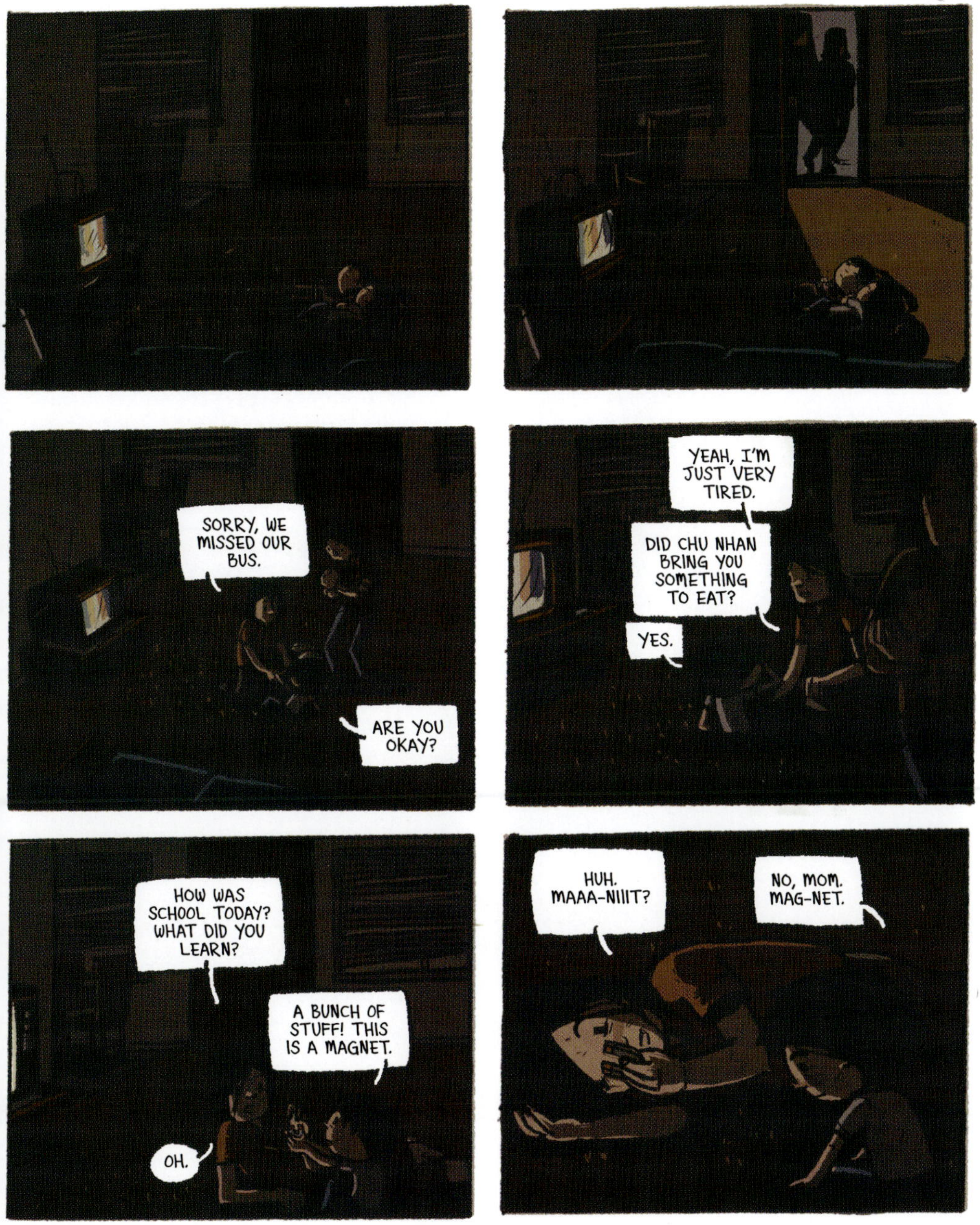
SORRY, WE MISSED OUR BUS.
ARE YOU OKAY?
YEAH, I'M JUST VERY TIRED.
DID CHU NHAN BRING YOU SOMETHING TO EAT?
YES.
HOW WAS SCHOOL TODAY? WHAT DID YOU LEARN?
A BUNCH OF STUFF! THIS IS A MAGNET.
OH.
HUH. MAAA-NIIIT?
NO, MOM. MAG-NET.

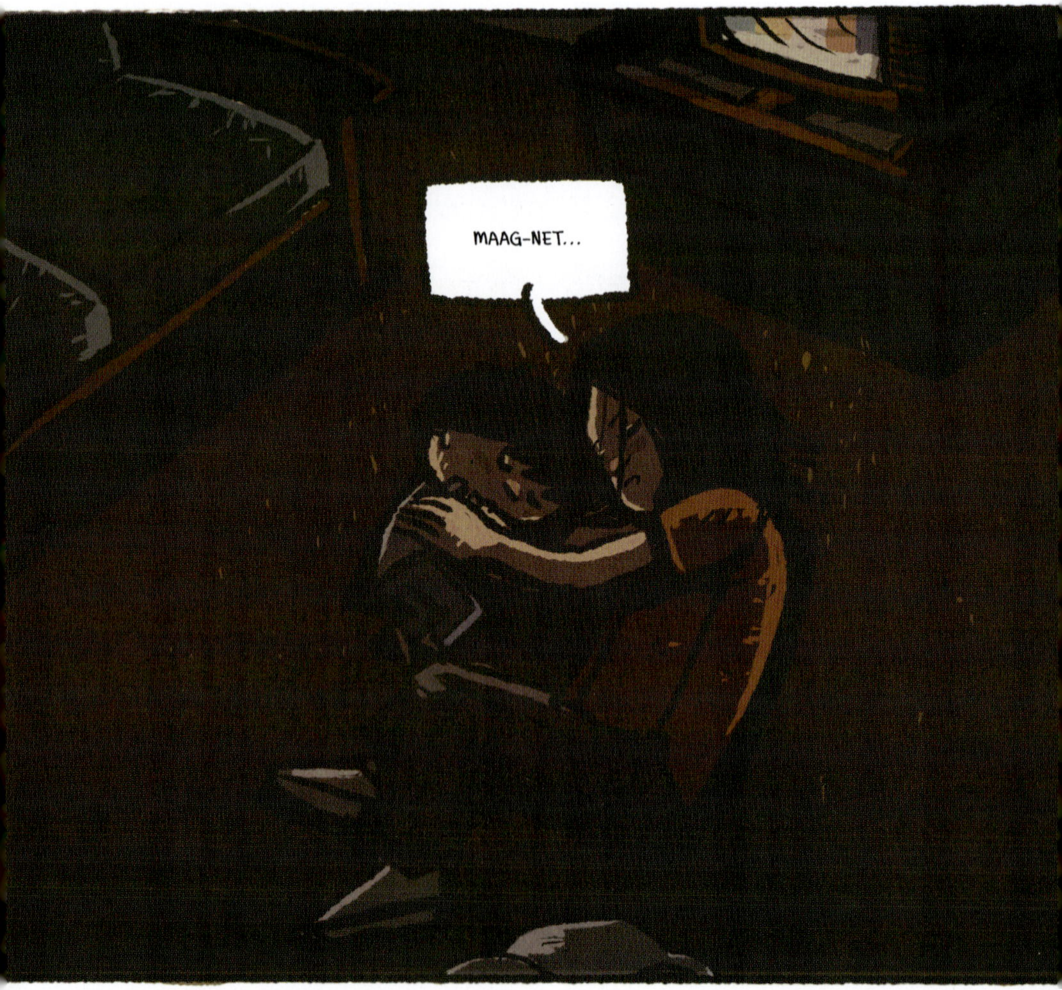
MAAG-NET...

CHAPTER 6: HAM AND CHEESE CROISSANT

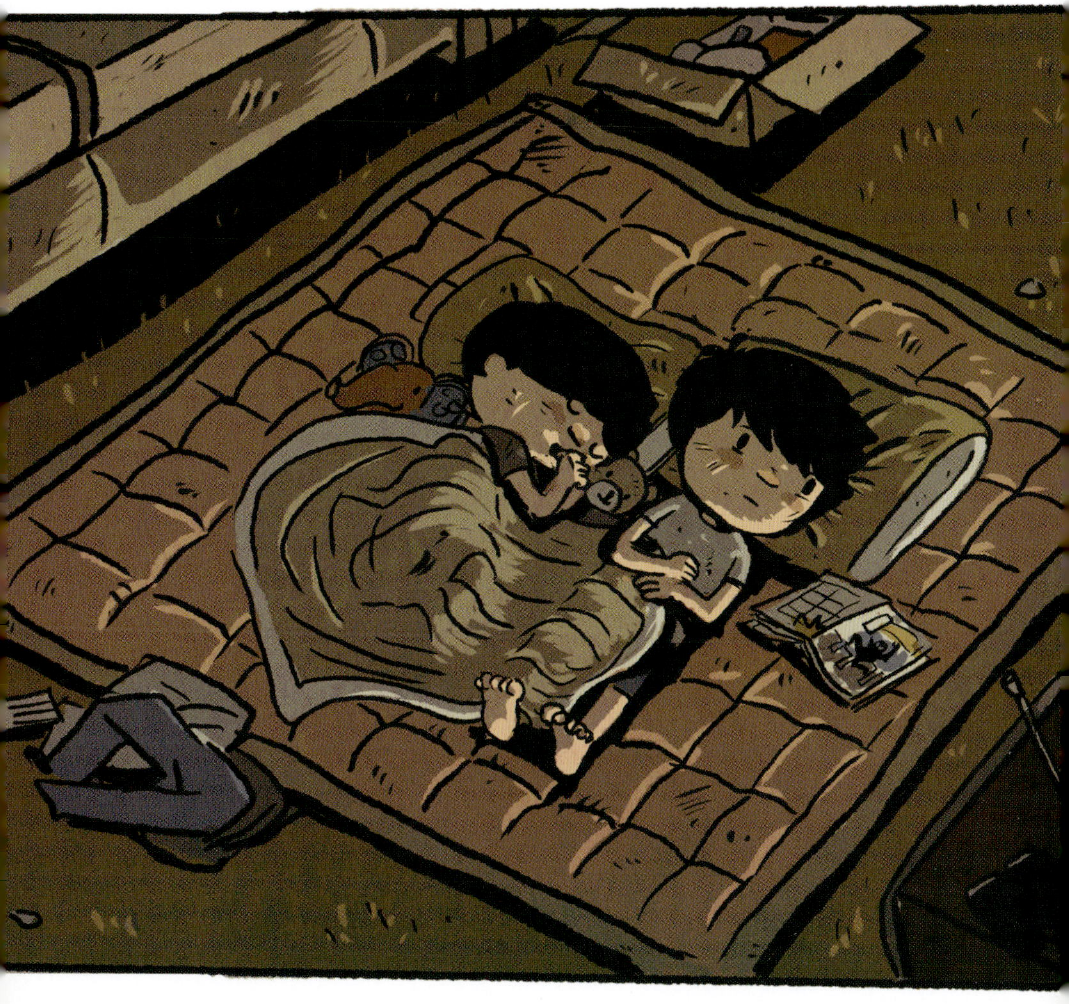

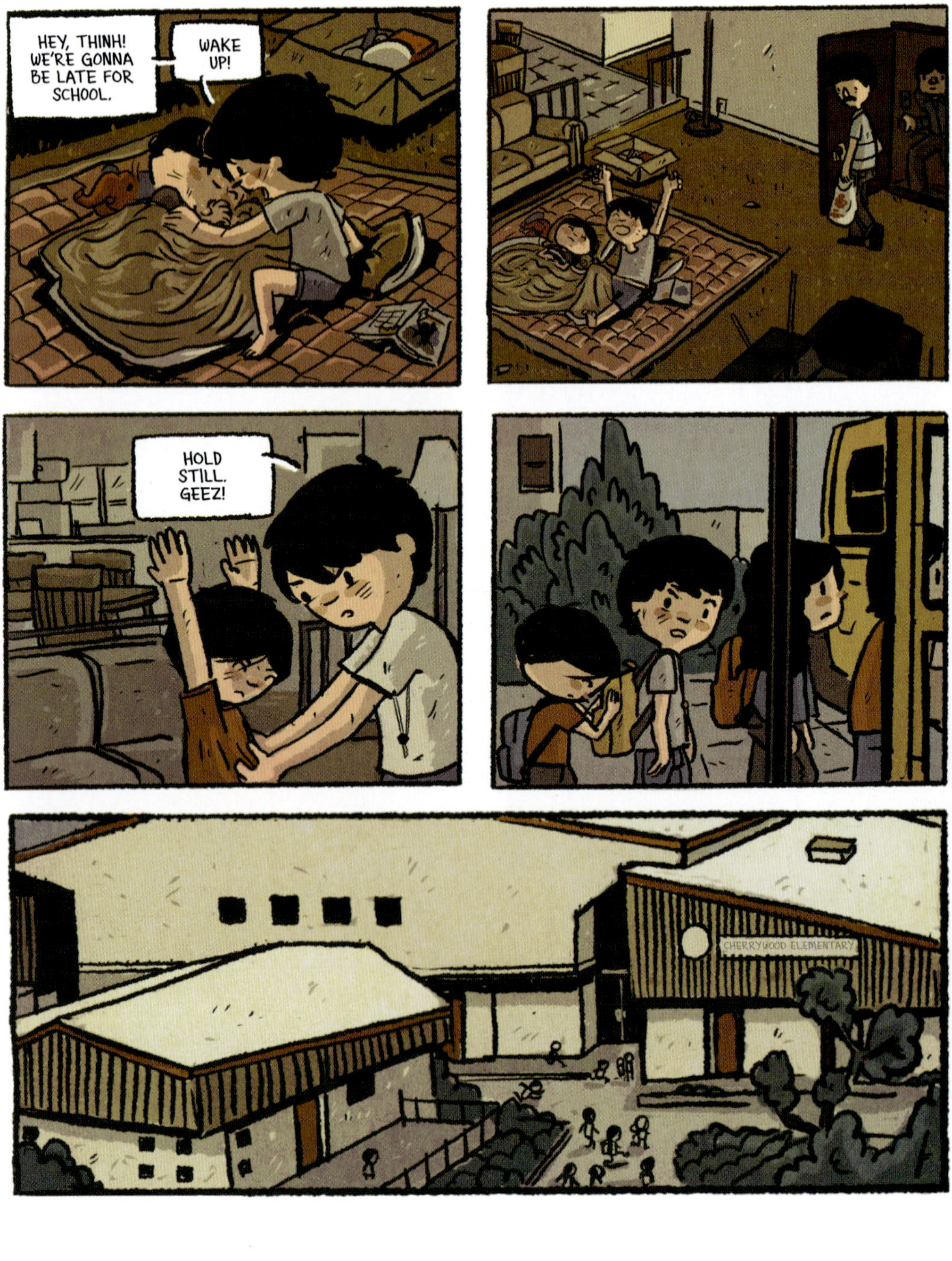
HEY, THINH! WE'RE GONNA BE LATE FOR SCHOOL.
WAKE UP!
HOLD STILL. GEEZ!
CHERRYWOOD ELEMENTARY

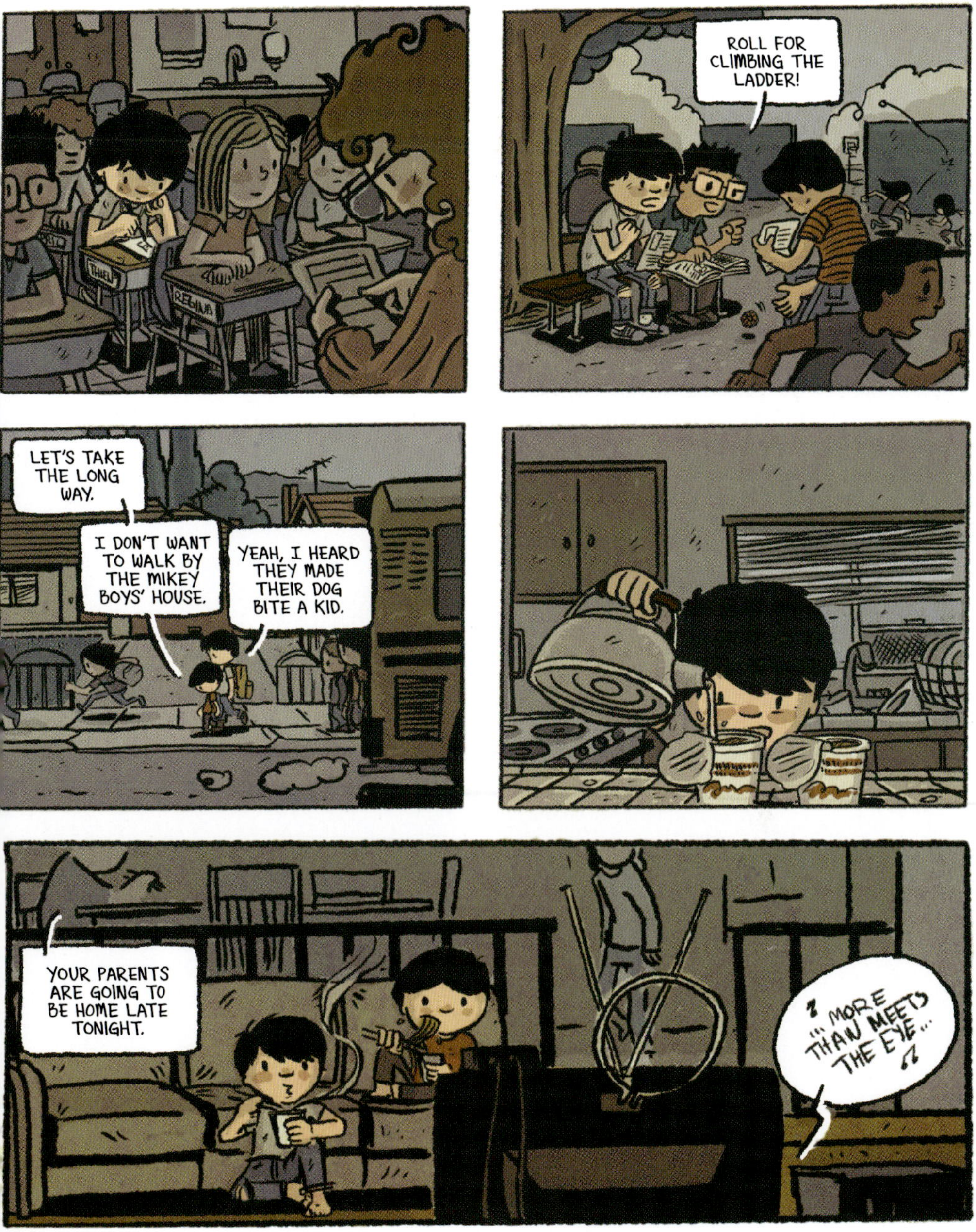

ROLL FOR CLIMBING THE LADDER!
LET'S TAKE THE LONG WAY.
I DON'T WANT TO WALK BY THE MIKEY BOYS' HOUSE.
YEAH, I HEARD THEY MADE THEIR DOG BITE A KID.
YOUR PARENTS ARE GOING TO BE HOME LATE TONIGHT.
... MORE THAN MEETS THE EYE...

MOM?
DAD?

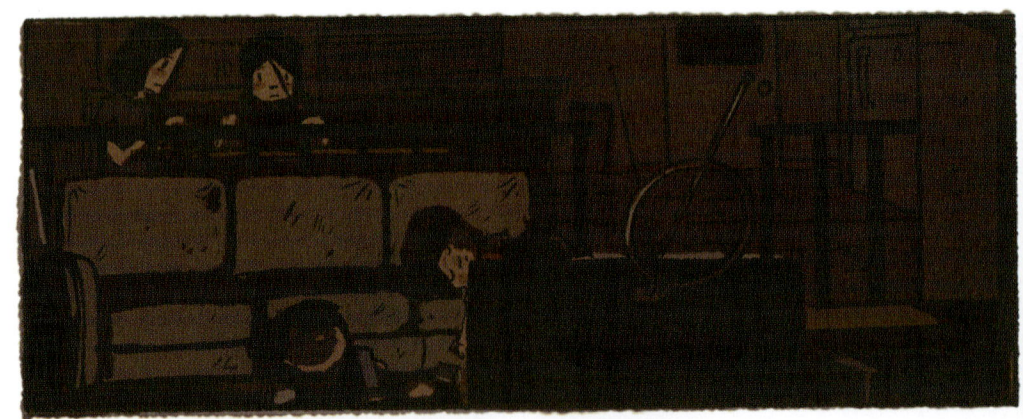

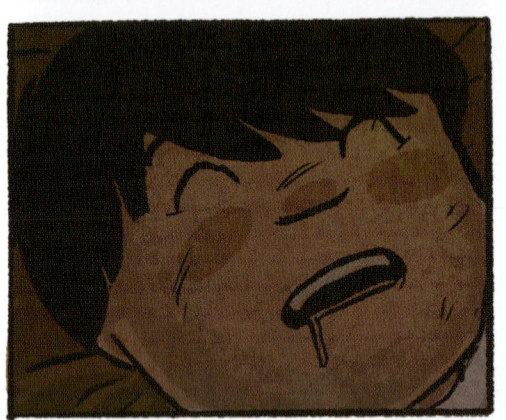

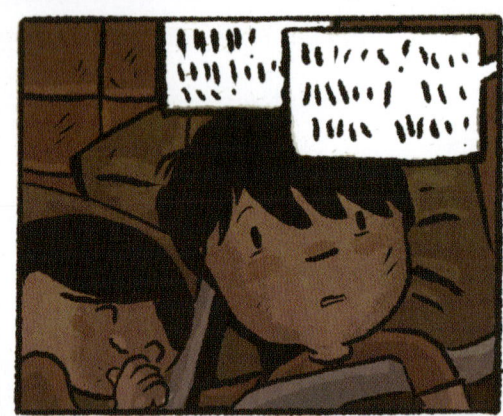

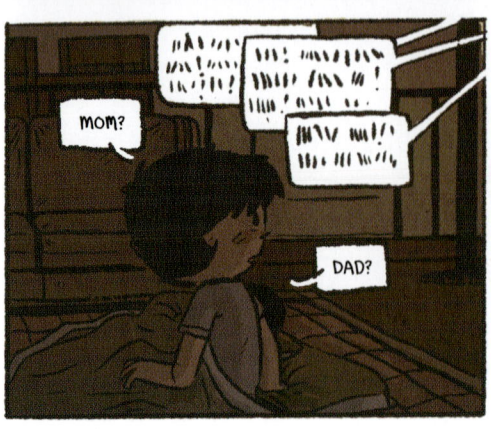

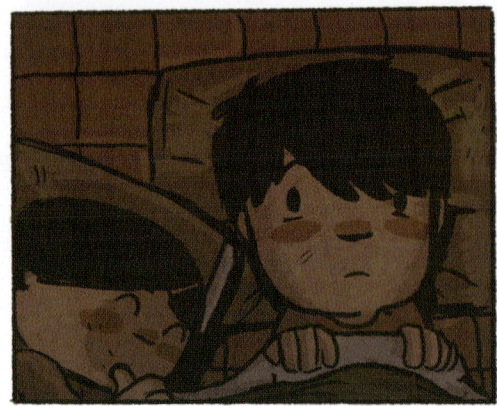

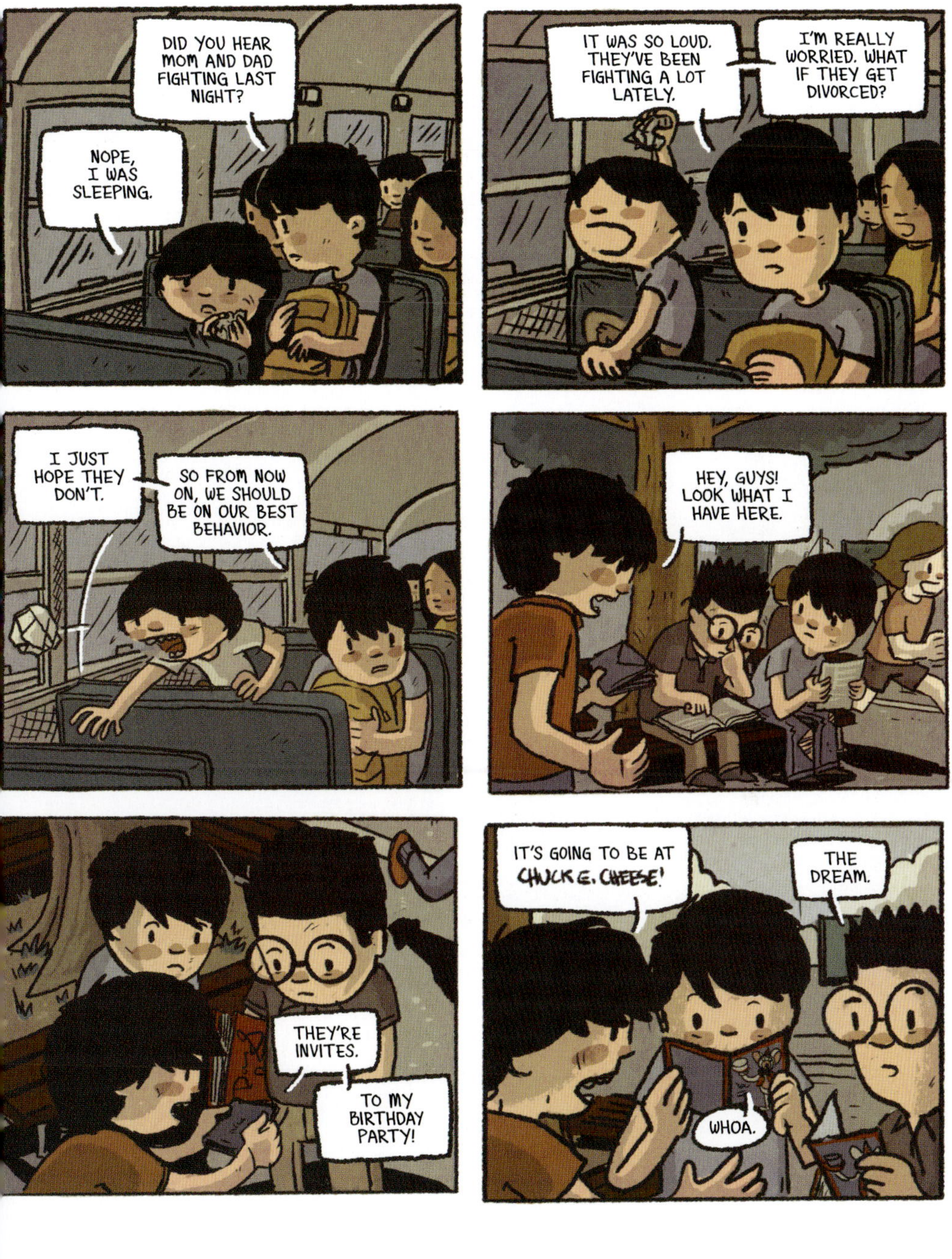
DID YOU HEAR MOM AND DAD FIGHTING LAST NIGHT?
NOPE, I WAS SLEEPING.
IT WAS SO LOUD. THEY'VE BEEN FIGHTING A LOT LATELY.
I'M REALLY WORRIED. WHAT IF THEY GET DIVORCED?
I JUST HOPE THEY DON'T.
SO FROM NOW ON, WE SHOULD BE ON OUR BEST BEHAVIOR.
HEY, GUYS! LOOK WHAT I HAVE HERE.
THEY'RE INVITES.
TO MY BIRTHDAY PARTY!
IT'S GOING TO BE AT CHUCK E. CHEESE!
THE DREAM.
WHOA.

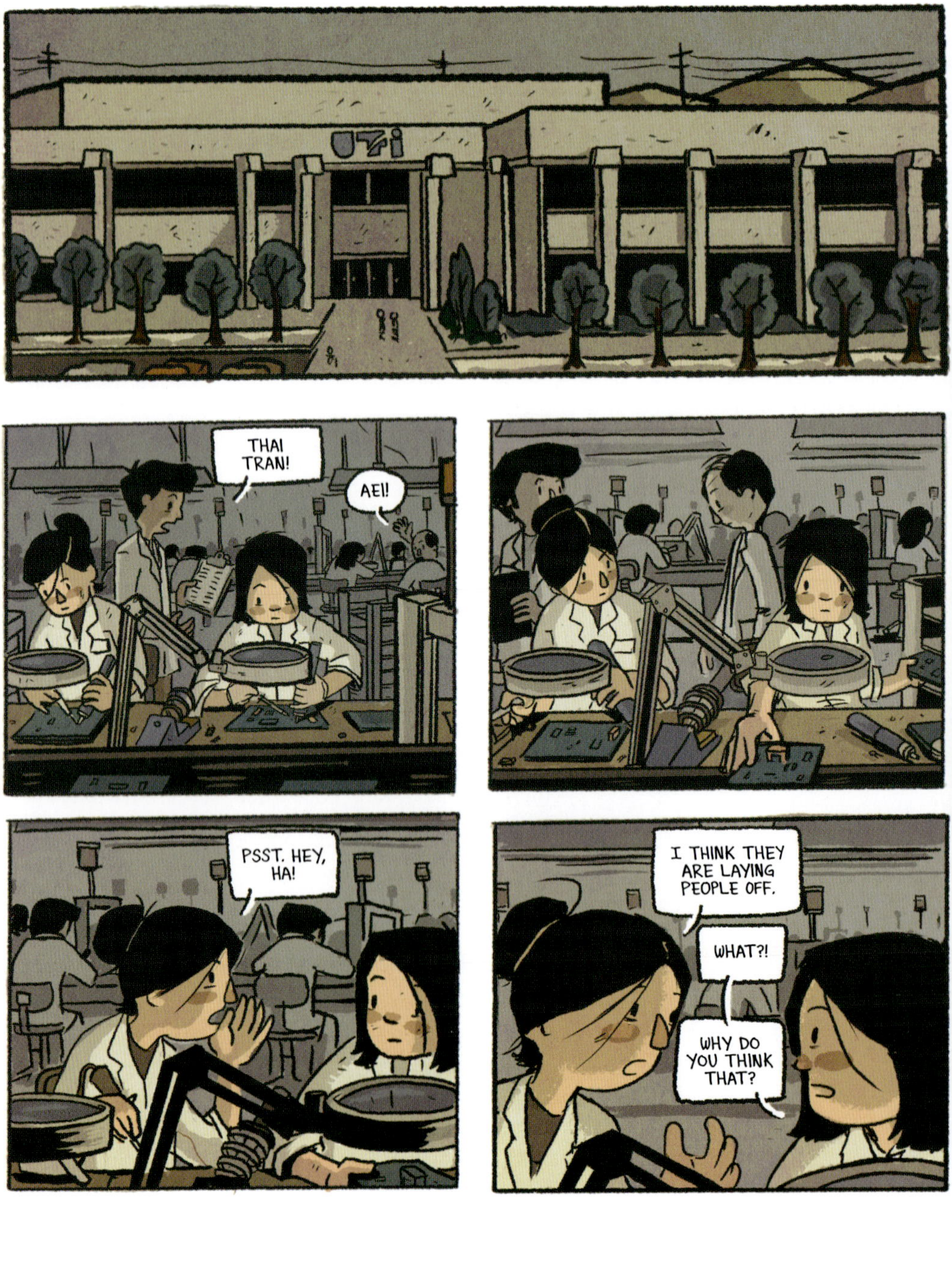
UTi
THAI TRAN!
AEI!
PSST. HEY, HA!
I THINK THEY ARE LAYING PEOPLE OFF.
WHAT?!
WHY DO YOU THINK THAT?

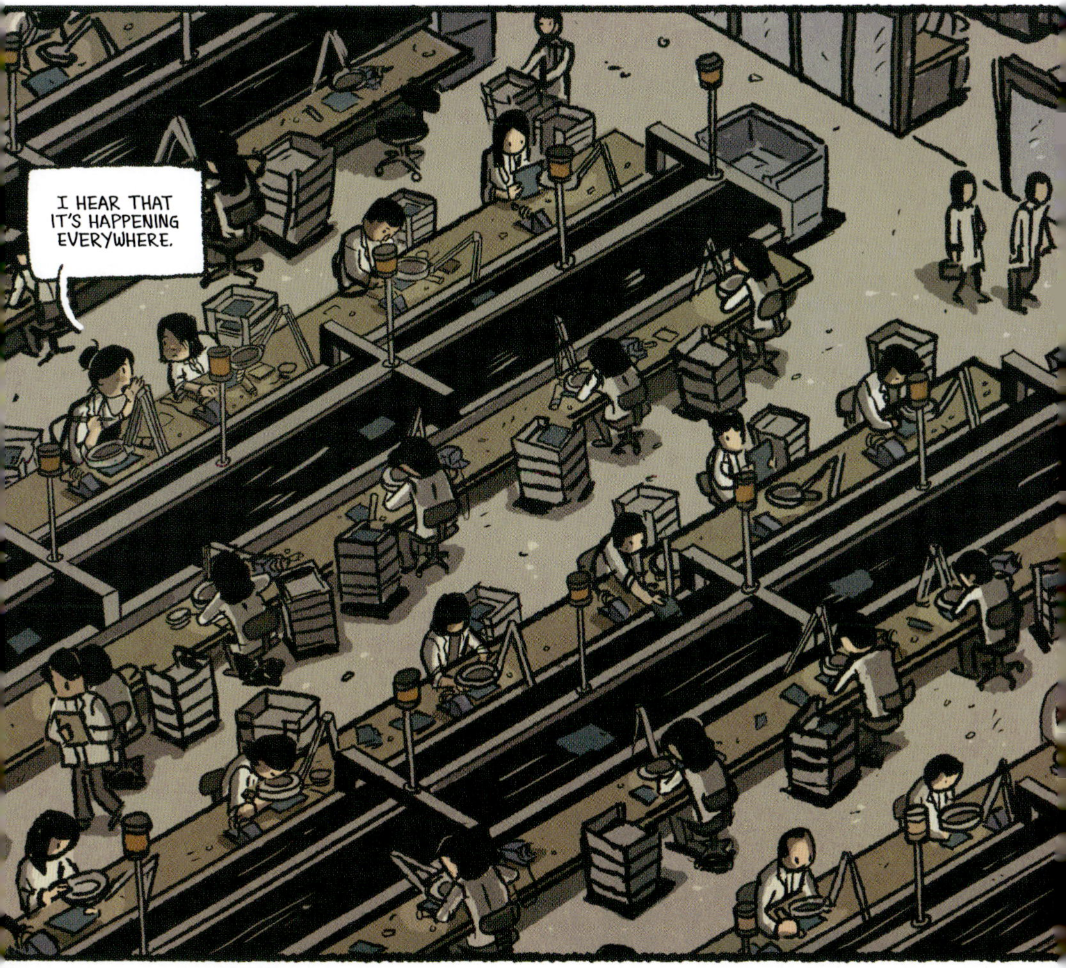
I HEAR THAT IT'S HAPPENING EVERYWHERE.

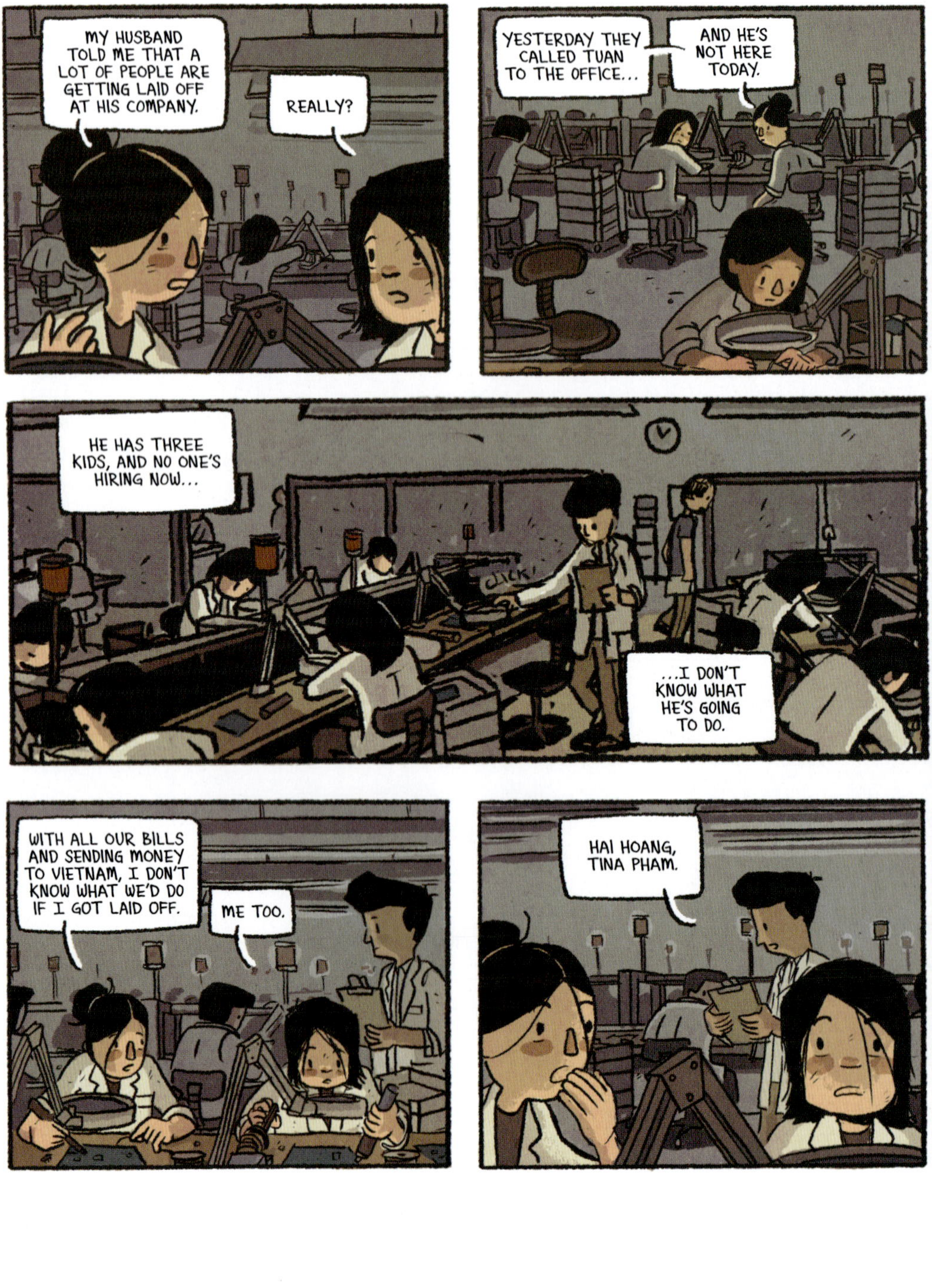
MY HUSBAND TOLD ME THAT A LOT OF PEOPLE ARE GETTING LAID OFF AT HIS COMPANY.
REALLY?
YESTERDAY THEY CALLED TUAN TO THE OFFICE...
AND HE'S NOT HERE TODAY.
HE HAS THREE KIDS, AND NO ONE'S HIRING NOW...
CLICK
...I DON'T KNOW WHAT HE'S GOING TO DO.
WITH ALL OUR BILLS AND SENDING MONEY TO VIETNAM, I DON'T KNOW WHAT WE'D DO IF I GOT LAID OFF.
ME TOO.
HAI HOANG, TINA PHAM.

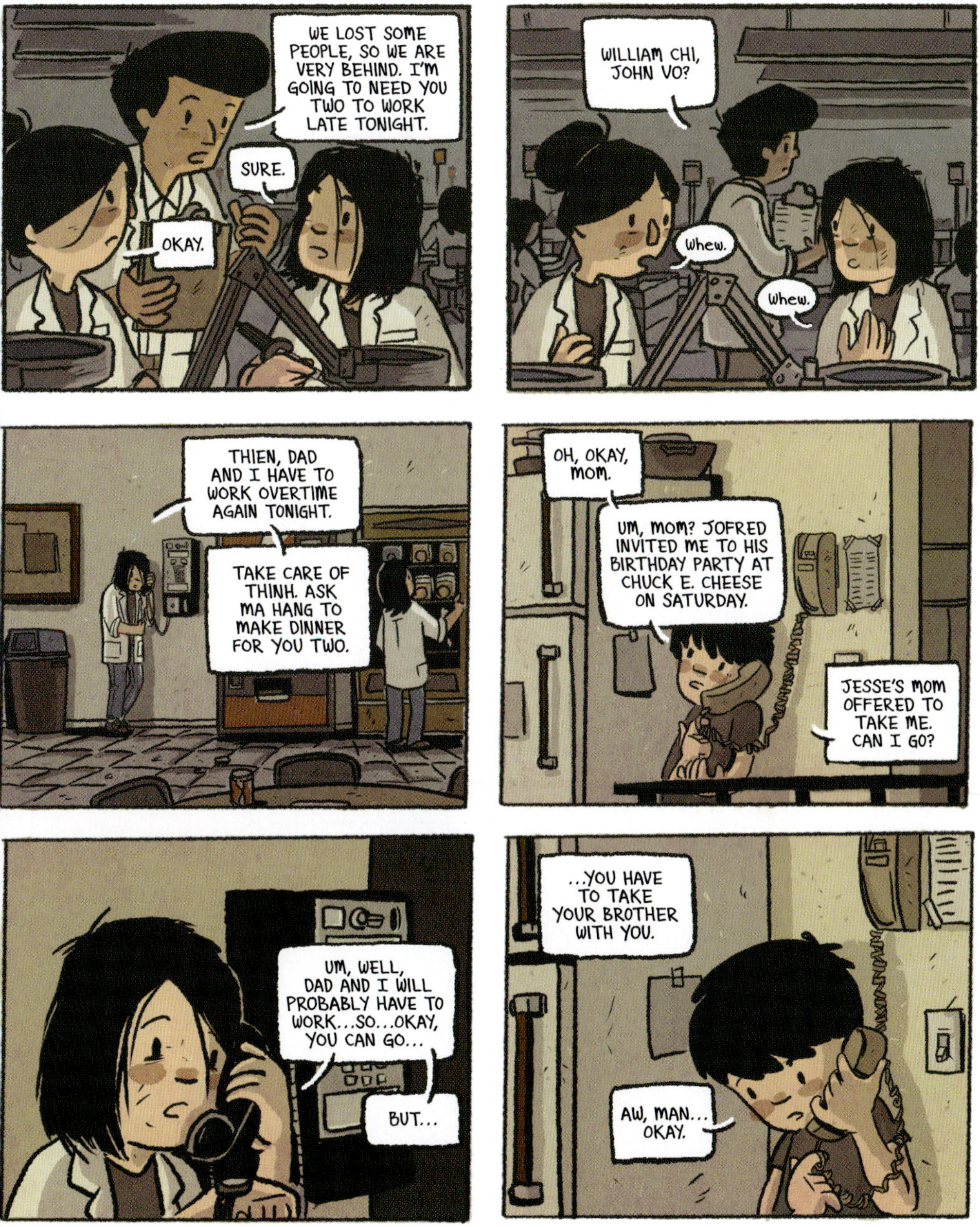

WE LOST SOME PEOPLE, SO WE ARE VERY BEHIND. I'M GOING TO NEED YOU TWO TO WORK LATE TONIGHT.
SURE.
OKAY.
WILLIAM CHI, JOHN VO?
Whew.
Whew.
THIEN, DAD AND I HAVE TO WORK OVERTIME AGAIN TONIGHT.
TAKE CARE OF THINH. ASK MA HANG TO MAKE DINNER FOR YOU TWO.
OH, OKAY, MOM.
UM, MOM? JOFRED INVITED ME TO HIS BIRTHDAY PARTY AT CHUCK E. CHEESE ON SATURDAY.
JESSE'S MOM OFFERED TO TAKE ME. CAN I GO?
UM, WELL, DAD AND I WILL PROBABLY HAVE TO WORK...SO...OKAY, YOU CAN GO...
BUT...
...YOU HAVE TO TAKE YOUR BROTHER WITH YOU.
AW, MAN... OKAY.

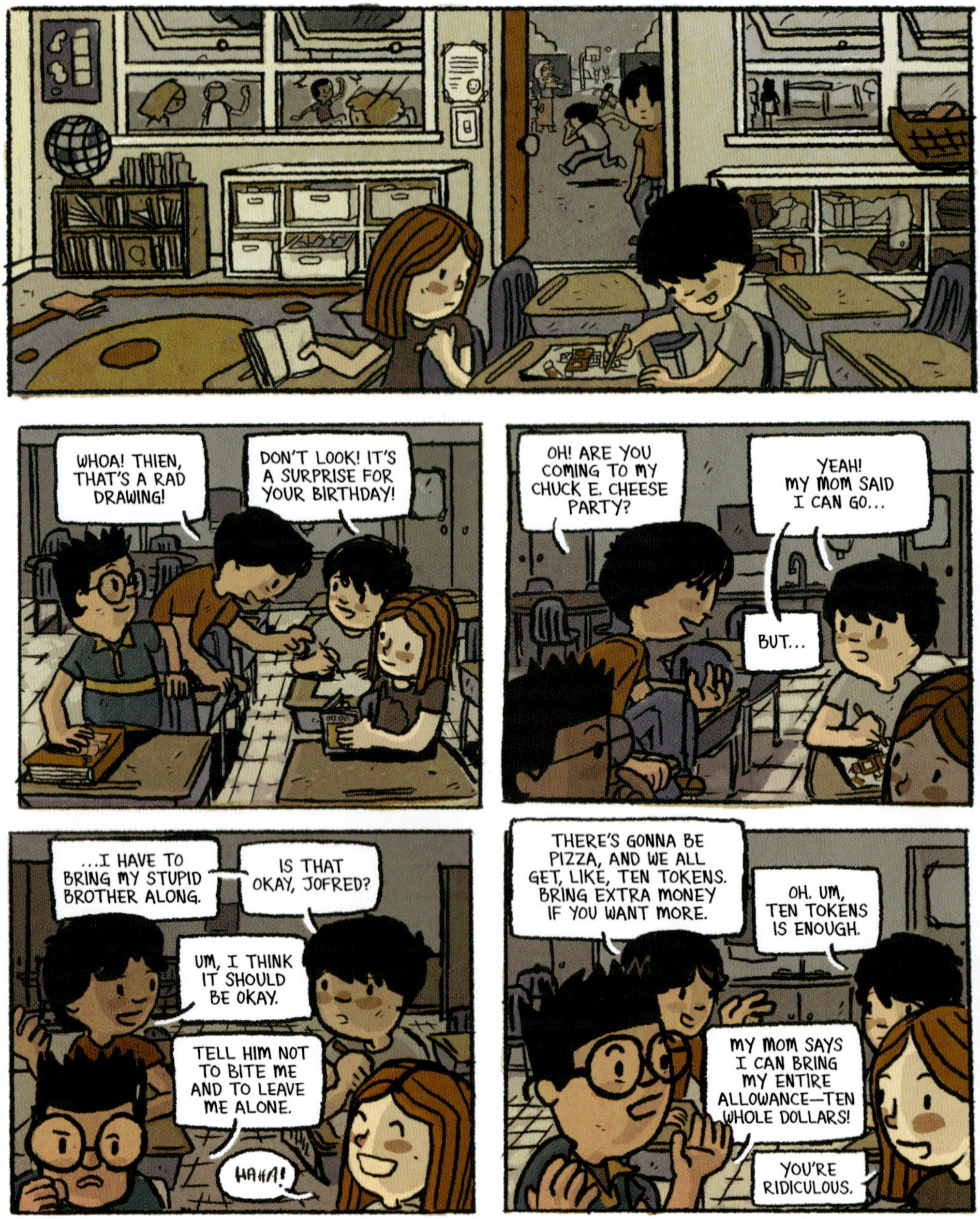
WHOA! THIEN, THAT'S A RAD DRAWING!
DON'T LOOK! IT'S A SURPRISE FOR YOUR BIRTHDAY!
OH! ARE YOU COMING TO MY CHUCK E. CHEESE PARTY?
YEAH! MY MOM SAID I CAN GO...
BUT...
...I HAVE TO BRING MY STUPID BROTHER ALONG.
IS THAT OKAY, JOFRED?
UM, I THINK IT SHOULD BE OKAY.
TELL HIM NOT TO BITE ME AND TO LEAVE ME ALONE.
HAHA!
THERE'S GONNA BE PIZZA, AND WE ALL GET, LIKE, TEN TOKENS. BRING EXTRA MONEY IF YOU WANT MORE.
OH. UM, TEN TOKENS IS ENOUGH.
MY MOM SAYS I CAN BRING MY ENTIRE ALLOWANCE—TEN WHOLE DOLLARS!
YOU'RE RIDICULOUS.

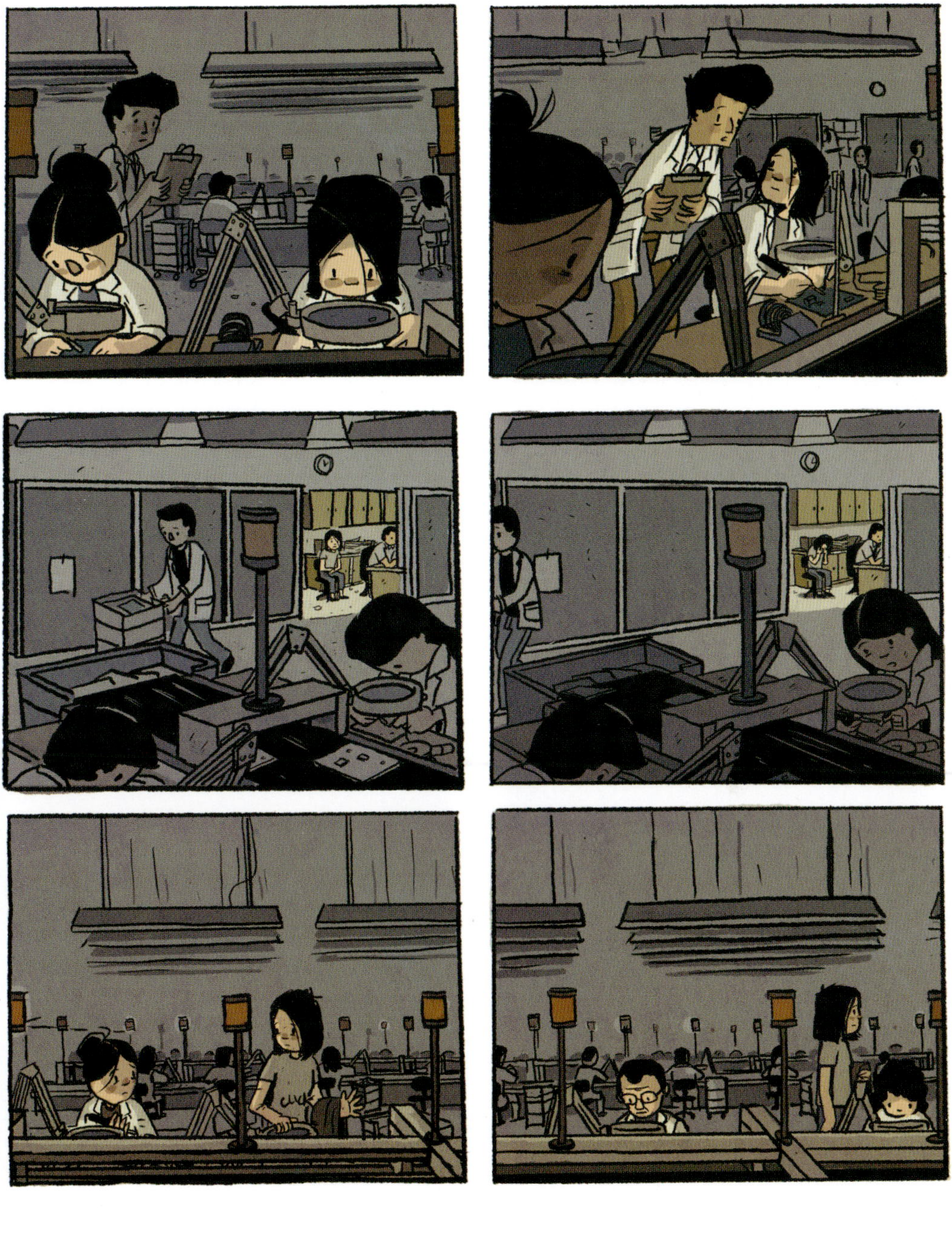
CLICK

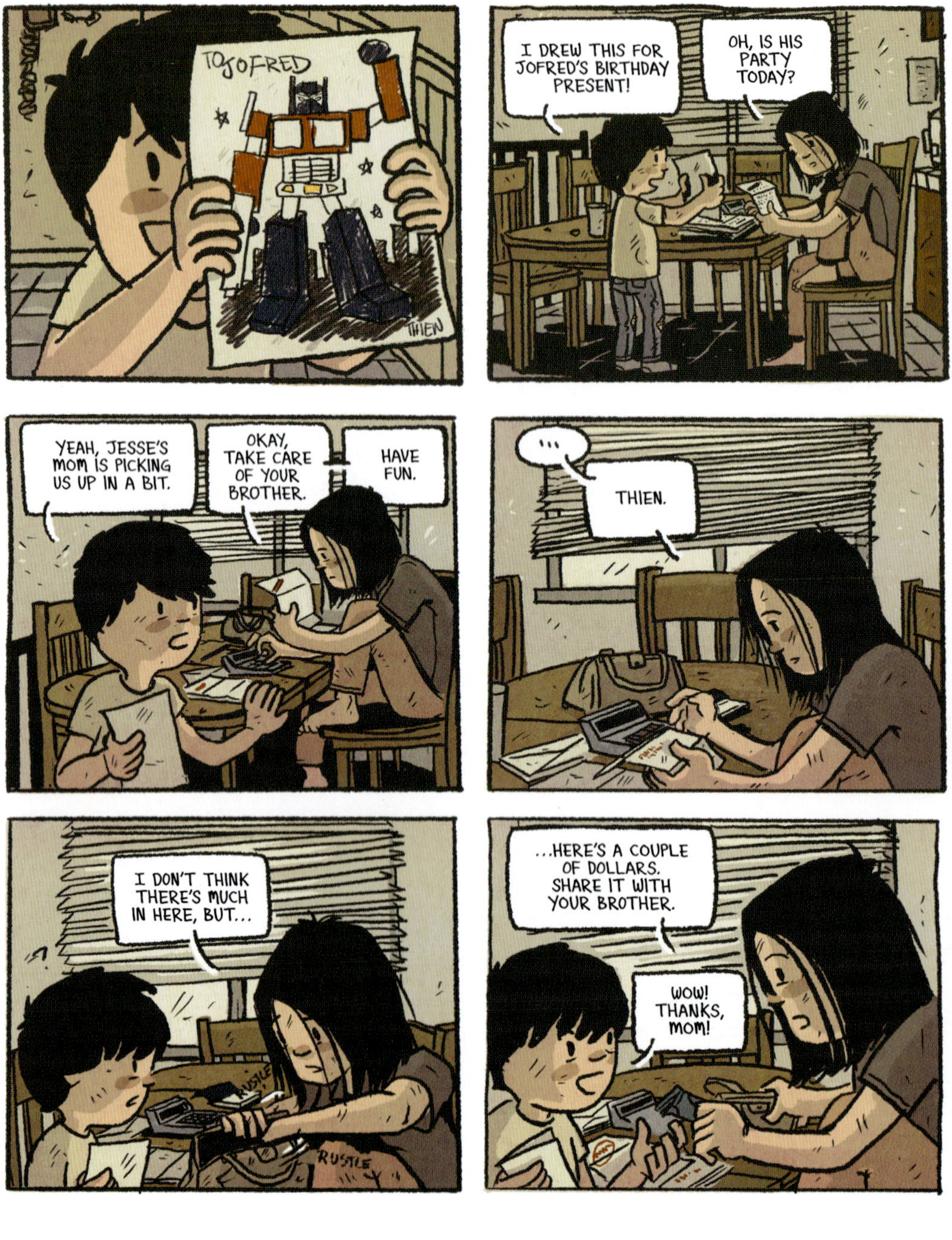
TO JOFRED
THIEN
I DREW THIS FOR JOFRED'S BIRTHDAY PRESENT!
OH, IS HIS PARTY TODAY?
YEAH, JESSE'S MOM IS PICKING US UP IN A BIT.
OKAY, TAKE CARE OF YOUR BROTHER.
HAVE FUN.
...
THIEN.
I DON'T THINK THERE'S MUCH IN HERE, BUT...
RUSTLE
RUSTLE
...HERE'S A COUPLE OF DOLLARS. SHARE IT WITH YOUR BROTHER.
WOW! THANKS, MOM!

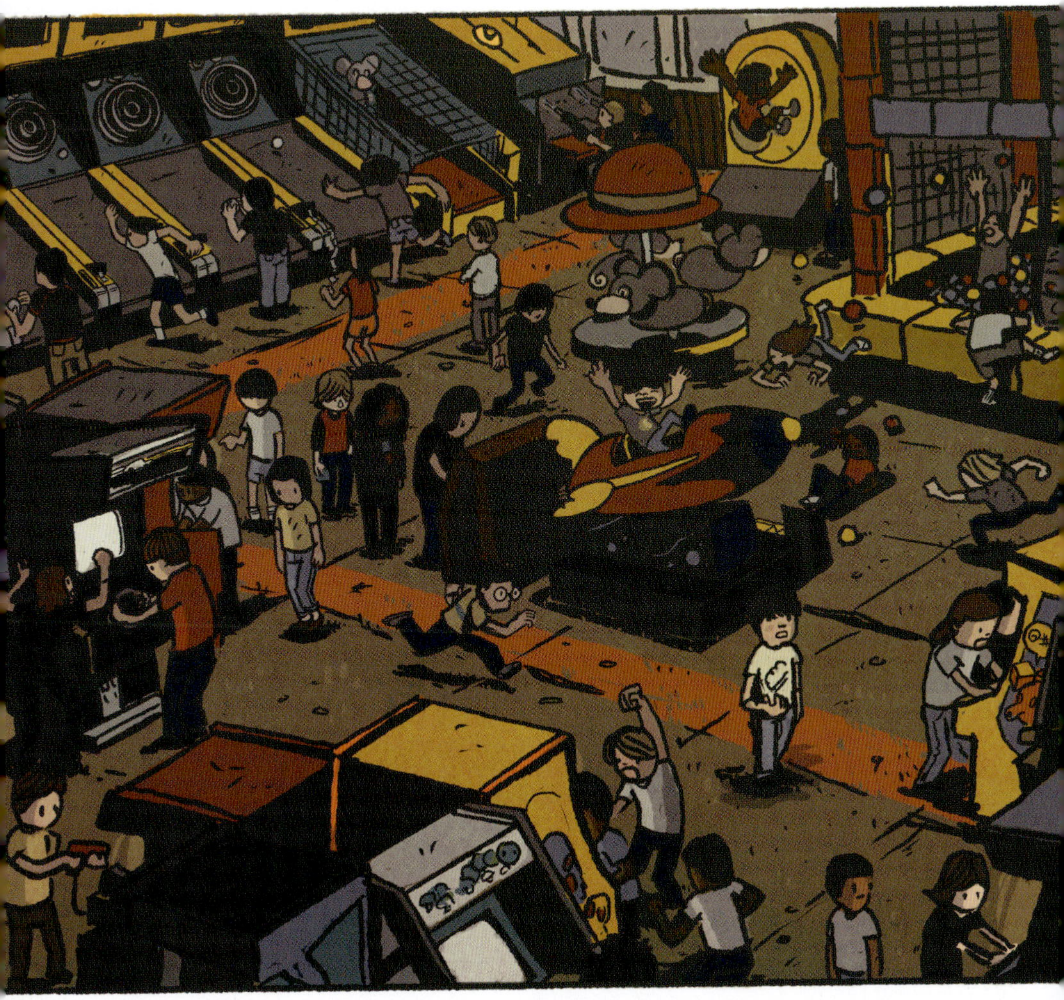

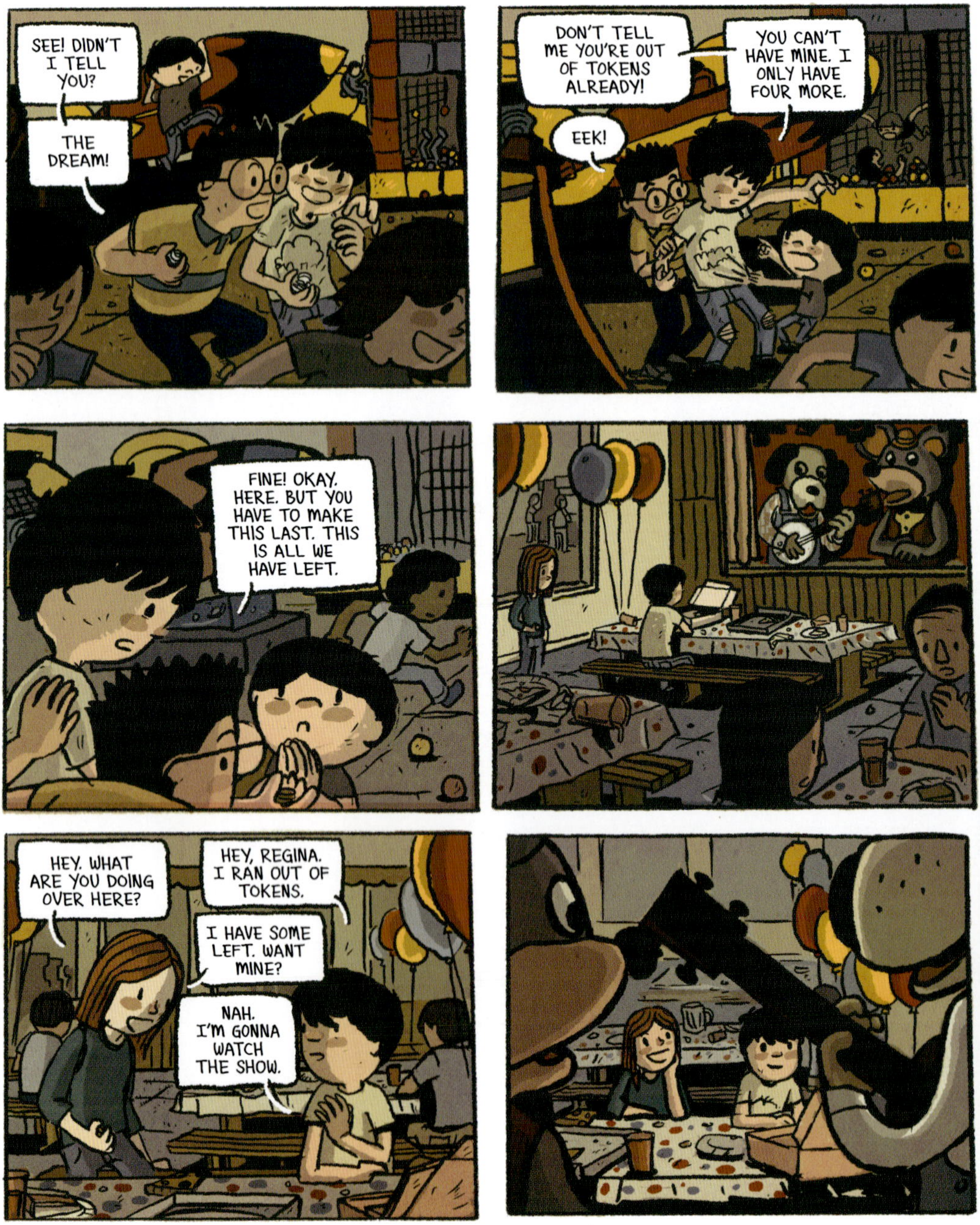
SEE! DIDN'T I TELL YOU?
THE DREAM!
DON'T TELL ME YOU'RE OUT OF TOKENS ALREADY!
YOU CAN'T HAVE MINE. I ONLY HAVE FOUR MORE.
EEK!
FINE! OKAY. HERE. BUT YOU HAVE TO MAKE THIS LAST. THIS IS ALL WE HAVE LEFT.
HEY. WHAT ARE YOU DOING OVER HERE?
HEY, REGINA. I RAN OUT OF TOKENS.
I HAVE SOME LEFT. WANT MINE?
NAH. I'M GONNA WATCH THE SHOW.

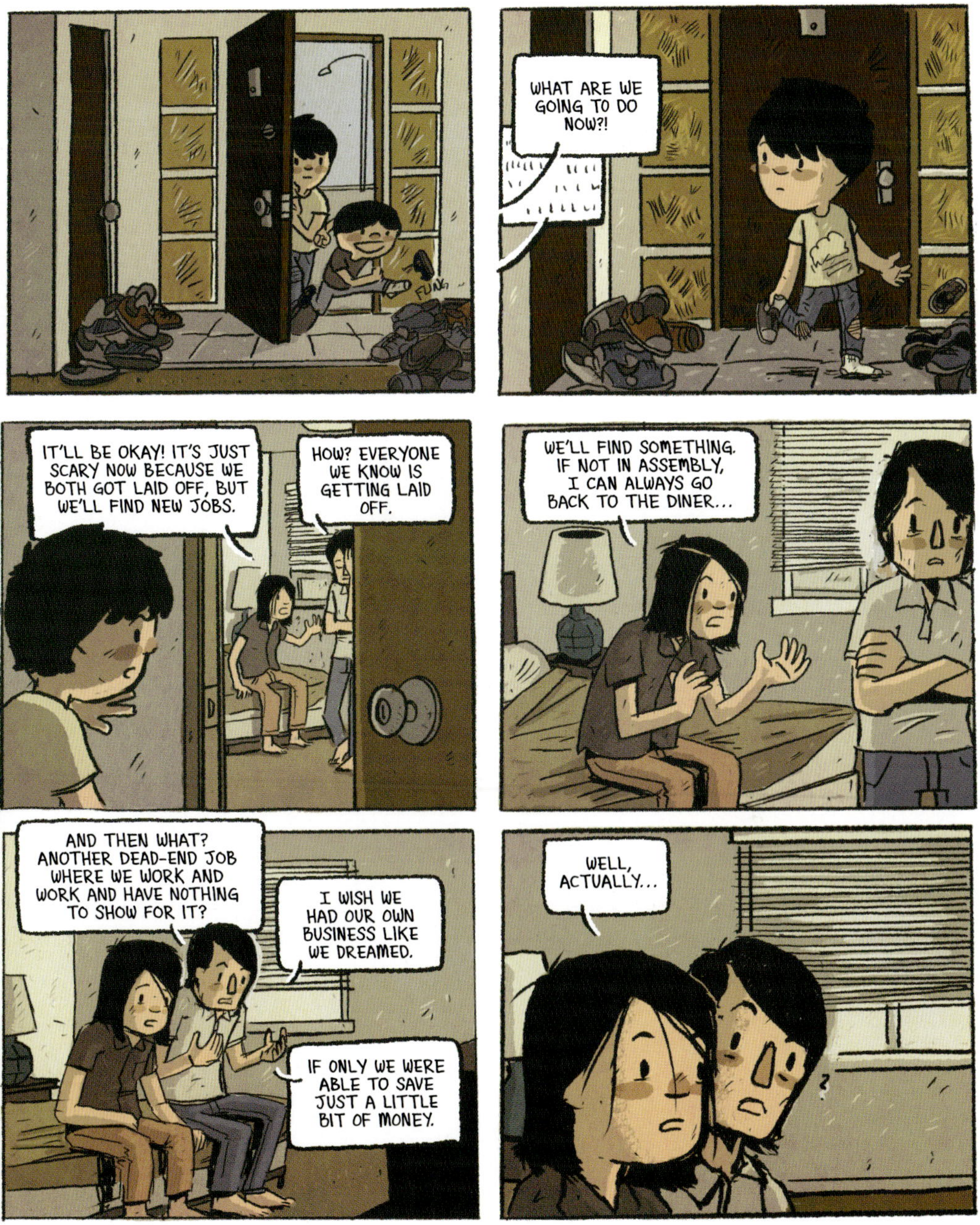
FLING
WHAT ARE WE GOING TO DO NOW?!
IT'LL BE OKAY! IT'S JUST SCARY NOW BECAUSE WE BOTH GOT LAID OFF, BUT WE'LL FIND NEW JOBS.
HOW? EVERYONE WE KNOW IS GETTING LAID OFF.
WE'LL FIND SOMETHING. IF NOT IN ASSEMBLY, I CAN ALWAYS GO BACK TO THE DINER...
AND THEN WHAT? ANOTHER DEAD-END JOB WHERE WE WORK AND WORK AND HAVE NOTHING TO SHOW FOR IT?
I WISH WE HAD OUR OWN BUSINESS LIKE WE DREAMED.
IF ONLY WE WERE ABLE TO SAVE JUST A LITTLE BIT OF MONEY.
WELL, ACTUALLY...

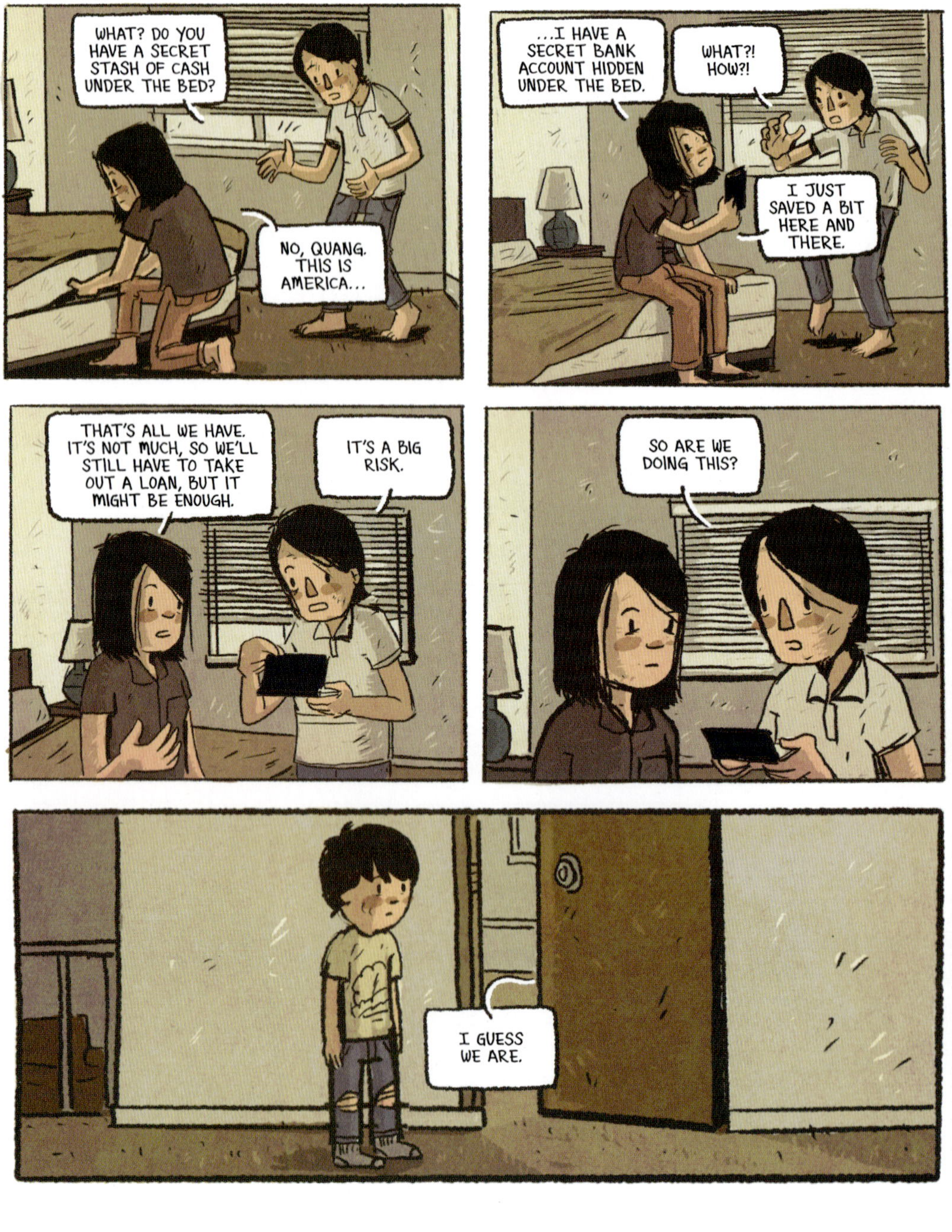
WHAT? DO YOU HAVE A SECRET STASH OF CASH UNDER THE BED?
NO, QUANG. THIS IS AMERICA...
...I HAVE A SECRET BANK ACCOUNT HIDDEN UNDER THE BED.
WHAT?! HOW?!
I JUST SAVED A BIT HERE AND THERE.
THAT'S ALL WE HAVE. IT'S NOT MUCH, SO WE'LL STILL HAVE TO TAKE OUT A LOAN, BUT IT MIGHT BE ENOUGH.
IT'S A BIG RISK.
SO ARE WE DOING THIS?
I GUESS WE ARE.

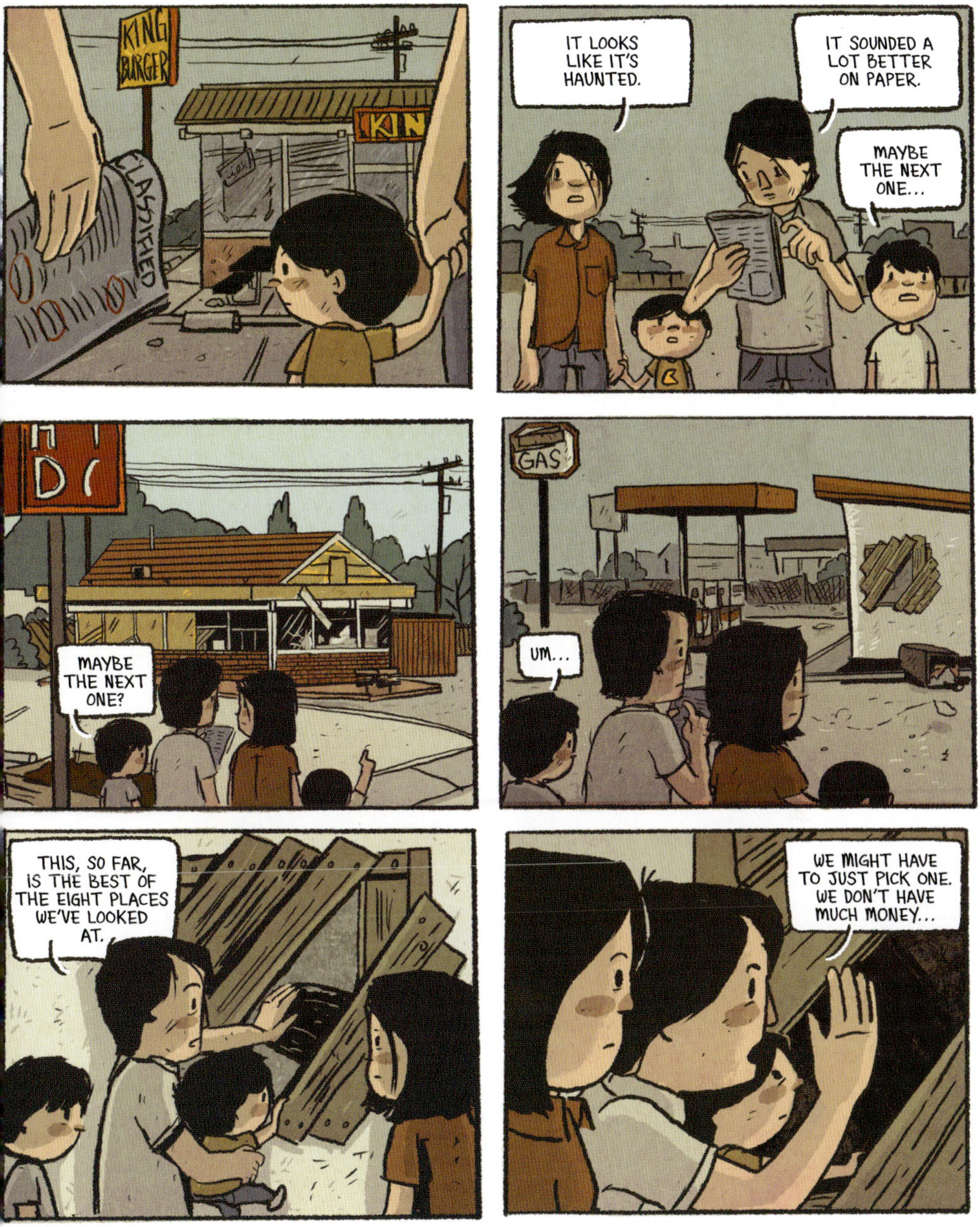
KING BURGER
CLASSIFIED
IT LOOKS LIKE IT'S HAUNTED.
IT SOUNDED A LOT BETTER ON PAPER.
MAYBE THE NEXT ONE...
MAYBE THE NEXT ONE?
GAS
UM...
THIS, SO FAR, IS THE BEST OF THE EIGHT PLACES WE'VE LOOKED AT.
WE MIGHT HAVE TO JUST PICK ONE. WE DON'T HAVE MUCH MONEY...

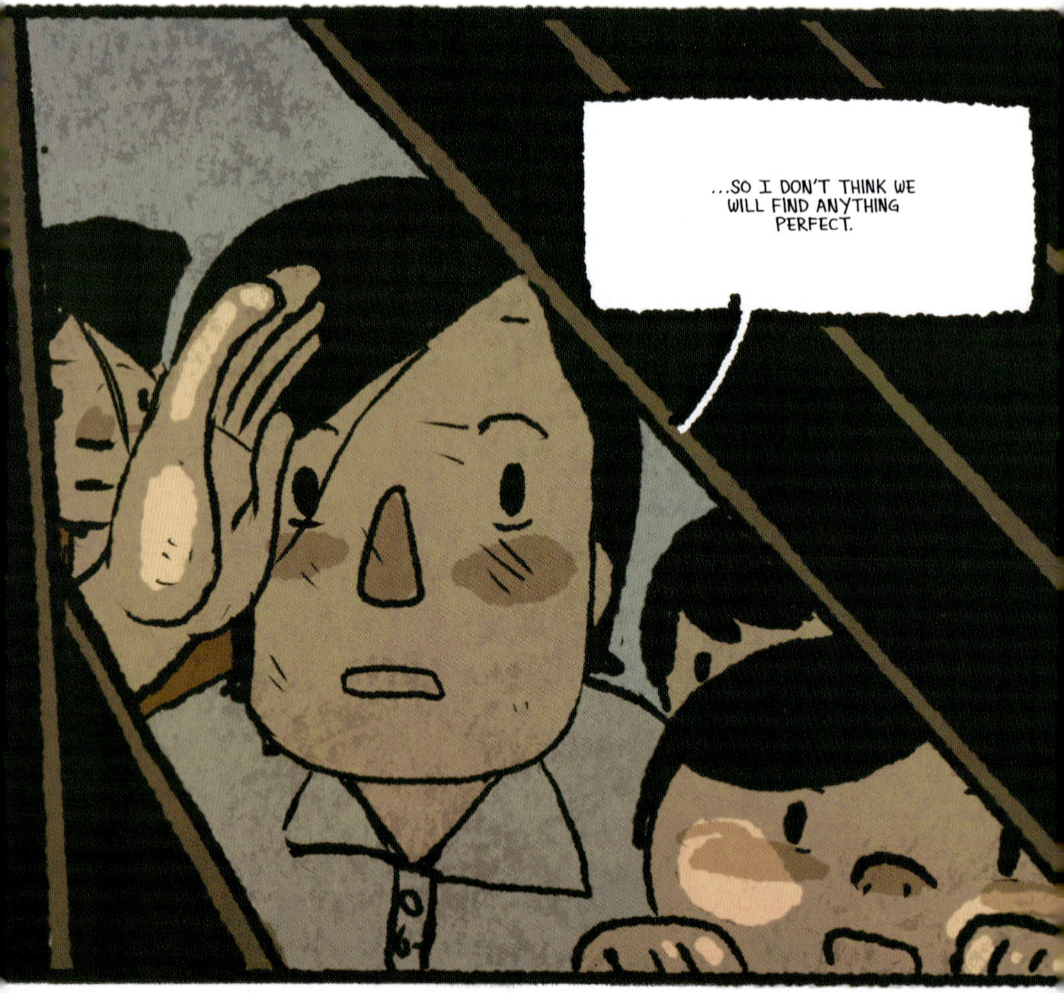
...SO I DON'T THINK WE WILL FIND ANYTHING PERFECT.

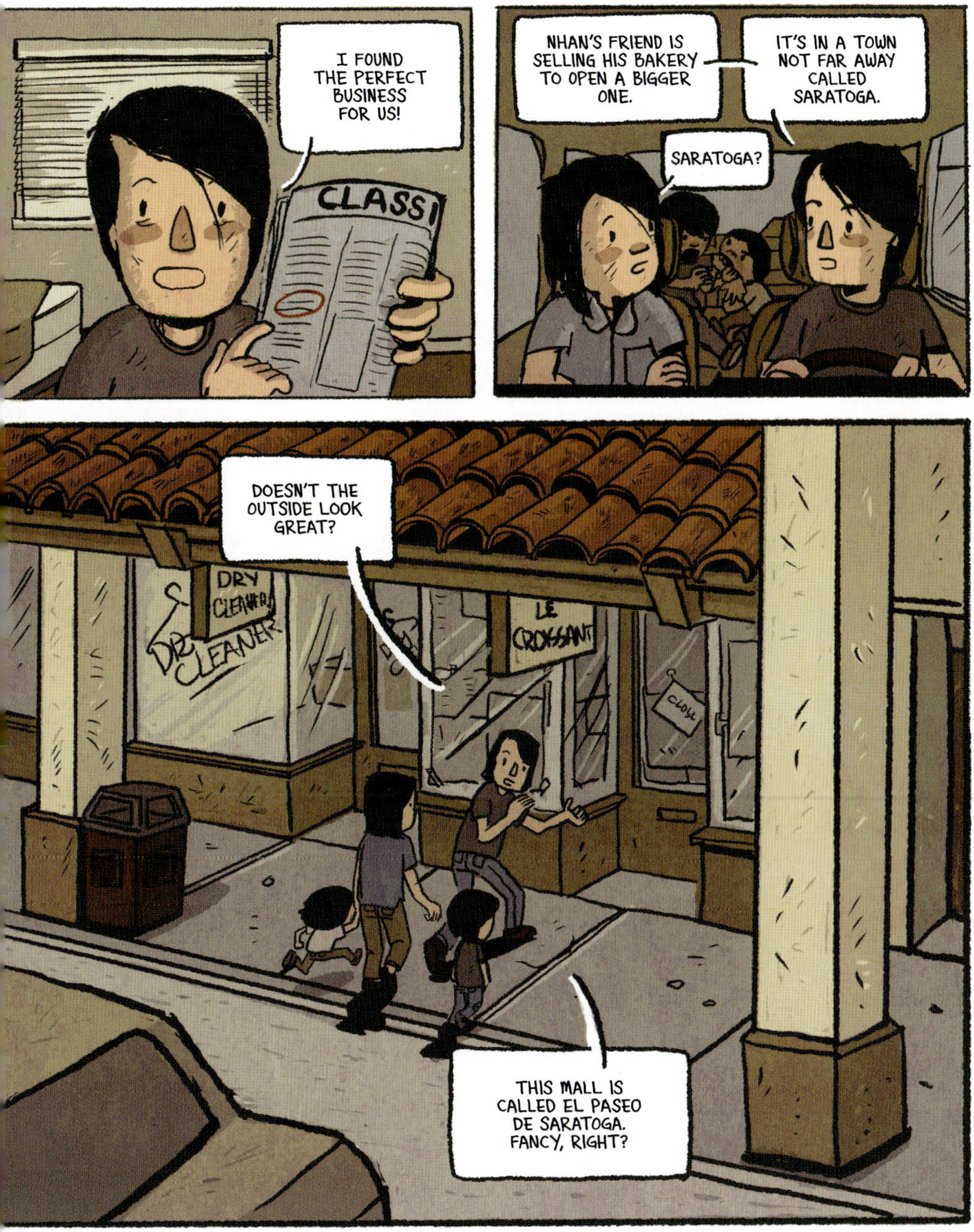
I FOUND THE PERFECT BUSINESS FOR US!
CLASSI
NHAN'S FRIEND IS SELLING HIS BAKERY TO OPEN A BIGGER ONE.
IT'S IN A TOWN NOT FAR AWAY CALLED SARATOGA.
SARATOGA?
DOESN'T THE OUTSIDE LOOK GREAT?
DRY CLEANERS
DRY CLEANERS
LE CROSSANT
CLOSE
THIS MALL IS CALLED EL PASEO DE SARATOGA. FANCY, RIGHT?

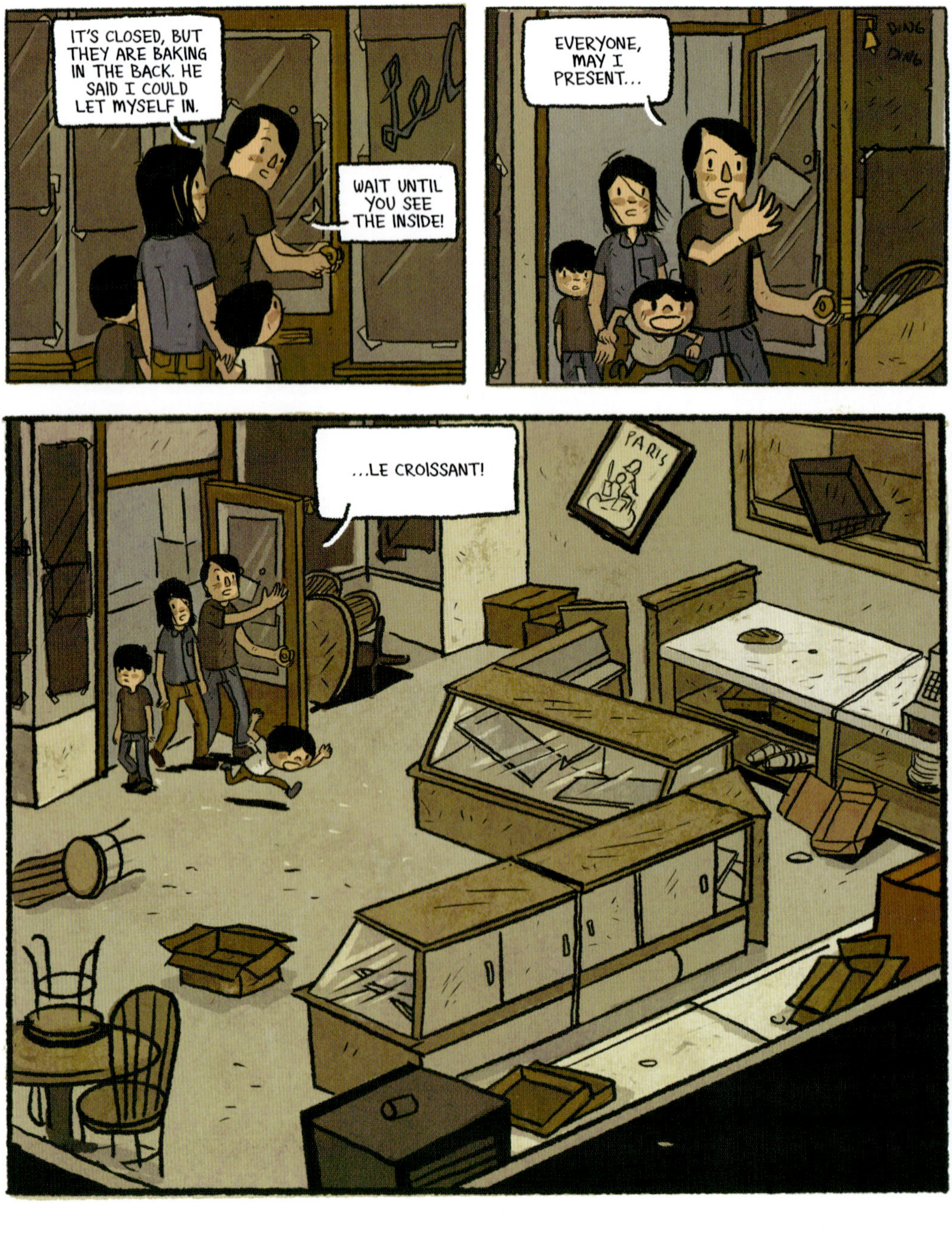
IT'S CLOSED, BUT THEY ARE BAKING IN THE BACK. HE SAID I COULD LET MYSELF IN.
WAIT UNTIL YOU SEE THE INSIDE!
EVERYONE, MAY I PRESENT...
DING
DING
...LE CROISSANT!
PARIS

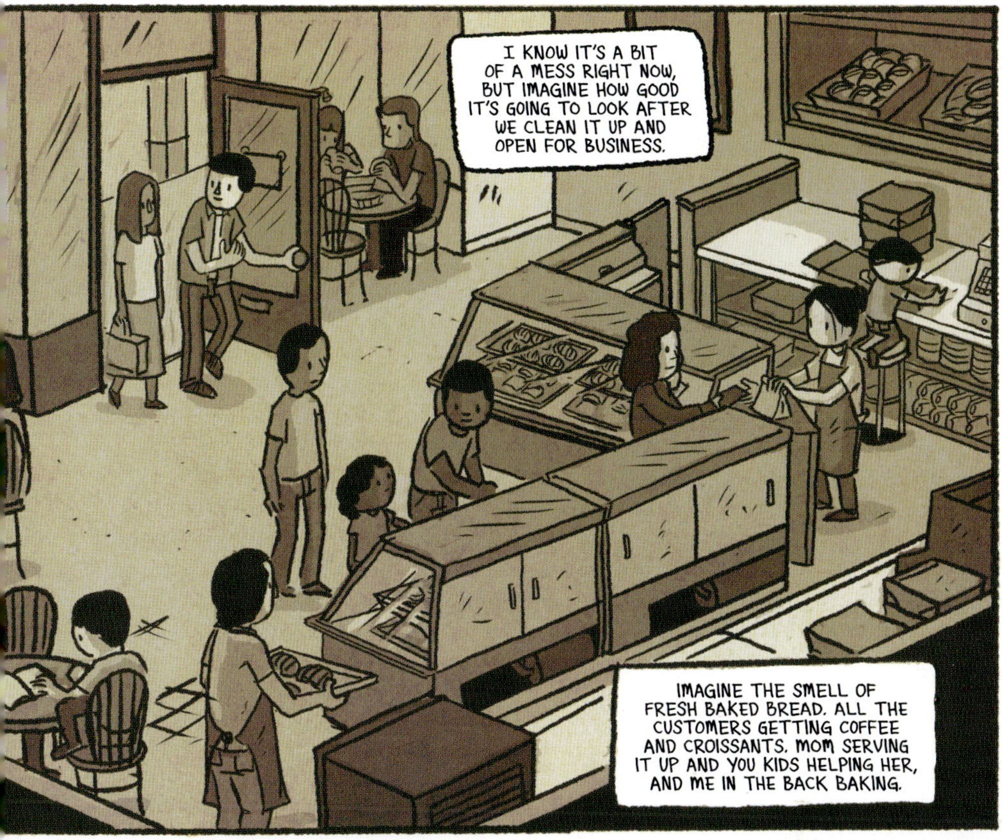
I KNOW IT'S A BIT OF A MESS RIGHT NOW, BUT IMAGINE HOW GOOD IT'S GOING TO LOOK AFTER WE CLEAN IT UP AND OPEN FOR BUSINESS.
IMAGINE THE SMELL OF FRESH BAKED BREAD. ALL THE CUSTOMERS GETTING COFFEE AND CROISSANTS. MOM SERVING IT UP AND YOU KIDS HELPING HER, AND ME IN THE BACK BAKING.

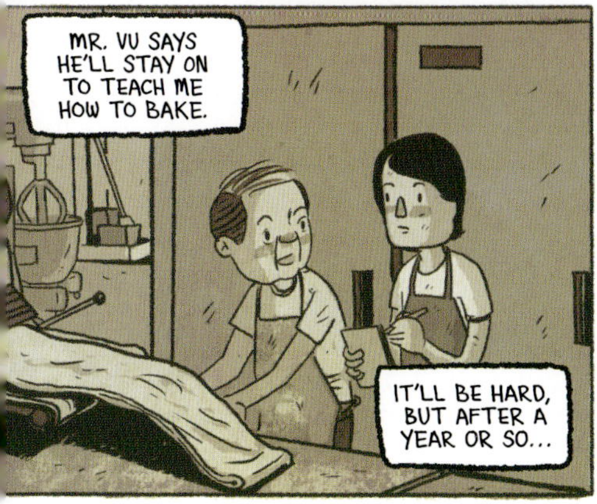
MR. VU SAYS HE'LL STAY ON TO TEACH ME HOW TO BAKE.
IT'LL BE HARD, BUT AFTER A YEAR OR SO...

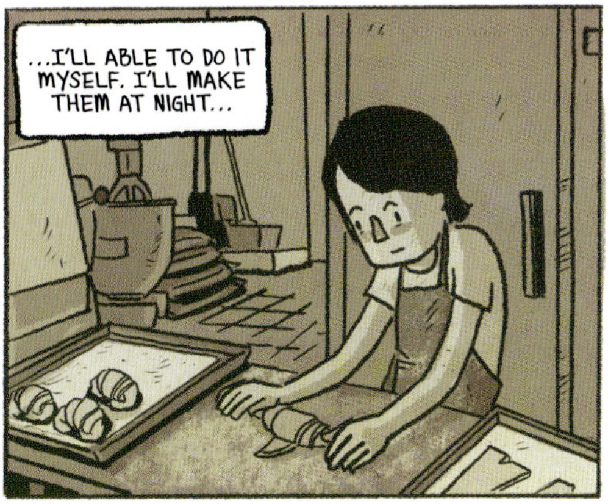
...I'LL ABLE TO DO IT MYSELF. I'LL MAKE THEM AT NIGHT...

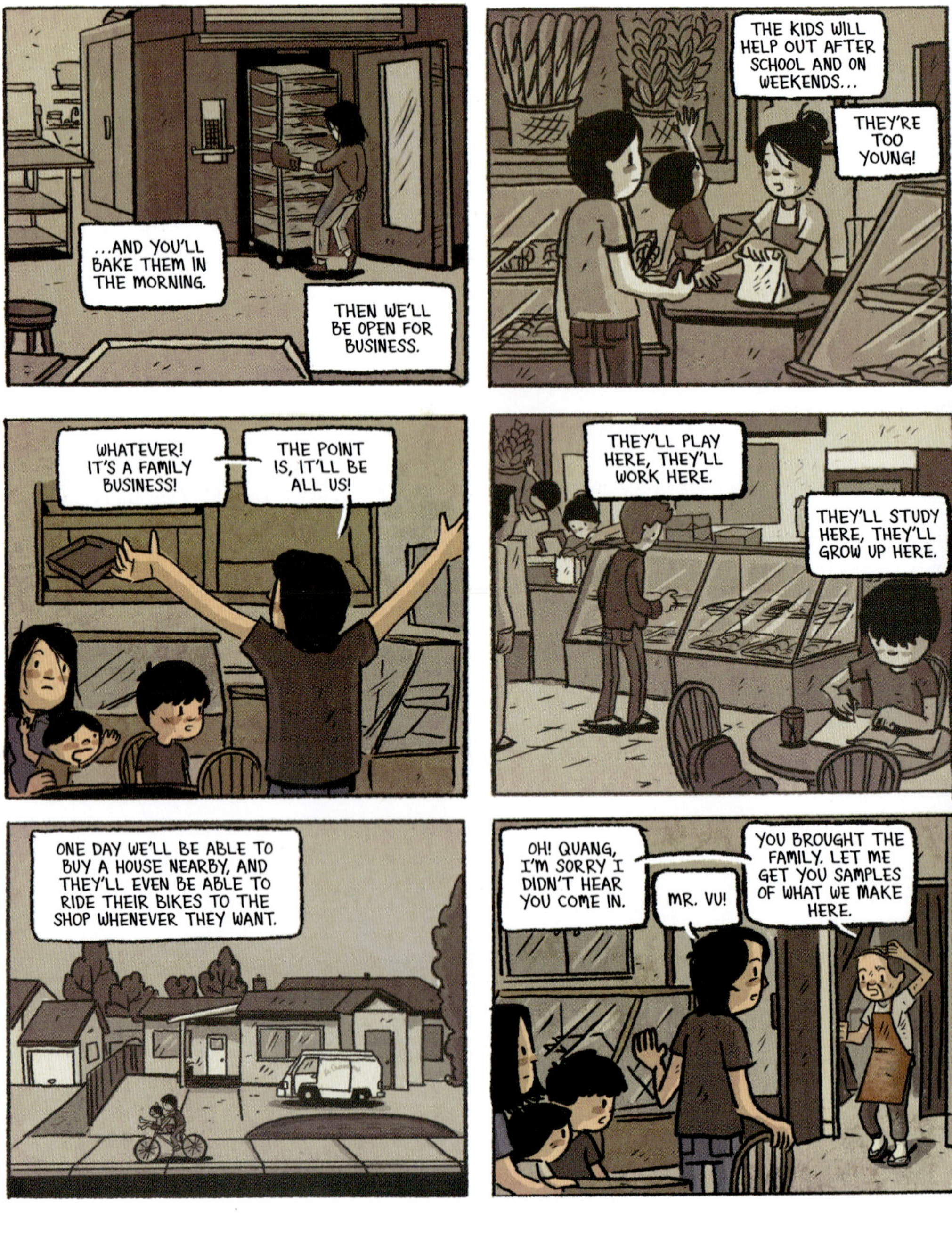
...AND YOU'LL BAKE THEM IN THE MORNING.
THEN WE'LL BE OPEN FOR BUSINESS.
THE KIDS WILL HELP OUT AFTER SCHOOL AND ON WEEKENDS...
THEY'RE TOO YOUNG!
WHATEVER! IT'S A FAMILY BUSINESS!
THE POINT IS, IT'LL BE ALL US!
THEY'LL PLAY HERE, THEY'LL WORK HERE.
THEY'LL STUDY HERE, THEY'LL GROW UP HERE.
ONE DAY WE'LL BE ABLE TO BUY A HOUSE NEARBY, AND THEY'LL EVEN BE ABLE TO RIDE THEIR BIKES TO THE SHOP WHENEVER THEY WANT.
OH! QUANG, I'M SORRY I DIDN'T HEAR YOU COME IN.
MR. VU!
YOU BROUGHT THE FAMILY. LET ME GET YOU SAMPLES OF WHAT WE MAKE HERE.

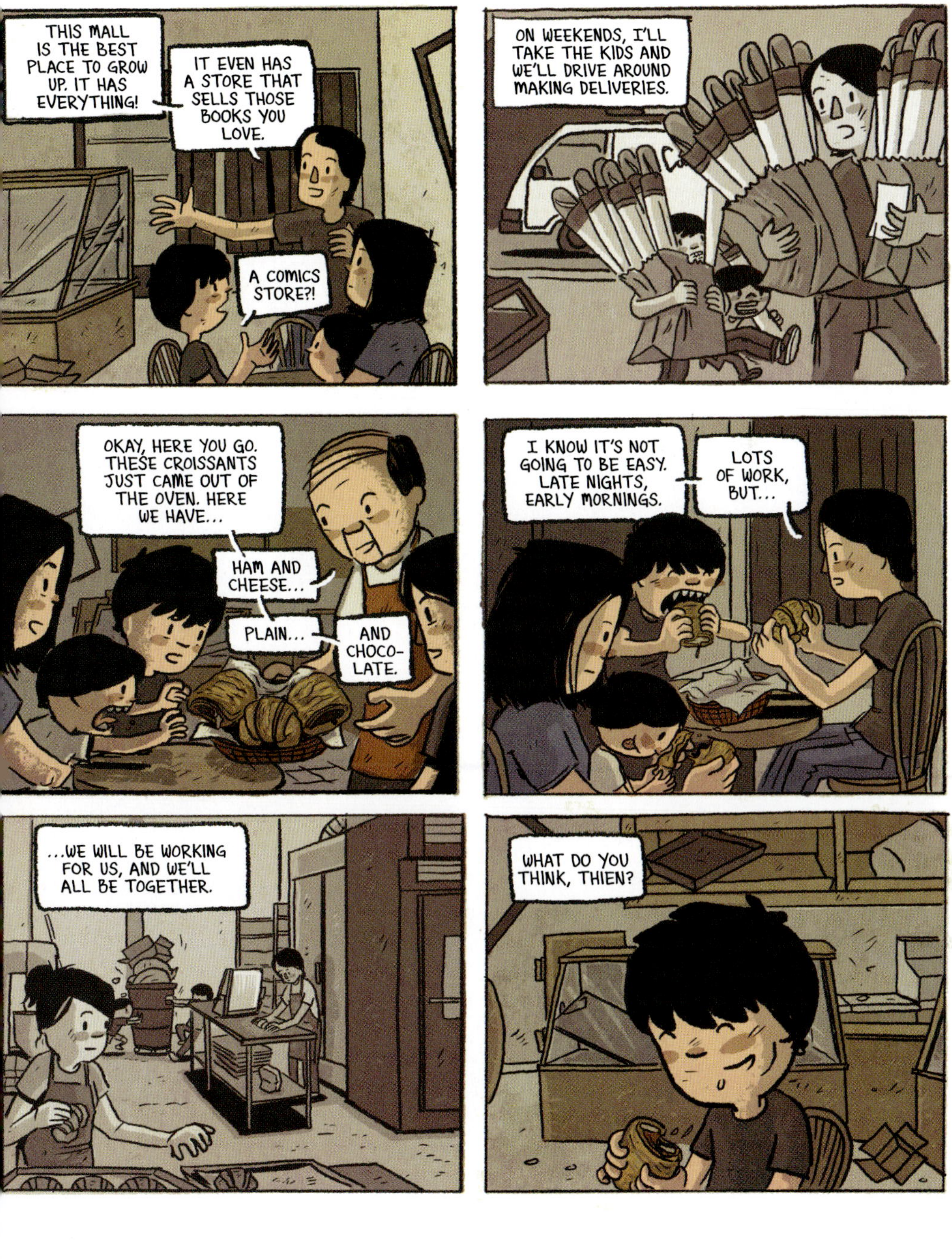
THIS MALL IS THE BEST PLACE TO GROW UP. IT HAS EVERYTHING!
IT EVEN HAS A STORE THAT SELLS THOSE BOOKS YOU LOVE.
A COMICS STORE?!
ON WEEKENDS, I'LL TAKE THE KIDS AND WE'LL DRIVE AROUND MAKING DELIVERIES.
OKAY, HERE YOU GO. THESE CROISSANTS JUST CAME OUT OF THE OVEN. HERE WE HAVE...
HAM AND CHEESE...
PLAIN...
AND CHOCO-LATE.
I KNOW IT'S NOT GOING TO BE EASY. LATE NIGHTS, EARLY MORNINGS.
LOTS OF WORK, BUT...
...WE WILL BE WORKING FOR US, AND WE'LL ALL BE TOGETHER.
WHAT DO YOU THINK, THIEN?

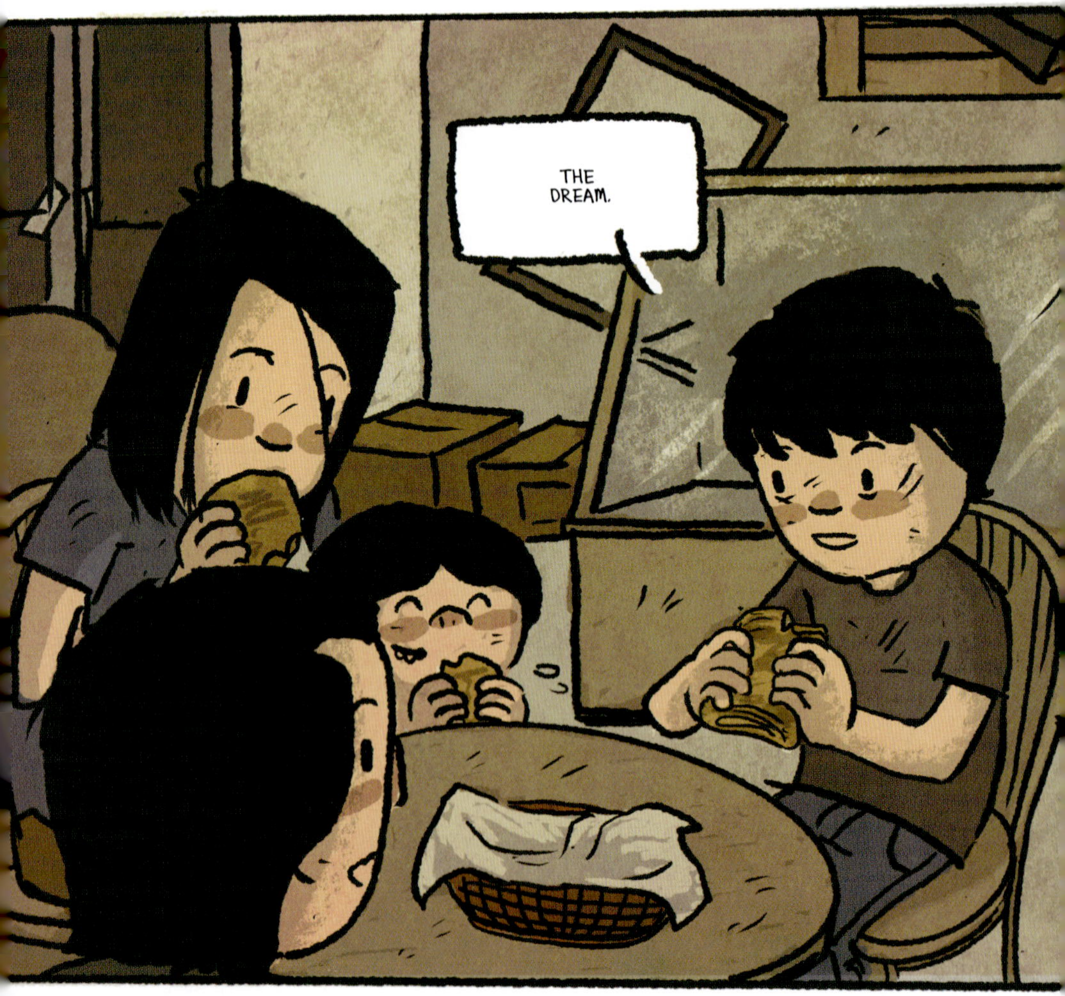
THE DREAM.

CHAPTER 7: CƠM TÂM ĐẶC BIỆT

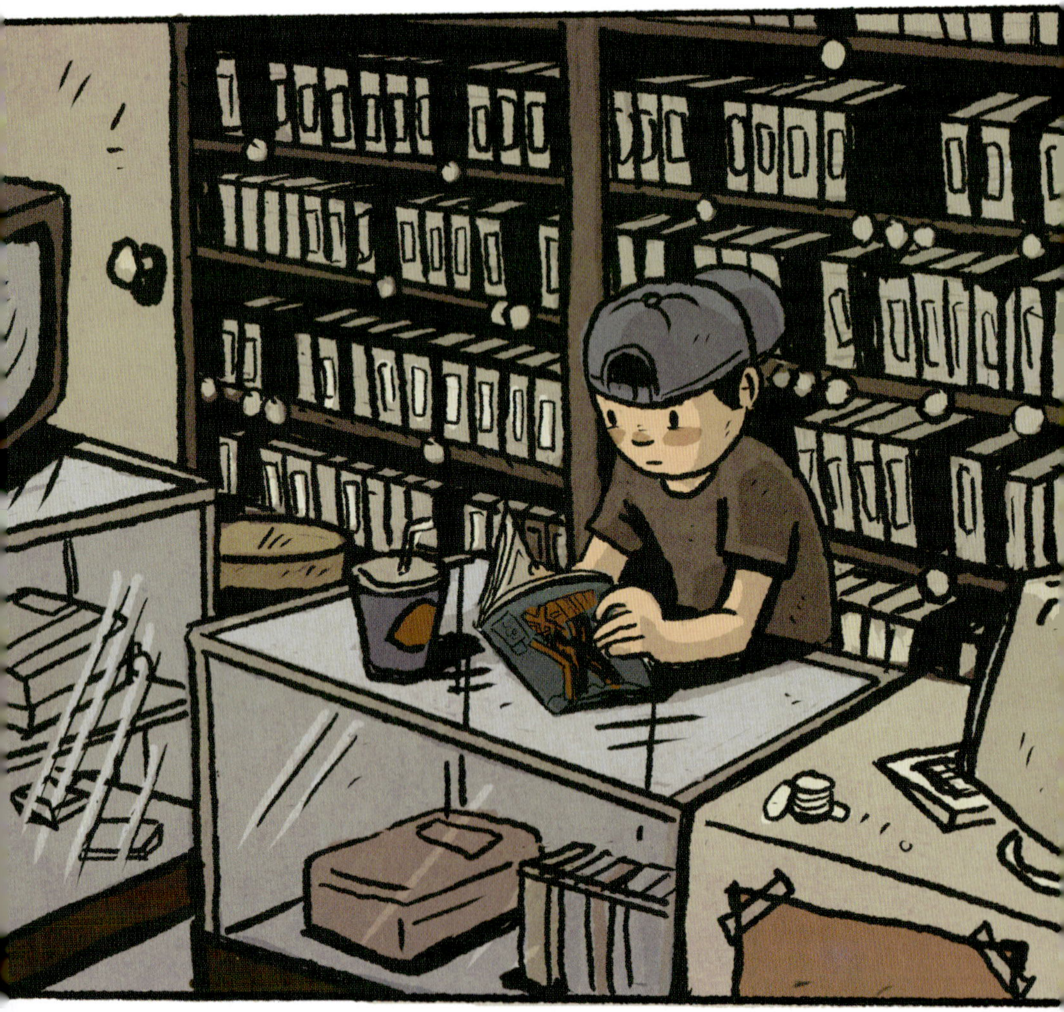

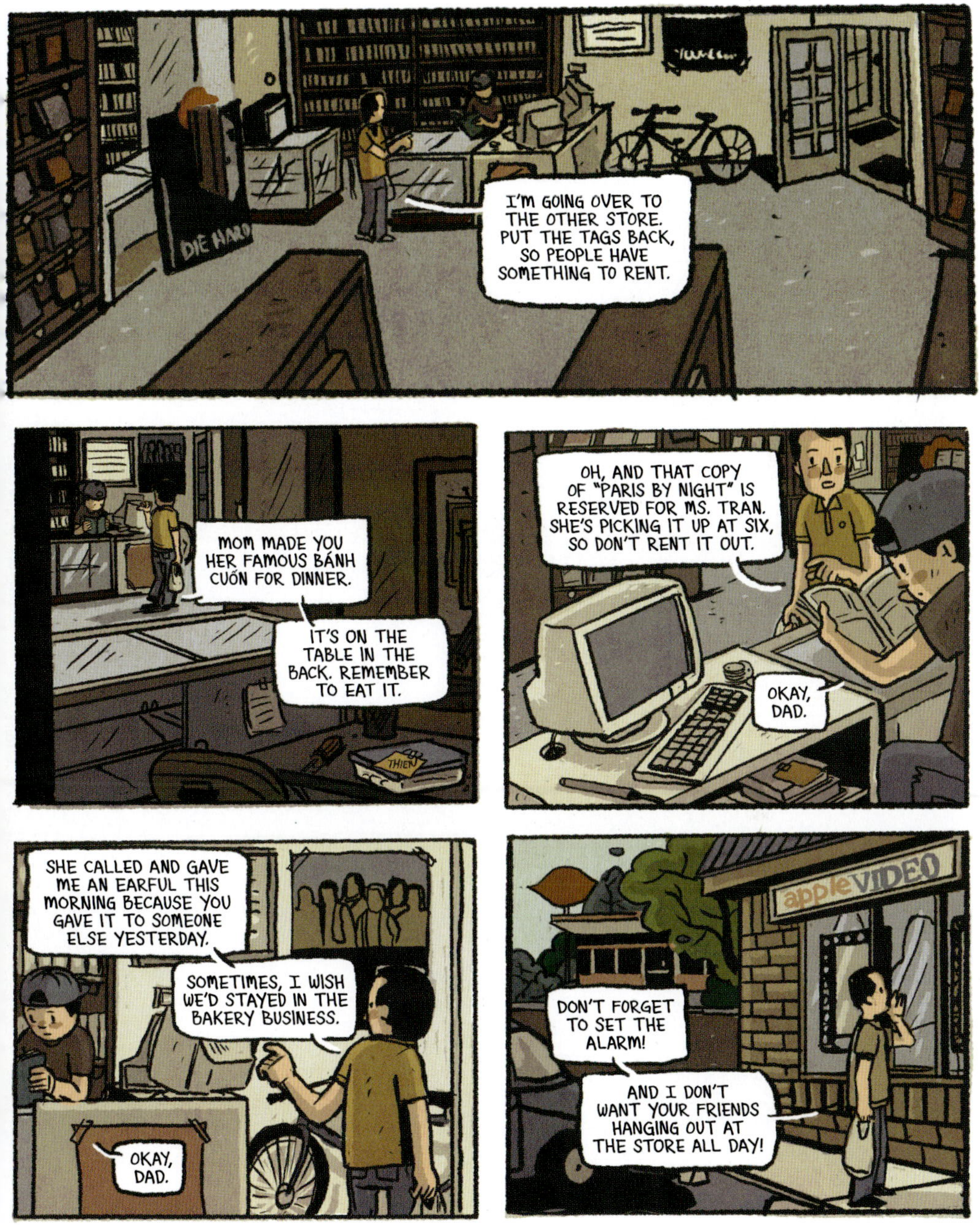
DIE HARD
I'M GOING OVER TO THE OTHER STORE. PUT THE TAGS BACK, SO PEOPLE HAVE SOMETHING TO RENT.
MOM MADE YOU HER FAMOUS BÁNH CUỐN FOR DINNER.
IT'S ON THE TABLE IN THE BACK. REMEMBER TO EAT IT.
THIEN
OH, AND THAT COPY OF "PARIS BY NIGHT" IS RESERVED FOR MS. TRAN. SHE'S PICKING IT UP AT SIX, SO DON'T RENT IT OUT.
OKAY, DAD.
SHE CALLED AND GAVE ME AN EARFUL THIS MORNING BECAUSE YOU GAVE IT TO SOMEONE ELSE YESTERDAY.
SOMETIMES, I WISH WE'D STAYED IN THE BAKERY BUSINESS.
OKAY, DAD.
apple VIDEO
DON'T FORGET TO SET THE ALARM!
AND I DON'T WANT YOUR FRIENDS HANGING OUT AT THE STORE ALL DAY!

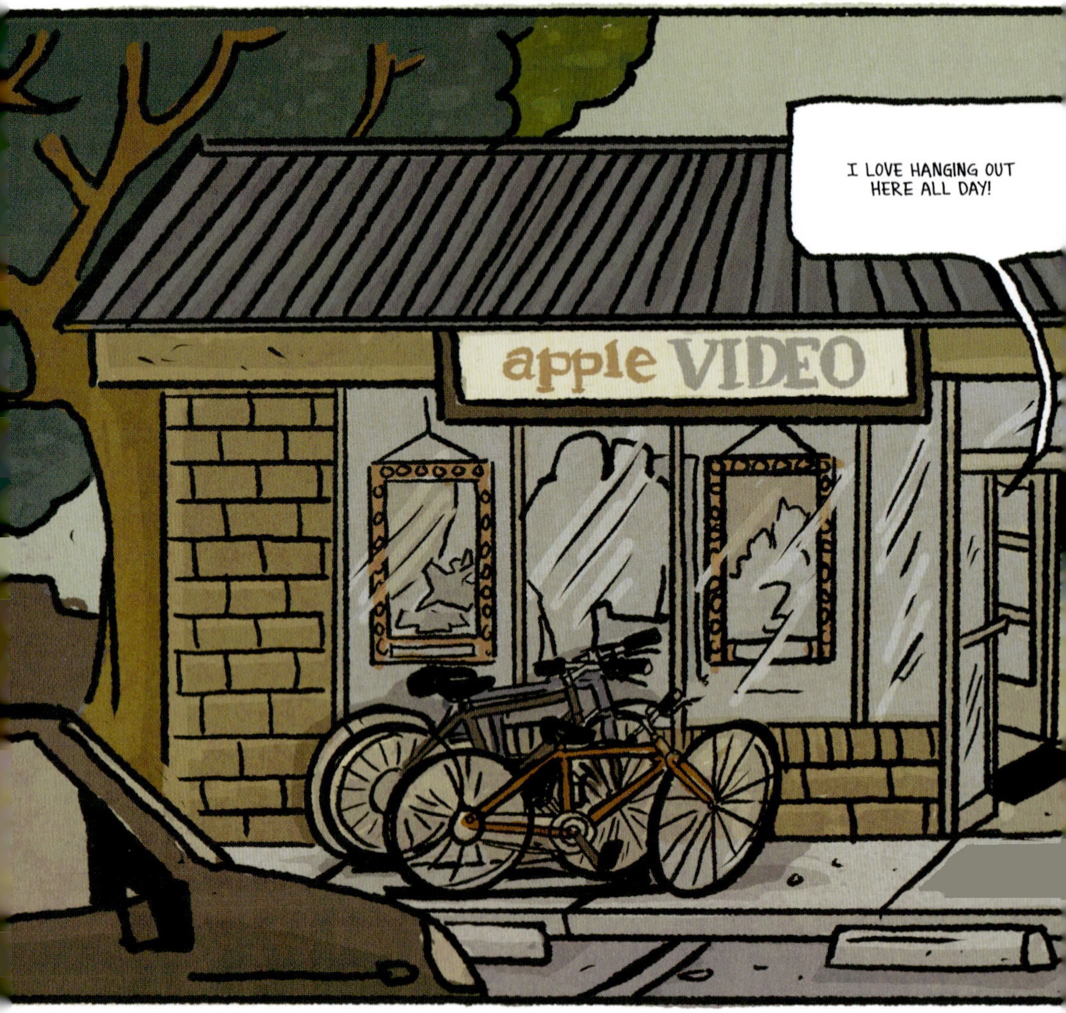
I LOVE HANGING OUT HERE ALL DAY!
apple VIDEO

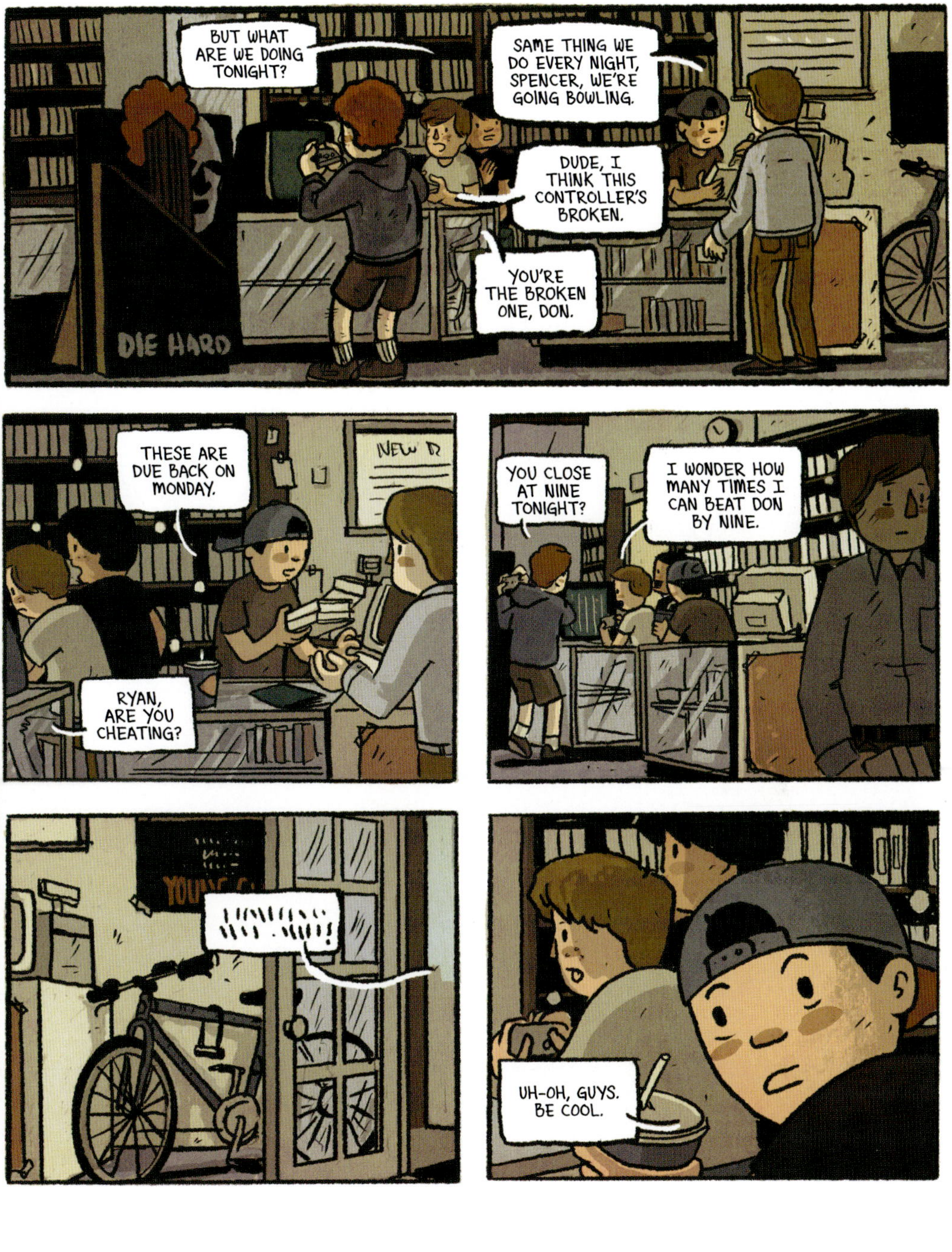
BUT WHAT ARE WE DOING TONIGHT?
SAME THING WE DO EVERY NIGHT, SPENCER, WE'RE GOING BOWLING.
DUDE, I THINK THIS CONTROLLER'S BROKEN.
YOU'RE THE BROKEN ONE, DON.
DIE HARD
THESE ARE DUE BACK ON MONDAY.
RYAN, ARE YOU CHEATING?
YOU CLOSE AT NINE TONIGHT?
I WONDER HOW MANY TIMES I CAN BEAT DON BY NINE.
UH-OH, GUYS. BE COOL.

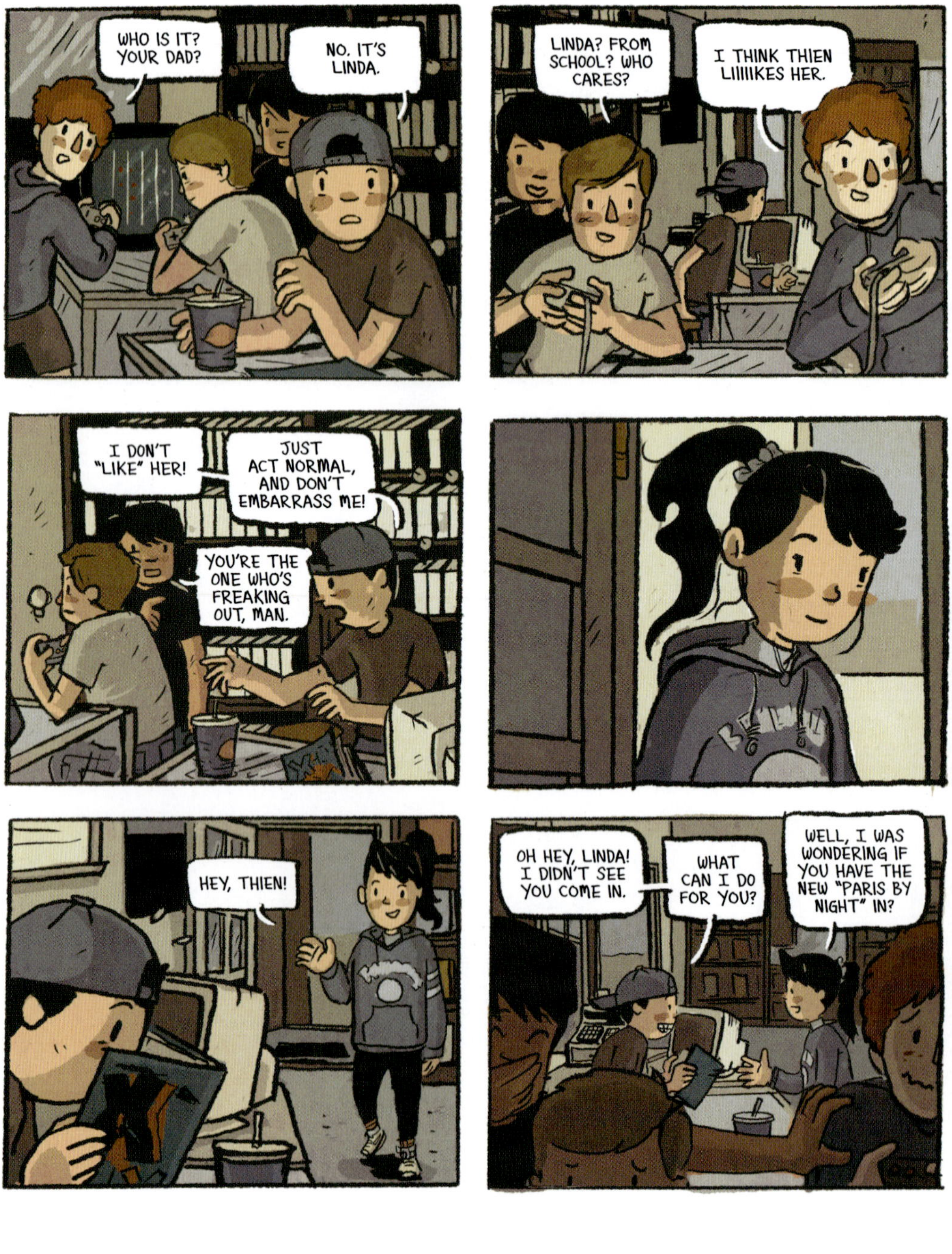
WHO IS IT? YOUR DAD?
NO. IT'S LINDA.
LINDA? FROM SCHOOL? WHO CARES?
I THINK THIEN LIIIIIKES HER.
I DON'T "LIKE" HER!
JUST ACT NORMAL, AND DON'T EMBARRASS ME!
YOU'RE THE ONE WHO'S FREAKING OUT, MAN.
HEY, THIEN!
OH HEY, LINDA! I DIDN'T SEE YOU COME IN.
WHAT CAN I DO FOR YOU?
WELL, I WAS WONDERING IF YOU HAVE THE NEW "PARIS BY NIGHT" IN?

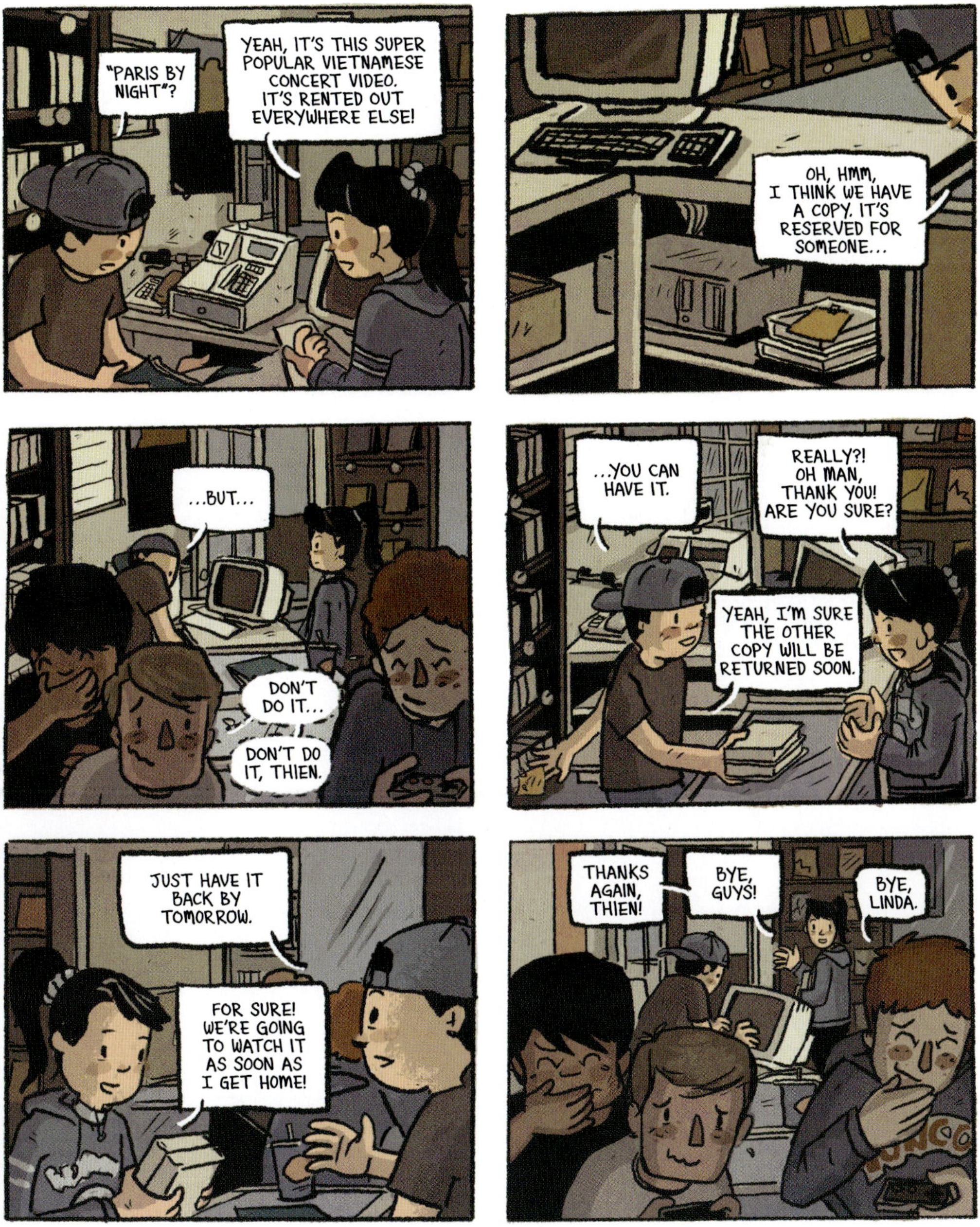
"PARIS BY NIGHT"?
YEAH, IT'S THIS SUPER POPULAR VIETNAMESE CONCERT VIDEO. IT'S RENTED OUT EVERYWHERE ELSE!
OH, HMM, I THINK WE HAVE A COPY. IT'S RESERVED FOR SOMEONE...
...BUT...
DON'T DO IT...
DON'T DO IT, THIEN.
...YOU CAN HAVE IT.
REALLY?! OH MAN, THANK YOU! ARE YOU SURE?
YEAH, I'M SURE THE OTHER COPY WILL BE RETURNED SOON.
JUST HAVE IT BACK BY TOMORROW.
FOR SURE! WE'RE GOING TO WATCH IT AS SOON AS I GET HOME!
THANKS AGAIN, THIEN!
BYE, GUYS!
BYE, LINDA.

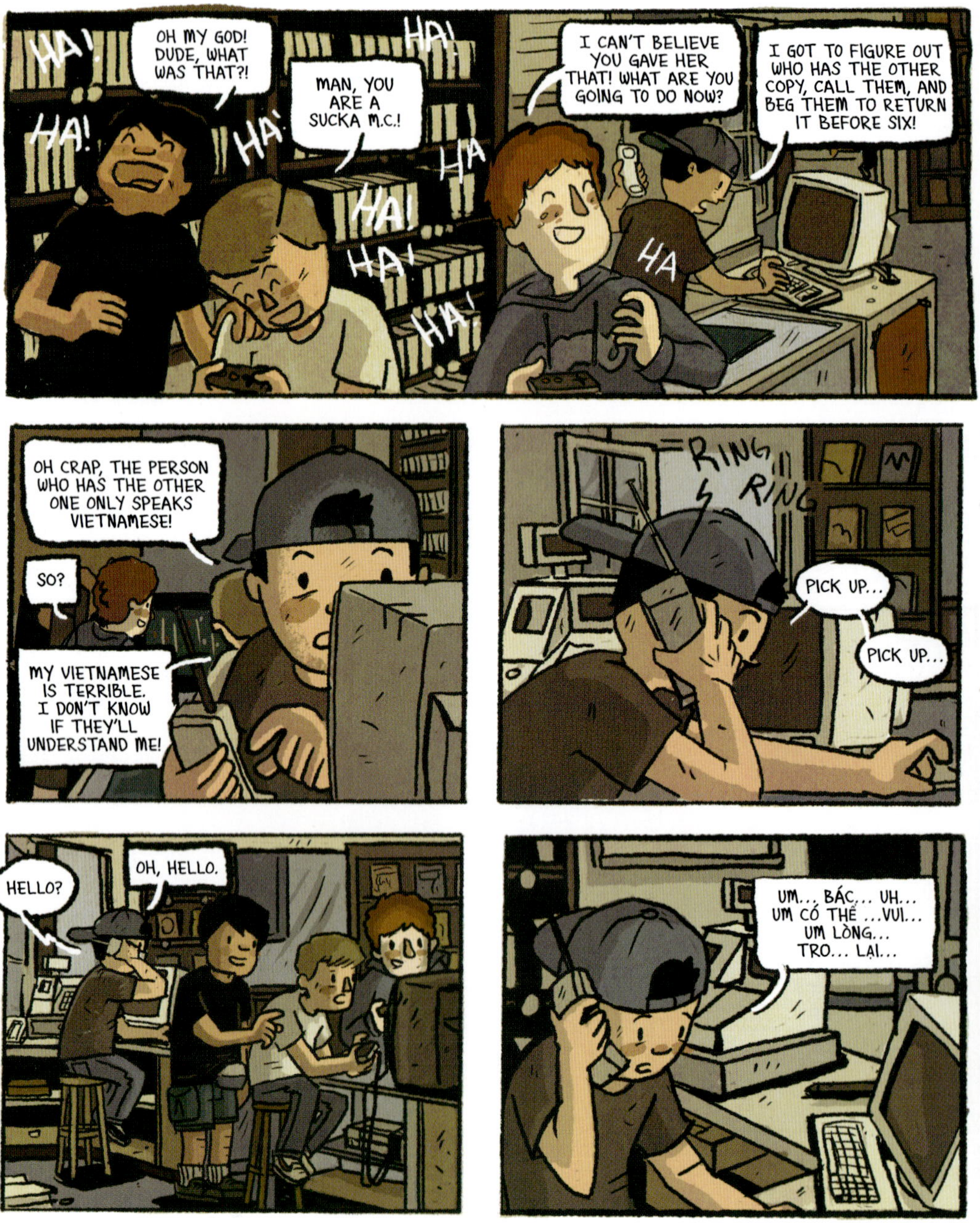
HA! HA!
OH MY GOD! DUDE, WHAT WAS THAT?!
HA!
MAN, YOU ARE A SUCKA M.C.!
HA! HA! HA! HA! HA!
I CAN'T BELIEVE YOU GAVE HER THAT! WHAT ARE YOU GOING TO DO NOW?
I GOT TO FIGURE OUT WHO HAS THE OTHER COPY, CALL THEM, AND BEG THEM TO RETURN IT BEFORE SIX!
HA
OH CRAP, THE PERSON WHO HAS THE OTHER ONE ONLY SPEAKS VIETNAMESE!
SO?
MY VIETNAMESE IS TERRIBLE. I DON'T KNOW IF THEY'LL UNDERSTAND ME!
RING RING
PICK UP...
PICK UP...
HELLO?
OH, HELLO.
UM... BÁC... UH... UM CÓ THỂ ...VUI... UM LÒNG... TRO... LẠI...

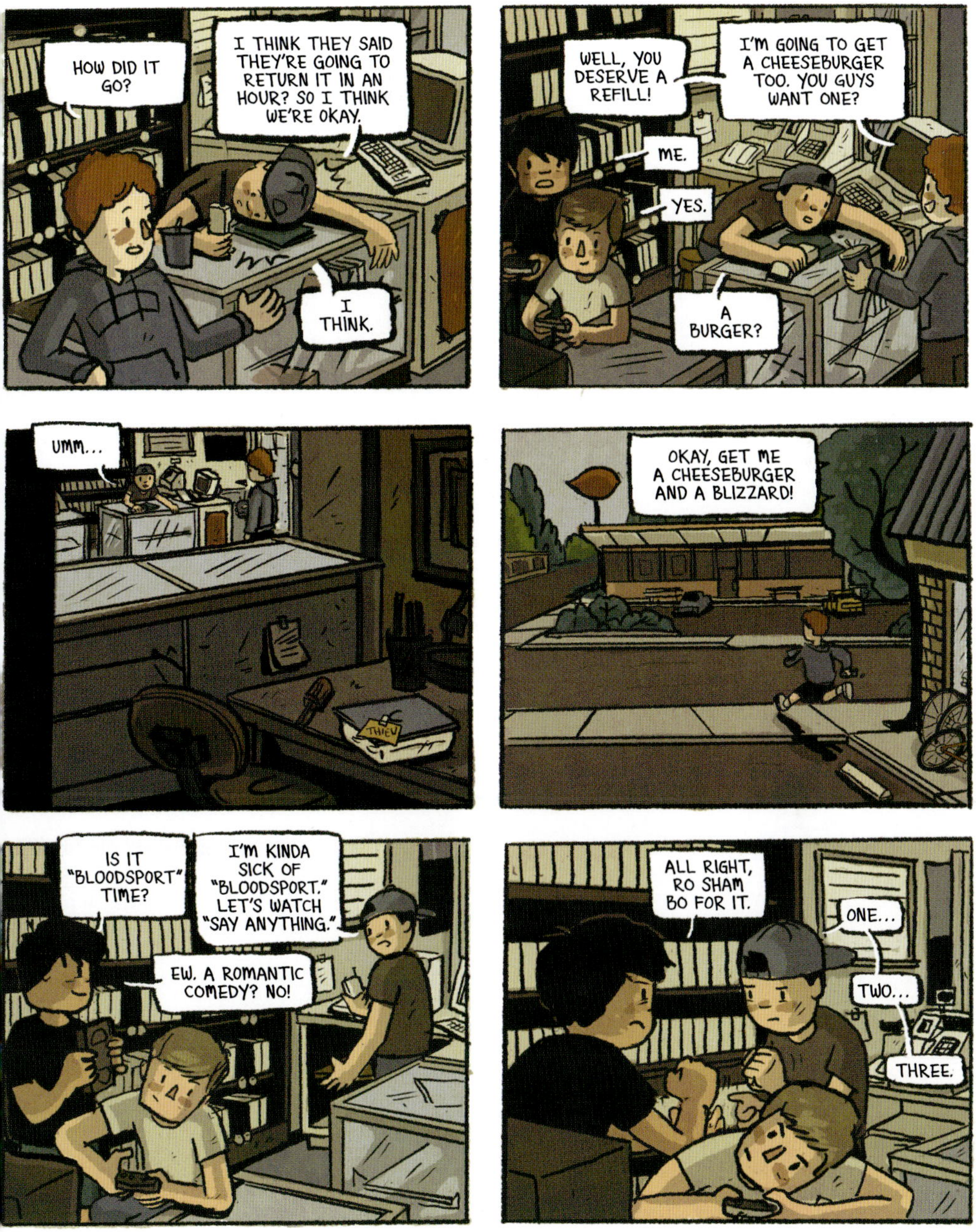
HOW DID IT GO?
I THINK THEY SAID THEY'RE GOING TO RETURN IT IN AN HOUR? SO I THINK WE'RE OKAY.
I THINK.
WELL, YOU DESERVE A REFILL!
I'M GOING TO GET A CHEESEBURGER TOO. YOU GUYS WANT ONE?
ME.
YES.
A BURGER?
UMM...
OKAY, GET ME A CHEESEBURGER AND A BLIZZARD!
IS IT "BLOODSPORT" TIME?
I'M KINDA SICK OF "BLOODSPORT." LET'S WATCH "SAY ANYTHING."
EW. A ROMANTIC COMEDY? NO!
ALL RIGHT, RO SHAM BO FOR IT.
ONE...
TWO...
THREE.

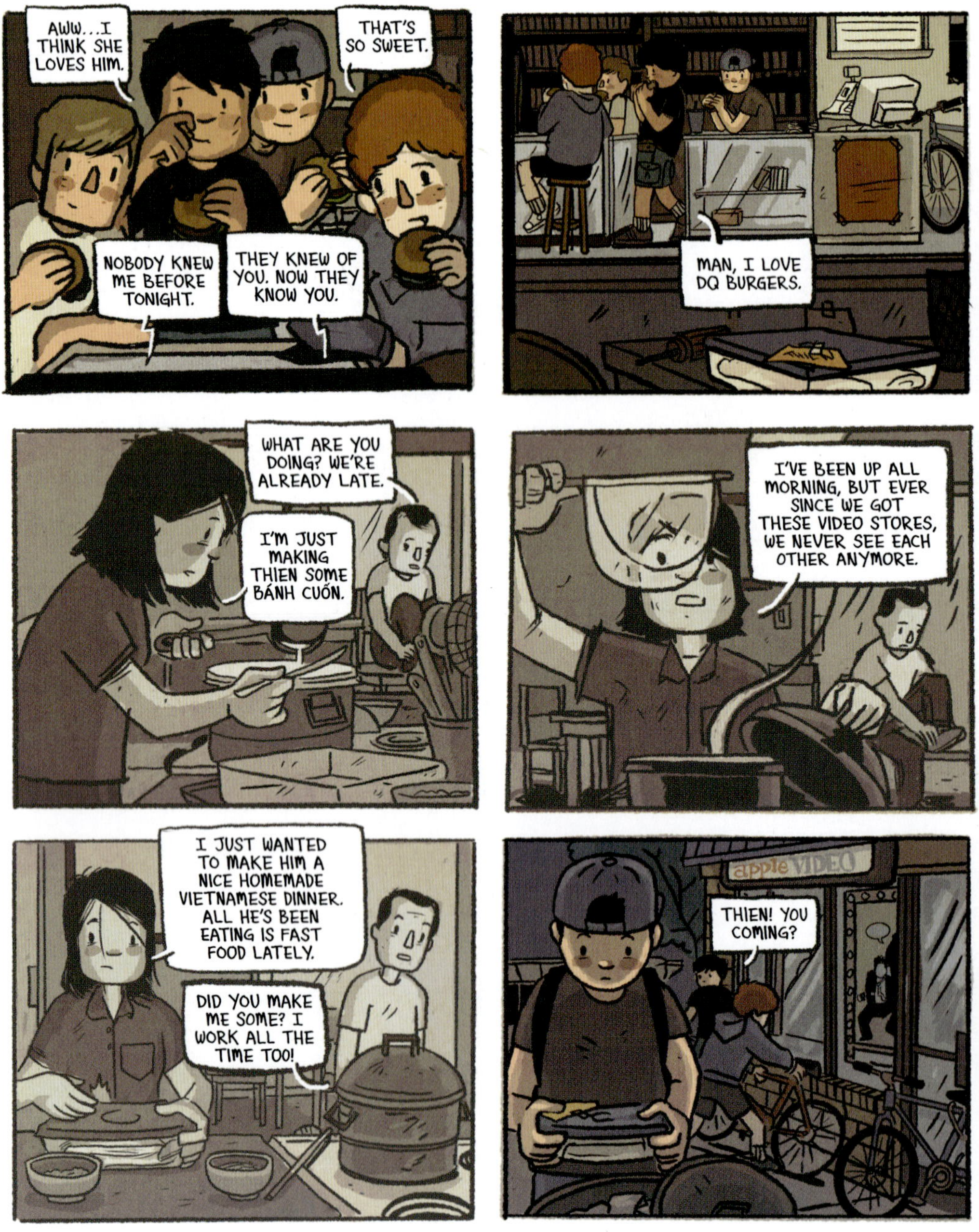
AWW...I THINK SHE LOVES HIM.
THAT'S SO SWEET.
NOBODY KNEW ME BEFORE TONIGHT.
THEY KNEW OF YOU. NOW THEY KNOW YOU.
MAN, I LOVE DQ BURGERS.
WHAT ARE YOU DOING? WE'RE ALREADY LATE.
I'M JUST MAKING THIEN SOME BÁNH CUỐN.
I'VE BEEN UP ALL MORNING, BUT EVER SINCE WE GOT THESE VIDEO STORES, WE NEVER SEE EACH OTHER ANYMORE.
I JUST WANTED TO MAKE HIM A NICE HOMEMADE VIETNAMESE DINNER. ALL HE'S BEEN EATING IS FAST FOOD LATELY.
DID YOU MAKE ME SOME? I WORK ALL THE TIME TOO!
apple VIDEO
THIEN! YOU COMING?

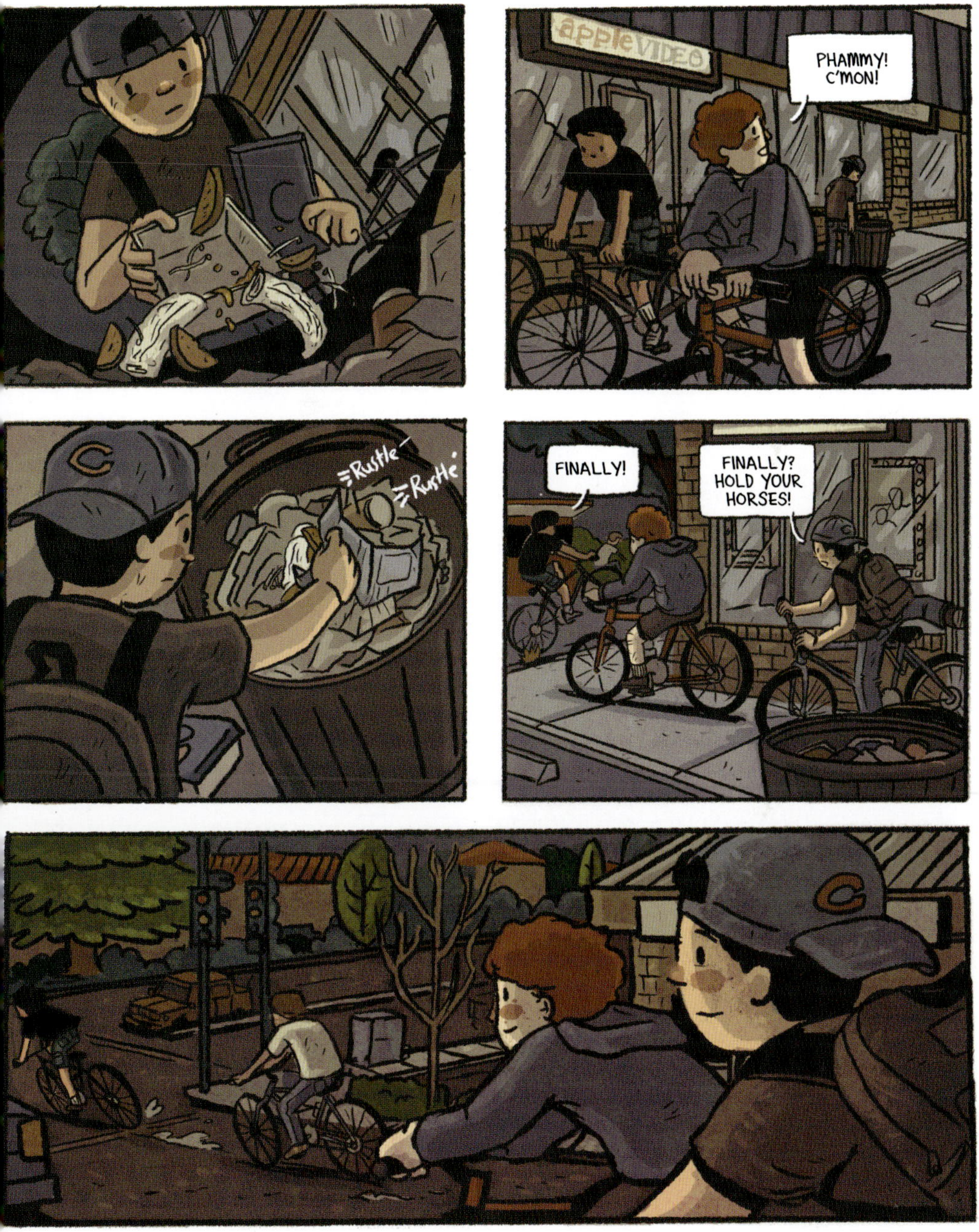
applevideo
PHAMMY! C'MON!
RUSTLE RUSTLE
FINALLY!
FINALLY? HOLD YOUR HORSES!

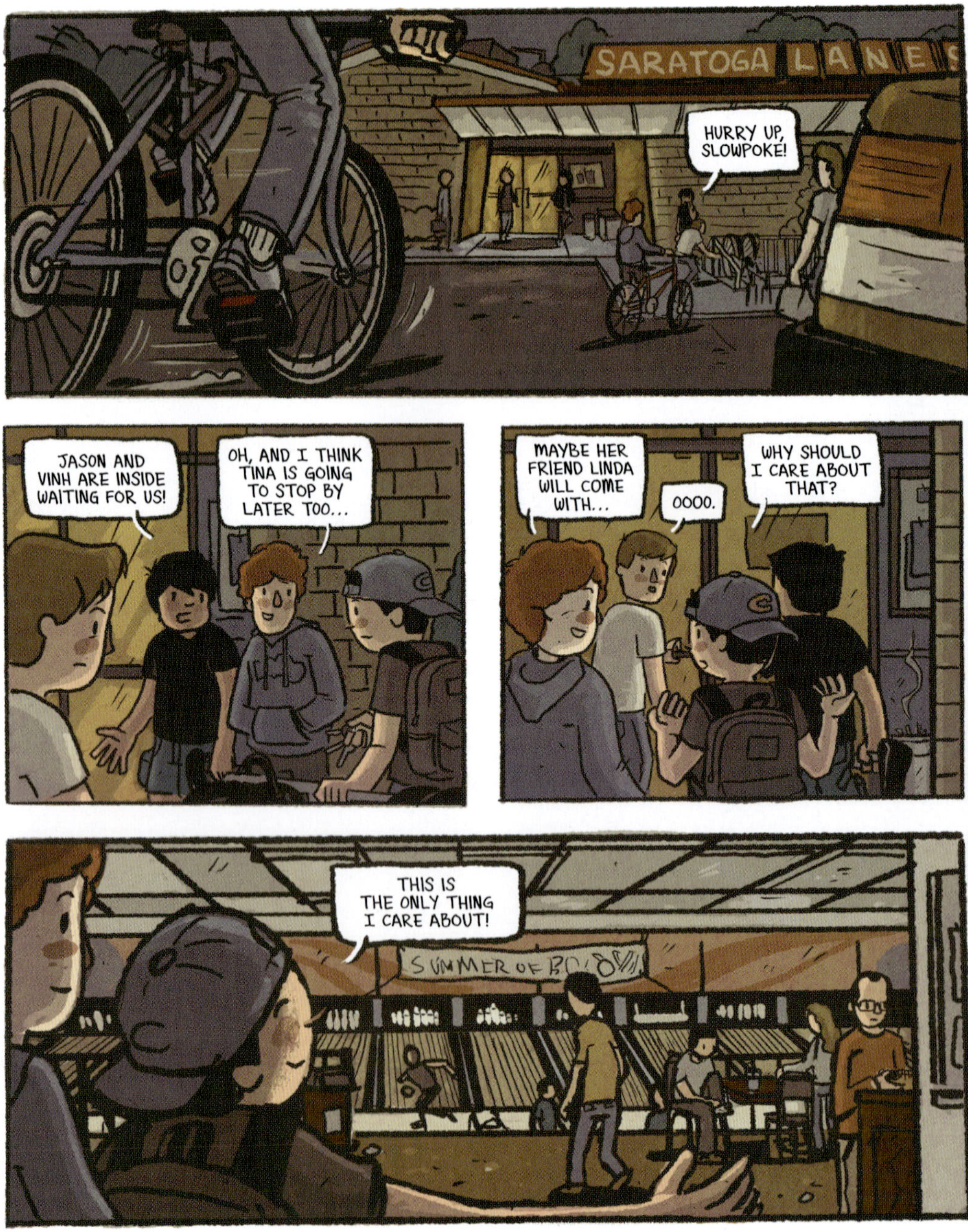
SARATOGA LANE
HURRY UP, SLOWPOKE!
JASON AND VINH ARE INSIDE WAITING FOR US!
OH, AND I THINK TINA IS GOING TO STOP BY LATER TOO...
MAYBE HER FRIEND LINDA WILL COME WITH...
OOOO.
WHY SHOULD I CARE ABOUT THAT?
THIS IS THE ONLY THING I CARE ABOUT!

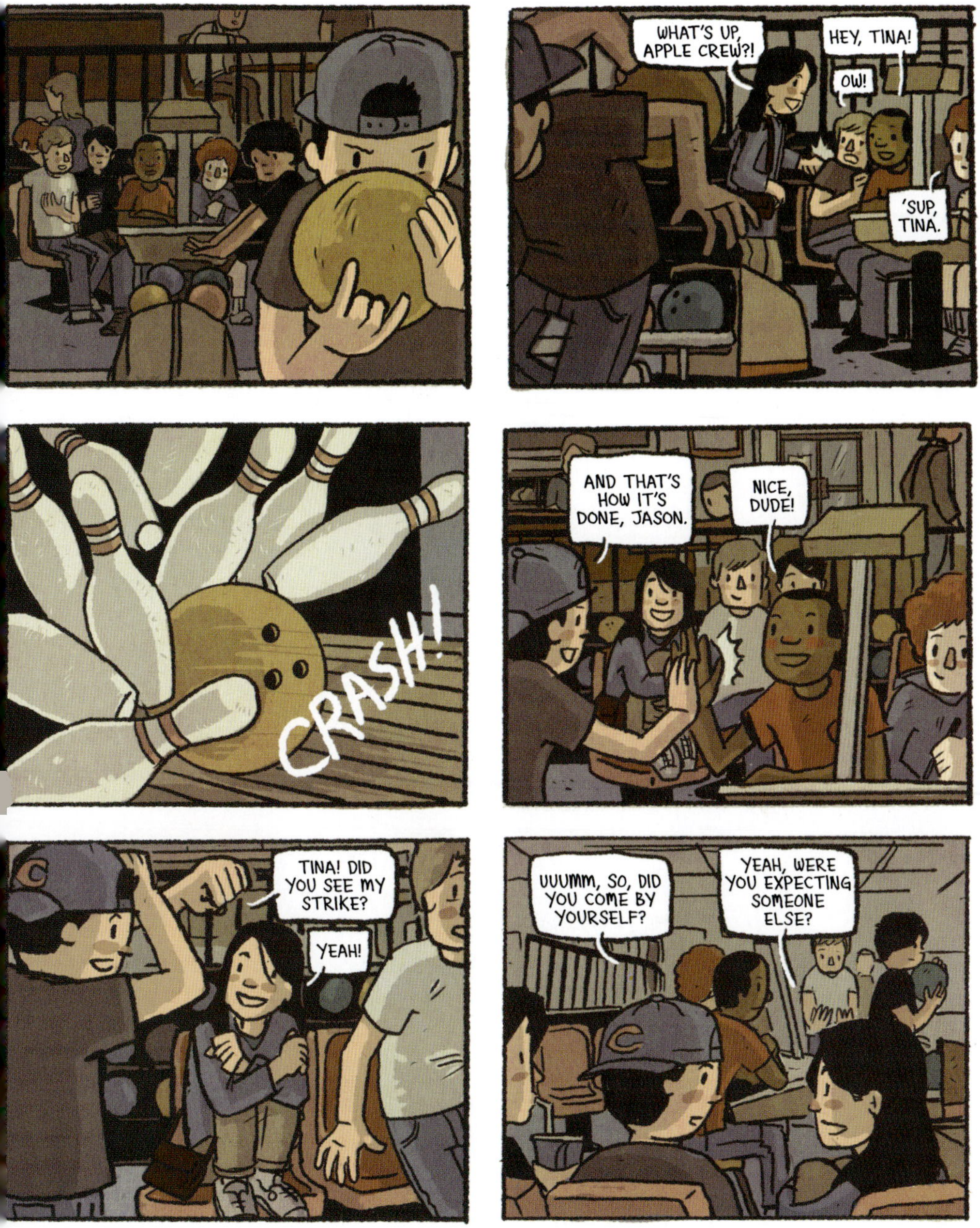
WHAT'S UP, APPLE CREW?!
HEY, TINA!
OW!
'SUP, TINA.
CRASH!
AND THAT'S HOW IT'S DONE, JASON.
NICE, DUDE!
TINA! DID YOU SEE MY STRIKE?
YEAH!
UUUMM, SO, DID YOU COME BY YOURSELF?
YEAH, WERE YOU EXPECTING SOMEONE ELSE?

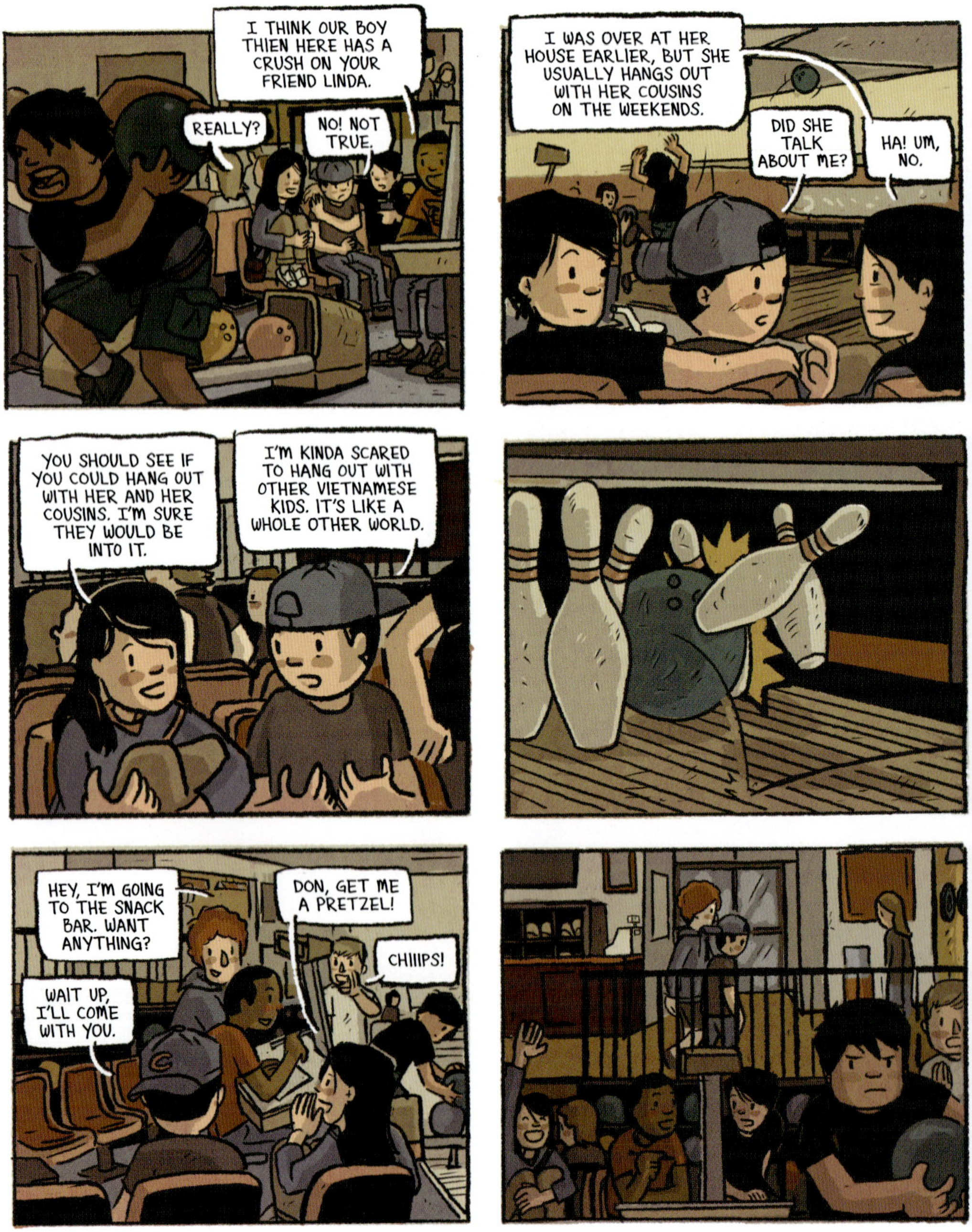
I THINK OUR BOY THIEN HERE HAS A CRUSH ON YOUR FRIEND LINDA.
REALLY?
NO! NOT TRUE.
I WAS OVER AT HER HOUSE EARLIER, BUT SHE USUALLY HANGS OUT WITH HER COUSINS ON THE WEEKENDS.
DID SHE TALK ABOUT ME?
HA! UM, NO.
YOU SHOULD SEE IF YOU COULD HANG OUT WITH HER AND HER COUSINS. I'M SURE THEY WOULD BE INTO IT.
I'M KINDA SCARED TO HANG OUT WITH OTHER VIETNAMESE KIDS. IT'S LIKE A WHOLE OTHER WORLD.
HEY, I'M GOING TO THE SNACK BAR. WANT ANYTHING?
DON, GET ME A PRETZEL!
CHIIIPS!
WAIT UP, I'LL COME WITH YOU.

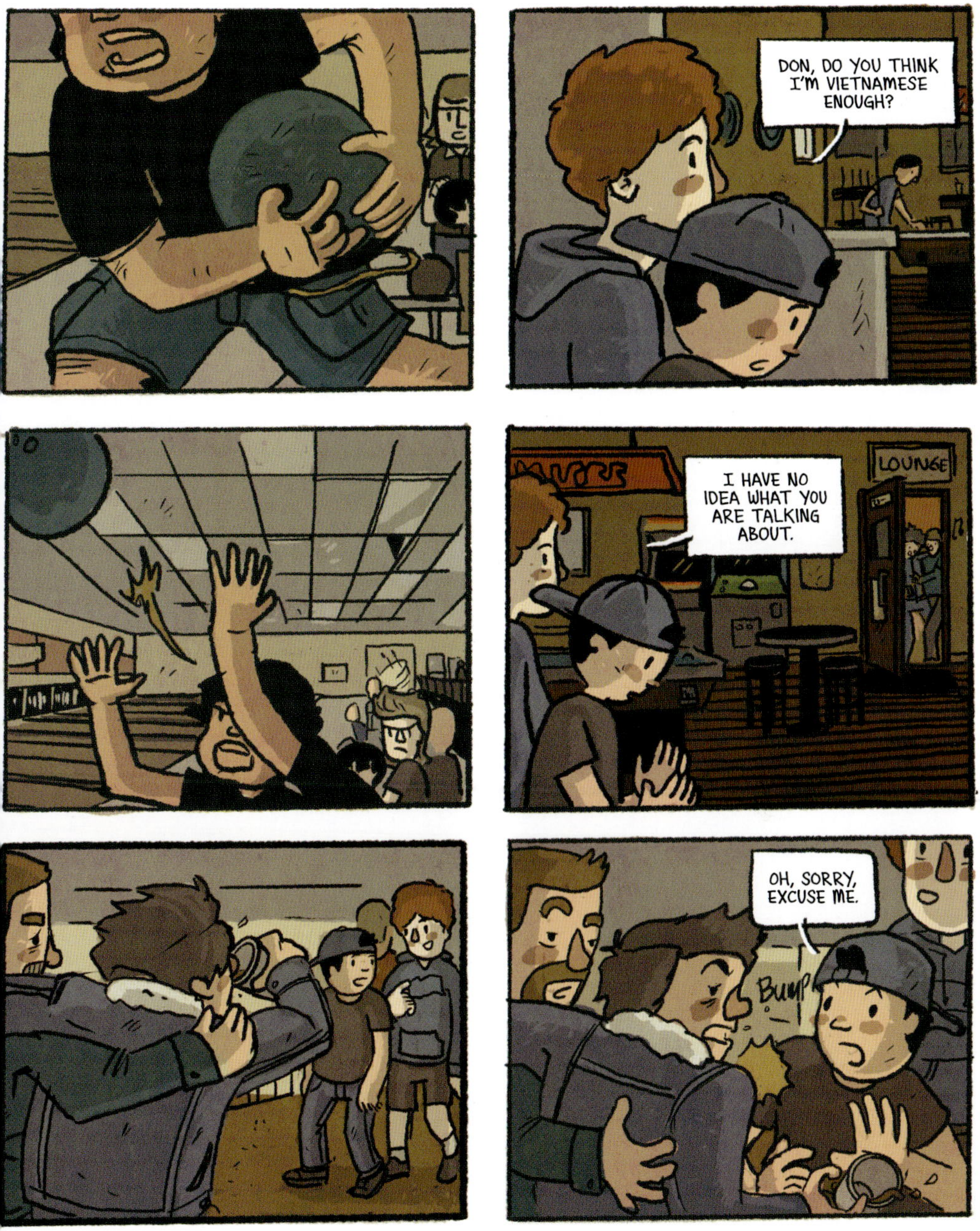
DON, DO YOU THINK I'M VIETNAMESE ENOUGH?
I HAVE NO IDEA WHAT YOU ARE TALKING ABOUT.
LOUNGE
OH, SORRY, EXCUSE ME.
BUMP

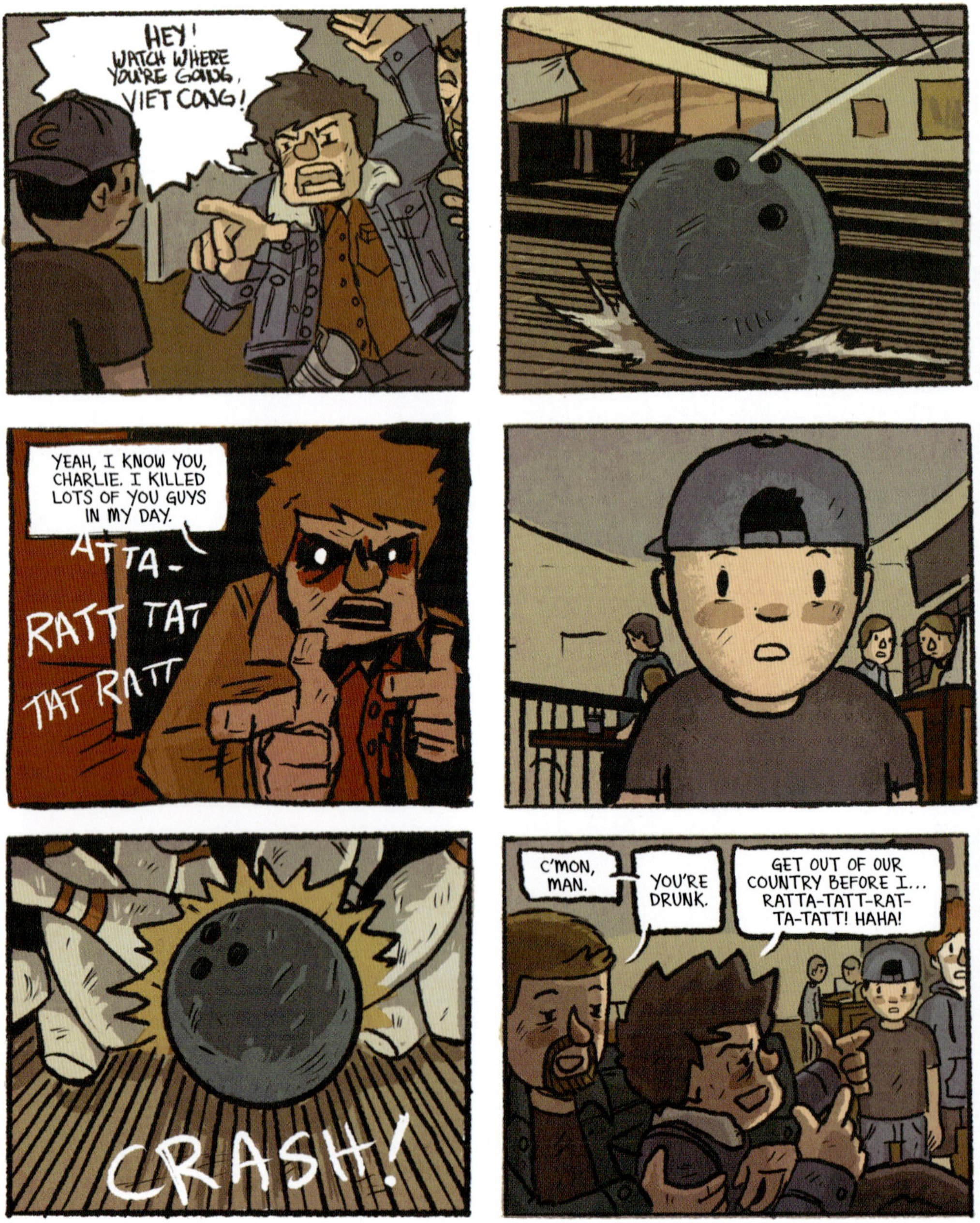
HEY! WATCH WHERE YOU'RE GOING, VIET CONG!
YEAH, I KNOW YOU, CHARLIE. I KILLED LOTS OF YOU GUYS IN MY DAY.
ATTA-
RATT TAT
TAT RATT
CRASH!
C'MON, MAN.
YOU'RE DRUNK.
GET OUT OF OUR COUNTRY BEFORE I... RATTA-TATT-RAT-TA-TATT! HAHA!

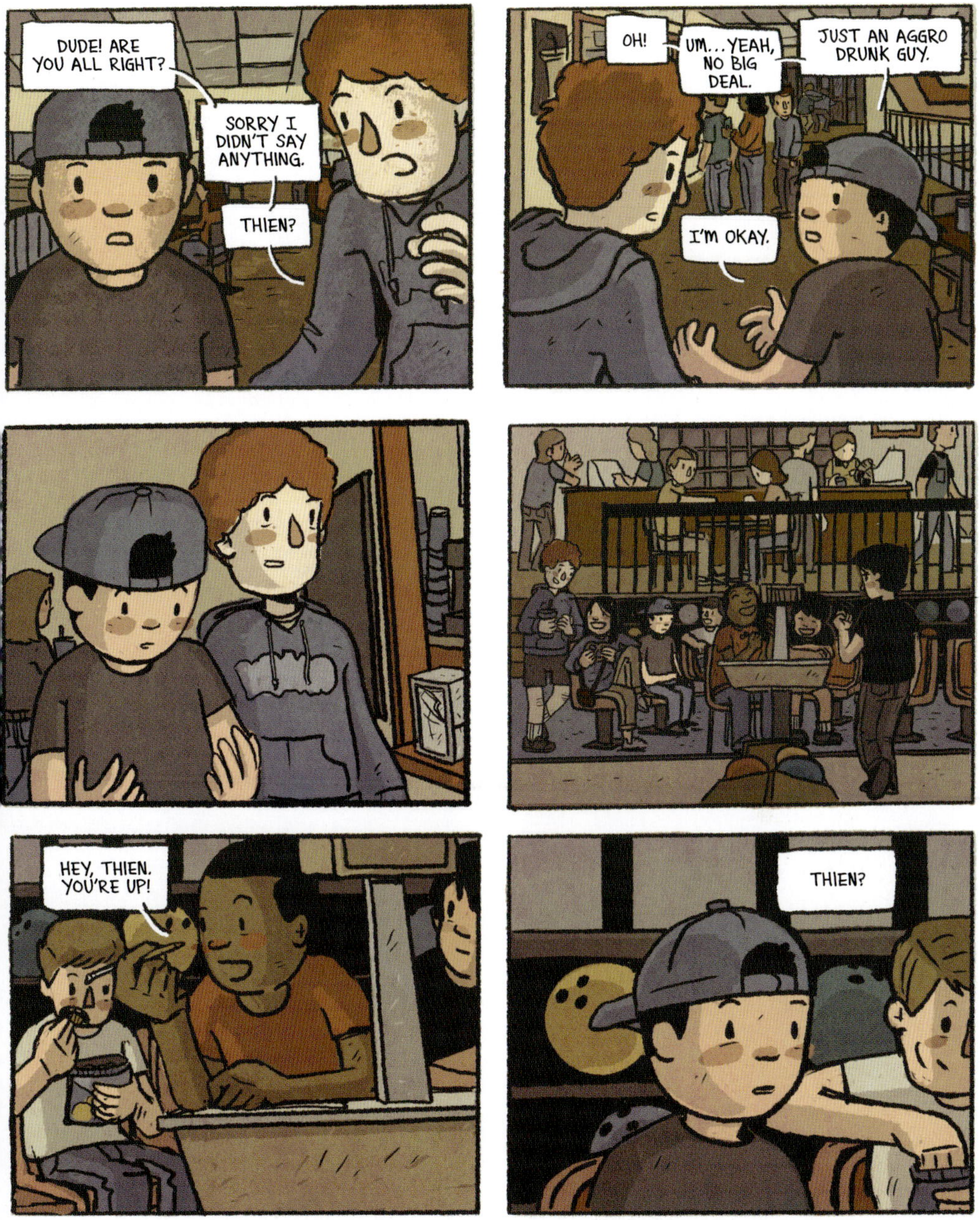
DUDE! ARE YOU ALL RIGHT?
SORRY I DIDN'T SAY ANYTHING.
THIEN?
OH!
UM...YEAH, NO BIG DEAL.
JUST AN AGGRO DRUNK GUY.
I'M OKAY.
HEY, THIEN. YOU'RE UP!
THIEN?

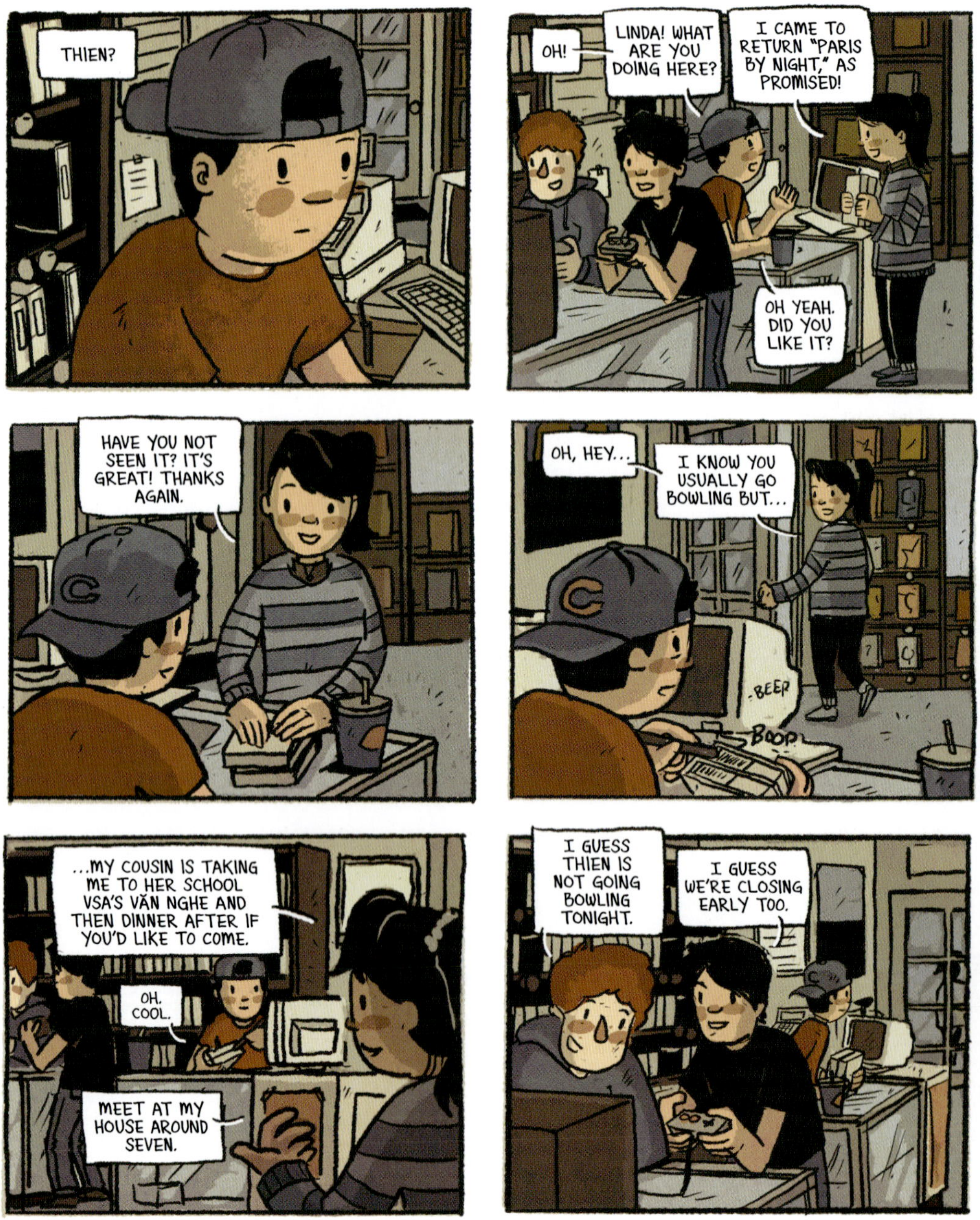
THIEN?
OH!
LINDA! WHAT ARE YOU DOING HERE?
I CAME TO RETURN "PARIS BY NIGHT," AS PROMISED!
OH YEAH. DID YOU LIKE IT?
HAVE YOU NOT SEEN IT? IT'S GREAT! THANKS AGAIN.
OH, HEY...
I KNOW YOU USUALLY GO BOWLING BUT...
BEEP
BOOP
...MY COUSIN IS TAKING ME TO HER SCHOOL VSA'S VĂN NGHE AND THEN DINNER AFTER IF YOU'D LIKE TO COME.
OH. COOL.
MEET AT MY HOUSE AROUND SEVEN.
I GUESS THIEN IS NOT GOING BOWLING TONIGHT.
I GUESS WE'RE CLOSING EARLY TOO.

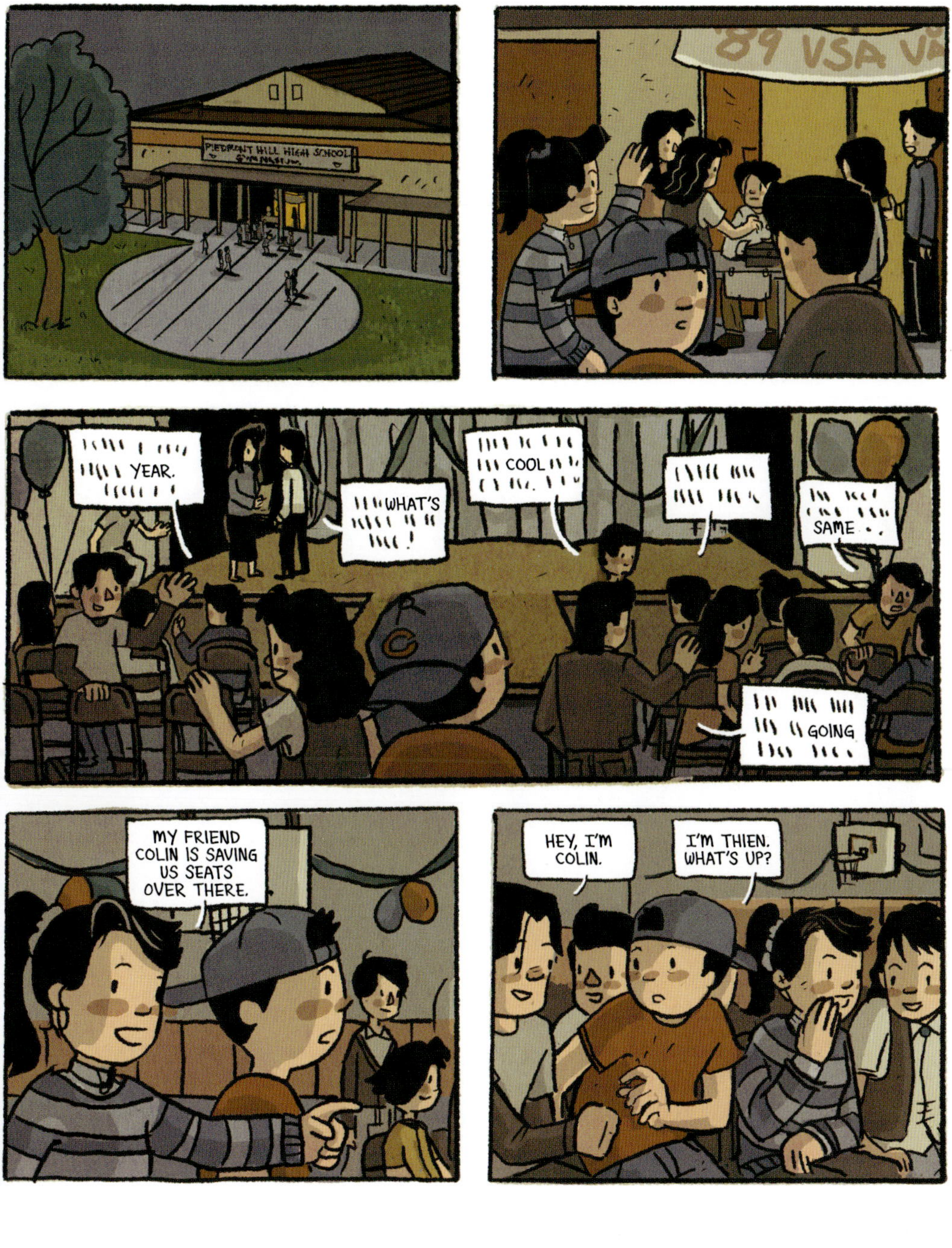
PIEDMONT HILL HIGH SCHOOL
'89 VSA
YEAR.
WHAT'S
COOL
SAME
GOING
MY FRIEND COLIN IS SAVING US SEATS OVER THERE.
HEY, I'M COLIN.
I'M THIEN. WHAT'S UP?

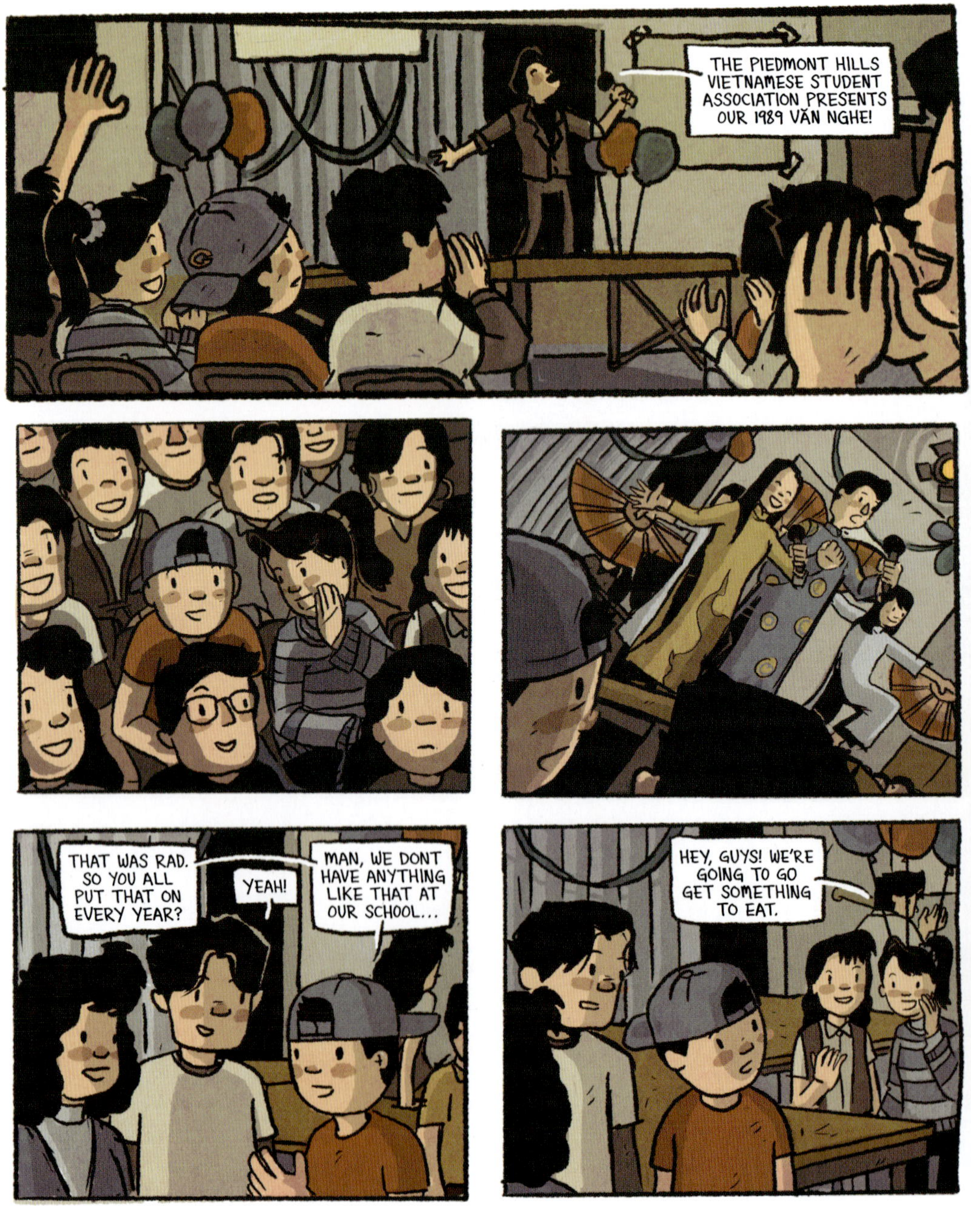
THE PIEDMONT HILLS VIETNAMESE STUDENT ASSOCIATION PRESENTS OUR 1989 VĂN NGHE!
THAT WAS RAD. SO YOU ALL PUT THAT ON EVERY YEAR?
YEAH!
MAN, WE DONT HAVE ANYTHING LIKE THAT AT OUR SCHOOL...
HEY, GUYS! WE'RE GOING TO GO GET SOMETHING TO EAT.

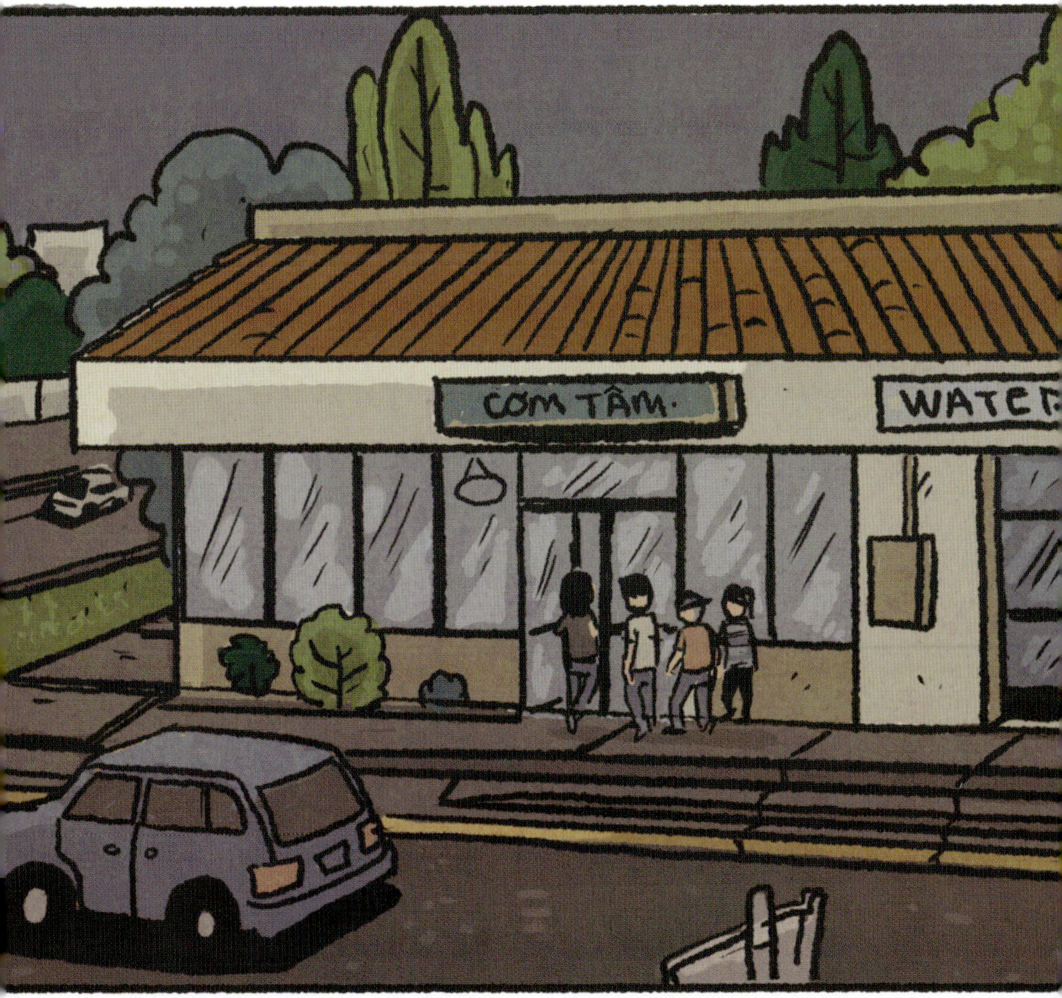
CƠM TẤM.
WATER

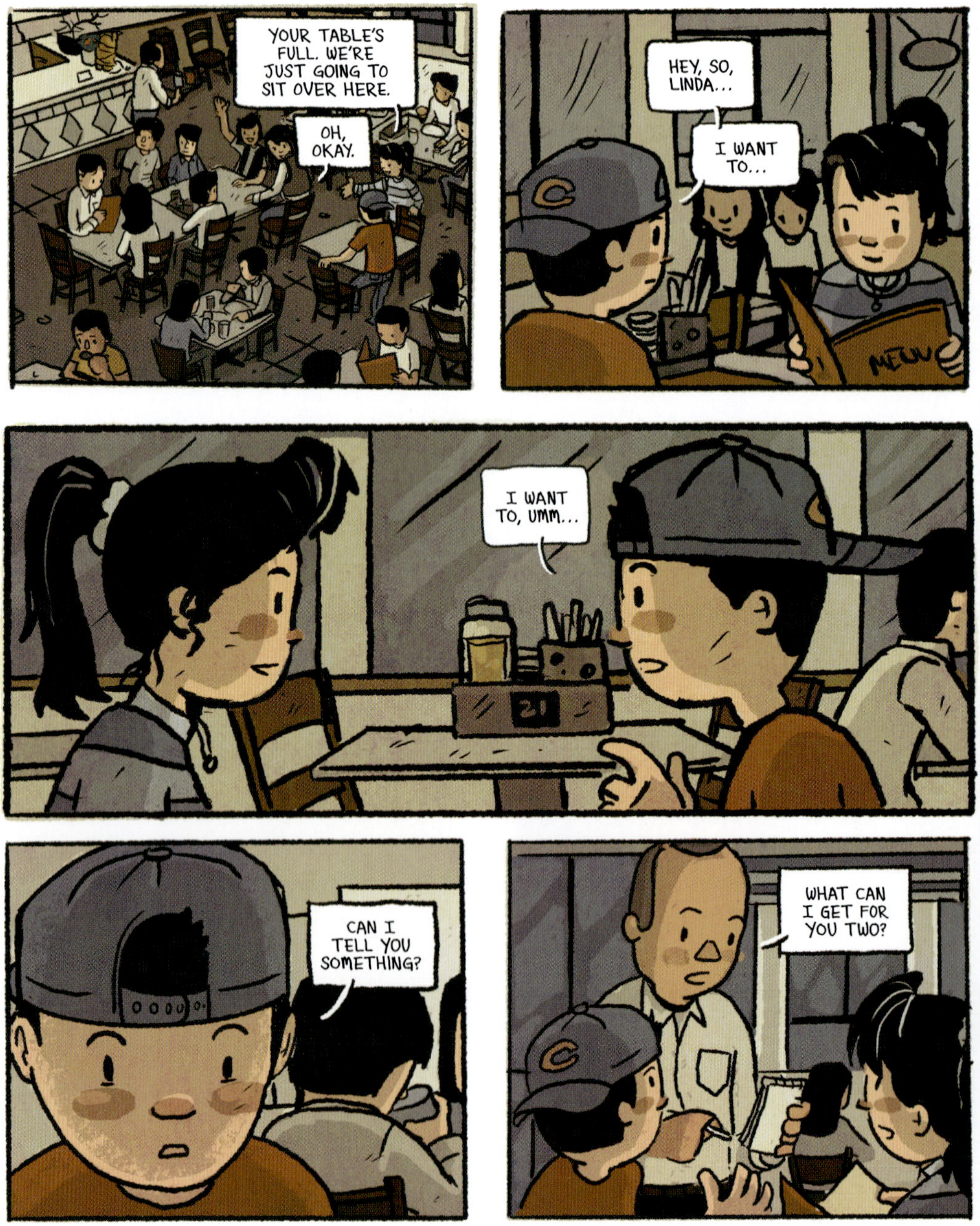
YOUR TABLE'S FULL. WE'RE JUST GOING TO SIT OVER HERE.
OH, OKAY.
HEY, SO, LINDA...
I WANT TO...
MENU
I WANT TO, UMM...
21
CAN I TELL YOU SOMETHING?
WHAT CAN I GET FOR YOU TWO?

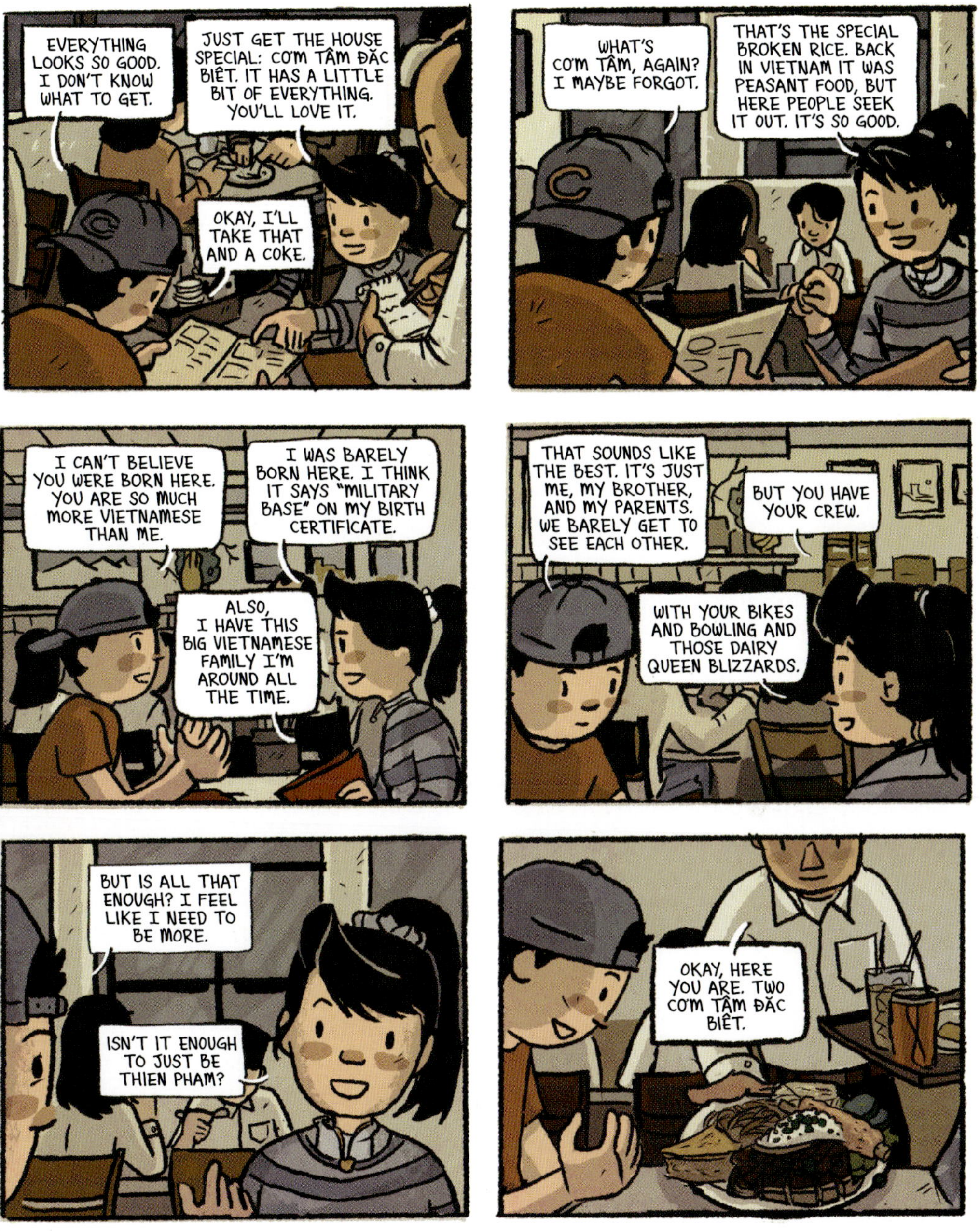
EVERYTHING LOOKS SO GOOD. I DON'T KNOW WHAT TO GET.
JUST GET THE HOUSE SPECIAL: CƠM TÂM ĐĂC BIÊT. IT HAS A LITTLE BIT OF EVERYTHING. YOU'LL LOVE IT.
OKAY, I'LL TAKE THAT AND A COKE.
WHAT'S CƠM TÂM, AGAIN? I MAYBE FORGOT.
THAT'S THE SPECIAL BROKEN RICE. BACK IN VIETNAM IT WAS PEASANT FOOD, BUT HERE PEOPLE SEEK IT OUT. IT'S SO GOOD.
I CAN'T BELIEVE YOU WERE BORN HERE. YOU ARE SO MUCH MORE VIETNAMESE THAN ME.
I WAS BARELY BORN HERE. I THINK IT SAYS "MILITARY BASE" ON MY BIRTH CERTIFICATE.
ALSO, I HAVE THIS BIG VIETNAMESE FAMILY I'M AROUND ALL THE TIME.
THAT SOUNDS LIKE THE BEST. IT'S JUST ME, MY BROTHER, AND MY PARENTS. WE BARELY GET TO SEE EACH OTHER.
BUT YOU HAVE YOUR CREW.
WITH YOUR BIKES AND BOWLING AND THOSE DAIRY QUEEN BLIZZARDS.
BUT IS ALL THAT ENOUGH? I FEEL LIKE I NEED TO BE MORE.
ISN'T IT ENOUGH TO JUST BE THIEN PHAM?
OKAY, HERE YOU ARE. TWO CƠM TÂM ĐĂC BIÊT.

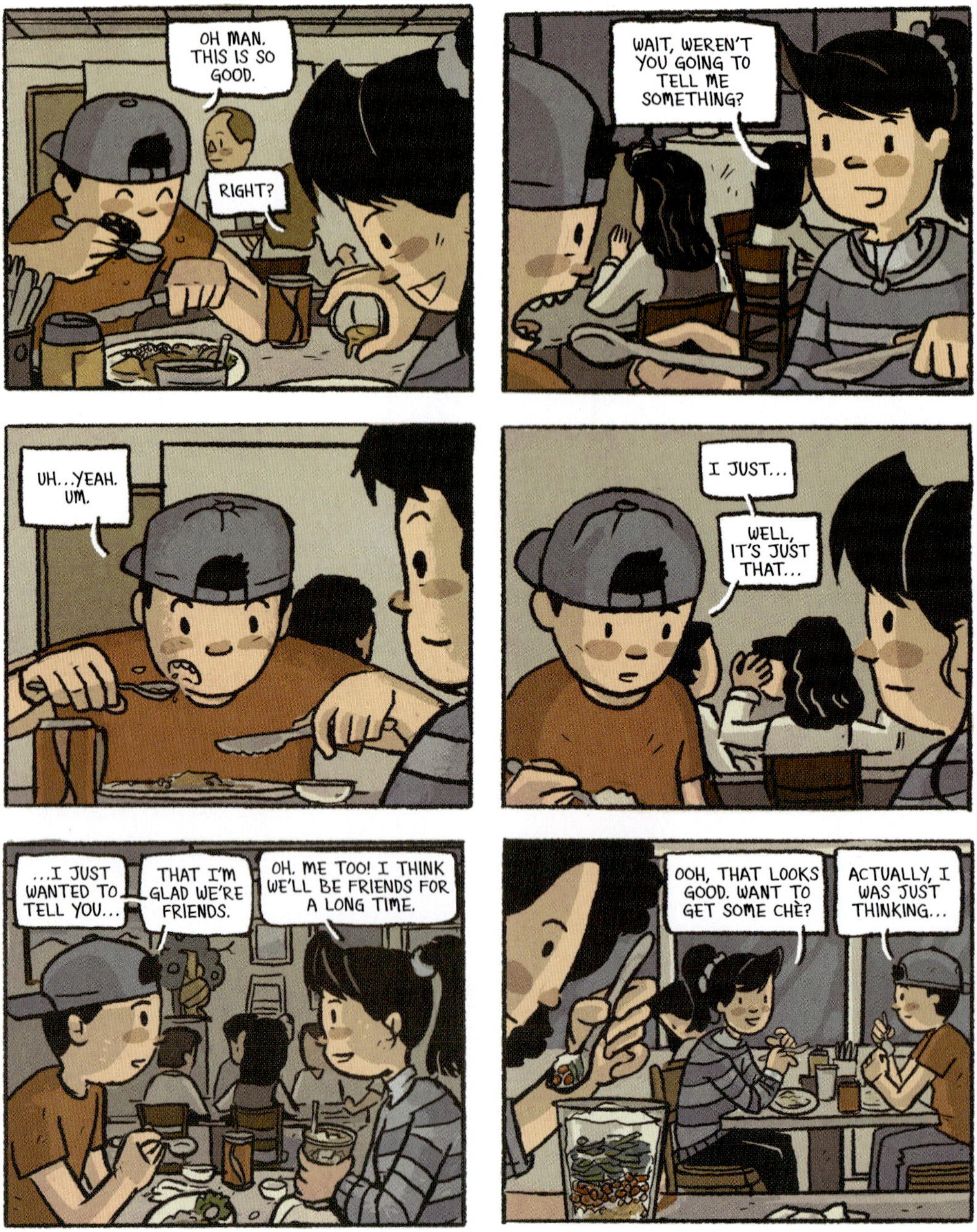
OH MAN. THIS IS SO GOOD.
RIGHT?
WAIT, WEREN'T YOU GOING TO TELL ME SOMETHING?
UH...YEAH. UM.
I JUST...
WELL, IT'S JUST THAT...
...I JUST WANTED TO TELL YOU...
THAT I'M GLAD WE'RE FRIENDS.
OH. ME TOO! I THINK WE'LL BE FRIENDS FOR A LONG TIME.
OOH, THAT LOOKS GOOD. WANT TO GET SOME CHÈ?
ACTUALLY, I WAS JUST THINKING...

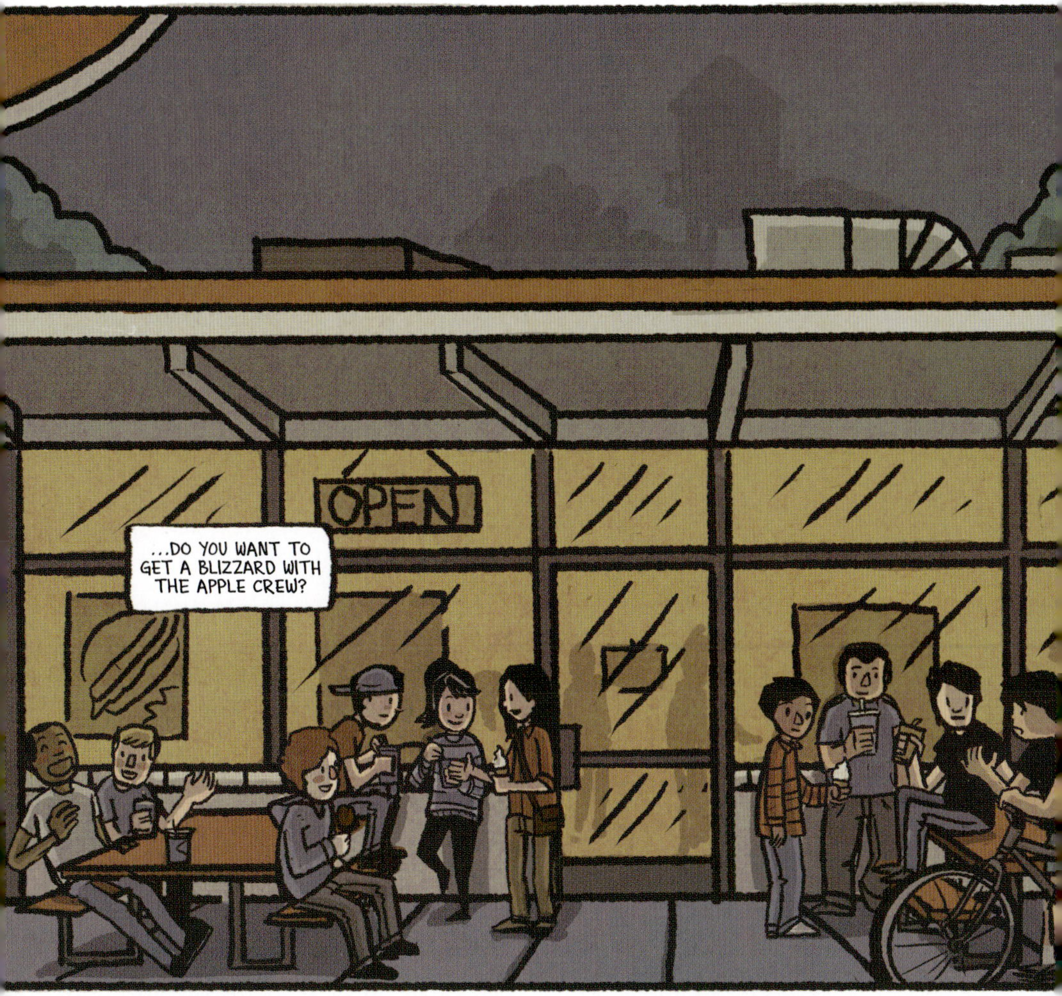
OPEN
...DO YOU WANT TO GET A BLIZZARD WITH THE APPLE CREW?

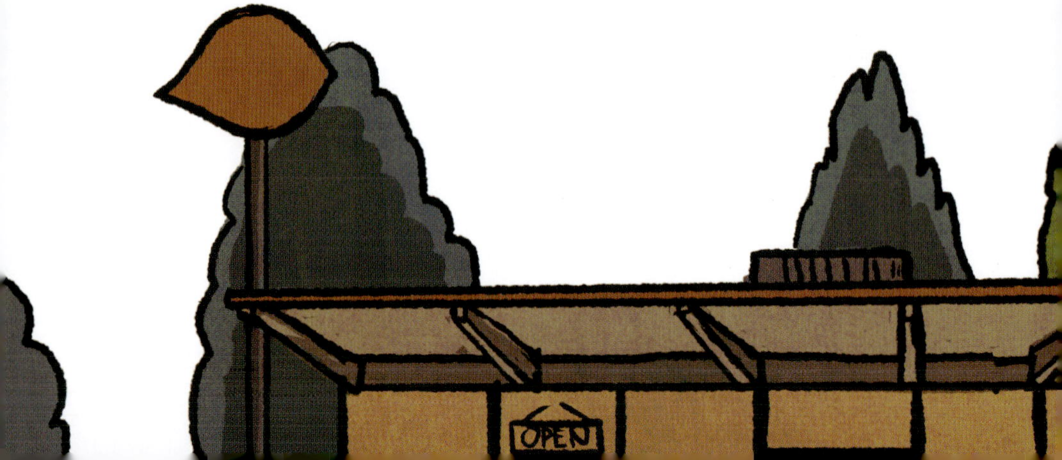
OPEN

CHAPTER 8: RICE AND FISH

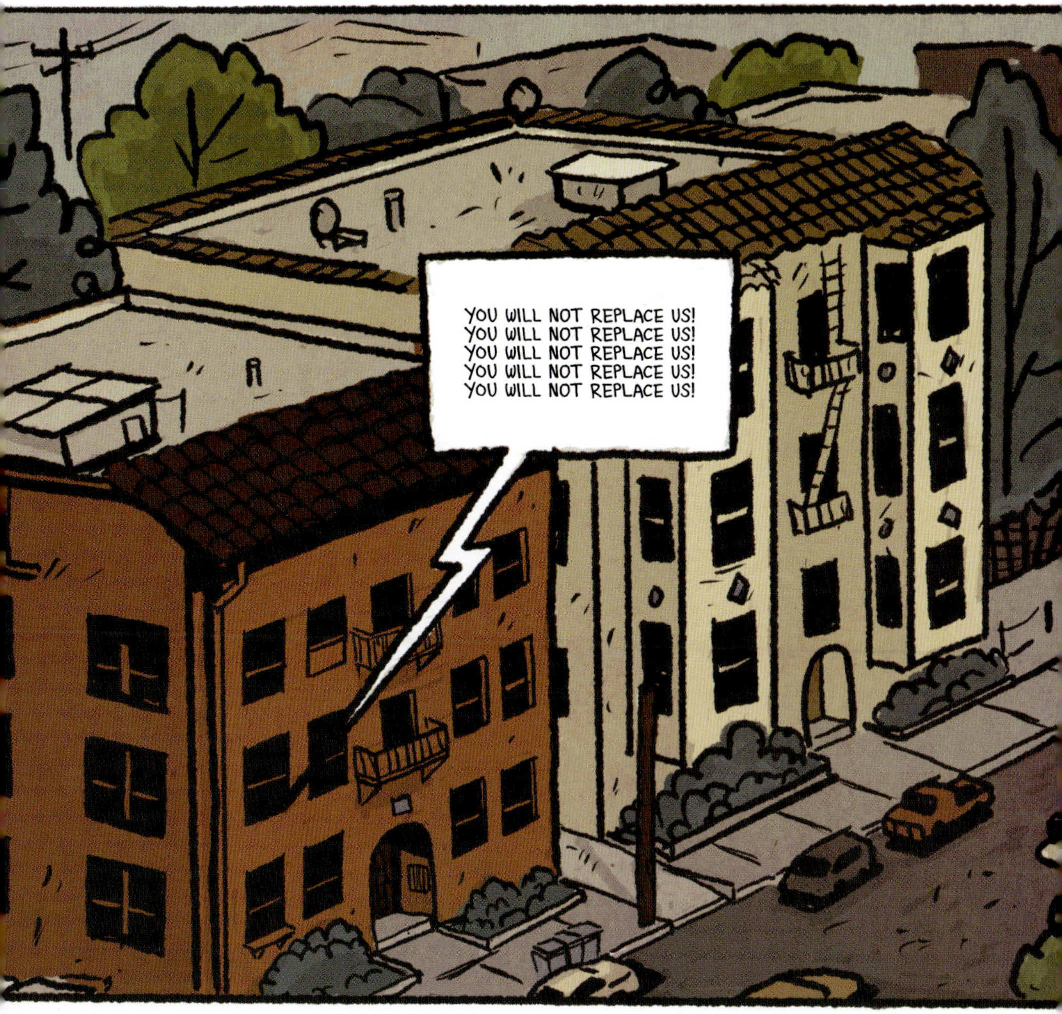
YOU WILL NOT REPLACE US!
YOU WILL NOT REPLACE US!
YOU WILL NOT REPLACE US!
YOU WILL NOT REPLACE US!
YOU WILL NOT REPLACE US!

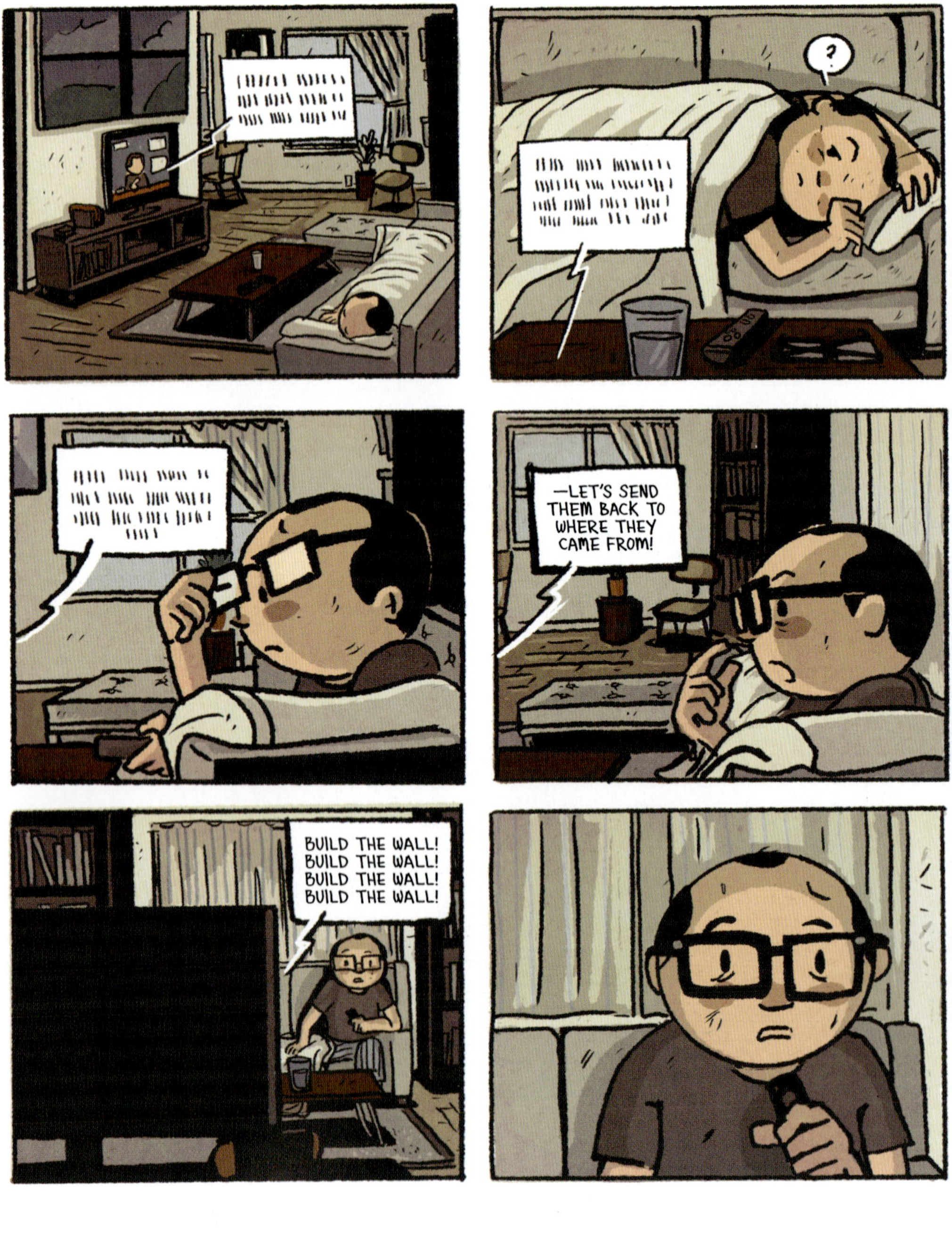
?
—LET'S SEND THEM BACK TO WHERE THEY CAME FROM!
BUILD THE WALL! BUILD THE WALL! BUILD THE WALL! BUILD THE WALL!

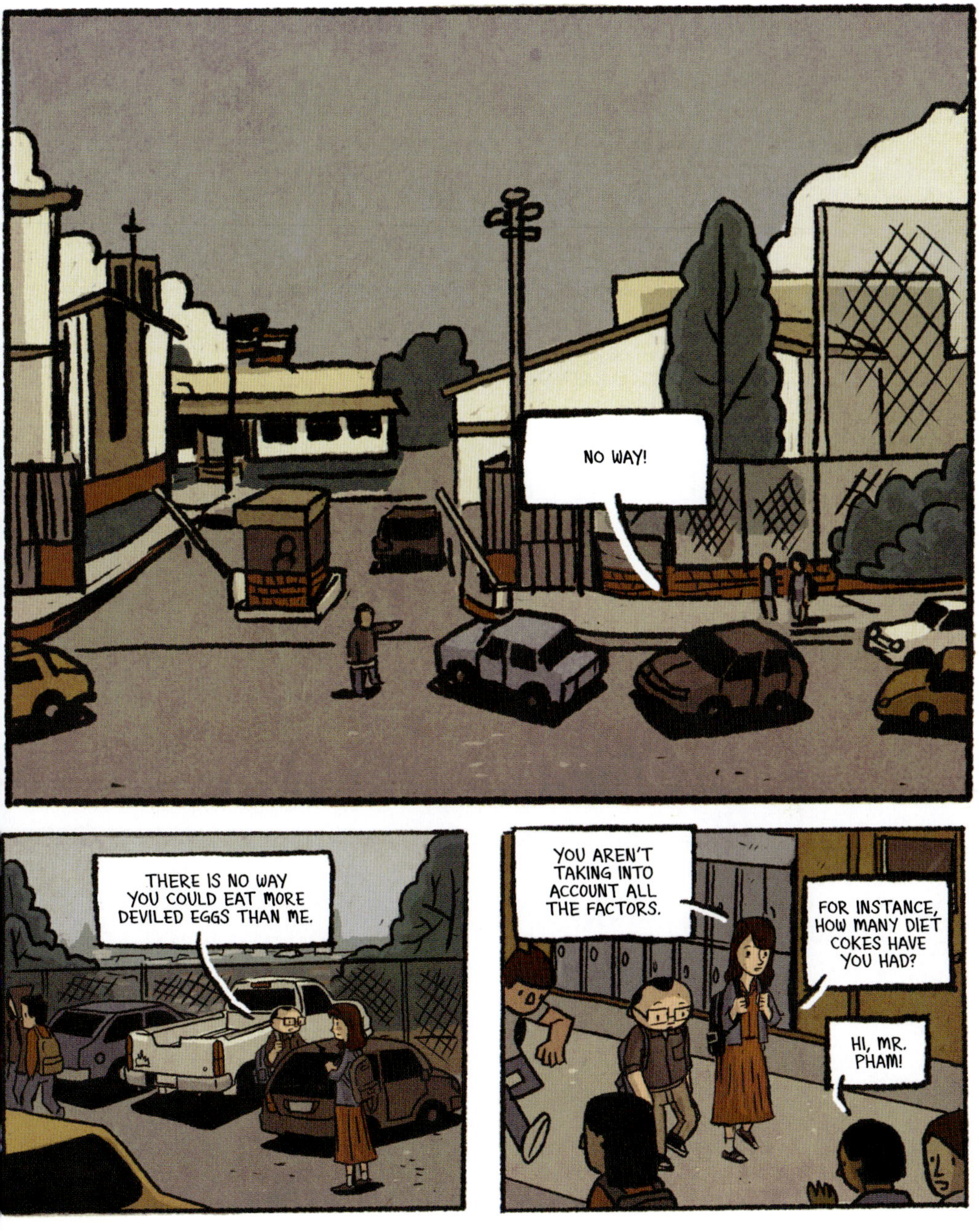
NO WAY!
THERE IS NO WAY YOU COULD EAT MORE DEVILED EGGS THAN ME.
YOU AREN'T TAKING INTO ACCOUNT ALL THE FACTORS.
FOR INSTANCE, HOW MANY DIET COKES HAVE YOU HAD?
HI, MR. PHAM!

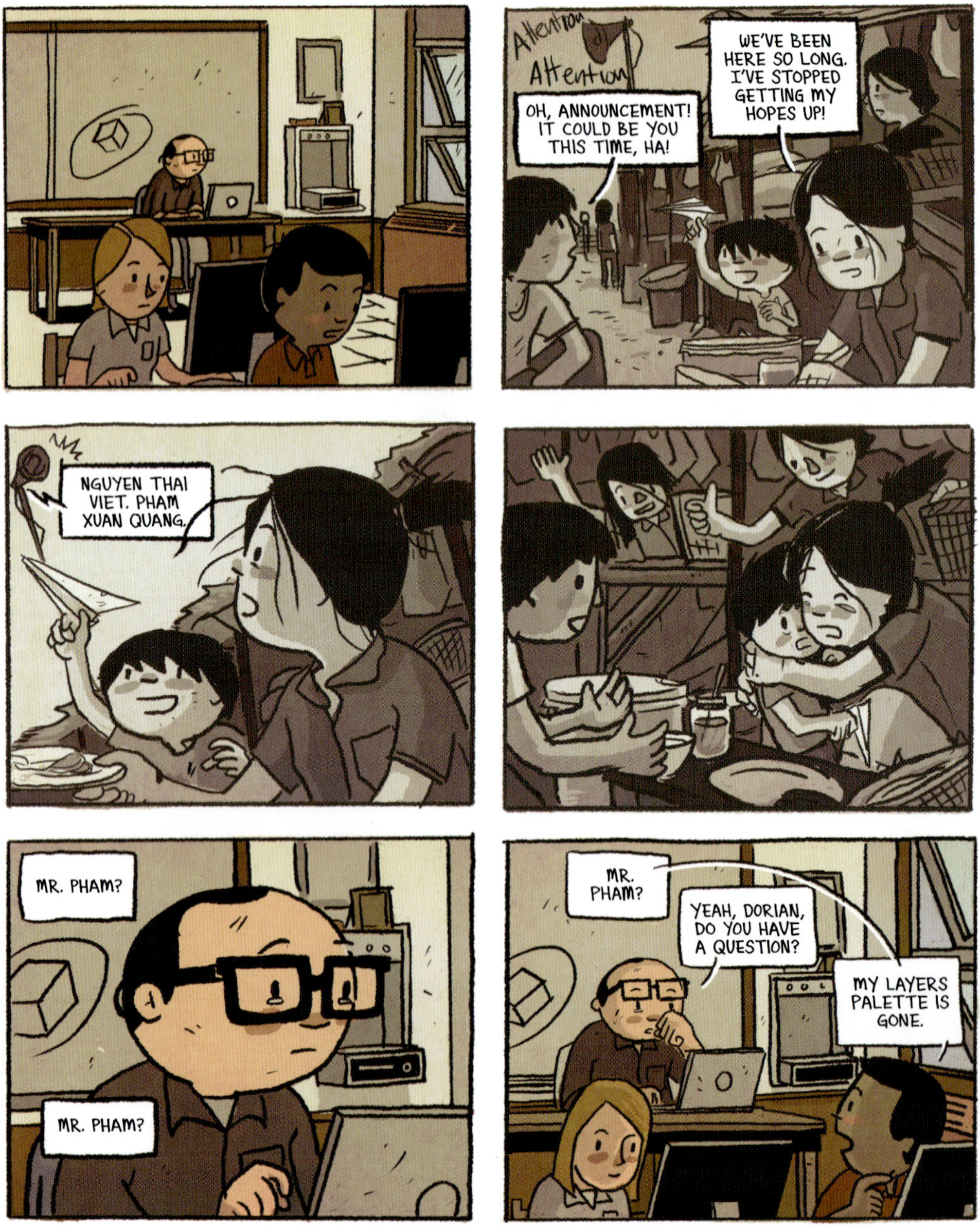

Attention
Attention
OH, ANNOUNCEMENT! IT COULD BE YOU THIS TIME, HA!
WE'VE BEEN HERE SO LONG. I'VE STOPPED GETTING MY HOPES UP!
NGUYEN THAI VIET. PHAM XUAN QUANG.
MR. PHAM?
MR. PHAM?
MR. PHAM?
YEAH, DORIAN, DO YOU HAVE A QUESTION?
MY LAYERS PALETTE IS GONE.

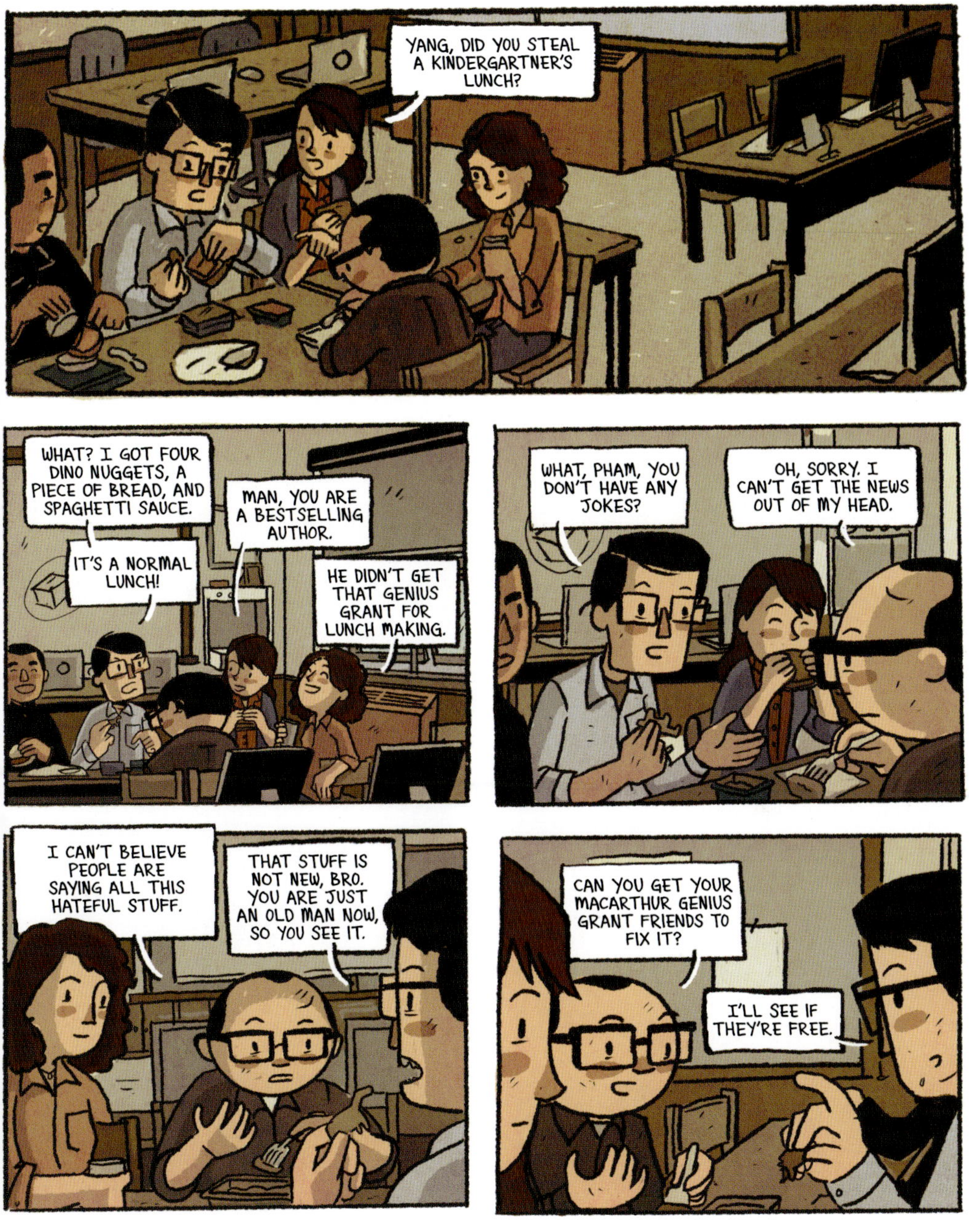
YANG, DID YOU STEAL A KINDERGARTNER'S LUNCH?
WHAT? I GOT FOUR DINO NUGGETS, A PIECE OF BREAD, AND SPAGHETTI SAUCE.
IT'S A NORMAL LUNCH!
MAN, YOU ARE A BESTSELLING AUTHOR.
HE DIDN'T GET THAT GENIUS GRANT FOR LUNCH MAKING.
WHAT, PHAM, YOU DON'T HAVE ANY JOKES?
OH, SORRY. I CAN'T GET THE NEWS OUT OF MY HEAD.
I CAN'T BELIEVE PEOPLE ARE SAYING ALL THIS HATEFUL STUFF.
THAT STUFF IS NOT NEW, BRO. YOU ARE JUST AN OLD MAN NOW, SO YOU SEE IT.
CAN YOU GET YOUR MACARTHUR GENIUS GRANT FRIENDS TO FIX IT?
I'LL SEE IF THEY'RE FREE.

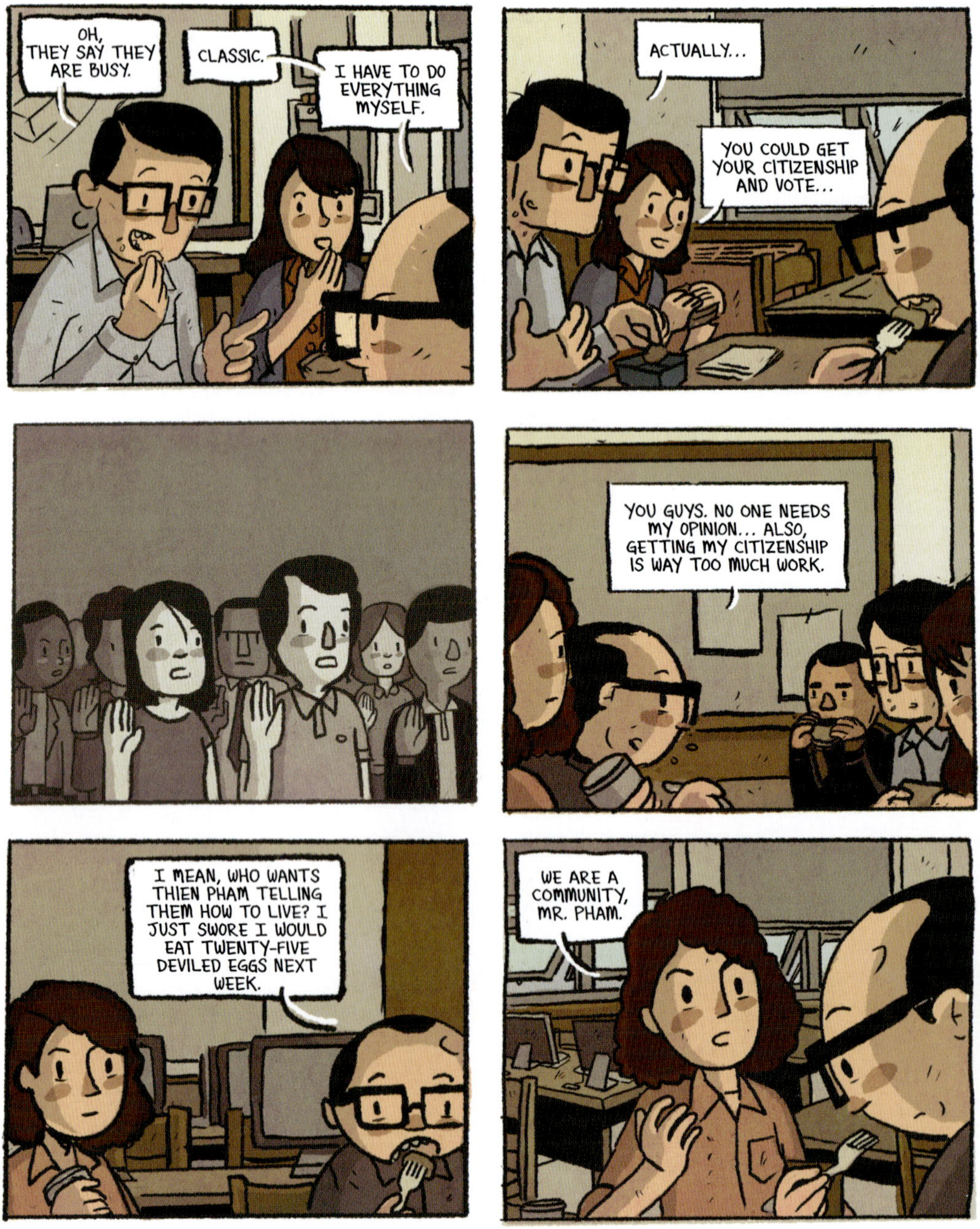
OH, THEY SAY THEY ARE BUSY.
CLASSIC.
I HAVE TO DO EVERYTHING MYSELF.
ACTUALLY...
YOU COULD GET YOUR CITIZENSHIP AND VOTE...
YOU GUYS. NO ONE NEEDS MY OPINION... ALSO, GETTING MY CITIZENSHIP IS WAY TOO MUCH WORK.
I MEAN, WHO WANTS THIEN PHAM TELLING THEM HOW TO LIVE? I JUST SWORE I WOULD EAT TWENTY-FIVE DEVILED EGGS NEXT WEEK.
WE ARE A COMMUNITY, MR. PHAM.

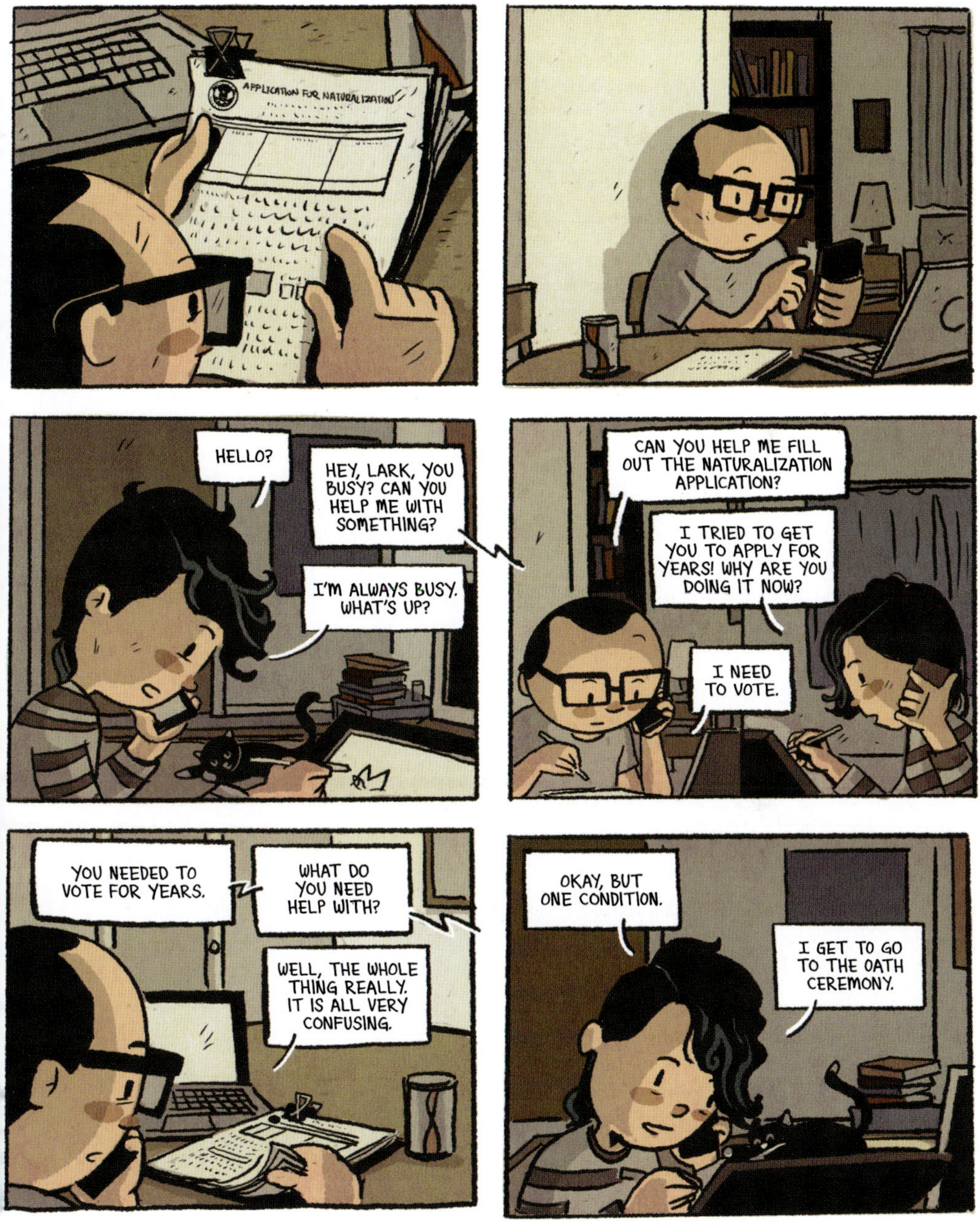
APPLICATION FOR NATURALIZATION
HELLO?
HEY, LARK, YOU BUSY? CAN YOU HELP ME WITH SOMETHING?
I'M ALWAYS BUSY. WHAT'S UP?
CAN YOU HELP ME FILL OUT THE NATURALIZATION APPLICATION?
I TRIED TO GET YOU TO APPLY FOR YEARS! WHY ARE YOU DOING IT NOW?
I NEED TO VOTE.
YOU NEEDED TO VOTE FOR YEARS.
WHAT DO YOU NEED HELP WITH?
WELL, THE WHOLE THING REALLY. IT IS ALL VERY CONFUSING.
OKAY, BUT ONE CONDITION.
I GET TO GO TO THE OATH CEREMONY.

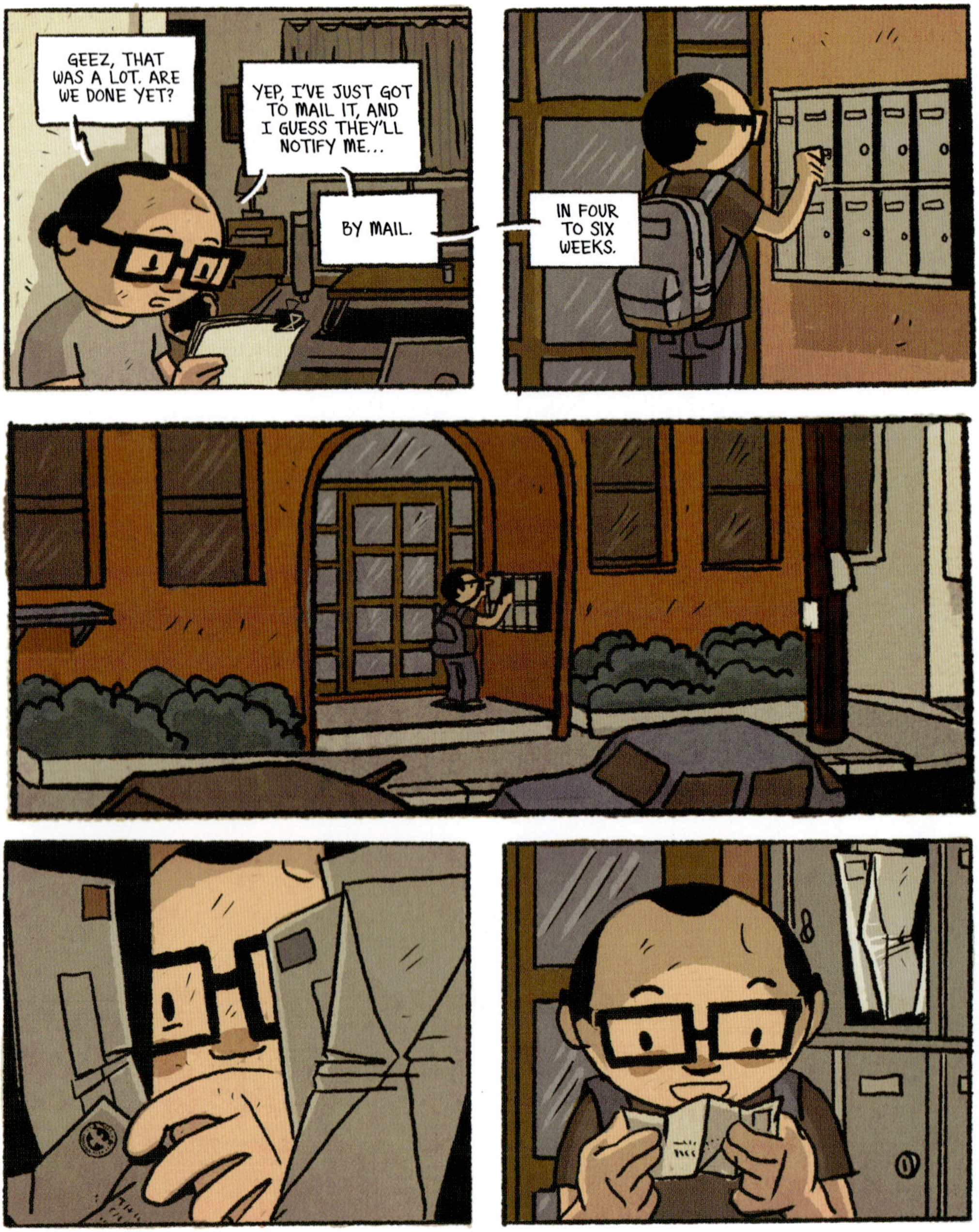
GEEZ, THAT WAS A LOT. ARE WE DONE YET?
YEP, I'VE JUST GOT TO MAIL IT, AND I GUESS THEY'LL NOTIFY ME...
BY MAIL.
IN FOUR TO SIX WEEKS.

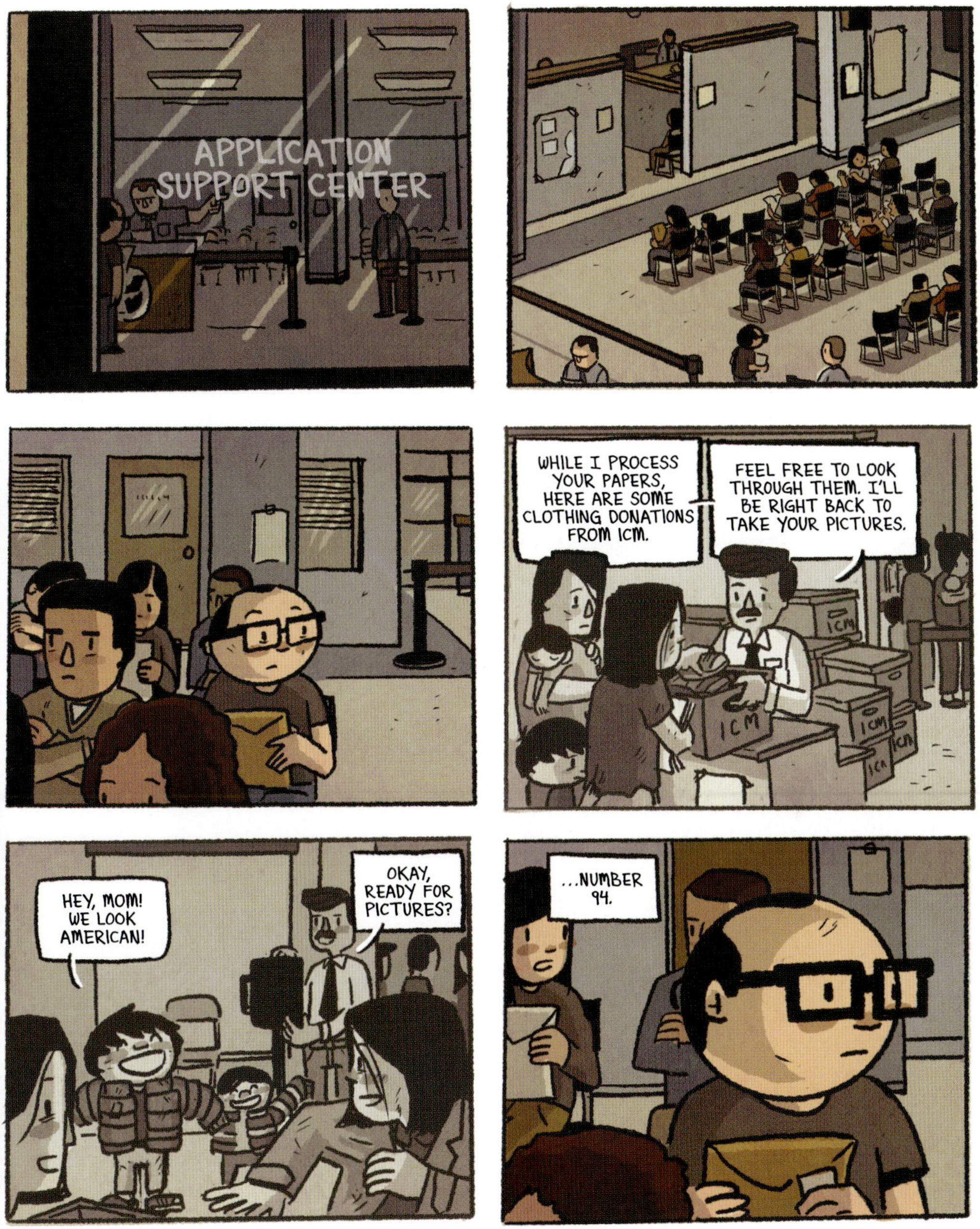
APPLICATION SUPPORT CENTER
WHILE I PROCESS YOUR PAPERS, HERE ARE SOME CLOTHING DONATIONS FROM ICM.
FEEL FREE TO LOOK THROUGH THEM. I'LL BE RIGHT BACK TO TAKE YOUR PICTURES.
ICM
HEY, MOM! WE LOOK AMERICAN!
OKAY, READY FOR PICTURES?
...NUMBER 94.

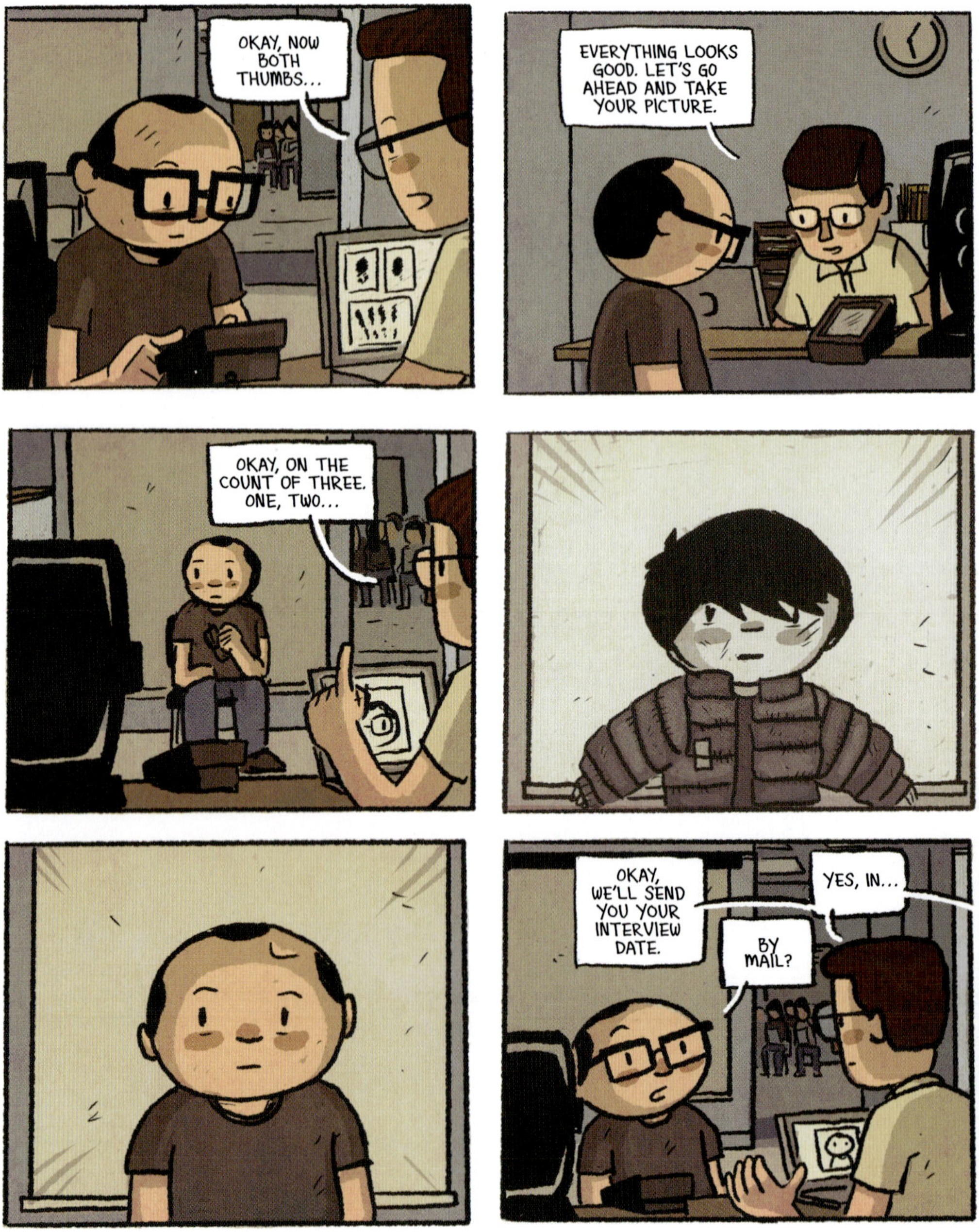
OKAY, NOW BOTH THUMBS...
EVERYTHING LOOKS GOOD. LET'S GO AHEAD AND TAKE YOUR PICTURE.
OKAY, ON THE COUNT OF THREE. ONE, TWO...
OKAY, WE'LL SEND YOU YOUR INTERVIEW DATE.
BY MAIL?
YES, IN...

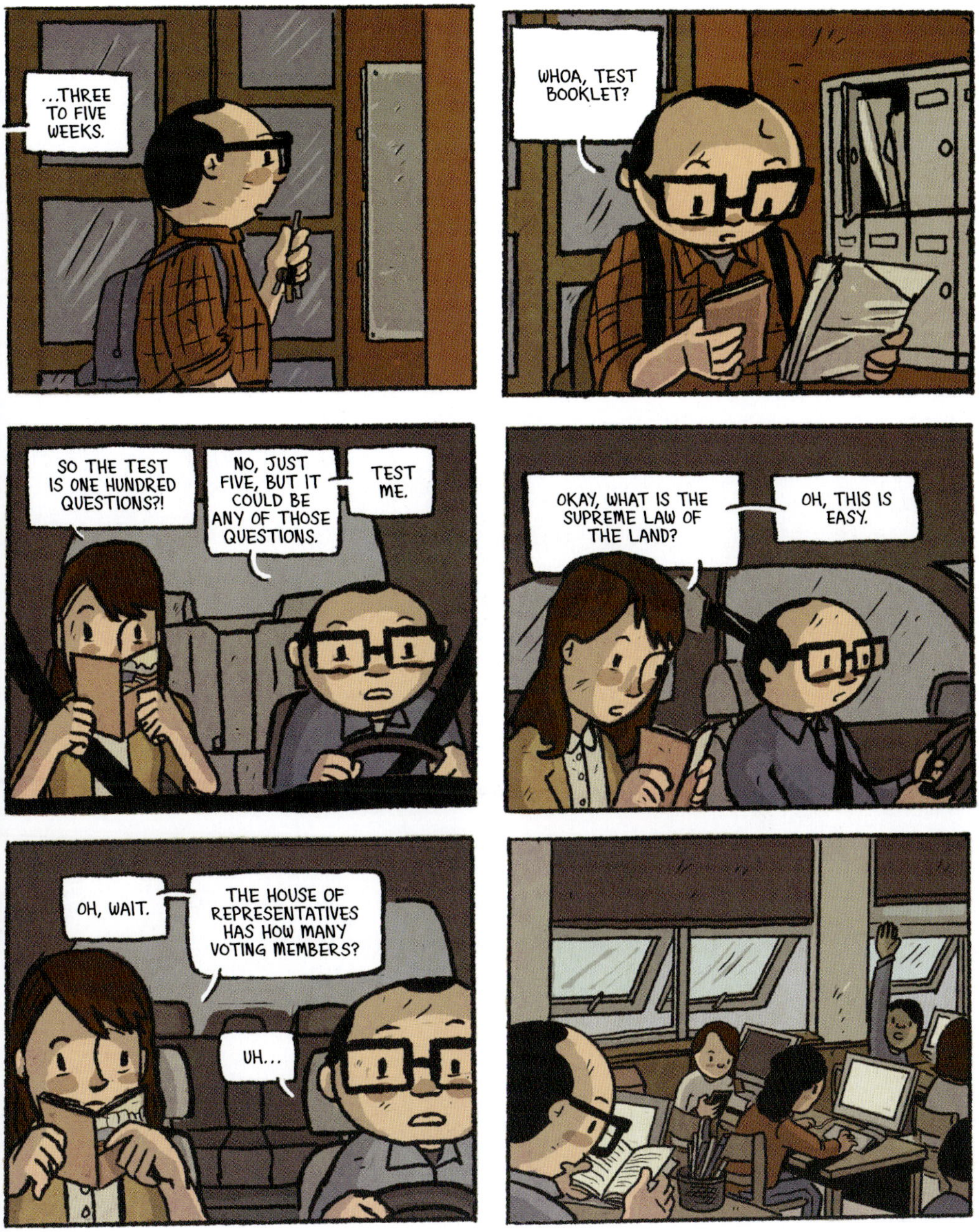

...THREE TO FIVE WEEKS.
WHOA, TEST BOOKLET?
SO THE TEST IS ONE HUNDRED QUESTIONS?!
NO, JUST FIVE, BUT IT COULD BE ANY OF THOSE QUESTIONS.
TEST ME.
OKAY, WHAT IS THE SUPREME LAW OF THE LAND?
OH, THIS IS EASY.
OH, WAIT.
THE HOUSE OF REPRESENTATIVES HAS HOW MANY VOTING MEMBERS?
UH...

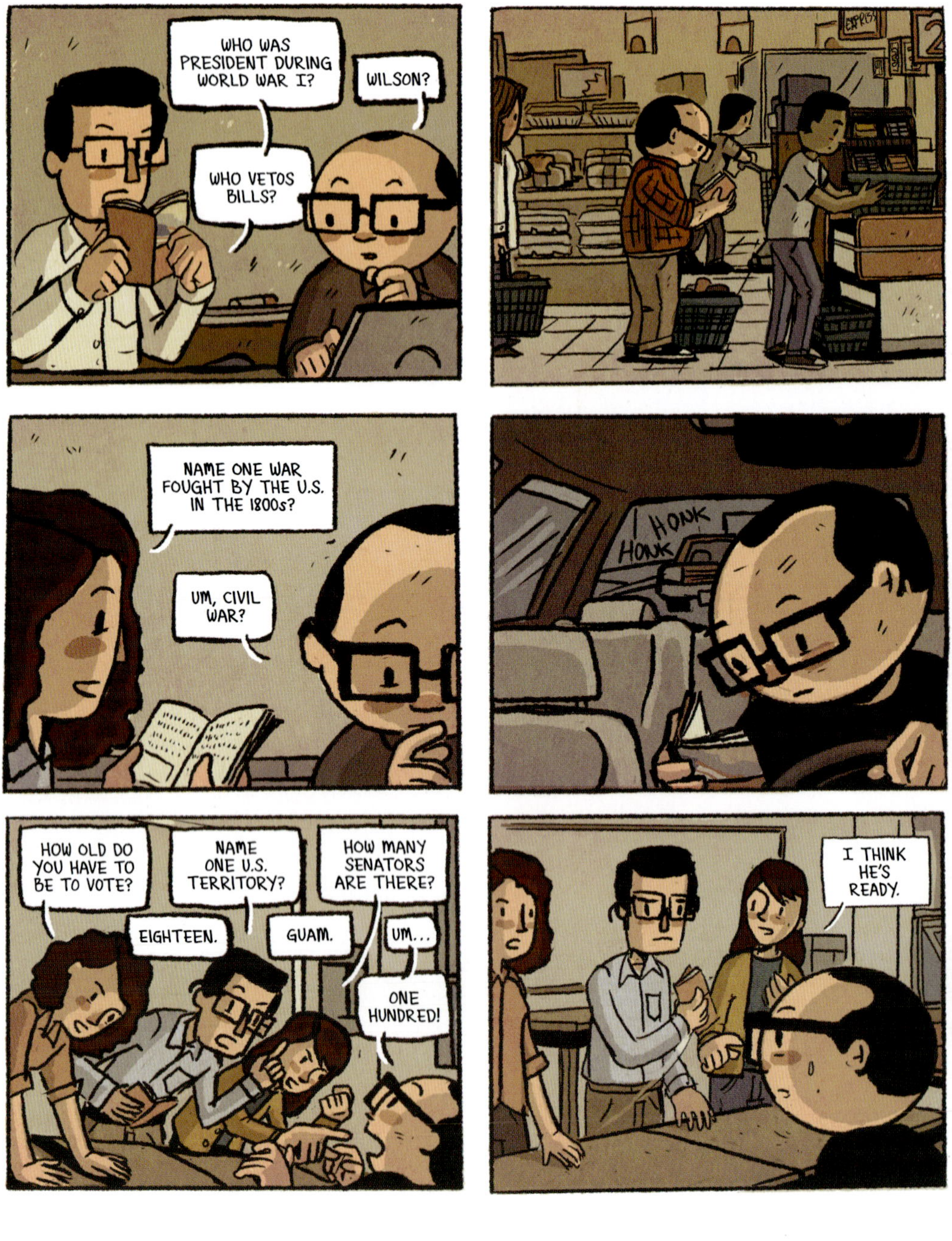
WHO WAS PRESIDENT DURING WORLD WAR I?
WILSON?
WHO VETOS BILLS?
NAME ONE WAR FOUGHT BY THE U.S. IN THE 1800s?
UM, CIVIL WAR?
HONK
HONK
HOW OLD DO YOU HAVE TO BE TO VOTE?
EIGHTEEN.
NAME ONE U.S. TERRITORY?
GUAM.
HOW MANY SENATORS ARE THERE?
UM...
ONE HUNDRED!
I THINK HE'S READY.

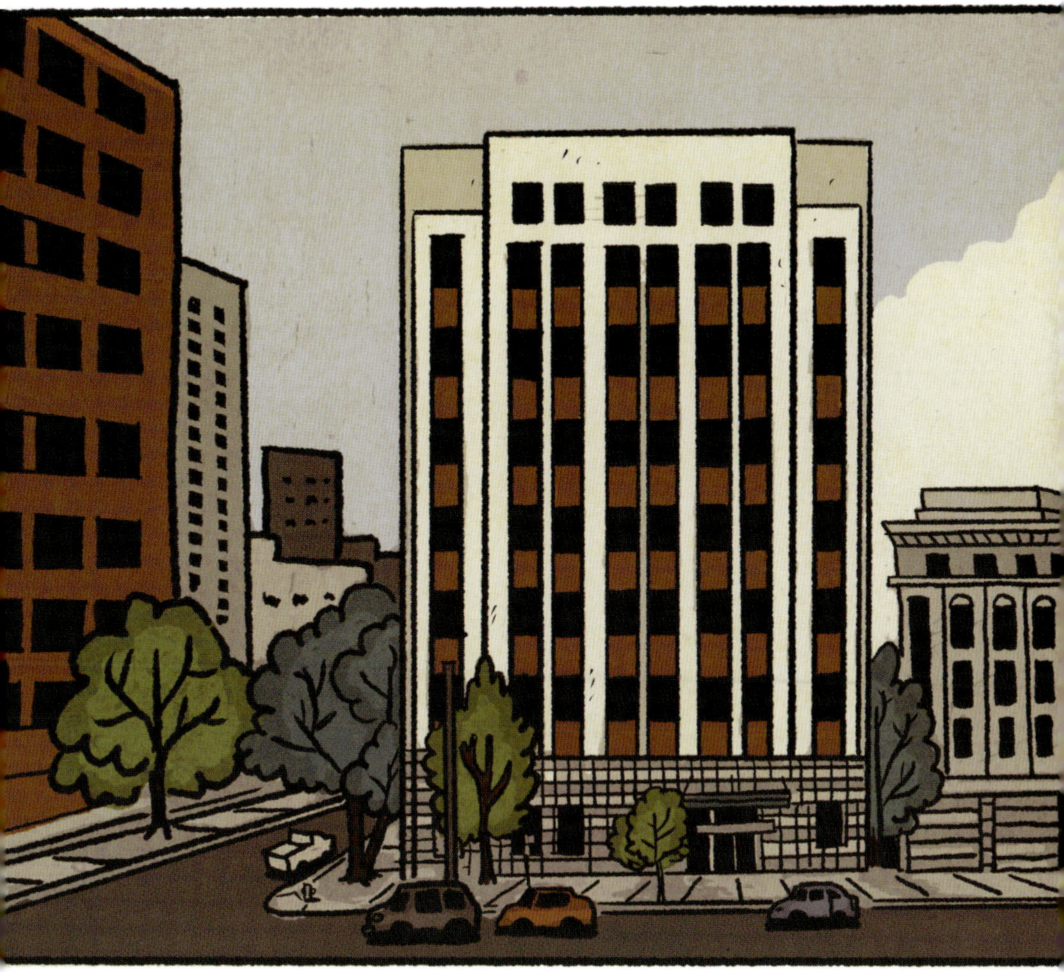

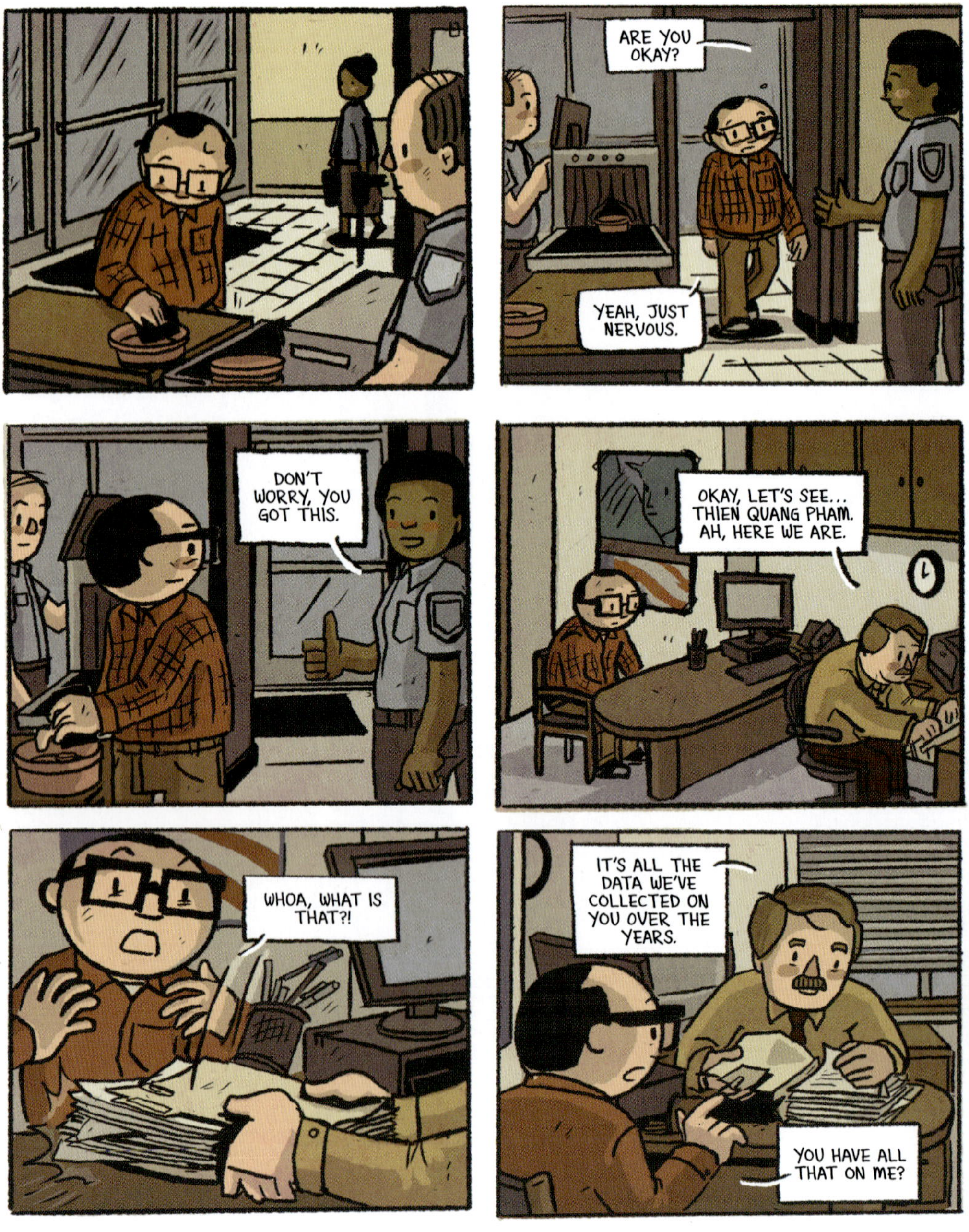
ARE YOU OKAY?
YEAH, JUST NERVOUS.
DON'T WORRY, YOU GOT THIS.
OKAY, LET'S SEE... THIEN QUANG PHAM. AH, HERE WE ARE.
WHOA, WHAT IS THAT?!
IT'S ALL THE DATA WE'VE COLLECTED ON YOU OVER THE YEARS.
YOU HAVE ALL THAT ON ME?

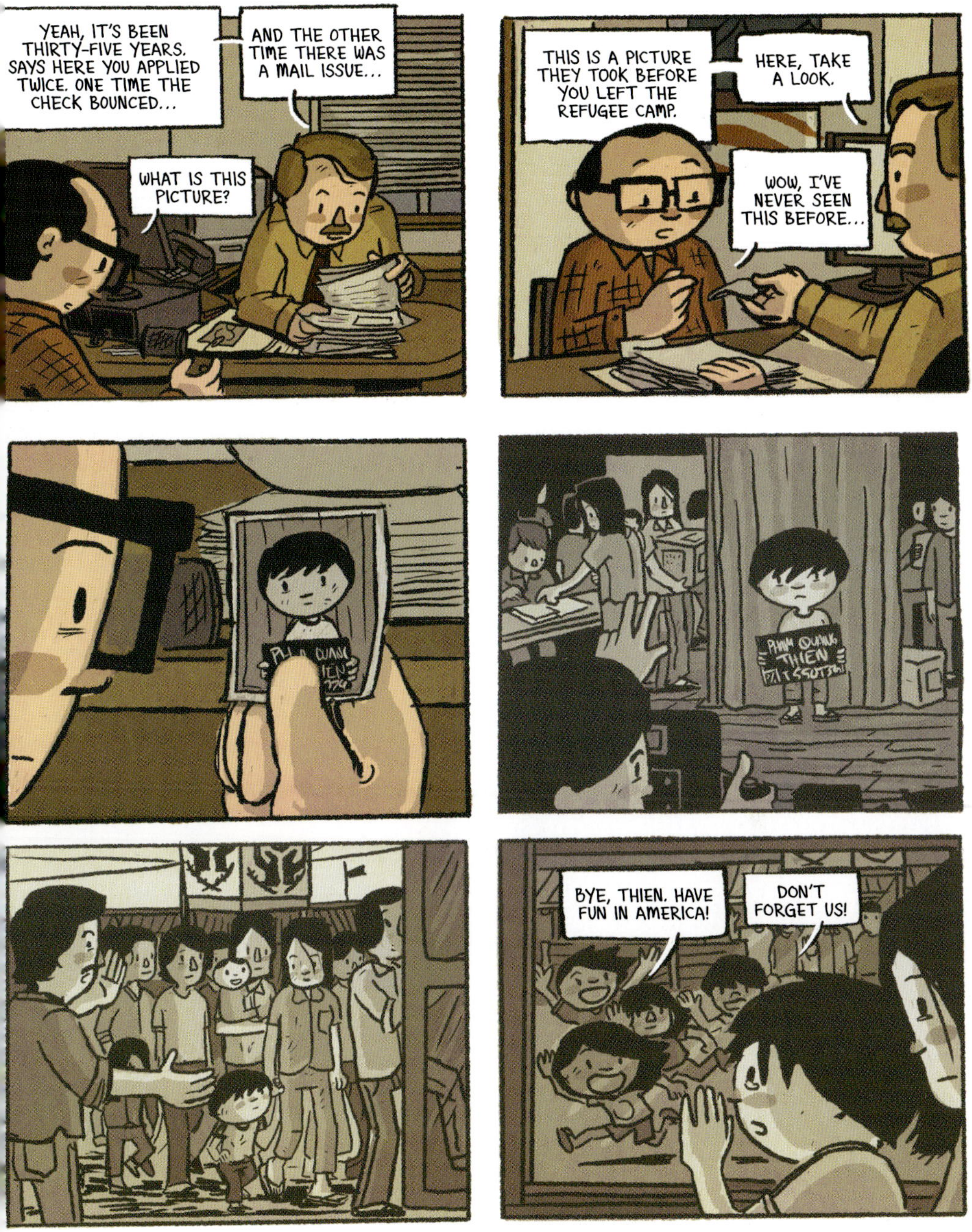
YEAH, IT'S BEEN THIRTY-FIVE YEARS. SAYS HERE YOU APPLIED TWICE. ONE TIME THE CHECK BOUNCED...
AND THE OTHER TIME THERE WAS A MAIL ISSUE...
WHAT IS THIS PICTURE?
THIS IS A PICTURE THEY TOOK BEFORE YOU LEFT THE REFUGEE CAMP.
HERE, TAKE A LOOK.
WOW, I'VE NEVER SEEN THIS BEFORE...
PHAM QUANG THIEN
BYE, THIEN. HAVE FUN IN AMERICA!
DON'T FORGET US!

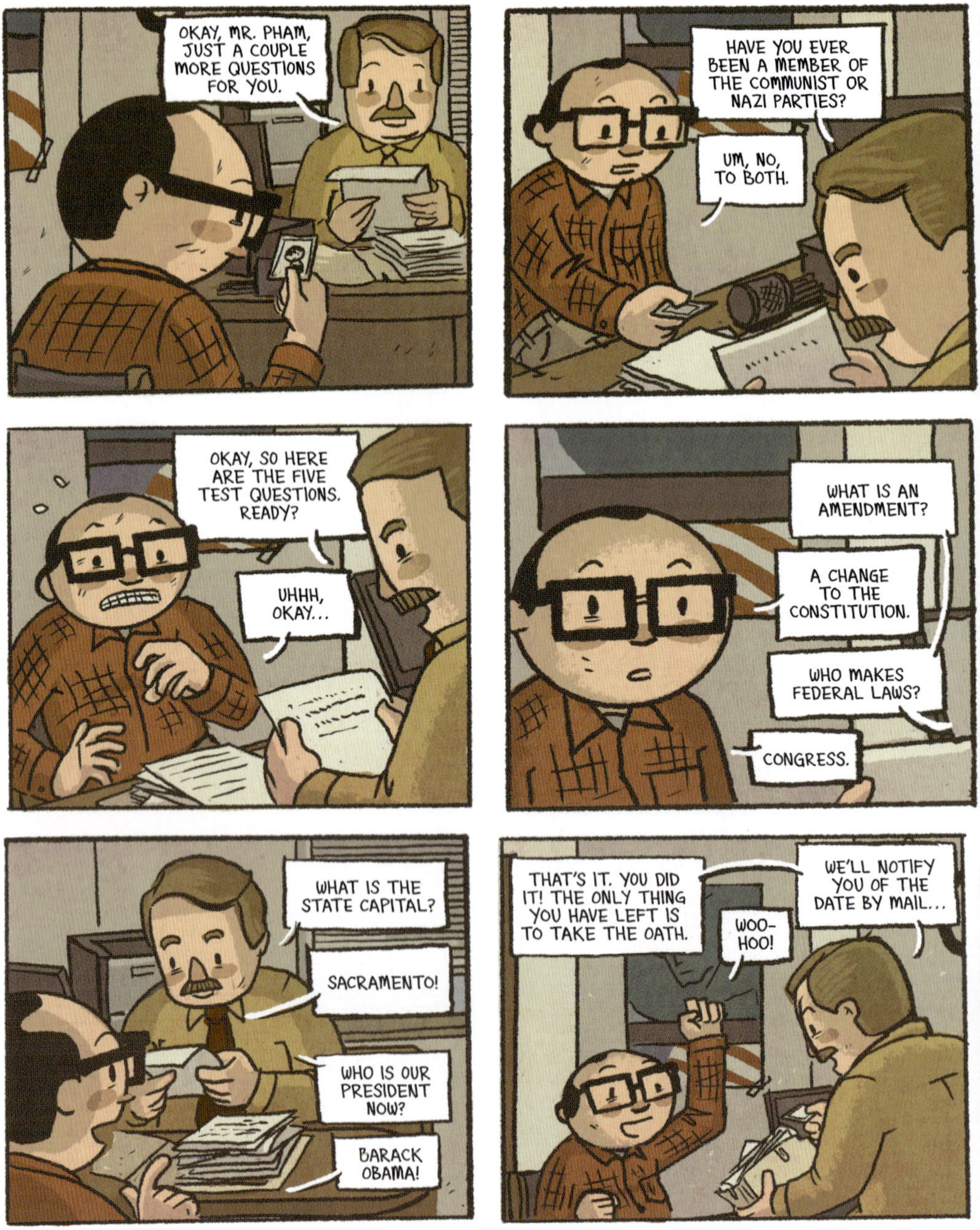

OKAY, MR. PHAM, JUST A COUPLE MORE QUESTIONS FOR YOU.
HAVE YOU EVER BEEN A MEMBER OF THE COMMUNIST OR NAZI PARTIES?
UM, NO, TO BOTH.
OKAY, SO HERE ARE THE FIVE TEST QUESTIONS. READY?
UHHH, OKAY...
WHAT IS AN AMENDMENT?
A CHANGE TO THE CONSTITUTION.
WHO MAKES FEDERAL LAWS?
CONGRESS.
WHAT IS THE STATE CAPITAL?
SACRAMENTO!
WHO IS OUR PRESIDENT NOW?
BARACK OBAMA!
THAT'S IT. YOU DID IT! THE ONLY THING YOU HAVE LEFT IS TO TAKE THE OATH.
WE'LL NOTIFY YOU OF THE DATE BY MAIL...
WOO-HOO!

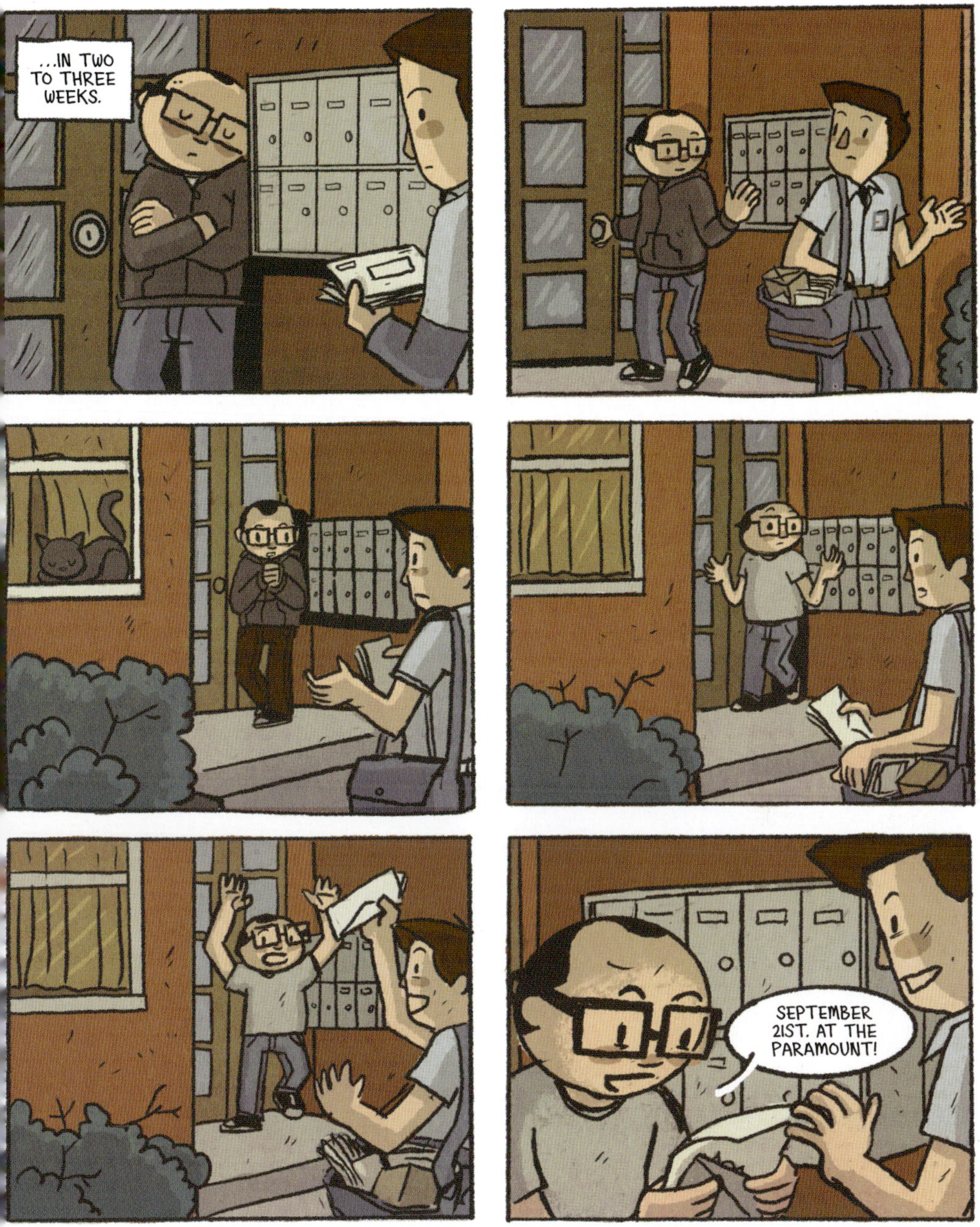
...IN TWO TO THREE WEEKS.
SEPTEMBER 21ST. AT THE PARAMOUNT!

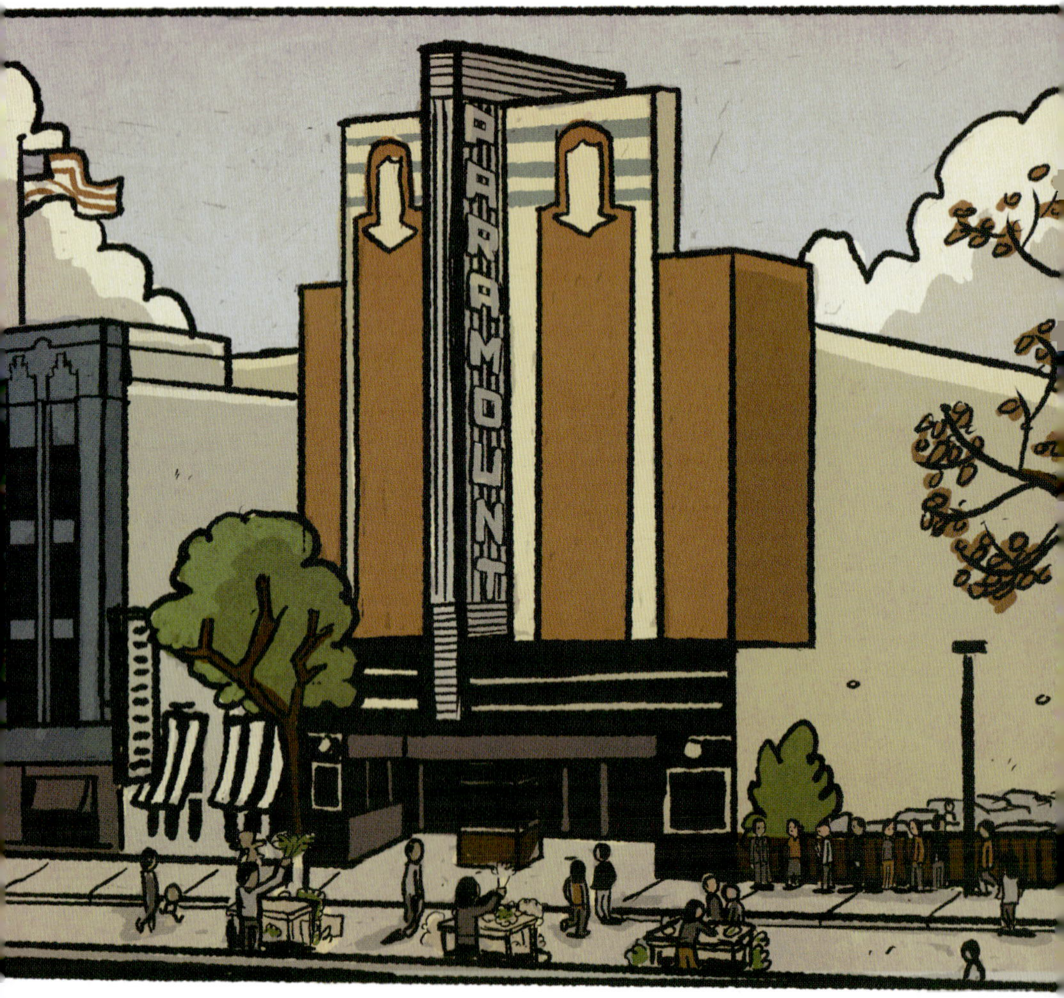
PARAMOUNT

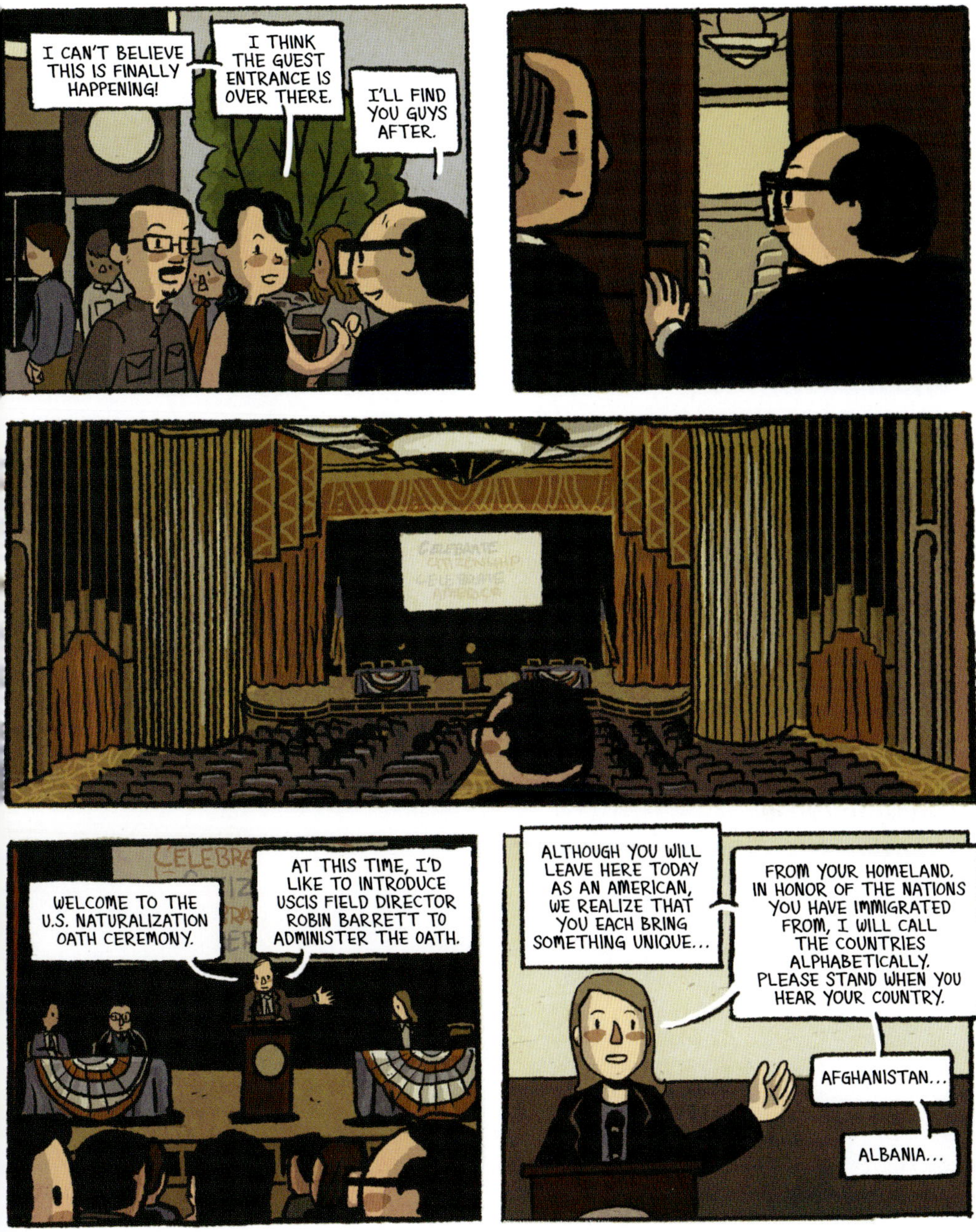
I CAN'T BELIEVE THIS IS FINALLY HAPPENING!
I THINK THE GUEST ENTRANCE IS OVER THERE.
I'LL FIND YOU GUYS AFTER.
WELCOME TO THE U.S. NATURALIZATION OATH CEREMONY.
AT THIS TIME, I'D LIKE TO INTRODUCE USCIS FIELD DIRECTOR ROBIN BARRETT TO ADMINISTER THE OATH.
ALTHOUGH YOU WILL LEAVE HERE TODAY AS AN AMERICAN, WE REALIZE THAT YOU EACH BRING SOMETHING UNIQUE...
FROM YOUR HOMELAND. IN HONOR OF THE NATIONS YOU HAVE IMMIGRATED FROM, I WILL CALL THE COUNTRIES ALPHABETICALLY. PLEASE STAND WHEN YOU HEAR YOUR COUNTRY.
AFGHANISTAN...
ALBANIA...

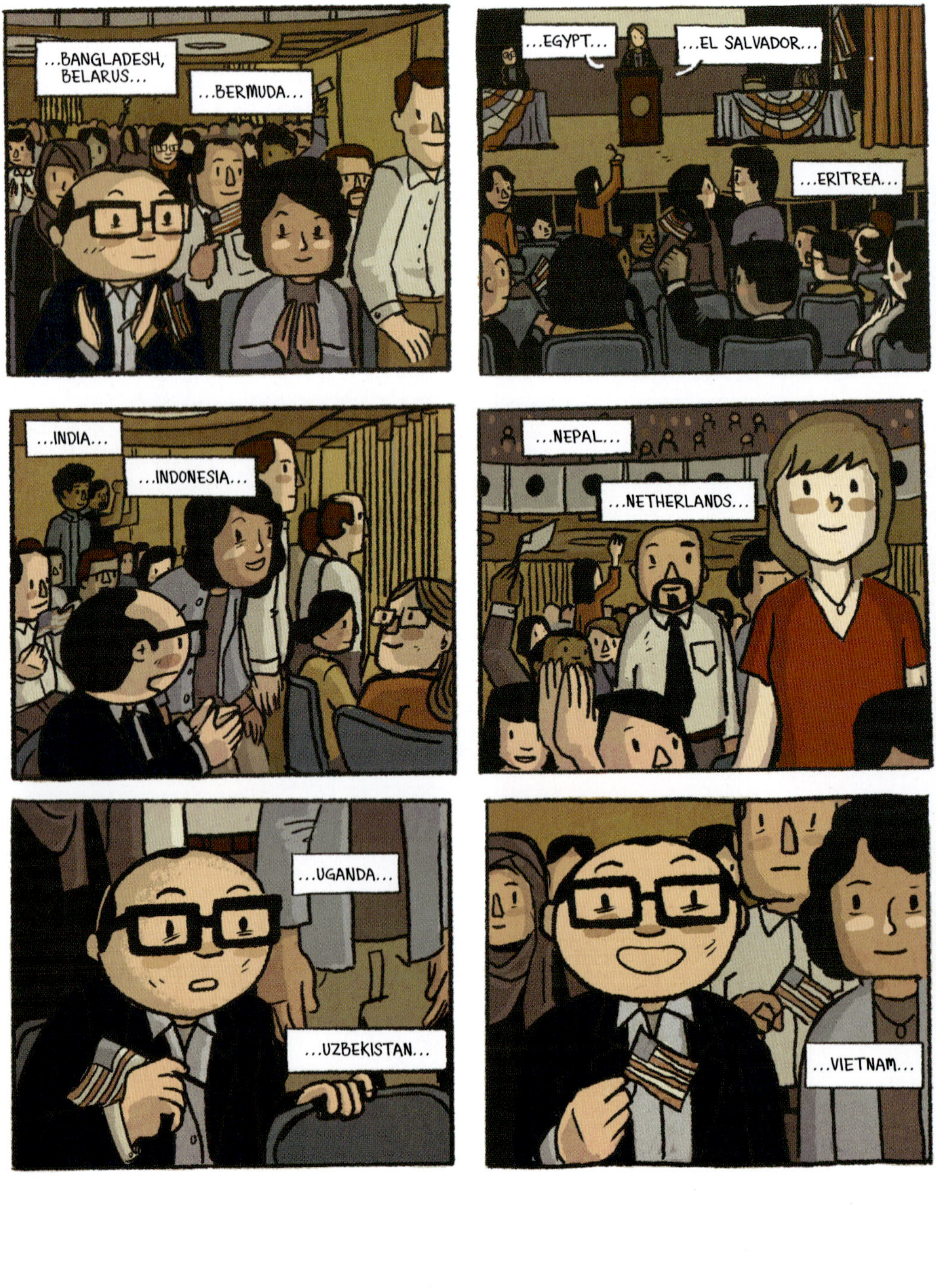
...BANGLADESH, BELARUS...
...BERMUDA...
...EGYPT...
...EL SALVADOR...
...ERITREA...
...INDIA...
...INDONESIA...
...NEPAL...
...NETHERLANDS...
...UGANDA...
...UZBEKISTAN...
...VIETNAM...

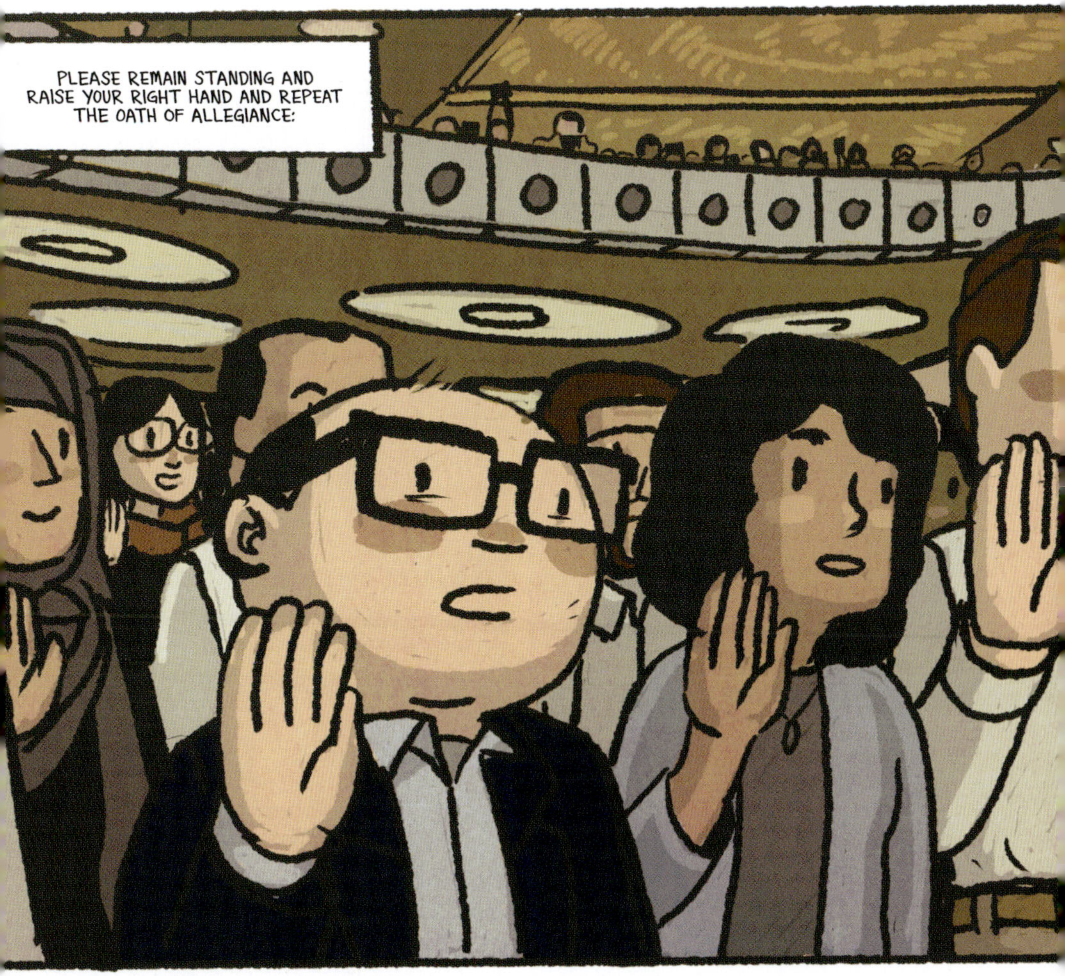
PLEASE REMAIN STANDING AND RAISE YOUR RIGHT HAND AND REPEAT THE OATH OF ALLEGIANCE:

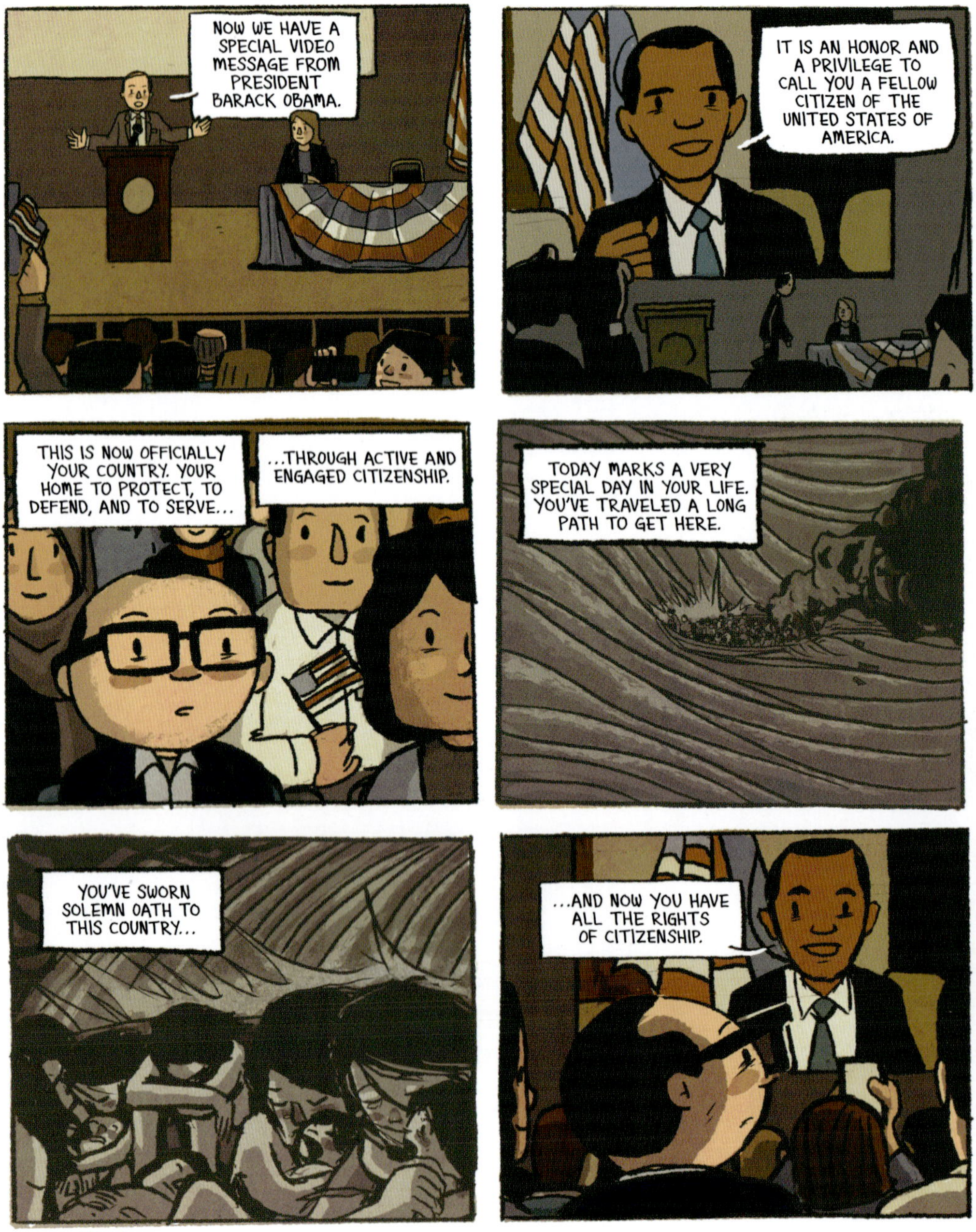
NOW WE HAVE A SPECIAL VIDEO MESSAGE FROM PRESIDENT BARACK OBAMA.
IT IS AN HONOR AND A PRIVILEGE TO CALL YOU A FELLOW CITIZEN OF THE UNITED STATES OF AMERICA.
THIS IS NOW OFFICIALLY YOUR COUNTRY. YOUR HOME TO PROTECT, TO DEFEND, AND TO SERVE...
...THROUGH ACTIVE AND ENGAGED CITIZENSHIP.
TODAY MARKS A VERY SPECIAL DAY IN YOUR LIFE. YOU'VE TRAVELED A LONG PATH TO GET HERE.
YOU'VE SWORN SOLEMN OATH TO THIS COUNTRY...
...AND NOW YOU HAVE ALL THE RIGHTS OF CITIZENSHIP.

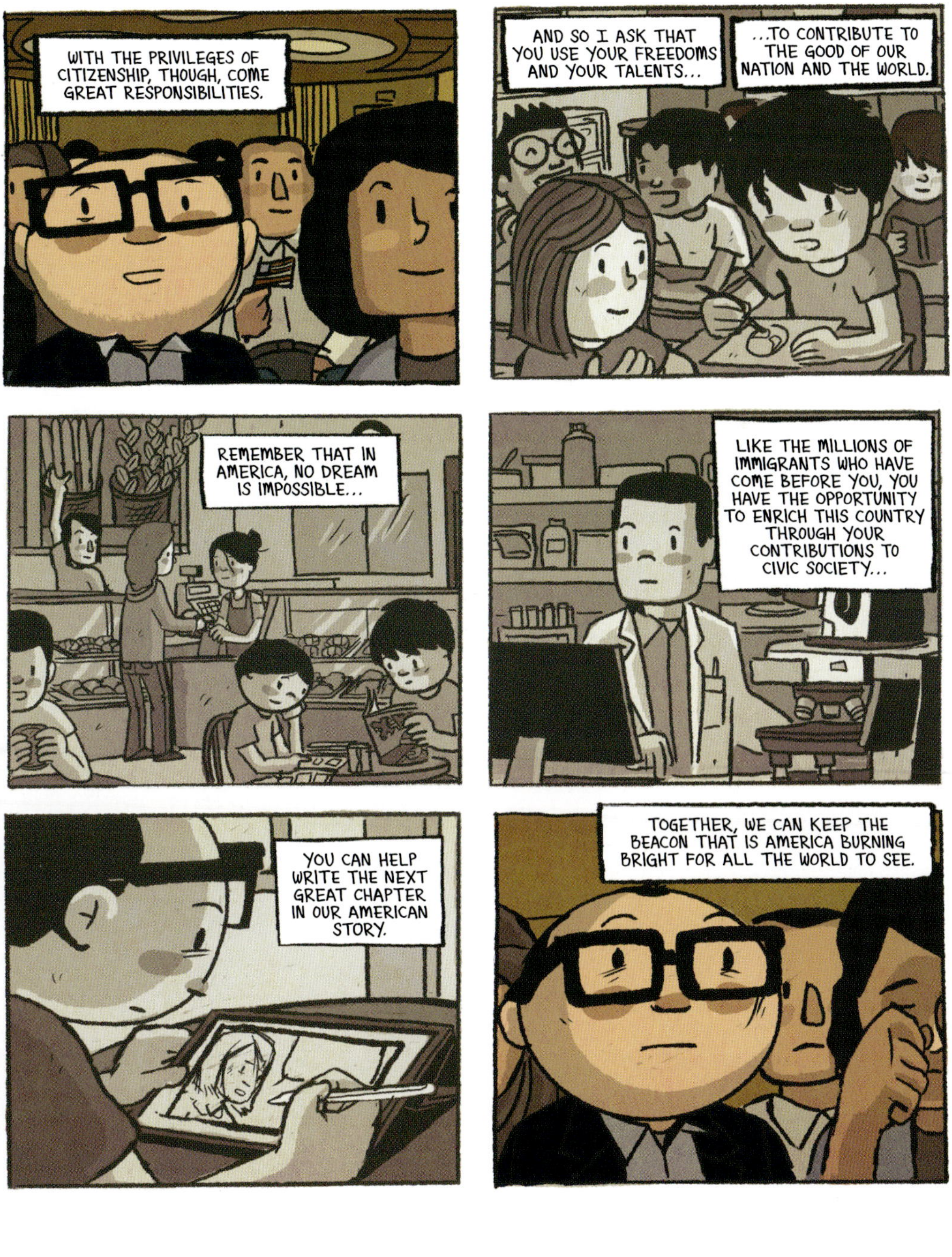
WITH THE PRIVILEGES OF CITIZENSHIP, THOUGH, COME GREAT RESPONSIBILITIES.
AND SO I ASK THAT YOU USE YOUR FREEDOMS AND YOUR TALENTS...
...TO CONTRIBUTE TO THE GOOD OF OUR NATION AND THE WORLD.
REMEMBER THAT IN AMERICA, NO DREAM IS IMPOSSIBLE...
LIKE THE MILLIONS OF IMMIGRANTS WHO HAVE COME BEFORE YOU, YOU HAVE THE OPPORTUNITY TO ENRICH THIS COUNTRY THROUGH YOUR CONTRIBUTIONS TO CIVIC SOCIETY...
YOU CAN HELP WRITE THE NEXT GREAT CHAPTER IN OUR AMERICAN STORY.
TOGETHER, WE CAN KEEP THE BEACON THAT IS AMERICA BURNING BRIGHT FOR ALL THE WORLD TO SEE.

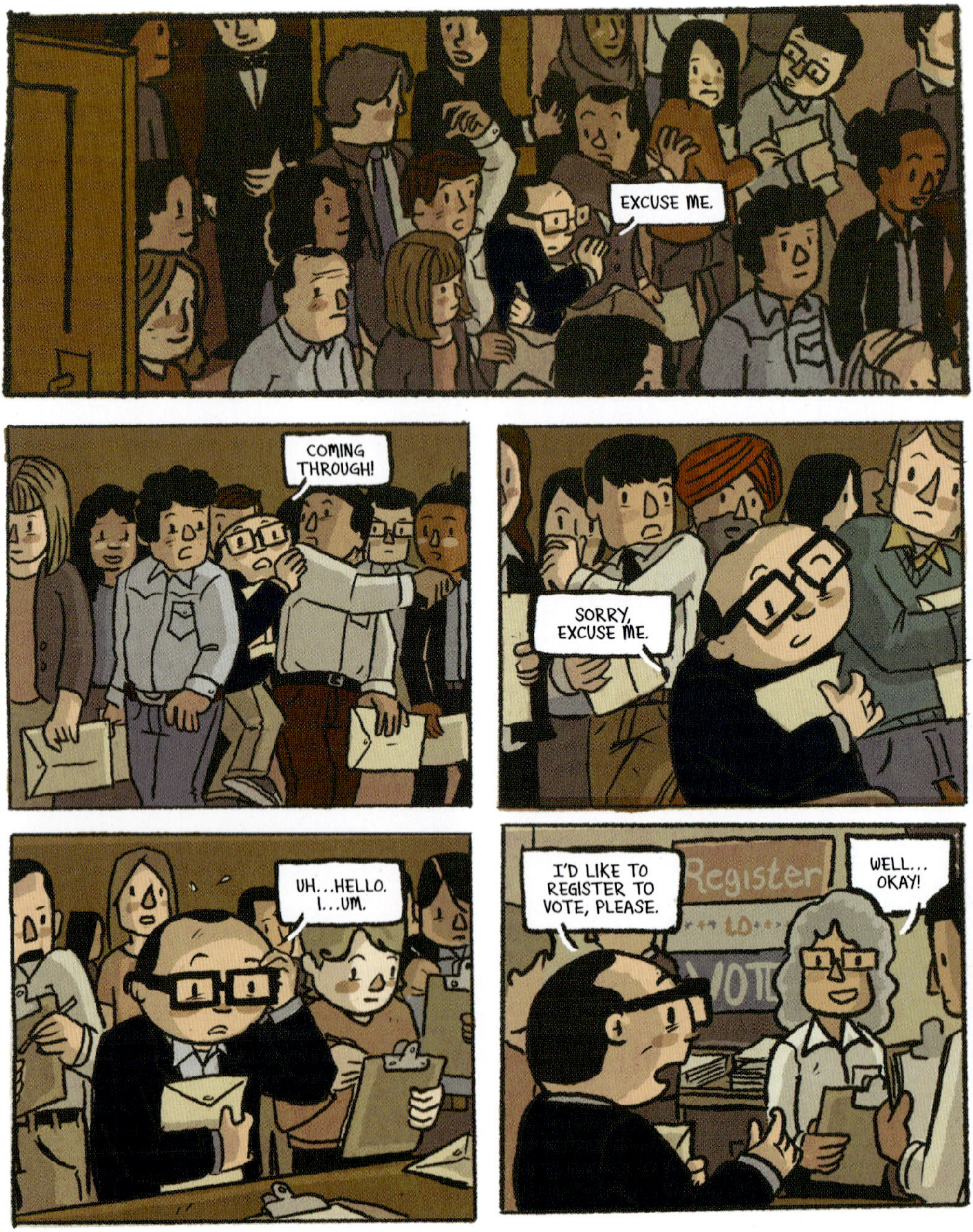
EXCUSE ME.
COMING THROUGH!
SORRY, EXCUSE ME.
UH...HELLO. I...UM.
I'D LIKE TO REGISTER TO VOTE, PLEASE.
Register to VOT
WELL... OKAY!

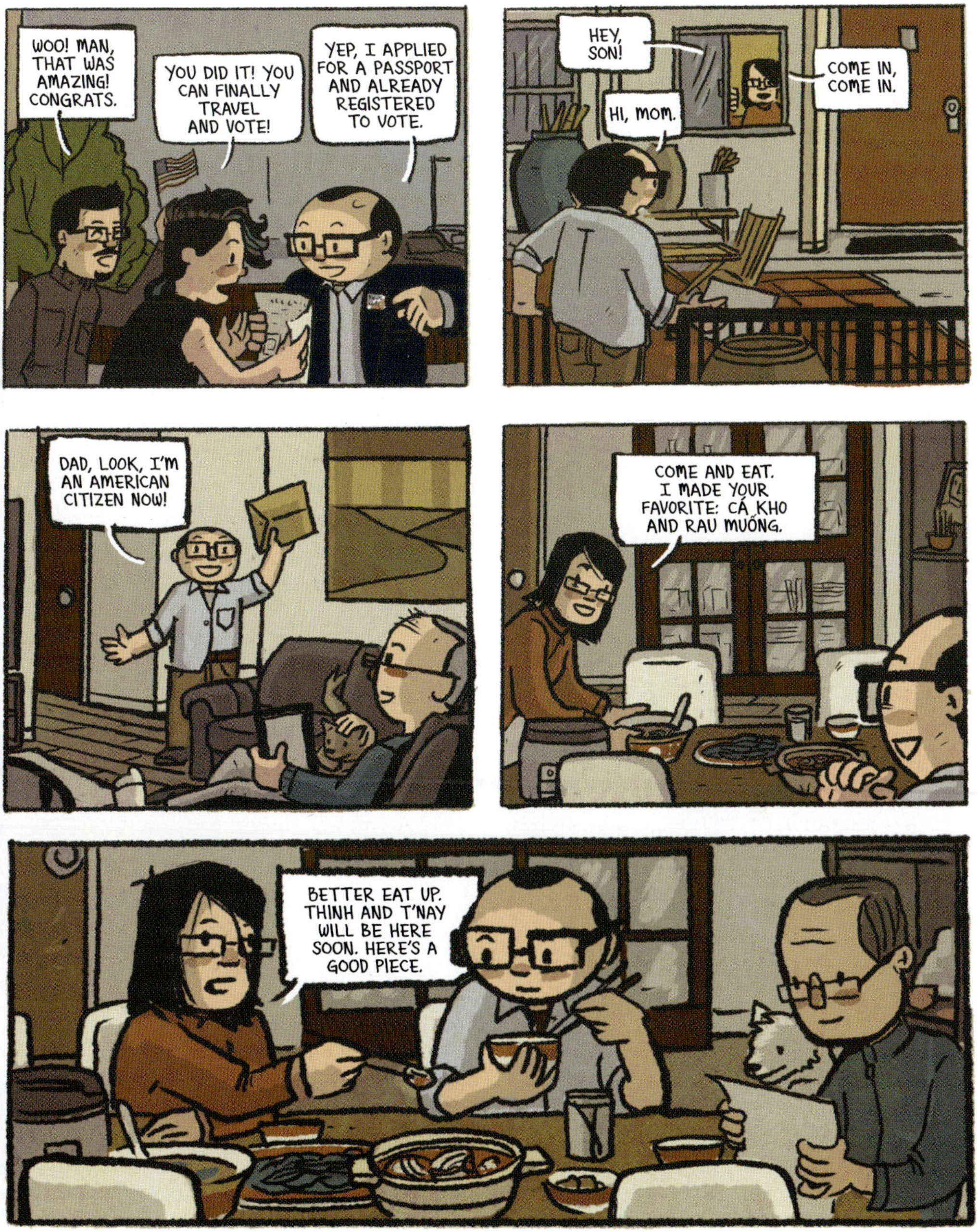
WOO! MAN, THAT WAS AMAZING! CONGRATS.
YOU DID IT! YOU CAN FINALLY TRAVEL AND VOTE!
YEP, I APPLIED FOR A PASSPORT AND ALREADY REGISTERED TO VOTE.
HEY, SON!
COME IN, COME IN.
HI, MOM.
DAD, LOOK, I'M AN AMERICAN CITIZEN NOW!
COME AND EAT. I MADE YOUR FAVORITE: CÁ KHO AND RAU MUỐNG.
BETTER EAT UP. THINH AND T'NAY WILL BE HERE SOON. HERE'S A GOOD PIECE.

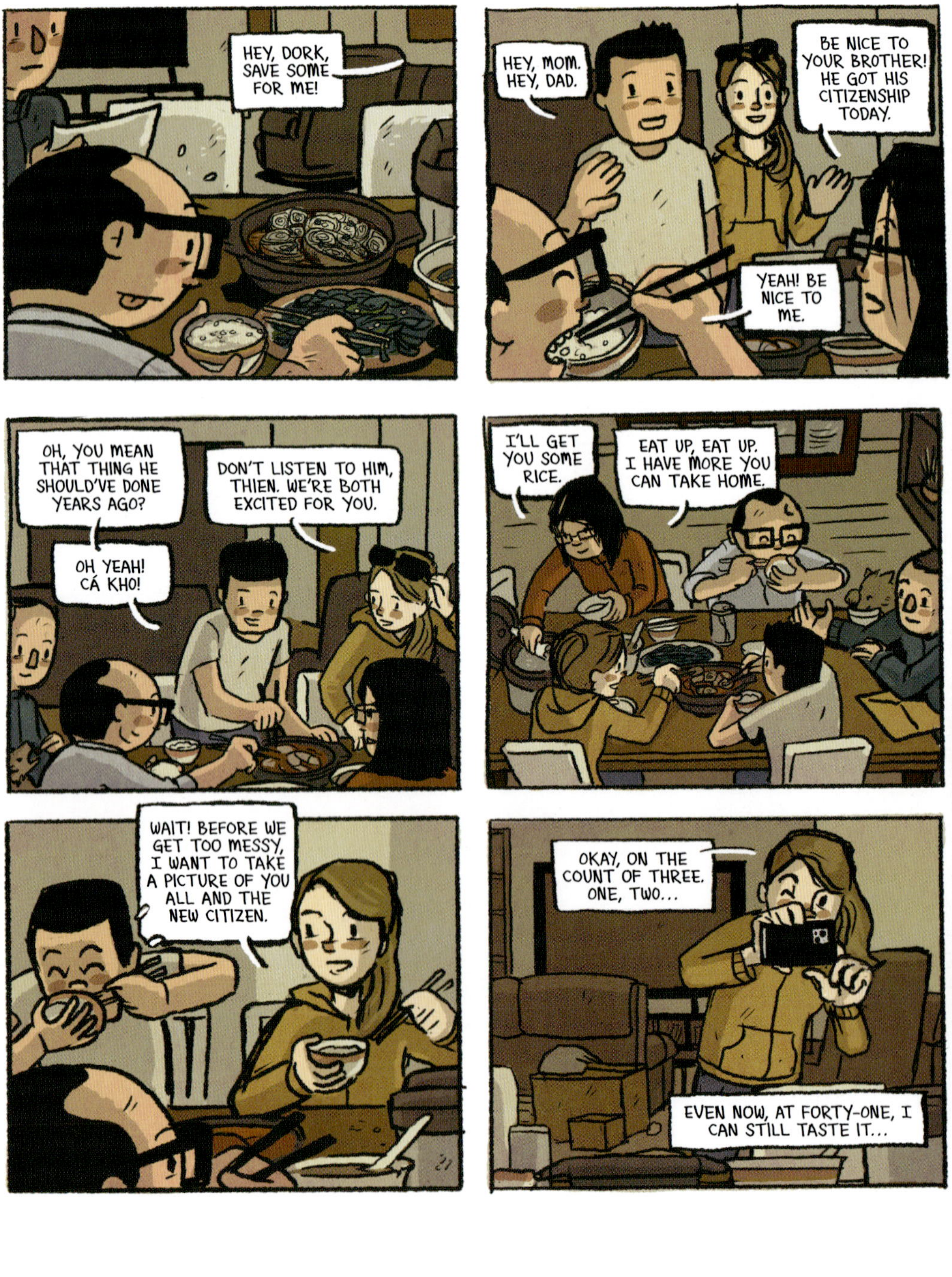
HEY, DORK, SAVE SOME FOR ME!
HEY, MOM. HEY, DAD.
BE NICE TO YOUR BROTHER! HE GOT HIS CITIZENSHIP TODAY.
YEAH! BE NICE TO ME.
OH, YOU MEAN THAT THING HE SHOULD'VE DONE YEARS AGO?
DON'T LISTEN TO HIM, THIEN. WE'RE BOTH EXCITED FOR YOU.
OH YEAH! CÁ KHO!
I'LL GET YOU SOME RICE.
EAT UP, EAT UP. I HAVE MORE YOU CAN TAKE HOME.
WAIT! BEFORE WE GET TOO MESSY, I WANT TO TAKE A PICTURE OF YOU ALL AND THE NEW CITIZEN.
OKAY, ON THE COUNT OF THREE. ONE, TWO...
EVEN NOW, AT FORTY-ONE, I CAN STILL TASTE IT...

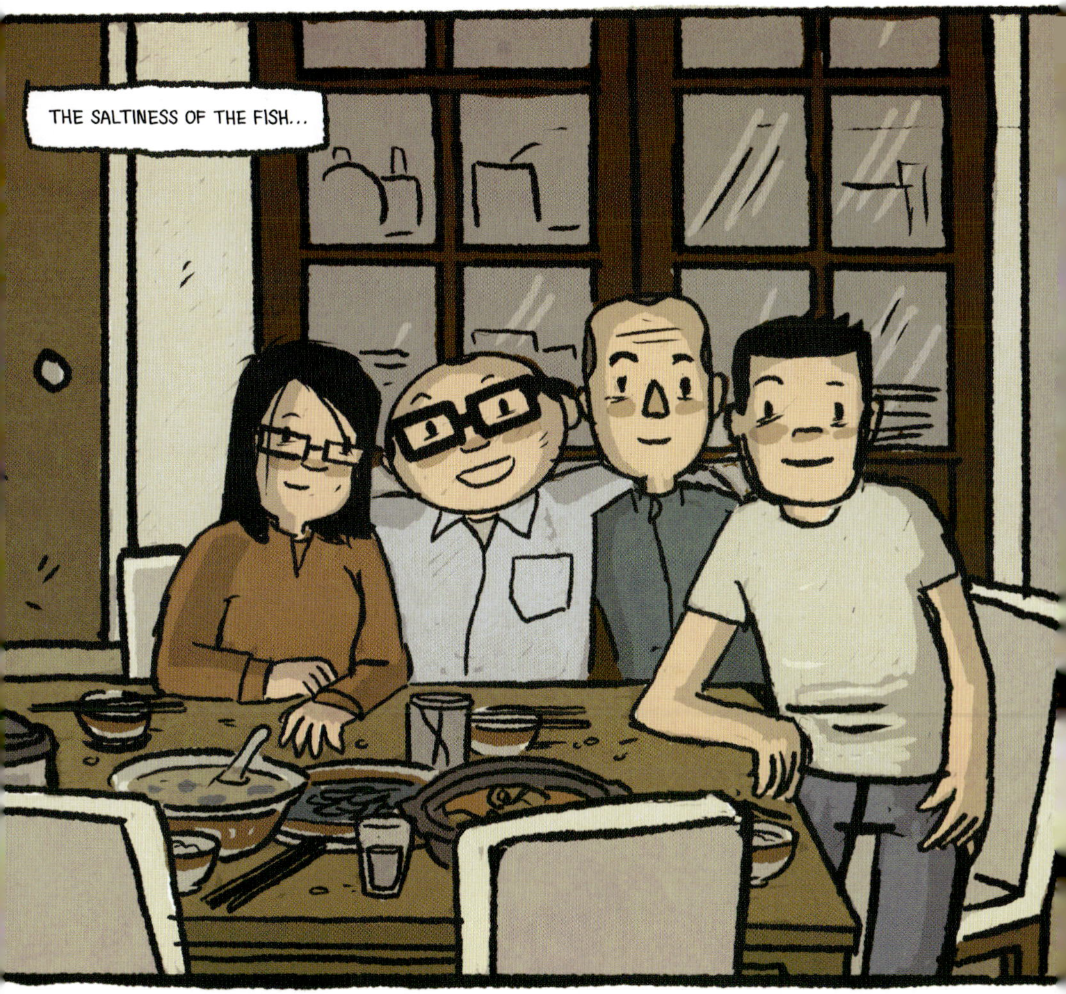
THE SALTINESS OF THE FISH...

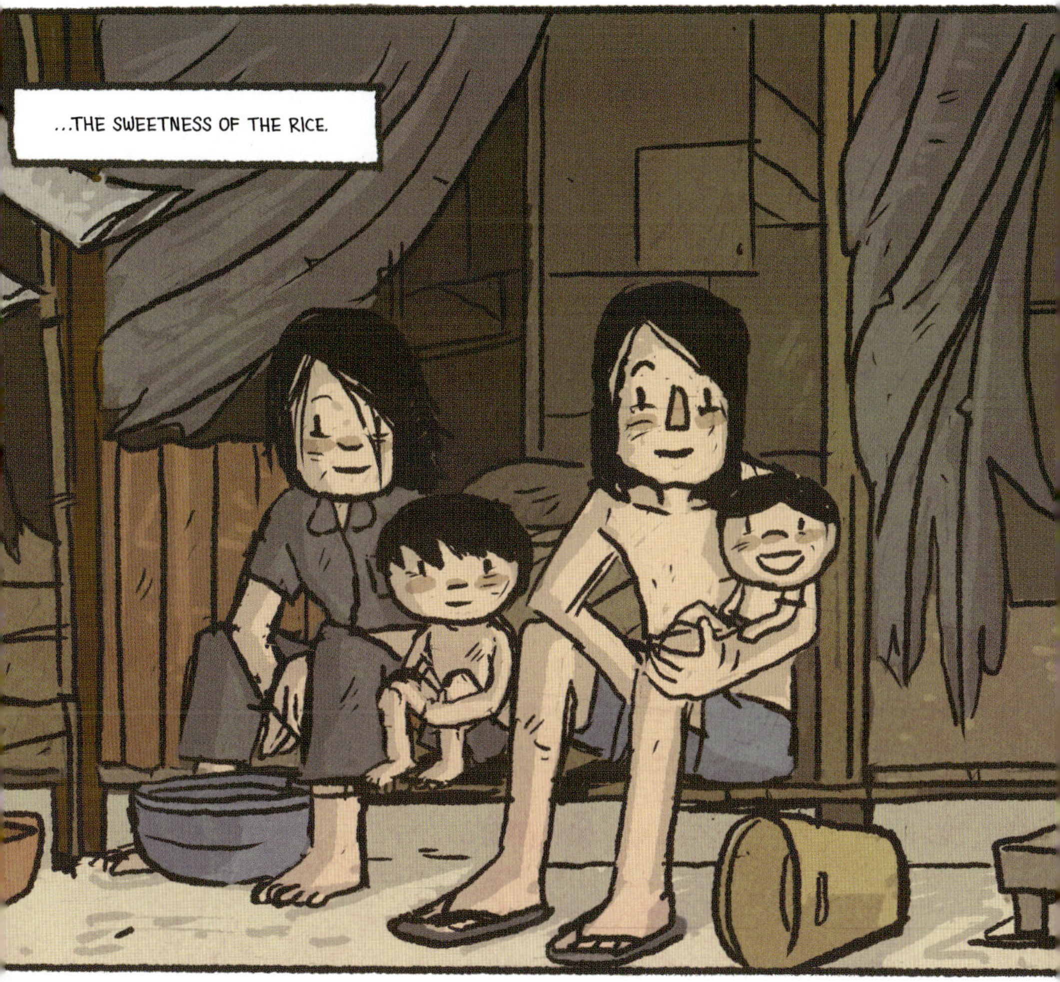
...THE SWEETNESS OF THE RICE.

FOR MY MOM AND DAD

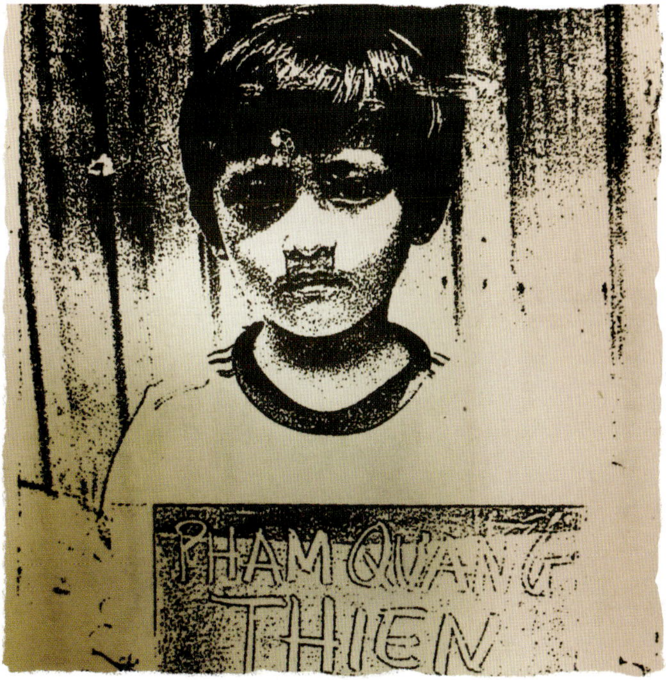
PHAM QUANG
THIEN

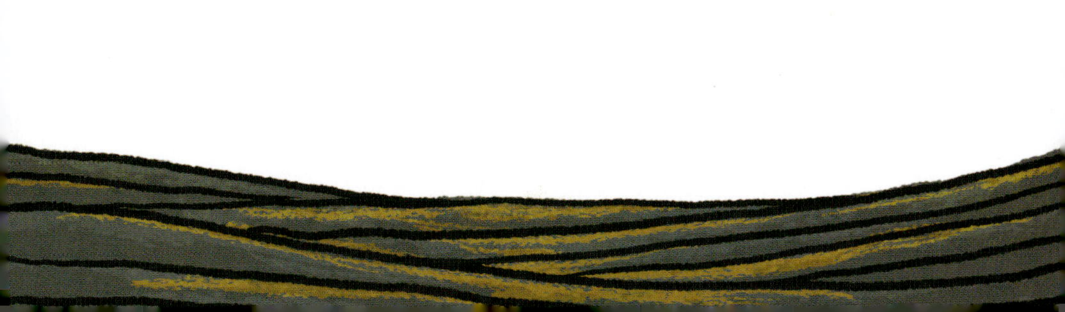

ENDNOTES

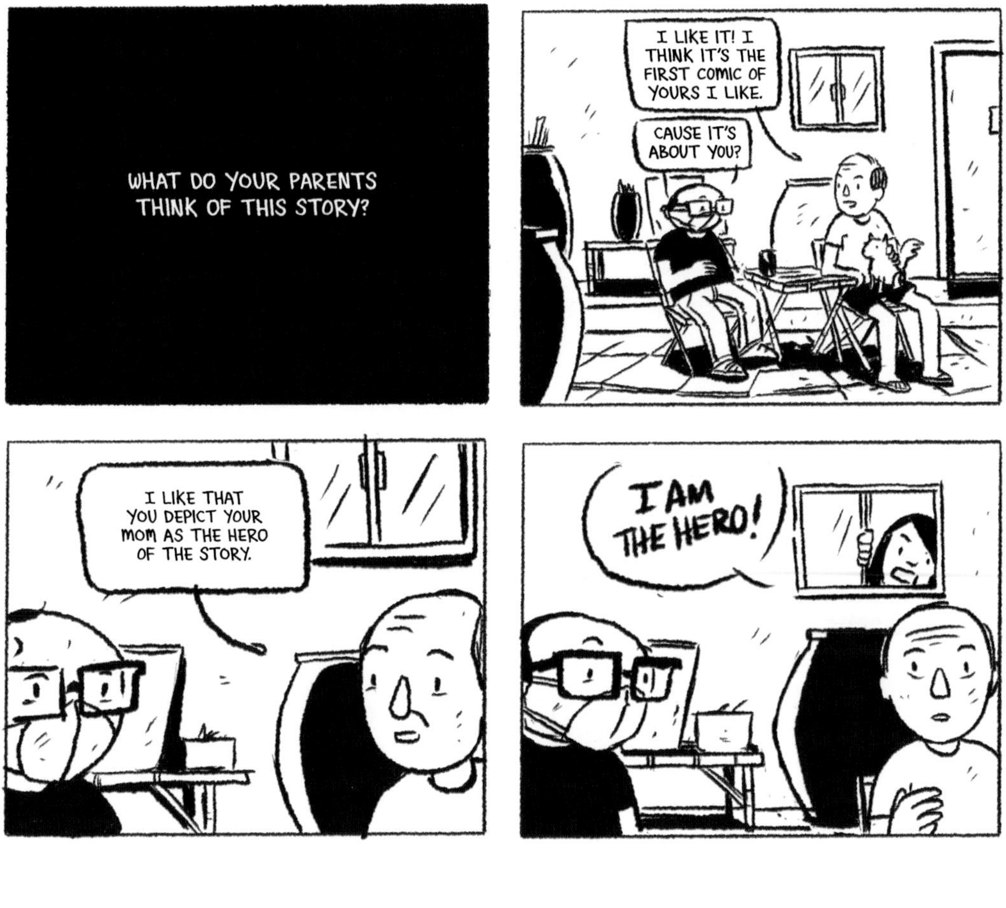
WHAT DO YOUR PARENTS THINK OF THIS STORY?
I LIKE IT! I THINK IT'S THE FIRST COMIC OF YOURS I LIKE.
CAUSE IT'S ABOUT YOU?
I LIKE THAT YOU DEPICT YOUR MOM AS THE HERO OF THE STORY.
I AM THE HERO!

WHAT WAS YOUR PROCESS FOR CREATING THIS BOOK LIKE?
I WAS TRYING TO DO A PAGE (SIX PANELS) A DAY. SO I USUALLY STARTED AT NINE A.M. I USUALLY ALREADY KNEW WHAT I WANTED TO CONVEY STORYWISE, SO I JUST HAD TO FIGURE OUT HOW TO TELL IT EFFECTIVELY.
THE OFFICE
iPAD
MR. SUN
FROSTED FLAKES
9:00 A.M.
AFTER I THUMBNAILED AND PENCILED A PAGE, IT WAS TIME TO TAKE A BREAK FOR LUNCH. I USUALLY TOOK ONE HOUR TO EAT AND WATCH A SHOW.
"THE OFFICE"
1:00 P.M.
THEN I INKED AND COLORED THE PAGE. THIS WAS THE MOST LABOR-INTENSIVE PART, SO I WAS USUALLY WORKING RIGHT UP UNTIL IT WAS TIME TO POST THE PAGE ON INSTAGRAM.
OH MAN! IT'S ALMOST SEVEN!

WHEN YOU LEFT VIETNAM, WHAT EXACTLY DID YOUR MOM SEW INTO YOUR SEAMS?
MOM.
WHAT?
WHAT WAS IT THAT YOU SEWED INTO OUR SEAMS?
WHY?
CAUSE IT'S INTERESTING!
...WELL, IT WAS JUST WHATEVER WE HAD, LIKE SOME SEAMS HAD PIECES OF A GOLD CHAIN...
...AND SOME MIGHT HAVE HAD ROLLED-UP PAPER MONEY.
BUT I HAVEN'T HIDDEN MONEY IN YOUR SEAMS FOR A WHILE NOW.
WAIT, A WHILE?
CLICK

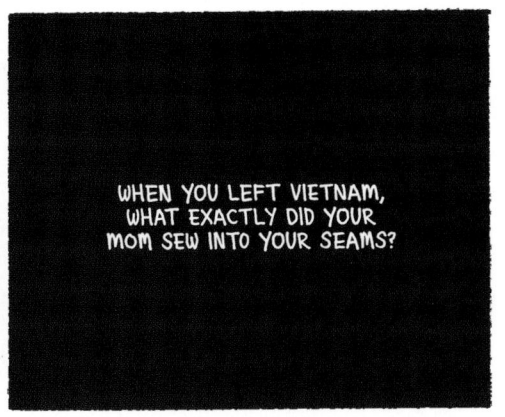

WHAT ARE SOME OF THE THINGS YOU GUYS PLAYED WITH IN THE REFUGEE CAMP?
WE DIDN'T HAVE MUCH AT THE REFUGEE CAMP. WE WERE ALWAYS MAKING TOYS AND FUN OUT OF THE THINGS AROUND US. THINGS LIKE:
BUG KITE!
AW, MY BUG IS A DUD!
WE WERE ALWAYS SCAVENGING FOR DISCARDED THINGS TO PLAY WITH.
OOO, BATTERIES!
MY MEMORIES OF MY TIME AT THE REFUGEE CAMP ARE KIND OF HAZY. BUT ONE THING I WILL ALWAYS REMEMBER VIVIDLY IS THIS. IT WAS OUR PRIZED POSSESSION.
WIRE
LIGHT BULB!
RUBBER BAND
BAMBOO STICKS
BATTERIES
HOMEMADE FLASHLIGHT!

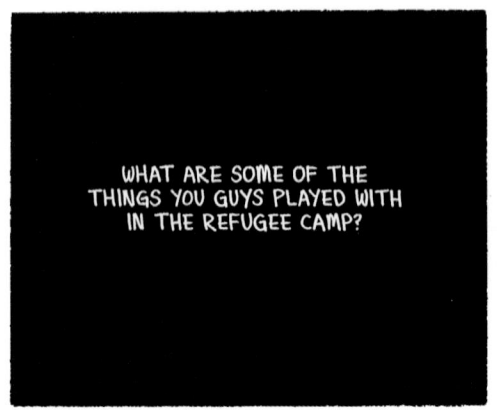

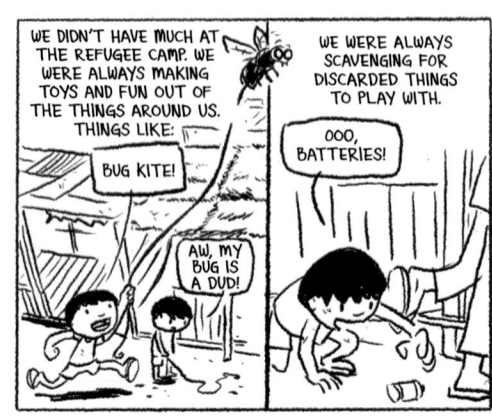

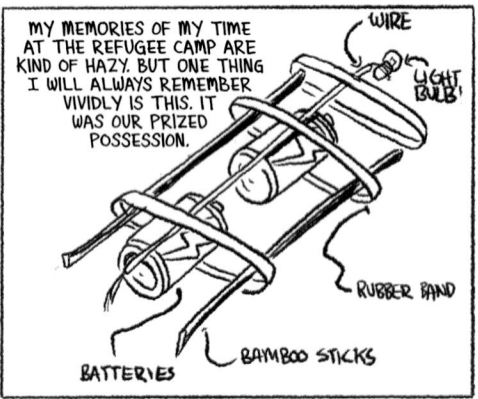

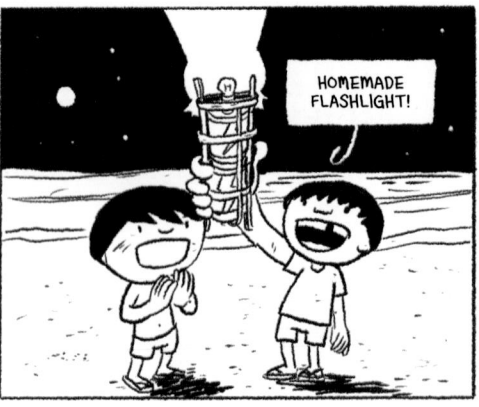

YOUR COMIC IS PRETTY GOOD, BUT THERE ARE SO MANY TYPOS!
ARE YOU GOING TO FIX THEM?
I'M DOING A PAGE A DAY, DAD! SORRY IF I MISS SOME TYPOS! A. PAGE. A. DAY!
BUT YES. WHEN I PUT THE BOOK TOGETHER, I'LL GO BACK AND EDIT EVERYTHING.
I HOPE SOMEONE HELPS YOU.
I'VE GOT TO GO!
BYE, SON.
WHATEVER, DAD!
I'M GLAD YOU TALKED TO HIM ABOUT THOSE TYPOS!
IT'S EMBARRASSING.
HI, I'M GENE, A FRIEND OF YOUR SON'S. I WAS HOPEING YOU COULD TALK TO YOUR SON ABOUT HIS TY—
WE KNOW, WE KNOW.
WE'RE ON IT!
YAAANG!

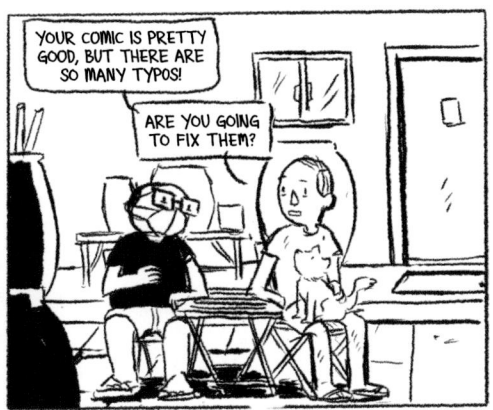

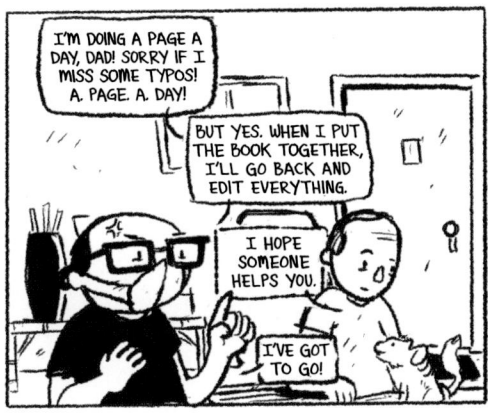

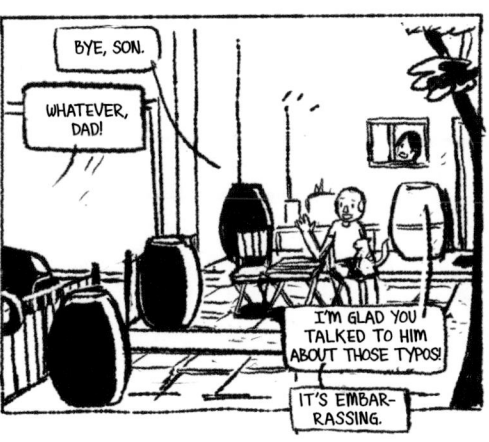

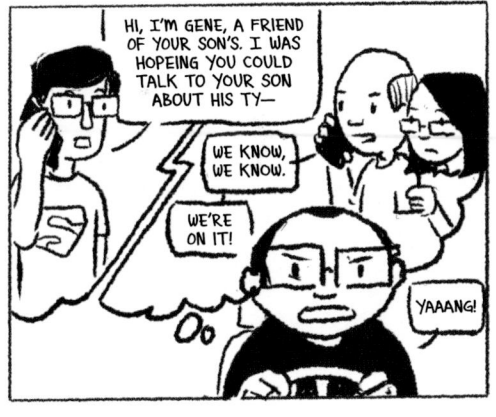

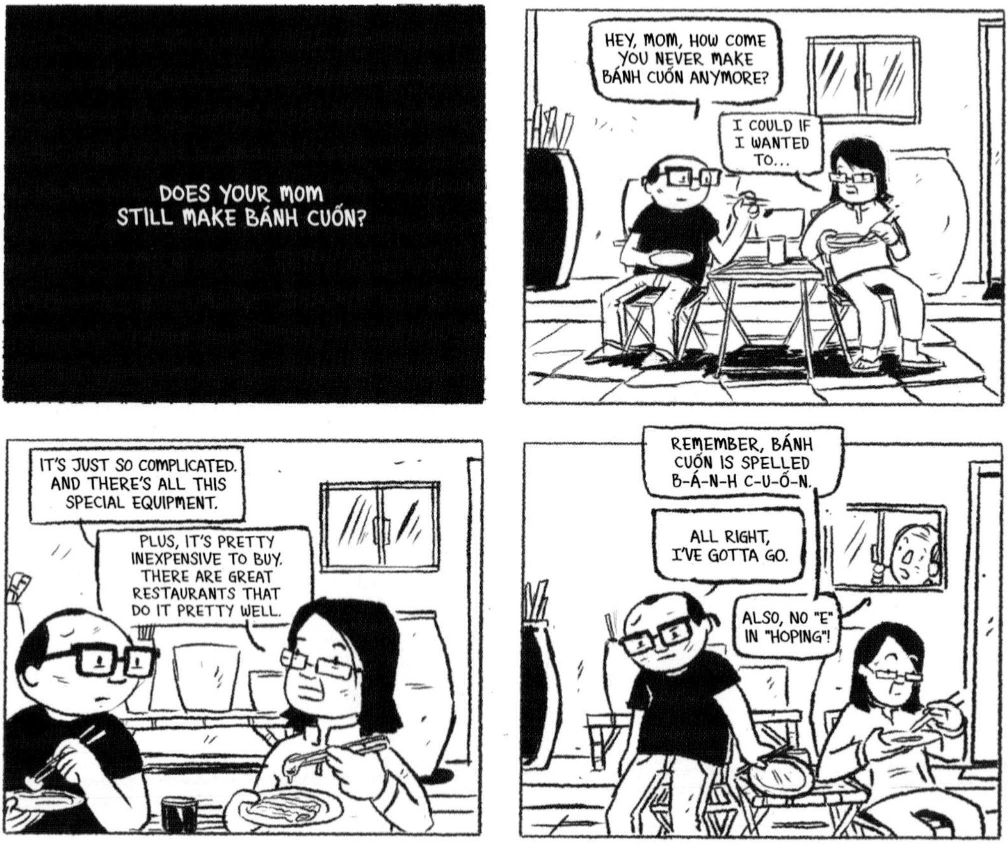
DOES YOUR MOM STILL MAKE BÁNH CUỐN?
HEY, MOM, HOW COME YOU NEVER MAKE BÁNH CUỐN ANYMORE?
I COULD IF I WANTED TO...
IT'S JUST SO COMPLICATED. AND THERE'S ALL THIS SPECIAL EQUIPMENT.
PLUS, IT'S PRETTY INEXPENSIVE TO BUY. THERE ARE GREAT RESTAURANTS THAT DO IT PRETTY WELL.
REMEMBER, BÁNH CUỐN IS SPELLED B-Á-N-H C-U-Ố-N.
ALL RIGHT, I'VE GOTTA GO.
ALSO, NO "E" IN "HOPING"!

WHAT DO YOUR PARENTS REMEMBER AS THE STRANGEST THING ABOUT AMERICA ON THEIR FIRST DAY?
HEY, DAD, ON OUR FIRST DAY IN AMERICA, WHAT DID YOU THINK WAS THE WEIRDEST THING?
HMM...EVERYTHING WAS JUST SO BIG, AND THERE WAS SO MUCH OF IT. THE BUILDINGS, THE CARS, THE STORES.
OH, ACTUALLY, I DO REMEMBER ONE THING THAT REALLY SCARED ME.
THAT FIRST NIGHT, WE WERE SLEEPING IN RUSS'S LIVING ROOM, AND I NOTICED THAT HE HAD ONE OF THOSE GAS WALL HEATERS. IT WAS FACING US, AND ALL OF A SUDDEN, IT TURNED ON!
A HEATER? WHAT HEATER? YOU DIDN'T TELL ME ABOUT A HEATER.
IT WAS JUST A HEATER. WHO CARES. LISTEN TO THE STORY!

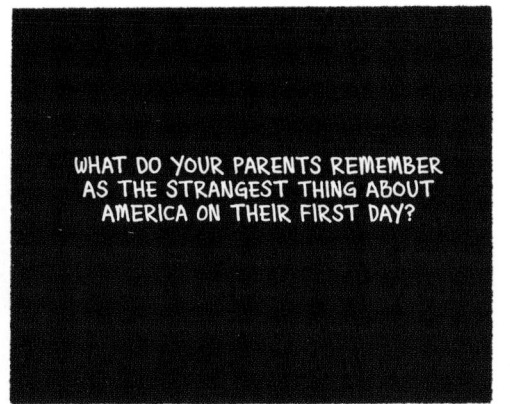

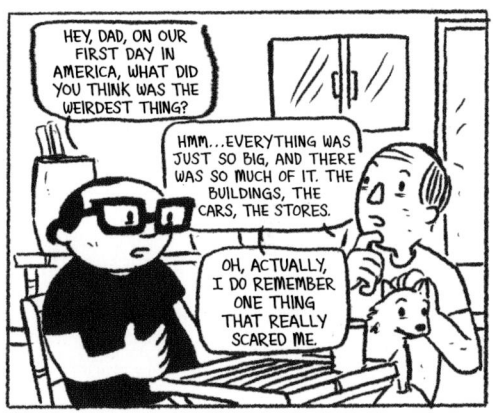

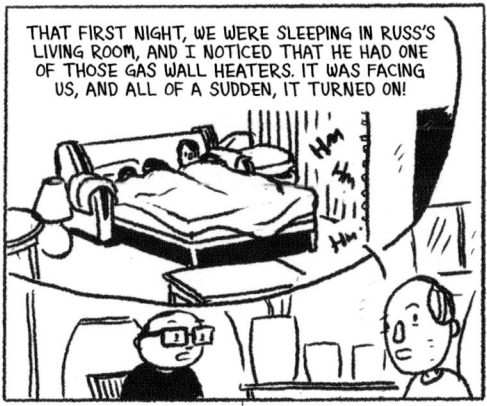

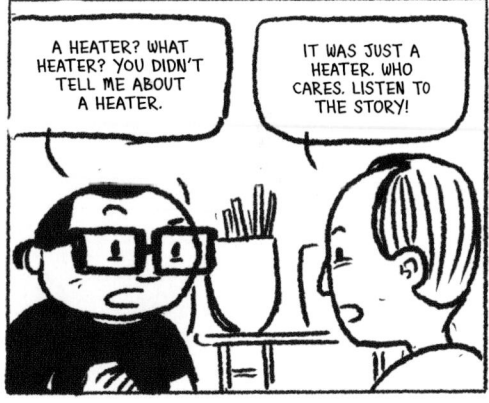

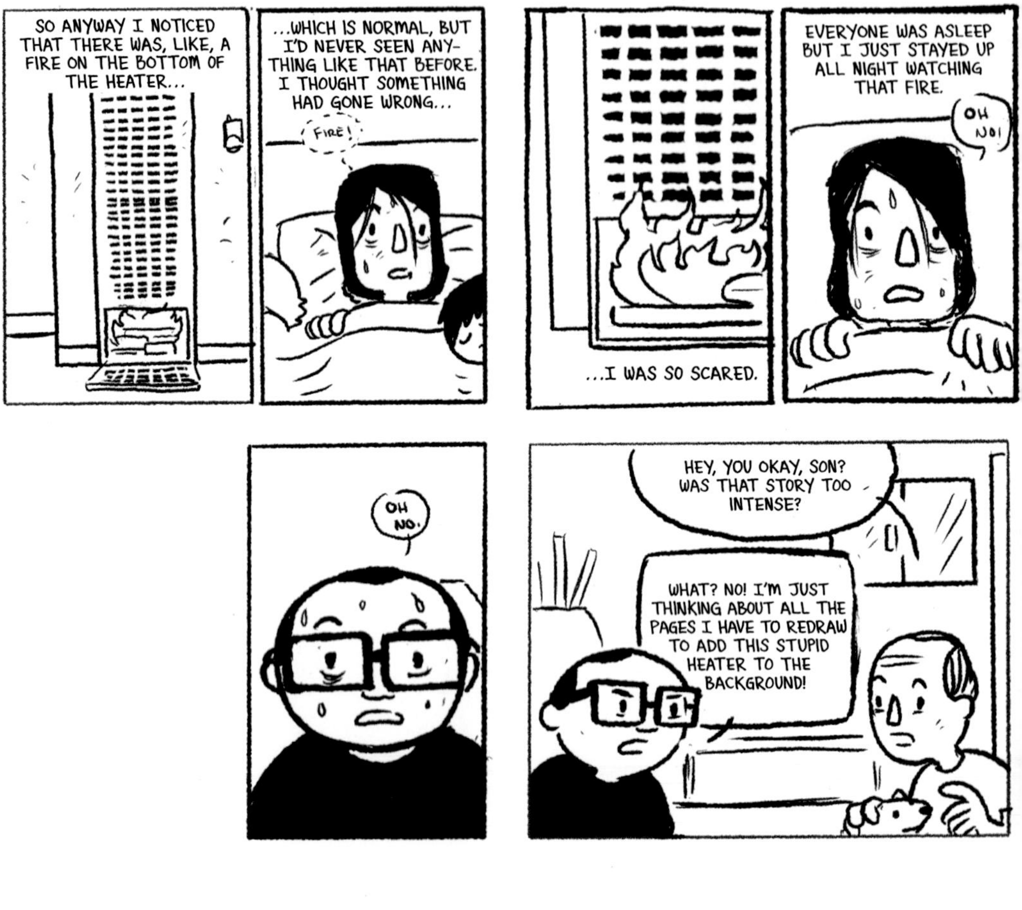
SO ANYWAY I NOTICED THAT THERE WAS, LIKE, A FIRE ON THE BOTTOM OF THE HEATER...
...WHICH IS NORMAL, BUT I'D NEVER SEEN ANYTHING LIKE THAT BEFORE. I THOUGHT SOMETHING HAD GONE WRONG...
FIRE!
...I WAS SO SCARED.
EVERYONE WAS ASLEEP BUT I JUST STAYED UP ALL NIGHT WATCHING THAT FIRE.
OH NO!
OH NO.
HEY, YOU OKAY, SON? WAS THAT STORY TOO INTENSE?
WHAT? NO! I'M JUST THINKING ABOUT ALL THE PAGES I HAVE TO REDRAW TO ADD THIS STUPID HEATER TO THE BACKGROUND!

DO YOU GUYS STILL KEEP IN TOUCH WITH RUSS?

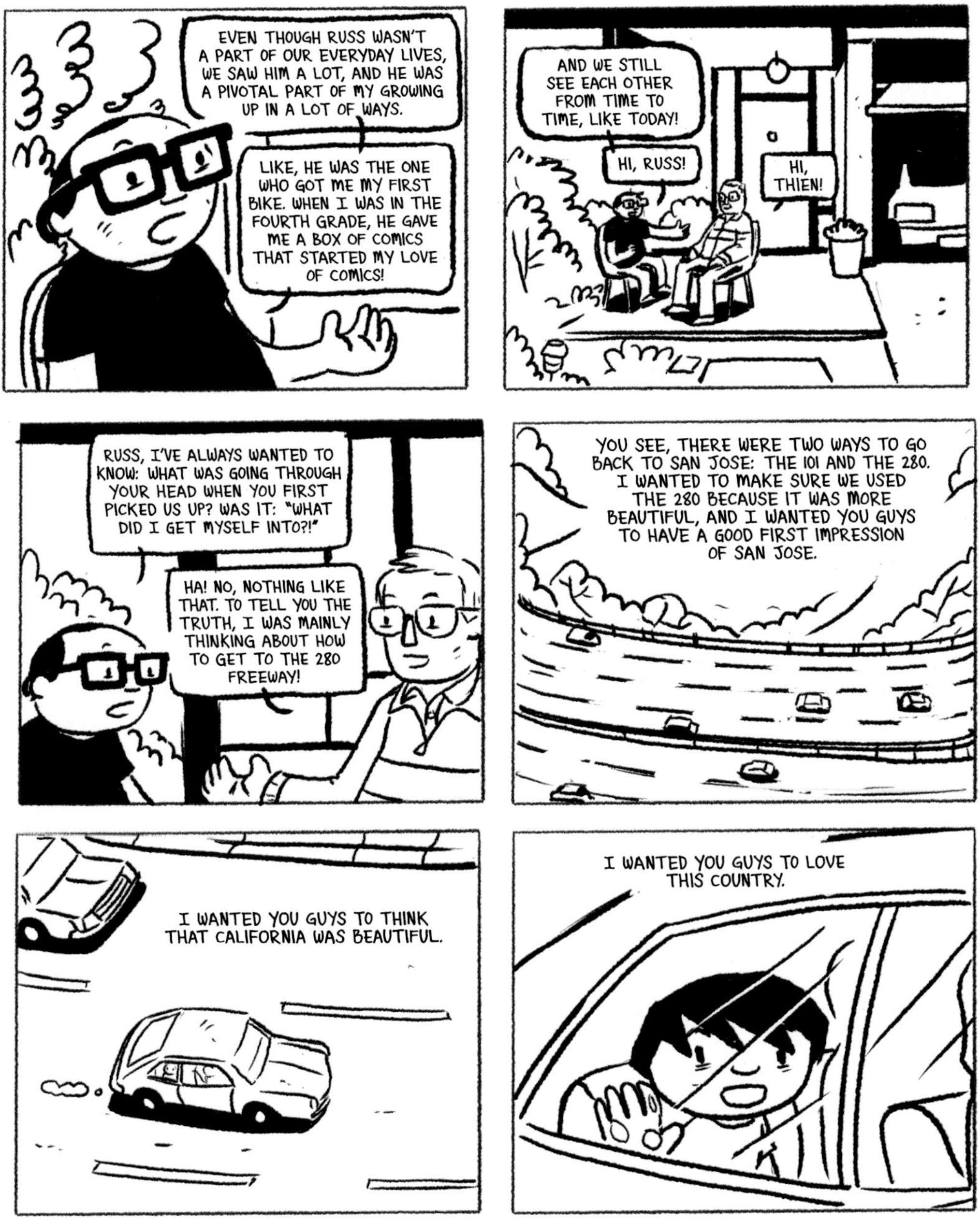
EVEN THOUGH RUSS WASN'T A PART OF OUR EVERYDAY LIVES, WE SAW HIM A LOT, AND HE WAS A PIVOTAL PART OF MY GROWING UP IN A LOT OF WAYS.
LIKE, HE WAS THE ONE WHO GOT ME MY FIRST BIKE. WHEN I WAS IN THE FOURTH GRADE, HE GAVE ME A BOX OF COMICS THAT STARTED MY LOVE OF COMICS!
AND WE STILL SEE EACH OTHER FROM TIME TO TIME, LIKE TODAY!
HI, RUSS!
HI, THIEN!
RUSS, I'VE ALWAYS WANTED TO KNOW: WHAT WAS GOING THROUGH YOUR HEAD WHEN YOU FIRST PICKED US UP? WAS IT: "WHAT DID I GET MYSELF INTO?!"
HA! NO, NOTHING LIKE THAT. TO TELL YOU THE TRUTH, I WAS MAINLY THINKING ABOUT HOW TO GET TO THE 280 FREEWAY!
YOU SEE, THERE WERE TWO WAYS TO GO BACK TO SAN JOSE: THE 101 AND THE 280. I WANTED TO MAKE SURE WE USED THE 280 BECAUSE IT WAS MORE BEAUTIFUL, AND I WANTED YOU GUYS TO HAVE A GOOD FIRST IMPRESSION OF SAN JOSE.
I WANTED YOU GUYS TO THINK THAT CALIFORNIA WAS BEAUTIFUL.
I WANTED YOU GUYS TO LOVE THIS COUNTRY.

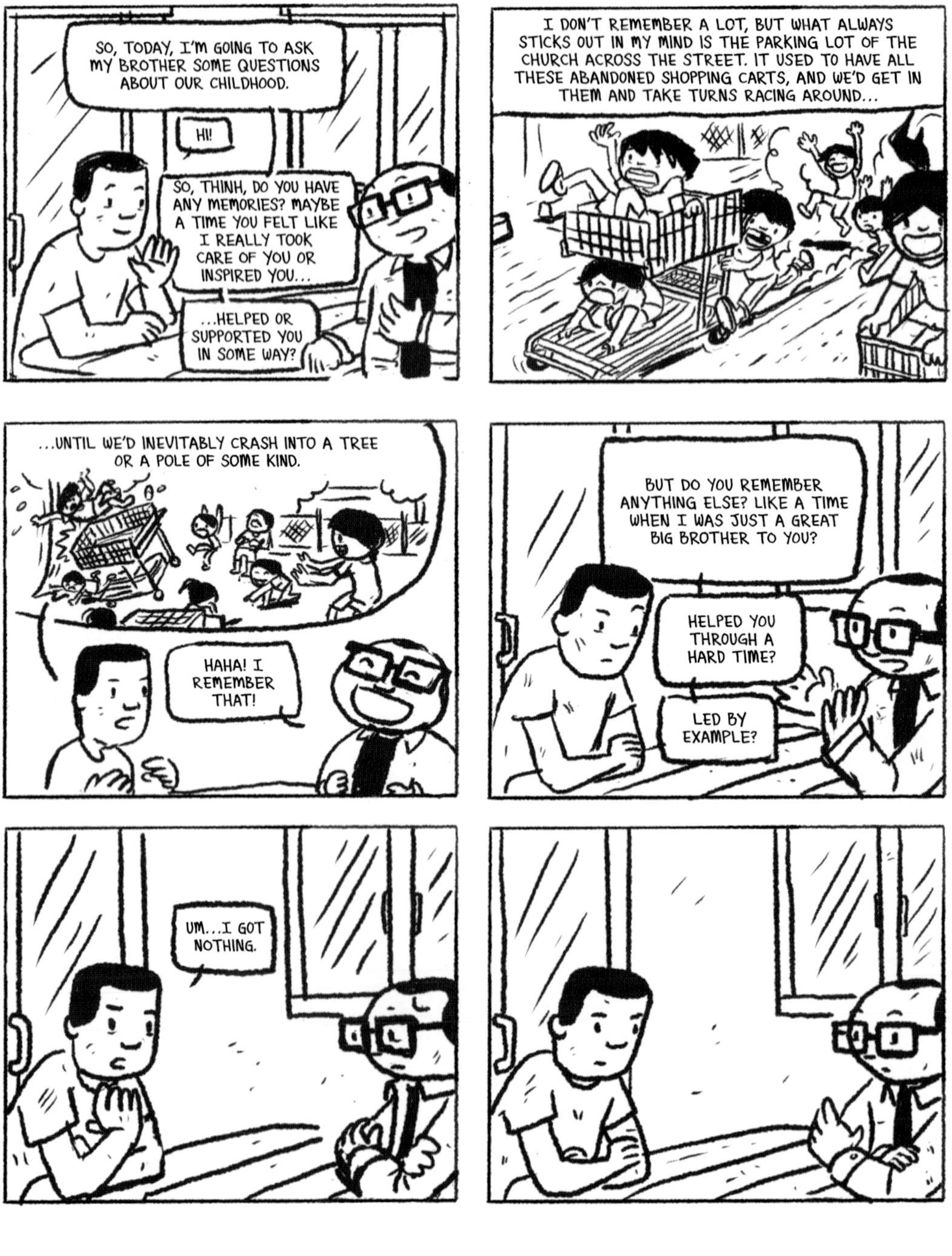
SO, TODAY, I'M GOING TO ASK MY BROTHER SOME QUESTIONS ABOUT OUR CHILDHOOD.
HI!
SO, THINH, DO YOU HAVE ANY MEMORIES? MAYBE A TIME YOU FELT LIKE I REALLY TOOK CARE OF YOU OR INSPIRED YOU...
...HELPED OR SUPPORTED YOU IN SOME WAY?
I DON'T REMEMBER A LOT, BUT WHAT ALWAYS STICKS OUT IN MY MIND IS THE PARKING LOT OF THE CHURCH ACROSS THE STREET. IT USED TO HAVE ALL THESE ABANDONED SHOPPING CARTS, AND WE'D GET IN THEM AND TAKE TURNS RACING AROUND...
...UNTIL WE'D INEVITABLY CRASH INTO A TREE OR A POLE OF SOME KIND.
HAHA! I REMEMBER THAT!
BUT DO YOU REMEMBER ANYTHING ELSE? LIKE A TIME WHEN I WAS JUST A GREAT BIG BROTHER TO YOU?
HELPED YOU THROUGH A HARD TIME?
LED BY EXAMPLE?
UM...I GOT NOTHING.

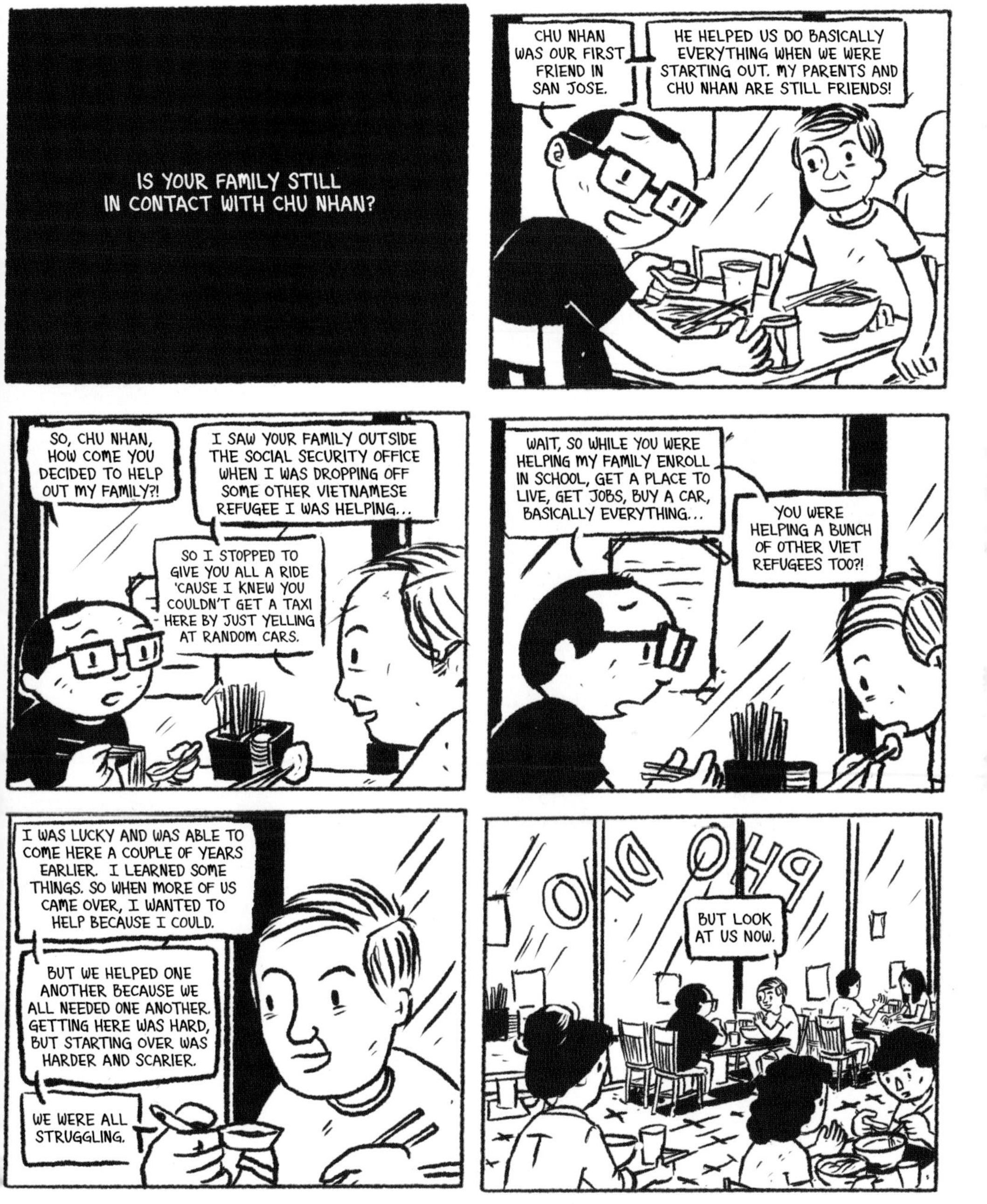
IS YOUR FAMILY STILL IN CONTACT WITH CHU NHAN?
CHU NHAN WAS OUR FIRST FRIEND IN SAN JOSE.
HE HELPED US DO BASICALLY EVERYTHING WHEN WE WERE STARTING OUT. MY PARENTS AND CHU NHAN ARE STILL FRIENDS!
SO, CHU NHAN, HOW COME YOU DECIDED TO HELP OUT MY FAMILY?!
I SAW YOUR FAMILY OUTSIDE THE SOCIAL SECURITY OFFICE WHEN I WAS DROPPING OFF SOME OTHER VIETNAMESE REFUGEE I WAS HELPING...
SO I STOPPED TO GIVE YOU ALL A RIDE 'CAUSE I KNEW YOU COULDN'T GET A TAXI HERE BY JUST YELLING AT RANDOM CARS.
WAIT, SO WHILE YOU WERE HELPING MY FAMILY ENROLL IN SCHOOL, GET A PLACE TO LIVE, GET JOBS, BUY A CAR, BASICALLY EVERYTHING...
YOU WERE HELPING A BUNCH OF OTHER VIET REFUGEES TOO?!
I WAS LUCKY AND WAS ABLE TO COME HERE A COUPLE OF YEARS EARLIER. I LEARNED SOME THINGS. SO WHEN MORE OF US CAME OVER, I WANTED TO HELP BECAUSE I COULD.
BUT WE HELPED ONE ANOTHER BECAUSE WE ALL NEEDED ONE ANOTHER. GETTING HERE WAS HARD, BUT STARTING OVER WAS HARDER AND SCARIER.
WE WERE ALL STRUGGLING.
BUT LOOK AT US NOW.

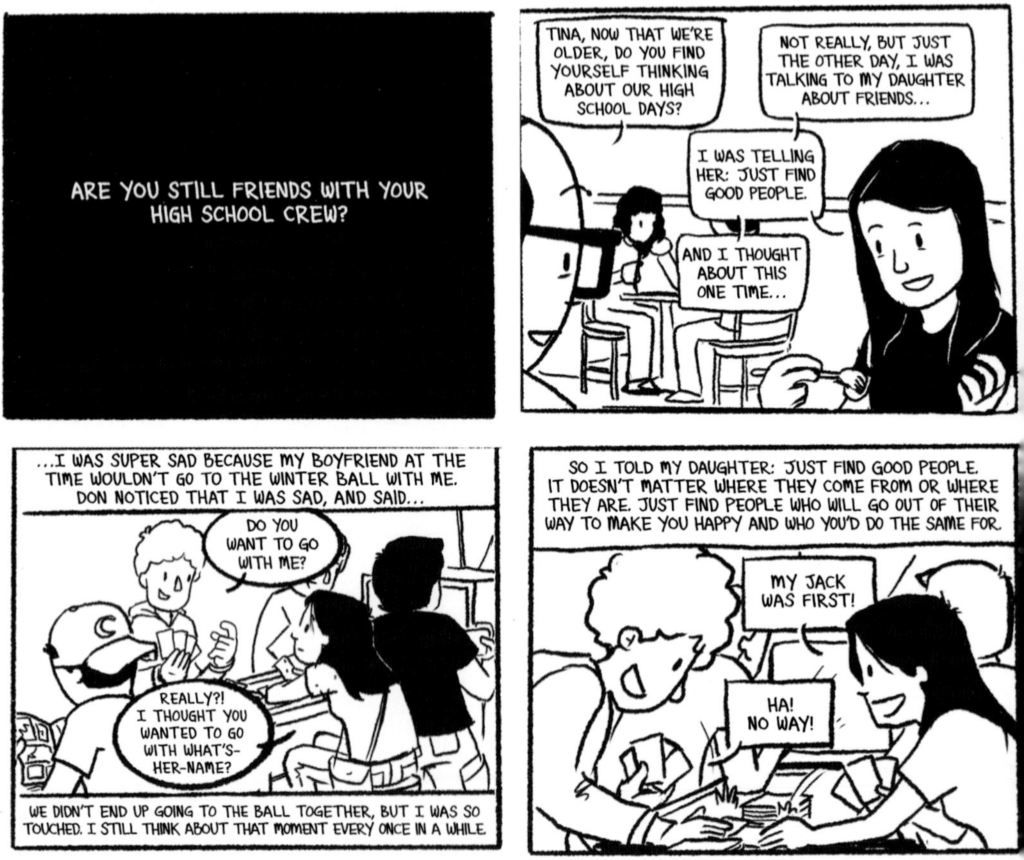
ARE YOU STILL FRIENDS WITH YOUR HIGH SCHOOL CREW?
TINA, NOW THAT WE'RE OLDER, DO YOU FIND YOURSELF THINKING ABOUT OUR HIGH SCHOOL DAYS?
NOT REALLY, BUT JUST THE OTHER DAY, I WAS TALKING TO MY DAUGHTER ABOUT FRIENDS...
I WAS TELLING HER: JUST FIND GOOD PEOPLE.
AND I THOUGHT ABOUT THIS ONE TIME...
...I WAS SUPER SAD BECAUSE MY BOYFRIEND AT THE TIME WOULDN'T GO TO THE WINTER BALL WITH ME. DON NOTICED THAT I WAS SAD, AND SAID...
DO YOU WANT TO GO WITH ME?
REALLY?! I THOUGHT YOU WANTED TO GO WITH WHAT'S-HER-NAME?
WE DIDN'T END UP GOING TO THE BALL TOGETHER, BUT I WAS SO TOUCHED. I STILL THINK ABOUT THAT MOMENT EVERY ONCE IN A WHILE.
SO I TOLD MY DAUGHTER: JUST FIND GOOD PEOPLE. IT DOESN'T MATTER WHERE THEY COME FROM OR WHERE THEY ARE. JUST FIND PEOPLE WHO WILL GO OUT OF THEIR WAY TO MAKE YOU HAPPY AND WHO YOU'D DO THE SAME FOR.
MY JACK WAS FIRST!
HA! NO WAY!

First Second

Published by First Second
First Second is an imprint of Roaring Brook Press, a division of
Holtzbrinck Publishing Holdings Limited Partnership
120 Broadway, New York, NY 10271
firstsecondbooks.com

© 2023 by Thien Pham
All rights reserved

Library of Congress Cataloging-in-Publication Data is available.

Our books may be purchased in bulk for promotional, educational, or business use.
Please contact your local bookseller or the Macmillan Corporate and Premium Sales
Department at (800) 221-7945 ext. 5442 or by email
at MacmillanSpecialMarkets@macmillan.com.

First edition, 2023
Edited by Calista Brill and Alex Lu
Cover design by Kirk Benshoff
Interior book design by Sunny Lee and Yan L. Moy
Production editing by Helen Seachrist

Drawn and colored entirely on an iPad Pro with an Apple Pencil using Procreate.
Layouts and lettering done with Photoshop CS on a MacBook Pro using a custom font
created by John Martz from the author's handwriting.

Printed in China by 1010 Printing International Ltd., Huizhou City, Guangdong Province

ISBN 978-1-250-80972-8 (paperback)
7 9 10 8 6

ISBN 978-1-250-80971-1 (hardcover)
5 7 9 10 8 6 4

Don't miss your next favorite book from First Second! For the latest updates go
to firstsecondnewsletter.com and sign up for our enewsletter.